Higher Education in the Caribbean

Higher Education in the Caribbean
Past, Present and Future Directions

Edited by

Glenford D. Howe

The University of the West Indies Press
Barbados ● *Jamaica* ● *Trinidad and Tobago*

The University of the West Indies Press
1A Aqueduct Flats, Mona
Kingston 7, Jamaica

© 2000 by Glenford D. Howe

All rights reserved. Published 2000

04 03 02 01 00   5 4 3 2 1

CATALOGUING IN PUBLICATION DATA

Higher education in the Caribbean: past, present and future directions / Glenford Howe, editor

p. cm.

IISBN 976-640-079-2

1. Education, Higher — Caribbean, English-speaking
2. University of the West Indies 3. Universities and colleges — Caribbean, English-speaking — Administration
I. Howe, Glenford

LB2329.8.C3H55 2000   378.9

Cover and book design by Prodesign Ltd, Red Gal Ring, Kingston

Contents

Foreword *by Sir Keith Hunte*	*vii*
Preface	*ix*
Introduction	*xii*
Abbreviations	*xvii*

1. The Historical Development of Higher Education in the Anglophone Caribbean
   Alan G. Cobley — *1*

2. Contrasting Problems Facing Universities in the Developed and Developing Worlds: The Same Difference
   Rex Nettleford — *24*

3. Higher Education and Caribbean Identity
   Orville Kean — *45*

4. Academic Travails and a Crisis-of-Mission of the University of the West Indies' Social Sciences: From History and Critique to Anti-Politics
   Don D. Marshall — *59*

5. The Politics of Caribbean Higher Education
   Bevis F. Peters — *85*

6. Access to Tertiary Education in the Commonwealth Caribbean in the 1990s
   Errol Miller — *117*

7. Higher Education and Agricultural Development in the Caribbean
   Carlisle A. Pemberton, Sarojini Ragbir and Rita Pemberton — *142*

Contents

8. A Vision of Transformational Leadership for the University *167*
   of the West Indies
   Glenford D. Howe and Earle Newton

9. Managing the Academy: Aspects of the Law Relating *186*
   to University Administration
   Jeff Cumberbatch

10. Changing a University: Reconciling Quantity with Quality *237*
    – The Case of the University of the West Indies
    Don Robotham

11. Future Directions for Research in Caribbean Higher Education *251*
    Institutions
    Roger Prichard

12. The University of the West Indies Press and Academic *266*
    and Textbook Publishing in the Caribbean: An Oral History
    Wenty Bowen

13. From Ideas to Practice: The Development of the University *306*
    of the West Indies Distance Education Policies and Programmes
    Glenford D. Howe

14. Current Issues in Distance Education in the English-Speaking *323*
    Caribbean: Challenges and Responses
    Claudia Harvey

15. Management Information Systems in Universities: Is the *342*
    University of the West Indies on Target?
    Gloria Barrett-Sobers

    Contributors *371*

Foreword

In every country in the Commonwealth Caribbean determined efforts are being made to establish higher education institutions or increase the capacity of existing ones. There is a sense of urgency that informs these developments. That sense of urgency was clearly reflected in the statement of goals contained in the strategic plan for human resource development endorsed by the Heads of Government of the Caribbean Community meeting in Montego Bay, Jamaica, in July 1997. The commitment to increase the level of participation in tertiary education from its annual state of less than 8 percent to 15 percent of those graduating from secondary schools, and to achieve this by 2005, clearly indicates that the heads of government recognize the need for the region to catch up with its competitors.

The University of the West Indies, in its Strategic Plan for the period 1996–2005, is seen to be responding to the urgent need to increase quantity and improve the quality of programmes in higher education. The university expresses its commitment to forming strategic alliances with other universities and colleges in the region and to using a variety of distance education delivery modes to achieve the desired result in a cost effective manner.

Given the magnitude of this undertaking and the need for the region to provide quality education through a variety of institutions and delivery modes, the publication of these essays on higher education is most timely. The essays identify and examine the issues that influenced the development of the present system of higher education. They demonstrate that there are important lessons to be learned from our relatively short but sustained effort to provide higher education to the region over the past fifty years. The essays are a valuable contribution to the continuing search for solutions to the problems faced by colleges and universities that are being asked to provide more with less.

Foreword

These issues include the need to increase access to higher education, keep costs within affordable limits, and develop a variety of delivery systems to meet the needs of a diverse student population comprising full-time students, employed persons and those who must study at home.

Notwithstanding the challenges and constraints, our institutions of higher education will be judged on their performance as producers of scholarship, higher level skills and competencies, knowledge, shared values and the quality and scope of their influence on society. Critical to the success of their efforts is their ability to recruit and maintain high quality staff and attract the brightest and best students. There is growing recognition of the need for the public and private sectors to pay more attention to research and development. The universities, via their research agendas, must be prepared to take the lead in converting policy making into action and demonstrating the importance of research in the development process.

A most refreshing aspect of this work is that the authors of the several essays were not rehearsed or given a party line. The widely different perspectives they bring to bear on the topics make the collection a useful source of ideas for further discussion. We are reminded in Rex Nettleford's chapter "Contrasting Problems Facing Universities in the Developed and Developing Worlds" that the issues we face in higher education are essentially similar to those faced by policy makers and administrators in countries more richly endowed than we are. In "The Politics of Caribbean Higher Education", Bevis Peters reminds us that the politics of getting things done in higher education is a further illustration of the truism that politics is the art of the possible.

For conceiving the idea of publishing a collection of essays on higher education in the Caribbean and for producing a publication that is undoubtedly a significant contribution to the relatively scarce literature on this important topic, Dr Howe deserves our thanks and congratulations.

Keith D. Hunte
University of the West Indies
Cave Hill, Barbados

Preface

Since its establishment in 1948, the University of the West Indies (UWI) has evolved into the premier provider of higher education in the anglophone Caribbean. However, as it attempts to achieve its primary developmental function of unlocking the potential of the peoples of the region, it too, as with universities around the world, is having to grapple with the diverse challenges of change spurred by global economic crises, technological change and globalization, among other difficulties. Today, as Professor Rex Nettleford observes in his contribution to the book, the UWI and related institutions of higher learning, as generators and transmitters of knowledge, find themselves at the heart not only of discourse but also of meaningful plans of action, targetting the development process and its relation to the human resource, as well as the paradigm shifts and quixotic changes attendant on the new situation.

The challenging regional and international sociocultural, political and economic changes are today reflected in the fact that theories and practices of higher education have become characterized by numerous controversial debates addressing, among other things, leadership, the role of research and publication, the role of graduate studies, the dilemmas of reconciling quantity and quality, school improvement, the teaching and learning processes, student and staff welfare and development, decision making practices and administration. The debates also encompass school climate and change, issues of gender, race and class, the school–community relationship, economic efficiency and effectiveness, student mobility, the legal context of higher education, and questions of access and democratization, among other things. These many issues have been at the heart of the restructuring efforts undertaken by various higher education institutions, not least the UWI, which underwent major restructuring in the 1980s and is currently in the throes of another initiated in the early 1990s.

Preface

Indeed, many countries in the anglophone Caribbean have been rethinking the role of higher education in national development and, as a result, the region has witnessed a proliferation of institutions of higher learning undreamed of in the colonial period of their development. Globally, higher education is having to grapple with the difficult task of meeting two of its major priorities: namely, adjusting to the changing and growing demands of the economies for adaptable workers who can readily acquire new skills, and secondly, maintaining its fundamental role of supporting the continued expansion of knowledge. It is in the context of these challenges of change that I thought about producing an edited collection of original essays that, among other things, reviewed and analysed the accomplishments, role and challenges of Caribbean higher education, focusing especially on the fifty years of the UWI's existence, and also considering the opportunities and alternatives facing the institution as it prepares to enter the twenty-first century.

The issues affecting higher education in the region are clearly numerous and complex and cannot be adequately addressed in any single volume. What this book does, however, is focus on some of the more critical and significant processes of change and the ways in which the UWI has been responding to and planning for them. The final product reflects the bringing together of some of the most talented and active academics and administrators in the region, to reflect on a number of these significant educational issues and dilemmas as they pertain to higher education in general, and in particular, to the UWI and the fulfilling of its developmental role within the region. In the final analysis, it is expected that this book will not merely document the changing and at times turbulent experience of an institution of higher learning in its quest for educational excellence, but more importantly, perhaps, offer some insights into the increasingly difficult and controversial educational issues, dilemmas and opportunities of our time. The essays in this collection also provide the basis for further reflection, inquiry and dialogue on not merely the role of the UWI, but more broadly about the lessons that may be derived for other universities in the developing world as they attempt educational reform in an uncertain external environment, and internal bureaucratic cultures which often militate against desirable reforms being successfully implemented.

Several individuals provided advice and support that helped to make this project a reality. These included Professor Woodville Marshall, Dr Alan Cobley and other members of the academic and administrative staff of the

Preface

UWI. Others who deserve recognition, since they were instrumental in assisting wherever possible and are a constant source of support, include Mrs Andrea Brice and Mrs Beverly Hinds, whose service and professionalism in dealing with all staff epitomize the type of excellence which the university should seek to acknowledge and reward more often. To these people, but especially my family and Carolyn Marshall, I express my sincerest thanks and appreciation for always being understanding and supportive.

Introduction

There is a new feeling of intensity in Caribbean development discourse. It is certainly different in its theoretical aspects from that associated with the anxieties of the 1970s, which seemed unquestionably more concerned about ideological issues such as social justice, economic inequalities, and cultural marginalization. The public sensation today is sharpened by deeper fears about macroeconomic backwardness and dependency as the principal state with which postcolonial society is about to entertain a new millennium. The dread of being, existentially speaking, an even poorer relation stripped of global respect in the twenty-first century embraces larger sections of the still ethnically fragmented and torn community. There is also a fair measure of guilt scattered among those who were sufficiently empowered in the 1970s to resist popular reforms, and who now feel somehow that the chickens have come home to do the expected, and are disturbingly messy and subversive in so doing.

At the centre of these divisive sentiments is a persisting admission by the majority of Caribbean people that their flight from crippling, oppressive pasts, and hectic journeys to modernity, have been fuelled by no other material than organized 'higher' education. It remains a self-degrading feature of the decision making of important sections of society (no longer the elite), however, to think of 'foreign' institutions, and their inculcations, as the faster vehicles to progress, though the locally made and maintained machinery has since proven second to none in terms of effectiveness and efficiency.

The colonial dispensation that conceived nothing immaculately would have it no other way. For despite a serious challenge from an increasingly confident popular movement that spoke after the war against Hitler about the end of an empire and the political rise of the 'small' man, it was contented with its arcane investment in the doctor–lawyer–postmaster education strategy. 'Development' was understood by it in terms of servicing the basic, and baser, colonial needs – just enough to keep up the cane fields and citrus groves, and to drive away pestilence from the gates of plantation great houses. Everywhere in the empire education for those on the 'ground' was projected in terms of 'nursing colonial words', and the concept of intellectual empowerment meant that 'you', meaning its indigenous collaborators, were expected to know how to do this yourself – without considering for a moment the real possibility of a liberating amputation.

But West Indians as a whole, for discernible reasons, and despite the Jamaican exclusive claim to the insight, knew that it was unintelligent to 'cut off your nose to spite your face', and protected, respected and cherished the university given them in 1948. There was, in fact, no need whatsoever among them for any debate about this revolutionary event as a mere token 'put-back' on Britain's part because the people knew at a much earlier time 'how it go'. Those few for whom the lilliputian university was intended behaved in a fashion that signalled the expressions of giants. All was well with them and 'it', and the glory days of the institution are etched now like commandments on the souls of those who were first to climb the Mona Mountain. Today, they are celebrated by subsequent alumni as founders of a great democratic tradition, and deservedly so.

The so-called radicals who followed did not intend to break down the barricades, but simply to 'untie the sheep' that wished to roam the open pastures of Mona in search of the greener stuff they knew was somewhere about. Development discourse turned to the left and broadened its base but education remained the theatre where the demand for inclusion was heard loudest throughout the region. There were no surprises here. A nation was making a move to sovereignty, and in so doing privileged the power of intellect while expecting larger numbers of citizens to hold their own in the structurally transforming nationalist offensive.

As schools for the poor multiplied in the rash of nation building exercises, and colleges of further education sprung up here and there, the University of the West Indies was called upon to be all things to all thinkers in 'development' anxieties. But the challenge of 'women in development' within the academy moved briskly in from the periphery of the discourse, creating a more equitable social circumstance. Democracy, as political reality, when translated into educational policy and planning meant, among other things, more education for less money, altogether very attractive when set out by fiscal quantifiers in the codes of cost-efficiency rhetoric. But West Indians are entirely correct to assert that they deserve better and more simply because they have laboured hard and long at the centre of the modernizing Atlantic system; they alone know fully about its 'old' secrets.

The social majority now wishes to share the modernizing experiences of the privileged few. Historically globalized, tugged and torn by market forces, driven by the universalism of their otherness, and with their tastes for mass produced commodities terribly tested by an unrelenting 'massive media', West Indian masses wish to live the next millennium as a people at the centre. But this is precisely who they are, a people globalized since the Columbus intervention and creators of the first village of this kind. Some, of course, long knew this world, and the likes of C.L.R. James, Rex Nettleford, and Derek Walcott were citizens of it long before the meaning of the term 'global village' was indigenized and its boundaries redrawn under national flags. The Atlantic minds of these 'space' travellers knew parameters that all of us now wish to embrace and claim – the 'space' of a specially remade people now stretching to their full potential in the agony of preparation for a new time.

And so, the essays in this volume – running to the centre from all parts of the perimeter – are concerned with the imaginations and imminent urgings of the West Indian citizen. Not surprisingly, the development discourse to which they all contribute remains loyal to the role of education, institutionally understood, within all new arrangements for the future. Some of them speak of a sense of crisis in the ideology underpinning public policy, as reflected in a lack of theoretical coherence; others focus on the challenges of bringing formal tuition to the many – issues of modes of delivery, costs, institutional frameworks, and general socioeconomic constraints. All assembled, they represent beads of sweat upon an intense Caribbean brow as it looks into a new age fully conscious of the traumas of 'old' times.

Only the evangelicals, however, seem confident in asserting, "we know where we are going, we know". But none of them are represented here, at least not in a formal sense. Senior university academics and managers freely set out the complexity of providing and promoting the culture of academia as a measurable productive output, and are determined to illustrate that scholarship is as indispensable to sustainable development as efficient agriculture and viable financial institutions. Educators debate the terms of tertiary teaching for a region that is at best nervous about its capacity to pay the piper downstream. These are all important statements that constitute, not so much a position from the West Indies, but proof of persistent passion for relevant knowledge within.

Development discourse, we are told, has moved away from banal considerations of end result gross domestic product (GDP) indicators, to issues such as the mass production of social-sensitive mentalities, citizens with a desire to feel and live the texture of a quality civic society and possessed with the willingness to generate new knowledges for their material support. 'Education', as a definition of these processes, is therefore about the methods used in sharpening the cutting edges of minds; not so much to separate one from another but to remove the trash and expose the core.

Nettleford shows skilfully that we are not alone in confronting the dilemmas crisply outlined by Robotham, Prichard and Cobley. For sure, the West Indian experience was part of a global circumstance after 1945 in which the larger part of the world grew frustrated with the nineteenth century about them, and did something about it. Whatever they did, however, ended in a reconciliatory discussion about knowledge, education, and their supportive infrastructures. Scattered far and wide by new national boundaries, and divided by rivers, mountains, seas, and ideologies, new-nation people of old civilizations have had to come face to face with modernity as a discourse about the knowledges of progress. The call for popular inclusion now drives policy initiatives in distance education. The theory and practice of settling this frontier, vigorously argued by Howe, Harvey, Peters and Miller, have as a core assumption the belief that greater access to formal education constitutes the key to development trajectories.

This is indeed a bold West Indian statement about the role and place of education in the modern age. The text contains the first systematic attempt to analyse the predicament of mass higher education in the West Indies. It ought to be a point of departure for discussion about how we might develop university research and higher education for the twenty-first century. Authors identify radically new modes of thinking about the future, and provide a discursive approach as a framework for making sense of recent changes in higher education. There is no sense of fatalism here about current thinking on the subject, but a powerful agreement that if the UWI is to be of value to future communities, it must also participate in defining those values, particularly as

Introduction

they relate to the impact of radical processes of globalization. The connections between the expansion and diversification of higher education – including the increasing emphasis on international collaboration and the recruitment of international students – are explored and set out with clarity as critiques of current orthodoxies in higher education.

While many of the technical innovations and policy expressions in education inherent in these chapters are imaginable within existing knowledge fare, the thread that links them to the realities of popular fantasies about the materialism of betterment is often broken though never lost from view. Here, the right of intellectuals to speak about the 'greater good' of future citizens is forcefully asserted, even if at times uncritically. The perception of an endemic theoretical crisis in much of the recent scholarship on planning 'further' education may be derived in part, also, from the absence of a tradition of intellectual self-criticism. If, however, these essays do not say clearly 'we know where we are going', it is because there is a general recognition of several possible futures and many rivers along which to travel – and cross! These acceptances constitute in themselves new forms of knowledge, always the best places from which to begin the process of thinking about different journeys.

Hilary McD. Beckles

Abbreviations

ACE	Association of Caribbean Economists
ACTI	Association of Caribbean Tertiary Institutions
ACH	Association of Caribbean Historians
AED	Academy of Educational Development
AICTA	Associateship of the Imperial College of Tropical Agriculture
AREP	Agricultural Research and Extension Project
BIAJ	Book Industry Association of Jamaica
BUCS	Bath University Computer Services
CAES	Caribbean Agro-Economic Society
CARCOST	Caribbean Regional Communications Study
CARDI	Caribbean Agricultural Research and Development Institute
CARICOM	Caribbean Economic Community
CASE	College of Agriculture, Science and Education
CAST	College of Arts, Science and Technology
CATIE	Tropical Agricultural Research and Training Institute
CDB	Caribbean Development Bank
CEAP	Caribbean Agricultural Extension Project
CET	Common external tariff
CEPAT	Continuing Education Programme in Agricultural Technology
CHEMS	Commonwealth Higher Education Management Services
CIS	Computer information systems
CJE	*Caribbean Journal of Education*
CMD	Centre for Management Development
CMS	Christian Missionary Society
COL	Commonwealth of Learning
CQ	*Caribbean Quarterly*
CRESACC	Centre for Higher Education in Latin America and the Caribbean
CRU	Cocoa Research Unit
CSA	Caribbean Studies Association
CUSA	Caribbean Universities Sports Association
DICTA	Diploma of the International College of Tropical Agriculture
DTA	Diploma in Tropical Agriculture
ECIAF	Eastern Caribbean Institute of Agriculture and Forestry
EMA	Environmental Management Agency
EPA	External Programme in Agriculture

Abbreviations

GATT	General Agreement on Trade and Tariffs
GDP	Gross domestic product
GSIFLC	Summer Institute for Future Global Leaders in the Caribbean
HEFC	Higher Education Funding Council
ICTA	Imperial College of Tropical Agriculture
IDB	Inter-American Development Bank
IICA	Inter-American Institute for Cooperation on Agriculture
ILO	International Labour Organization
IMF	International Monetary Fund
IPGRI	International Board for Plant Genetic Resources Institute
ISER	Institute of Social and Economic Research
ISTRC	International Society for Tropical Root Crops
IUC	Inter-University Council
JISC	Joint Information Systems Committee
JTA	Jamaica Teachers' Association
MIS	Management information systems
MUCIA	Midwest Universities Consortium for International Activities
NASA	National Aeronautics and Space Administration
NCC	Noncampus Country
NIHERST	National Institute of Higher Education Science and Technology
OECS	Organization of Eastern Caribbean States
OUS	Office of University Services
QM	Quantum Mechanics
RARECC	Regional Agricultural Research and Extension Coordinating Committee
RECU	Regional Extension Communications Unit
RRC	Regional Research Centre
RTP	Regional Transformation Programme
SCME	Standing Committee of Ministers Responsible for Education
SCMA	Standing Committee of Ministers of Agriculture
SCS	School of Continuing Studies
SES	*Social and Economic Studies*
TER	Tertiary enrolment ratio
TLI	Tertiary level institution
UAC	University Academic Committee
UAG	Université des Antilles et de Guyane
UCCA	Universities Central Council on Admissions
UCWI	University College of the West Indies
UAC	University Academic Committee
UFS	University Field Station
UGC	University Grants Committee
UNA	University of the Netherlands Antilles
UNICA	Association of Caribbean Universities and Research Institutes
USAID	United States Agency for International Development
UVI	University of the Virgin Islands
UWI	University of the West Indies
UWIDEC	University of the West Indies Distance Education Centre

Abbreviations

UWIDITE	University of the West Indies Distance Teaching Experiment
UWIPA	University of the West Indies Publishers Association
VCU	Virtual Caribbean university
WIGUT	West Indies Group of University Teachers
WIMJ	*West Indian Medical Journal*

1

The Historical Development of Higher Education in the Anglophone Caribbean

Alan G. Cobley

Introduction

The roots of higher education in the Caribbean, as in other regions of the world, can be traced to the role of the sage in traditional societies. The sage was a person who was consulted on the grounds of superior knowledge or wisdom on matters of importance in the community in which she or he lived. The sage could be an adviser, a counsellor, an arbitrator, a diviner, a healer, a rainmaker. Drawing on evidence for the African case, Ajayi, Goma and Johnson argue that the capacity of the sage to be a leader of thought in the community derived from what they call the "formal or informal processes of indigenous higher education".[1] These usually involved the attachment and apprenticeship of specially chosen candidates to elders, who taught their charges by a variety of methods, including oral instruction and, above all, through example: "Indigenous higher education produced and transmitted new knowledge necessary for understanding the world, the nature of man, society, God and various divinities, the promotion of agriculture and health, literature and philosophy."[2]

The historiography of the precolonial Caribbean is not as developed as that on precolonial Africa, and it is still fashionable to assert that the organization of the Amerindian communities of the islands before the colonial era was too simple and on too small a scale to admit such specialization of function: "everybody tended to learn the same skills and values; there was no need for education to serve as a vehicle for upward social mobility".[3] Archaeological evidence, however, complemented by anthropological data from surviving

Amerindian communities, has begun to reveal that this judgement has been too hasty, and that forms of 'indigenous higher education' were practised here too. Amerindian communities had their elders and their chiefs (*caciques*), and the rhythm of life, the vagaries of climate and food supply, of trade and occasional warfare, all required the attention of the 'wise ones' if they were to survive and prosper.

The colonization of the Caribbean by Europeans, and the African slaves they brought with them, introduced new concepts and experiences of higher education to the region. Africans carried with them their own systems of thought and modes of transmission derived from indigenous patterns of education. Some also brought the experience of more formal education through contact with Islam. By the beginning of the transatlantic slave trade, for example, the West African city of Timbuktu had become a holy city of learning, attracting thousands of students from all over the Sudan and Sahel regions. It was by no means rare to find sophisticated and articulate products of Islamic education among the ranks of slaves imported into the Caribbean.[4]

Western concepts of education brought to the region by Europeans also tended to be religious in inspiration. Indeed, the first higher education institution in the Caribbean was an Anglican school called Codrington College, established in Barbados in 1743 to train priests. The main concern of European settlers in the sphere of education was access to tuition for their children, but during the eighteenth century missionary activity increasingly turned attention to the question of instruction for slaves and former slaves. By the time of emancipation in the British West Indies in 1834, there were three Protestant religious groups, in addition to the Anglicans, active in the educational field in the anglophone Caribbean; these were the Moravians, the Baptists and the Methodists.[5] Codrington College, however, which was the result of a benefaction left under the terms of the will of Christopher Codrington, a wealthy Barbadian plantation and slave owner, remained unique for nearly two hundred years. It was the only college offering higher education in the English-speaking Caribbean until 1921, when the Imperial College of Tropical Agriculture (ICTA) was established in Trinidad.

The paucity of higher education colleges in the early colonial Caribbean is in stark contrast to developments in colonial America, where there were nine such colleges by 1770. John Figueroa suggests that there were two reasons for this pattern of neglect and 'underdevelopment' in early Caribbean education. First, he suggests that those among the settler community who had the resources and the interest to sponsor higher education preferred to pursue education outside the region: "It does seem hard to overstress the importance for social and educational thought in the Anglophone West Indies of this feeling, on the part of the important people [sic], that home was elsewhere."[6] Secondly, Figueroa points out that there was a remarkably small number of university graduates among the settlers who came to the West Indies when compared to the American colonies, a total of probably less than 150 by 1750.[7] With such a small and scattered group of university alumni it was not surprising that there was little support for tertiary education in the region. To these points we may add a third, which is that many planters and settlers were actively hostile to the notion of developing an extensive education system in the Caribbean, partly on grounds of cost, but mainly because they believed education of any sort for the majority black population was inappropriate and even dangerous. Such attitudes remained a serious brake on the development of education in parts of the Caribbean long after the formal end of slavery. As late as 1951, Dr Eric Williams felt it necessary to reject the notion of siting a university in Barbados partly because it "still exists too much in the shadow of the sugar plantation, with all the consequences, economic, social and political, that such an economy entails".[8]

A University for the West Indies: The Evolution of the Idea to 1920

Despite the unfavourable climate of opinion among the planter and colonial settler elite, there were repeated proposals for the development of higher education facilities in the English-speaking Caribbean during the colonial period. Indeed, the first recorded call for a university in the region dates to early in the eighteenth century when Bishop Berkeley proposed the conversion of the embryonic colony of Bermuda "into a university island for the British and American colonies".[9] In the nineteenth century, emancipation, and especially the provision of a 'Negro Education Grant' by the British government to assist missionary societies in the education of newly freed slaves, set the scene for a flurry of new proposals. In Jamaica, for example, the Baptist Missionary Society established Calabar College in 1843 for the training of ministers, and followed this up in 1844 with a call for the establishment of a nondenominational university to teach a range of secular subjects. Such proposals were driven by the concerns of missionaries, as well as by the desire of the colonial authorities directed from London to develop new systems of social control over (and encourage the growth of new markets among) the liberated black masses in the West Indies. They also reflected, however, a growing demand among the black population for new opportunities and for the alternatives that higher education could provide to unskilled agricultural labour.

The most articulate call for a 'University of the West Indies' made in the latter half of the nineteenth century came from Patrick Joseph Keenan, chief of the Inspection Board of National Education in Ireland. In 1869 Keenan was sent out to the West Indies by the British government to report on the state of education in Trinidad. In his report he dwelled on the lack of opportunities for higher education in the West Indies and the consequent anguish of parents who were forced to send their children to Europe to complete their education. Apart from the human dimension, he pointed out that this method was a cumbersome, inefficient and costly way of providing higher education. He proposed the establishment of a 'University of the West Indies' that would hold no classes and have no teachers, but which would set examinations and award degrees to students who pursued their studies at local colleges and seminaries in their home territories throughout the region. The idea received a cool reception on both sides of the Atlantic, perhaps because the notion of a nonteaching university was too radical for its time. In one regard, however, Keenan's scheme showed remarkable prescience: as Wellington Friday points out, with the exception of the Bahamas, the list of territories Keenan proposed for inclusion in his scheme included all of the territories that would eventually come together in 1948 to form the University College of the West Indies (UCWI). The Bahamas became a contributing territory of the university in 1964.[10]

At the same time as aspirations for an improved education system were growing in the British West Indies, a parallel demand for western style education was growing in parts of British Africa. As in the Caribbean, this was sponsored partly by the missionaries, who saw education as the key to the propagation of Christianity and as a necessity for training 'native agents' of the missions, such as teachers and evangelists, and partly by the colonial authorities, who were seeking to promote trade. But it was also sponsored by indigenous rulers seeking to ensure their survival against the inroads of colonialism by acquiring new skills and new technology. In West Africa, Fourah Bay College had been established in Sierra Leone by the Christian Missionary Society (CMS) in 1826, and Liberia College had been established in 1862. In one of many cross-fertilizations between West Africa and the West Indies under British rule, one of the founding faculty at Liberia College was an American-educated West Indian scholar named Edward Wilmot Blyden. It was Blyden who first proposed a 'University of West Africa' in 1872, as a form of restitution from the colonial authorities for the depredations on the region of the transatlantic slave trade. His proposal was supported by other leading West African scholars, including James Johnson and Africanus Horton. As in the West Indies, however, the reception from the authorities to the idea of a regional university was cool.

With the failure of the Colonial Office to provide a coordinated policy or funding for higher education in the West Indies in the wake of the Keenan Report, individual territories were left to pursue their own plans. In Jamaica, for example, the governor attempted to launch a public university college in 1873, but this effort quickly collapsed (another attempt made to set up a university college in Jamaica between 1889 and 1898 was equally unsuccessful). In Barbados, meanwhile, Bishop Mitchinson made a series of proposals on the direction of higher education in the island in a report published in 1876. In the report he praised Oxford and Cambridge universities as "the acme of academic excellence" and recommended that one or two scholarships should be granted each year by the Barbados government to allow the best students from the island to attend one or other of these institutions of higher learning. This recommendation was quickly put in place, as were similar schemes in Jamaica (1879) and Trinidad, so that the 'Island Scholarships' quickly became established as the apex of academic achievement in the British West Indies. While this development undoubtedly allowed a number of brilliant young West Indians (at first exclusively male, and almost all white) access to higher education which they might not otherwise have had, the scholarships had the less positive effect over the years of elevating an Oxbridge education to the status of a Holy Grail for West Indian students, and, by implication, tended to belittle the efforts of local institutions to offer a quality education. Thus the scholarships may be seen in some senses as another step in the underdevelopment of higher education in the region.

Another important recommendation put forward by Mitchinson was that the programme offered by Codrington College should be broadened to allow students who did not win scholarships to study secular subjects there. Accordingly, in 1878 the college began teaching a number of courses leading to degrees of the University of Durham. This development had an exact parallel in West Africa, where the failure of the proposal for a University of West Africa had led to a move to upgrade Fourah Bay College in Sierra Leone. The college authorities had entered discussions with the University of London seeking affiliation in 1876 but when the link between Durham and Codrington became known it was decided to approach Durham instead. Like Codrington, Fourah Bay began teaching courses leading to degrees of the University of Durham in 1878. Also like Codrington, until 1948 it was the only institution in its region offering instruction leading to the award of university degrees.

The idea of a regional university for the West Indies lay fallow in the early part of the twentieth century as economic stagnation consequent on the decline of sugar precipitated social and political stagnation. It was only after World War I that the issue was revived. The only initiative in the interim had been a more modest call for a publicly funded West Indian teacher training college.

The Interwar Period

After the war, efforts were made to make British policy towards the colonies more consistent and comprehensive. The war had shown that such an approach was needed if the British Empire was to survive as an economic and political entity. One symptom of this new, more systematic approach was the establishment of the ICTA in Trinidad in 1921. The college was intended to provide postgraduate training in tropical agriculture to key personnel from all over the empire, with the aim of improving the profitability of the sector, although it also offered diploma courses in agriculture to locals. It thus became only the second higher education institution in the anglophone Caribbean.

Generally, the postwar period saw a shift in attitudes concerning the demand for improved education systems in the colonies. A key role in this shift after 1923 was played by the British Advisory Committee on Education in the Colonies. This committee had been formed by the secretary of state for the colonies as a response to the report of a commission sent out in 1922 by an American philanthropic foundation, the Phelps-Stokes Fund, to examine education policy and practice towards Africans in South and West Africa. Although its primary focus was on elementary and secondary education, by the early 1930s the committee found itself considering a series of proposals for higher education facilities in the colonies. Within the West Indies, the Standing Conference on Education in the West Indian Colonies had renewed consideration of the establishment of a university in 1926; the first West Indian Conference held under the auspices of the Colonial Office in 1929 also urged further discussion of the idea.

Growing support among British colonial officials for the establishment of colonial universities in various parts of the empire in the interwar period was based on three points. The first was a recognition of the obvious shortage of well trained local personnel in the colonies to serve in the lower levels of the colonial administration, as teachers and in the nascent professions; without provision for university education at local level demand would always exceed supply. Secondly, colonial officials were increasingly concerned by the growing political consciousness among the rising elites in the colonies. Demands for self-determination were growing, fuelled in Africa and the West Indies by Garveyite and Pan-Africanist ideas. Officials feared that the continuing flow of students from West Africa and the Caribbean to institutions in Europe and the United States would further radicalize them and inspire nationalist aspirations when they returned home. The third point relates particularly to the socioeconomic and political climate in Britain in these years and perhaps requires a little more explanation.

During the war years, a large influx of black and brown people from all corners of the empire had been welcomed into Britain to assist the war effort; following the war, however, this welcome wore thin as the job market contracted and economic depression ensued. A wave of race riots in 1919 was followed by a series of measures designed to repatriate and restrict the entry of black and brown colonial citizens during the 1920s. Although students from the Caribbean and Africa were exempted from such measures, they could not be insulated from the prevailing racist climate in Britain. The potential repercussions in the colonies of the exposure of members of the educated West Indian and African elite to racism on the streets of Britain were all too obvious.

If the Colonial Office had any doubts about the matter, they were rapidly dispelled by a string of complaints it received from colonial students in Britain during these years. Many of these complaints were articulated through two significant black organizations of this period in Britain; these were the League of Coloured Peoples and the West African Students Union.[11] Other complaints were sent directly to the authorities. In 1929, for example, a group of fourteen West Indian students – mostly doctors and lawyers completing their training – wrote to Lord Passfield, the secretary of state, to protest the treatment they were receiving:

In recent months we are being made to feel that there is a rising tendency in some quarters in London to accord us the treatment of undesirable aliens; and we desire emphatically to protest against the growing inclination to discriminate against students of colour in public places of amusement, in restaurants, hotels and boarding houses . . .

They went on to detail an incident involving one of their number, a postgraduate student at the London School of Tropical Medicine, who had been ejected from the Locarno Dance Hall in Streatham on the grounds of colour. They concluded their letter with a polite but unambiguous warning:

We feel it unnecessary to point out to your lordship that such far-reaching acts of discrimination in Great Britain are likely to have far-reaching repercussive effects in different parts of the Empire, and that colonial legislation compels us to come to Great Britain and Ireland to qualify for the professions. We may be permitted to add that in order to prepare ourselves for constructive work in different parts of the Empire we should not be hindered in the enjoyment of our full rights of British citizenship; and that we should like very much to return to our homes with none but pleasant memories of our student days in Great Britain.[12]

For Colonial Office officials, however, who professed themselves powerless to remove the colour bar "or to exorcise the spirit which gives rise to it", the problem did not lie with British society, but with the policy of encouraging too many coloured students to come to Britain: "The toleration accorded to a few will not extend to a number. The remedy seems to be to provide them with higher education in their own homes, and thus discourage them from coming here."[13]

The growing official consensus on the need for colonial universities was reinforced by two reports in the early 1930s. The Mayhew–Marriott Report in 1932 on aspects of West Indian education focused mainly on the promotion of elementary, secondary and vocational education. It favoured much greater cooperation between the islands, however, and proposed a West Indian university as the crowning institution of an upgraded West Indian education system: "We feel that the future of West Indian secondary education depends largely on local provision being made for University training in all the main subjects of the secondary school curriculum."[14] At the same time it did not go so far as to suggest that such a university should be publicly funded. Instead it argued that it "would be the most appropriate object of private benefaction".

A year later a subcommittee of the British Advisory Committee on Education in the Colonies, chaired by Sir James Currie, was set up to review the parallel case for higher education in the colonies of tropical Africa. His report warned of "a grave danger" if the reasonable aspirations of the rising African elite for advancement were not met. He recommended that Gordon's College in Khartoum and Makerere College be pushed towards university college status to serve the needs of East and Central Africa, while Achimota and Yaba Colleges, together with Fourah Bay, should be groomed for a similar role in West Africa. In the event, neither report was implemented, killed off largely by the exigencies of the Depression of the early 1930s, but the principle of establishing colonial universities which both had advocated gained wide currency.

The Asquith Report and the Birth of the UCWI

The latter part of the 1930s was a period of rising labour unrest and anticolonial agitation in many parts of the British Empire. This was no more apparent than in the West Indies, where a wave of riots involving the black working class swept through the islands. In the wake of the troubles, a Royal Commission, under the chairmanship of Lord Moyne, was sent in 1938 to review conditions in the West Indies and to investigate the causes of the riots. The resulting report proposed sweeping reforms to political and administrative structures as well as improvements to the education system, and led to the establishment of the Colonial Development and Welfare Fund to finance improvements in education and other spheres. Despite the outbreak of World War II in 1939, which delayed the implementation of many of the recommendations of the Moyne Commission, both the Colonial Office and the British Advisory Committee on Education in the Colonies recognized that the need for the provision of higher education for the rising colonial elites was becoming an urgent matter. To add to earlier considerations, rising nationalist aspirations among the colonial elites, combined with Britain's desperate need for support from the colonies during the war, forced the British government to concede that there would have to be some degree of self-determination for the colonies after the war. Accordingly, colonial officials turned their attention to the practicalities of how university education could be developed in the colonies in a way that would serve the interests of Britain, as well as those of the colonial peoples in these changing times.

The critical breakthrough came in 1943, after an internal report had persuaded officials that colonial university colleges could be sponsored using the syllabuses and awarding degrees of the University of London. Thereafter, the colonial secretary, Colonel Oliver Stanley, moved rapidly to call for the appointment of a commission:

to consider the principles which should guide the promotion of higher education, learning, and research and the development of universities in the Colonies; and to explore means whereby universities and other appropriate bodies in the United Kingdom may be able to cooperate with institutions of higher education in the Colonies in order to give effect to these principles.[15]

The political reasoning behind this plan to develop colonial universities under the tutelage of British universities was explicit; the linkage would be used "to rear the local leaders of the future". By this means, indigenous elites would not only receive the training they required for effective leadership, they would remain intellectually and ideologically tied to Britain.

The Commission on Higher Education in the Colonies, appointed under the chairmanship of Mr Justice Cyril Asquith at the end of 1943, was charged with the responsibility for developing a scheme for higher education for West, Central and East Africa, as well as the West Indies. To cover these disparate geographical areas the commission lost no time in delegating authority to two committees, one under Sir Walter Elliot to consider the issue in relation to West Africa, and the other, under Sir James Irvine, to examine the issue in the West Indies. Subsequently, the findings of these two committees were absorbed into the main Report of the Asquith Commission, published in June 1945. The Asquith Report became the blueprint for the establishment of university colleges in Africa and the West Indies in the years that followed.[16]

The Irvine Committee was appointed in January 1944 and left Britain for the West Indies a month later, without holding any preliminary meetings. Such meetings were hardly necessary since the terms of reference were straightforward: they were "to review existing facilities for higher education in the British Colonies in the Caribbean and to make recommendations regarding future university development for those colonies".[17] Two members of the commission were highly experienced university administrators: the chairman, Sir James Irvine, was principal and vice chancellor of the University of St Andrews, while Raymond Priestley was principal and vice chancellor of the University of Birmingham. The third member was Margery Perham, a fellow of Nuffield College and reader in colonial administration at the University of Oxford, who had vast experience of West African conditions. The secretary was Thomas R. Rowell, an assistant educational adviser in the Colonial Office. However, perhaps the most interesting members of the committee were two West Indians, Hugh Springer, then a trade unionist and member of the House of Assembly in Barbados, and Philip Sherlock, secretary of the Institute of Jamaica. It was the first time West Indians had been asked to serve on such a committee, and the committee's report emphasized "the effect their presence had in enabling us to get into rapid and sympathetic touch with witnesses and the public generally". Both would go on to have a seminal influence in the formative years of the university.[18]

Over the next three months the Irvine Committee visited Trinidad, British Guiana, Jamaica and Barbados. They also spent five days on a fact finding mission at the University of Puerto Rico. Subsequently, they visited West Indian students studying at Howard University in Washington and at McGill University in Montreal. Their findings were unequivocal:

After a careful consideration of the evidence put before us and after enquiry into the needs and conditions of the West Indies, the number of potential candidates for higher education and the absorptive capacity of the colonies, we have come to a unanimous decision.

We recommend the establishment of a single University of the West Indies at the earliest possible date.[19]

The committee reported that the arguments it had heard against the establishment of a single university boiled down to two basic points. The first was that the economic state of the British West Indies would not support the expense of a university. The committee responded to this practical objection by recommending that the imperial government should provide funds to meet the capital cost for setting up the university, "as well as some part of the recurrent cost", and by suggesting that further funds might be found through private benefactions. The other argument was that the smallness and isolation of the islands required that students should be sent out into the wider world to complete their education and broaden their intellectual horizons. The committee's response to this was that it would be more suitable and more effective for West Indian students to proceed abroad for postgraduate training, and that, in any case, the number of undergraduate places available for overseas students would be squeezed by a rapid expansion in domestic student numbers in Britain after the war. As for the argument that the establishment of a university was desirable but that it should be delayed pending improvement in the standards of elementary and secondary education, the committee felt to the contrary that the existence of a university might help to raise standards elsewhere in the education system.

Having swept aside these criticisms, the committee then went on to make its case for a single, unitary and residential University of the West Indies. The most important argument was that such a university would develop "a West Indian outlook":

We believe that if West Indian students could work together in surroundings of dignity and beauty, living in close community with each other and with teachers of the highest intellectual quality, and enjoying all the culture and athletic activities possible in such conditions, they would develop fully, not only as individuals, but as West Indians. Many of them might thus so strengthen their desire to serve their own people that it would not weaken when they went on to complete and broaden their experience overseas. This is, perhaps, the only means by which the present divisions and insularities can be broken down.[20]

Other arguments along these lines for the establishment of the university included the immediate need for responsible and well informed leaders in the Caribbean as it passed through a process of democratization and progress towards self-determination, and the need to improve the position of women in Caribbean society. The committee also argued that a single University of the West Indies could become "the intellectual centre" of the region, and an agency for the promotion of research pertinent to the needs of West Indian people.

Despite the fine words, however, it is important to realize that the university envisaged by the Irvine Committee in the West Indies was completely in keeping with the aims of the wider Asquith Commission, of which it was part. The overriding mission was to ensure that the obligation of the British government to guide the colonies towards self-rule through the promotion of higher education was met without sacrificing continuing British interest and influence. The UCWI was thus only one of several colonial universities proposed by the Asquith Commission to serve different parts of the empire. Together, they were intended to provide intellectual training for a greater proportion of the indigenous elites of the colonies than had been possible hitherto, and at relatively low cost. They would end the politically undesirable practice of sending students overseas for training, where they might be exposed to radical anticolonial influences. The financing of these universities from imperial coffers (through the Colonial Development and Welfare Fund), plus the control over the syllabus and the awarding of degrees by the University of London (overseen by a new body, the Inter-University Council [IUC] for Higher Education in the Colonies), would ensure that their programmes would not stray too far from the models and standards laid down in Britain, as would the appointment of staff recruited via the IUC from British universities. As an added refinement to the new system, the Asquith Commission insisted, over local objections, that staff recruited from Britain for these 'Asquith Colleges' (as they became known) should receive special allowances that would set them apart from local staff.[21]

The new UCWI was finally opened at Mona in a suburb of Kingston, Jamaica, in 1948. All of the other Asquith Colleges were located in Africa. They included Khartoum University College, opened in 1947; the University College of Ibadan, opened in January 1948; the University College of Ghana, opened in October 1948; Makerere University College, opened in 1949, and the University College of Rhodesia and Nyasaland, opened in 1955. The only other higher education institution in West Africa, Fourah Bay College, continued as a university college affiliated to the University of Durham until

1960 when it became the University of Sierra Leone. Ajayi et al. have written thus of the Asquith Colleges:

They were colonial universities in the sense defined by John Hargreaves of an institution which 'paid greater attention to its standing in the eyes of foreigners than to the relevance of its activities to the needs of its own country.' The two essential characteristics of the Colleges, therefore, were the search for equivalence with European university standards and the attendant control of both curriculum and personnel by the colonial authorities acting in partnership with the metropolitan universities.[22]

When the circumstances and conditions under which they were established are taken into consideration, it is certainly difficult to escape the conclusion that – whatever other benefits they may have brought – the Asquith Colleges were designed by the British authorities chiefly to help manage the transition from colonial to neocolonial regimes during the 1940s and 1950s.

The Early Development of UCWI

The origins of the new UCWI as an autonomous institution of higher learning had been less than auspicious. Essentially, it had been designed as part of a much larger colonial project to contain and (to some extent) coopt rising anticolonial elites. Nevertheless, from the beginning there were ambiguities in the make-up of the UCWI which meant that it was never wholly the child of colonial policy. It seems paradoxical, for example, that the mission of the university college to serve the region as a whole and to promote West Indian identity as a single, unitary institution – as articulated by the colonially inspired Irvine Committee – was entirely in accord with the agenda of West Indian nationalists. From their differing perspectives, both Colonial Office officials and West Indian nationalists during the 1950s hoped that the university college would become, in Eric Williams words, "a spearhead for Federation". Both believed this would make the region easier to manage. Yet while the British hoped that a federal West Indian state would remain locked into a relationship as a subordinate partner of Britain, West Indian nationalists such as Williams argued that federation was the only means through which the many small island states scattered across the anglophone Caribbean could achieve true economic and political independence from British rule.

There was another important, politically ambiguous feature in the make-up of the UCWI. The strong centralizing assumptions of the Irvine Committee, which were reflected in the early administrative structures and programmes of the university, contradicted the powerful decentralizing force of local island identities and aspirations. Recognition of this fact had been implicit in a decision dating back to 1945 to establish a Department of Extra Mural Studies of the University College with centres in the noncampus territories. Ironically, whatever success the UCWI had in nurturing a West Indian historical, cultural and intellectual renaissance had the effect of promoting the very diversity of identity and aspiration it was pledged to subsume. Thus, from the outset, the stage was set for a political and ideological struggle for the soul of the university in the region. This would come to the fore with the collapse of the West Indies Federation in 1962, and continues to the present day.

During the late 1940s and 1950s, the UCWI had only limited success in establishing itself as the natural destination for West Indians in search of higher education. The initial enrolment in 1948 of 33 students (23 men and 10 women) had risen to 555 (354 men and 201 women) by 1957–58, an increase of more than sixteen times in ten years. But this was still only a fraction of the university college's potential. A committee under the chairmanship of A.S. Cato, appointed in 1957 by the new Federal administration to review the policy of the UCWI found that of 494 applicants in that year who held the minimum qualifications for admission only 179 were admitted, or 36.23 percent. The main reason for turning away so many qualified students was the lack of scholarships and other aid to support them at the university college.[23] At the same time there was a continuing preference on the part of many potential students to go to universities and colleges overseas. The same committee estimated the number of students from the anglophone Caribbean in universities and colleges in the United Kingdom, Canada and the United States in 1956–57 at "not less than 2,370".[24] Ironically, given the financial constraints limiting student numbers at the UCWI, at least 260 of these were on government scholarships. As if these problems were not enough, the UCWI further limited its potential enrolments by setting entry requirements that were simply too high for the bulk of West Indians graduating from the region's secondary schools. Some of those students who went overseas to study did so because the UCWI did not consider them qualified for admission; they found that institutions of higher learning elsewhere were not so exclusive. In an aside the Cato Committee noted:

> It cannot be assumed that increase in the amount of government financial aid for students proceeding to the University College will substantially change the number of West Indies students proceeding to North America. Lower admission requirements, the prospect of 'working their way' through University or College, and the inducement of financial aid, will continue to attract many students.[25]

Another handicap to the growth of the UCWI was a high failure rate. It soon became clear that in the anxiety to deliver good quality education, standards had been set at a punitive level, so that many of those who did matriculate found it difficult to progress through the university system. Once this pattern was established, however, faculty members at the UCWI – many of whom were expatriates – seemed to take a perverse pride in holding to it, to the detriment of their students and of the development of the university college as a whole. The report of an IUC committee chaired by Dame Lillian Pension in 1953, which praised the high academic standards achieved at the UCWI in its first five years, merely served to perpetuate the trend. Perhaps the most worrying aspect for the university was the fact that many of those students who did not meet its exacting standards and so had been refused admission, or who later dropped out, went on to complete degrees successfully in other institutions in Britain, Canada or the United States.

It was small comfort that similar problems were being experienced by the other Asquith Colleges.[26] By the end of the 1950s, there was a growing realization that if the UCWI was to grow beyond the parameters established at its origins, it had to throw off the strait-jacket of British influence in these and in other critical areas of its operation.

Independence and the Decentralization of Higher Education in the Anglophone Caribbean

By the 1960s, criticisms of the UCWI were becoming increasingly vocal in various parts of the Caribbean. Critics argued that far from broadening access to higher education in the region, it had succeeded thus far only in educating a relatively narrow neocolonial elite. This problem had been compounded by the fact that its programmes were too limited, focused mainly on general degrees in arts and science and on medicine (through the University College Hospital), and by the fact that the structure of its degrees was locked into British models of doubtful utility. Generally, the university college community was perceived as having locked itself away in its ivory towers at Mona and as having become separated from the concerns and aspirations of the people of the region. This critical mood was no doubt associated with the collapse of the West Indian Federation and the subsequent spread of independence for individual island states throughout the anglophone Caribbean during these years. The collapse of the Federation in 1962 also called into question the validity of the unitary model on which the UCWI had been founded. One of the contributing territories, Guyana, withdrew forthwith from the university and moved to set up its own institution, the University of Guyana, in 1963.[27]

In response to these many challenges, the university college, under the leadership of its first West Indian principal, Arthur Lewis, sought to remake itself.[28] The possibility of ending the 'special relationship' whereby matriculation requirements and adaptations to the syllabuses were approved by, and the degrees awarded were those of, the University of London, had first been raised by the Pension Report in 1954. Four years later the Cato Report strongly supported the proposal that the university college should seek university status in its own right. It based this recommendation on a review of the UCWI's structures of governance, its teaching standards, its research output, the "corporate social life" of its students, and its relationship with the wider West Indian community. Even as the Federation collapsed in 1962, the university received a new Royal Charter which established it as an autonomous degree awarding body, no longer dependent on its 'special relationship' with the University of London for validation. Reborn as the University of the West Indies (UWI) it moved quickly to unmake other aspects of its earlier incarnation.

One of the key features of the university college, as noted earlier, was its unitary nature. In the early days of the UCWI's existence this aspect of its character had been relatively uncontroversial, although there had been some interisland argument about the site chosen. The only concession to decentralizing pressures had been the appointment of two 'resident tutors' to represent the Extra Mural Department in the noncampus territories, one for the Windward Islands and one for the Leewards.[29] The Cato Committee, which had met under the auspices of the West Indies Federation, had not thought to challenge the assumption that the new UWI would retain a unitary structure. It did recommend, however, that the UCWI should merge with the ICTA, so that the ICTA would become the Faculty of Agriculture of the university. Despite the efforts of the Cato Committee to integrate agriculture into the activities of the university at the Mona site, the inevitable result of this decision would be the beginnings of a second campus in Trinidad. The merger duly took place in 1960, and for the first time the UCWI found itself operating in two widely separated locations. The premier of Trinidad, Dr Eric Williams, had helped to promote this development in the hope – quickly to be disappointed – that this strengthening of the 'Jamaica–Trinidad axis' might help prop up the crumbling Federation. Instead it pointed the way forward for the new UWI in a rapidly changing social and political environment.

The break-up of the Federation in May 1962, barely a month after the UWI had received its Royal Charter, was followed almost immediately by the granting of independence to Jamaica and Trinidad and Tobago. From the university's perspective, if it was to meet the challenge of the new political realities whilst retaining its deeply valued regional character, it had to move quickly to increase its presence in the southern Caribbean. Arthur Lewis proposed not only that the university should expand the programmes it offered in Trinidad, but that it should add a third campus to serve the so-called little eight – the smaller Eastern Caribbean states that had been left isolated by the collapse of the Federation. At a meeting of the University Council chaired by Eric Williams in February 1963 both these proposals were approved. Less than nine months later the university's third campus was opened in sheds at the Bridgetown harbour in Barbados. Subsequently it moved to a purpose-built site at Cave Hill. At the same council meeting in 1963 the residential requirement, which had operated since the inception of the UCWI, was dropped to allow the introduction of evening programmes at Mona and St Augustine in order to widen the access to higher education to nonresidential and part-time students in those islands.[30]

Over the next thirty years, the reports of numerous commissions and committees on its operations would launch the university on an almost continuous process of what Rex Nettleford has called "the sort of piecemeal institutional engineering which was facilitated by the heritage of British muddling, though coupled with a native Caribbean facility to function on several levels simultaneously".[31] While some of these commissions and committees focused on the more prosaic, but vital, matters of administrative structures and finance, others reviewed and revised its academic programmes. Although space does not allow a full discussion of the process and results of this "piecemeal institutional engineering", it may be noted that the overall thrust of these efforts was to attempt to make the university more responsive to its constituency and to throw off the more blatant features of its colonial past. They also sought to maintain and, if possible, enhance, its growing international reputation as an institution of higher learning.

The pressure for decentralization of the university did not end with the opening of the third campus in Barbados, however. Nationalist agendas in the various island states, both large and small, ate away at the concept of a single West Indian nation, and operated as a centrifugal force in university affairs. The 'noncampus territories', as they were known, demanded an increased physical presence by the university in their territories, not only in order to broaden access to higher education locally, but also to ensure that the financial and other benefits accruing to the campus territories as a result of their association with the university would be shared more equitably with the other islands. Since the university was now funded by a University Grants Committee on which the governments of all fourteen contributing territories were represented, these were pressures it could not ignore. As one response, between 1967 and 1972 the number of resident tutors was increased from two to seven, and university centres were established in Antigua, Dominica, Grenada, Montserrat, St Kitts, St Lucia and St Vincent.[32]

Although these developments helped to preserve UWI's regional character during the politically stormy days of the late 1960s and 1970s, when several more of the contributing territories moved towards independence from Britain, they were still not sufficient to meet the rising aspirations of all of the region's people for access to higher education. Recognizing this, the Caribbean Heads of Government Conference in 1974 set up an Intergovernmental Committee on Caribbean University Education under the chairmanship of William Demas. Among its recommendations were calls for further devolution and democratization of the management structures of the university. Most significantly, however, the Demas Report included a call for the establishment of community colleges in the noncampus territories.

The Organization of Eastern Caribbean States (OECS), established in 1981, consisted of the seven smaller anglophone territories of the Eastern Caribbean (Barbados – the most populous of the original 'little eight' – was not included). In addition to the UWI, two other institutions in the region were providing access to higher education for students from these territories by the mid 1970s. These were the University of the Virgin Islands, established in 1963 with campuses in St Thomas and St Croix, which was sponsored by the United States, and the College of Arts, Science and Technology in Jamaica, opened in the early 1970s. Mainly due to financial constraints, however, only a small proportion of potential students from the OECS went on to higher education at any of these institutions. At the same time the OECS was experiencing an acute shortage of trained manpower.

In these circumstances, it became urgent for the OECS territories to develop their own domestic institutions.[33] The lead was taken by Antigua and Barbuda, where, in 1977, the government amalgamated the hotel school, the technical institute and the sixth forms of the local secondary schools into the Antigua State College. The Clifton Dupigny Community College was established in Dominica in 1983 along similar lines. These were followed by the Sir Arthur Lewis Community College in St Lucia (1986), St Kitts College of Further Education (1988), and the Grenada National College (1988).[34] In 1988, the Antigua State College and the Sir Arthur Lewis Community College began offering the first year of degree programmes of the UWI through a process of accreditation with UWI that recalled its own origins in the 'special relationship' with the University of London.

Elsewhere in the anglophone Caribbean, other national and community colleges had been, or were being, established. By the 1990s they included such institutions as the Barbados Community College, the College of the Bahamas, and the Herman Lavity Stoutt Community College in Tortola, British Virgin Islands, among others. An Association of Caribbean Tertiary Institutions (ACTI) was formed to coordinate and consolidate these various efforts in November 1990.

Conclusion

By the 1990s the anglophone Caribbean was witnessing a proliferation of institutions of higher learning undreamed of in the colonial period. This has the potential to democratize access to higher education regionwide for the first time since the onset of colonialism disrupted the pattern of indigenous education practised by the Amerindian communities. At the same time, however, the neglect and underdevelopment of higher education in the region over centuries has left its mark in the manner in which that proliferation has occurred, and in the continuing debates in the region about the nature and role of higher education. It remains to be seen to what extent this historical legacy will shape the development of higher education in the region into the next century.

Notes

1. J.F. Ade Ajayi, Lameck K.H. Goma and G. Ampah Johnson, *The African Experience with Higher Education* (Accra: Association of African Universities; London: James Currey; Athens: Ohio University Press, 1996), 4.
2. Ajayi, Goma and Johnson, *The African Experience with Higher Education*, 5.
3. Carl Campbell, *Colony and Nation: A Short History of Education in Trinidad and Tobago 1836–1986* (Kingston, Jamaica: Ian Randle Publishers, 1992), 1.
4. See, for example, Carl Campbell, "Mohammed Sisei of Gambia and Trinidad c.1788–1838", *African Studies Association of the West Indies Bulletin*, no.7 (December 1974): 29–38
5. There was also some minor participation in education at this time by the Roman Catholic Church in Trinidad and in other islands that were formerly Spanish or French
6. John J Figueroa, *Society, Schools and Progress in the West Indies* (Oxford: Pergamon Press, 1971), 14.
7. Figueroa, *Society, Schools and Progress in the West Indies*, 15.
8. Eric Williams, *Education in the British West Indies* (first published 1951) quoted in Wellington R.L. Friday, *Restructuring Higher Education in the Non-Campus Territories of the British Caribbean as a Strategy for Development: Problems and Prospects* (EdD diss., University of Southern California, 1975), 107.
9. Quoted in Friday, *Restructuring Higher Education*, 83.
10. Ibid., 86.
11. For background on the West African Students Union and the League of Coloured Peoples see Peter Fryer, *Staying Power. The History of Black People in Britain* (London: Pluto Press, 1984), 324–34
12. Letter from fourteen British West Indian students to Lord Passfield, Secretary of

State for the Colonies, 12.10.29: Colonial Office files ref: CO318/396/6.
13. Lord Passfield to Walter J. Thompson BA, 4.11.29; see also handwritten note on file (initials illegible); file ref: CO318/296/6.
14. Quoted in Figueroa, *Society, Schools and Progress in the West Indies*, 26.
15. Quoted in Ajayi, Goma and Johnson, *The African Experience with Higher Education*, 55.
16. Ibid., 55. For the full text of the report see Great Britain, *Report of the Commission on Higher Education in the Colonies* (Cmd. 6647, HMSO, London, June 1945).
17. Great Britain, *Report of the West Indies Committee of the Commission on Higher Education in the Colonies* (Cmd. 6634, HMSO, London, June 1945), para. 8.
18. Philip Sherlock was the first director of the UCWI's Department of Extra Mural Studies, acting principal of the UCWI from 1958 to 1960, first principal of the St Augustine campus and vice principal of the UCWI 1960–1963, and vice chancellor of the University of the West Indies in succession to Arthur Lewis from 1963 to 1968. Hugh Springer was the first registrar of the UCWI from 1948 to 1963 and served as first director of the Institute of Education of the University of the West Indies from 1963 to 1968.
19. *Report of the West Indies Committee*, paras. 21 and 22.
20. Ibid., para. 42.
21. Ajayi, Goma and Johnson, *The African Experience with Higher Education*, 55. In the West Indian case it was notable that Margery Perham, the expert from West Africa, insisted on the importance of these differential rates of pay, while the two West Indian members of the Irvine Committee, Springer and Sherlock, registered a dissenting view, and argued that "there should never be a distinction" between overseas and local staff. One of the more popular legacies of this period is that all academic and senior administrative staff at the university still receive an entitlement to a study and travel grant, the value of which is calculated according to the cost of a return air ticket to England.
22. Ibid., 67.
23. West Indies (Federation), *Report of the Committee Appointed to Review the Policy of the University College of the West Indies December 1957–January 1958* (Bridgetown, Barbados. The Advocate Printers, 1958), para. 20.
24. *Report of the Committee Appointed to Review the Policy of the University College of the West Indies*, para. 19.
25. Ibid., para. 19, note 6.
26. These problems were highlighted at a conference of the heads of the Asquith Colleges held in Jamaica under the auspices of the IUC in 1955; Ajayi, Goma and Johnson, *The African Experience with Higher Education*, 70.
27. Gem Fletcher, Lynette France and Iris Sukdeo, *Higher Education in Guyana (University of Guyana)* (Caracas: UNESCO Regional Centre for Higher Education in Latin America and the Caribbean [CRESACC], 1987).
28. Arthur Lewis from St Lucia, later a Nobel Prize winning economist, had been a member of the League of Coloured Peoples during his student days in London, and served as economic adviser to Kwame Nkrumah in Ghana. He formally took up

his appointment as principal on 1 April 1960. He became the first vice chancellor of the UWI on 2 April 1962. He resigned in 1963 to take a professorship in Economics at Princeton.
29. Friday, *Restructuring Higher Education*, 193.
30. Ibid., 194–95
31. Philip Sherlock and Rex Nettleford, *The University of the West Indies: A Caribbean Response to the Challenge of Change* (London: Macmillan Caribbean, 1990), 212.
32. The work of the university centres was coordinated by the Office of University Services (OUS). Two offices were established, one at Mona and one at Cave Hill, in 1984. Recently (1996) the OUS has been reconstituted under the university's Board for Non-Campus Countries and Distance Education as the Tertiary Level Institutions Unit (TLIU).
33. Bevis Peters, *The Emergence of Community, State and National Colleges in the OECS Member Countries: An Institutional Analysis* (Cave Hill, Barbados: Institute of Social and Economic Research, UWI, 1993), 7–9.
34. Ibid., 15–16.

2

Contrasting Problems Facing Universities in the Developed and Developing Worlds: The Same Difference

Rex Nettleford

Introduction

Locating the prospects of higher education in the Commonwealth Caribbean against the background of developments in the wider world is particularly useful at this time when the phenomenon known as *globalization* is being seen as the cause, occasion and result of what is otherwise termed the 'knowledge economy'. The university and related institutions of higher learning, as generators and transmitters of knowledge, find themselves at the heart not only of the discourse but also of meaningful plans of action targeting the development process and its relation to the human resource as well as the paradigm shifts and quixotic changes attendant on the new situation. One is here tempted to address contrasting problems (and possibilities) evident in the developing two-thirds of the world of which the Caribbean is an acknowledged charter member and the developed world which continues to preside over and control the mobilization and distribution of the wealth on planet Earth.

Paradoxically, the approach to the problematique is in some ways misleading; for if there is contrast, or difference, in the experience of universities operating in both worlds, which must now meet the challenges on the threshold of a new millennium, it is the same difference that is to be found for the most part in both of these worlds. It is better, then, to speak of *traditional* universities and *nontraditional* places of higher learning, both of which, as products of the human intellect, are to be found in both the developed and the developing worlds.

Yet, whatever may be the claims to progress and educational revolutionism, persons who teach in, manage and attend universities anywhere seem to be agreed that such institutions are intended for the production, transmission and application of knowledge. Within this neat and cosy definitional framework different emphases have long vied for supremacy – whether it is advocacy for teaching over research and vice versa, or the assertion of the autonomous principle (knowledge for knowledge's sake and all that) over the service function of the university expressed at times in a ferocious theological commitment to relevance, utility and the like.[1] None of these concerns, which have been evident among institutions of higher learning since the 1960s, is exclusive to the developed world which, admittedly, had some of its most dramatic confrontations between agitated students and incarcerated staff members as well as between the radical constituents and the long arm of the law, ending in violence and a fatal shooting or two in some places. The developing world also had its share of protest, and it is remarkable how similar were the problems and grouses articulated in the affluent advanced North and those expressed in the poverty-stricken and technologically backward South. This was so even when boredom with Western rationalism and the scientific tradition was a major cause of unrest among the student populace in industrialized countries, and while that tradition remained the hope and much hankered-after prize for developing-country counterparts aspiring to social mobility and what they perceived to be 'civilization'.

The reason for the similarities in the problems may very well rest in the nature of the university institution itself, which was, after all, exported to most of the developing world from Europe, as well as in the fact that most of the developing-world universities are still run by those who have been trained in the values, rubrics and intellectual dogma of the continent of origin. The problems faced by universities in the United Kingdom today, for example, are very much the sort of problems encountered by many universities in the developing Commonwealth. In many cases the contrasts are more of degree than of kind.

Plotted against political, economic, cultural, and philosophical points of reference, reflections on the fate of the university in the foreseeable future do give clues, however, to those critical issues that the institution as a special organizational species, and substantively as the generator and transmitter of knowledge, must face if it is to survive. The sense of urgency imposed on us by the problems immediately under our noses often blurs the vision needed for a long-range view of the total landscape – in this case, of higher education and its relation to the entire society and the world at large.

I

This is particularly true in the contemplation of *political* forces that militate against the autonomous claims of the university or that apply pressure on the institution to function in the national interest or in the interest of some cluster of professional needs associated with economic growth and recovery or, by implication, in the interest of those who take political decisions and have reason to want to hold on to power whether by the ballot or the bullet. Immediately we could run to the conclusion that this is specifically the problem of the developing countries with their record of endemic poverty and unemployment, of institutionalized marginality and the powerlessness of the impoverished masses, and of a chronic ambivalence to ideas that may not legitimate the programmes and policies of a particular set of people in power. But this is a misreading of reality. True, an account of the state of social science research in Central America in the eighties put forward the view that meaningful research suffers restrictions by dictatorships or private sector interests, which feel they are not being positively served by such intellectual indulgences;[2] and the call for the continuing internationalization of the university tradition was seen as an antidote to the poison injected into the body politic of such developing-country universities. But not even the land that houses the mother of parliaments, and regards itself as the bedrock of the free market of ideas escapes charges of political hanky-panky. Marinated as it is in the Cartesian philosophy and the liberal traditions of the Enlightenment, the democratic state of Great Britain and Northern Ireland has stuck to the rhetoric of political liberalism while pressing economic variables into the service of some bully-boy politics. The refusal by Oxford to confer an honorary doctorate on Margaret Thatcher in protest against such anti-higher education politics was small comfort to those who treasured the sanctity of 'academic freedom'.

Universities in their traditional form, if truth be told, can be rather an embarrassment to the best laid plans emerging out of vote catching manifestos; and however much one may be committed to free discussion and dialogue for dialogue's sake, the urgency of consensus over conflict, especially in time of crisis, is always at a premium for any government, developed or developing. The politics of it all is so often hidden behind the economics of the matter; shortage of funds is now the main obstacle facing many developed-country universities. But this is exactly the same crisis being faced in many developing-country universities. The contrast may come (here again more in degree than kind) in terms of the background against which such a shortage exists in a developed country like Britain or the United States. For the political ideology that rears its head in the circumstances is one that renders public spending increasingly illegitimate.

In the face of this resurgence of supply-side economics, Keynesian welfare statism which it defies and purports to supersede is naturally in decline. The mandatory cut-back in public spending is designated 'monetarist' – Thatcherian in its iron-will persistence and charmingly Reaganomic in its resolute stubbornness. Both seemed to take on much that is to be found in the Puritan spirit that insists that God is exclusively on one's side. Universities as defenders of tolerance have to be more modest than that. As public enterprises they fall under the monetarist or neoliberal axe. Private endowments and private enterprises they can be – yes! Public parasites – no! The vulnerability of universities rests not only on the fact that they are public enterprises of an eleemosynary character (and therefore 'nonproductive' to some),[3] but also on some of their own internal weaknesses, which could well do with self-correction, as well as their undoubted inner strengths (usually associated with the comradeship of an exclusive club), which are the butt of envy from competing power centres of many a society. But there is no doubt that the university in the developed Western democracies on either side of the Atlantic is the victim of the political conviction of parties in power committed to the conscious limiting of the growth of money supply. For the argument soon develops that it is easy to train fewer doctors, engineers and teachers and certainly easier to do less pure and applied research rather than allow an economic enterprise that is productive to go bankrupt.[4] The implication here is that a university is not productive and is therefore expendable.

In this, the developing-country universities and their employers, the governments of those countries, experience a real dilemma. For though in some places (for example, the Caribbean)[5] supply-side economics, and with it liberal-corporate politics, has sought to knock Keynesian welfarism together with various forms of socialist politics off the agenda, the university in such places has had to be taken seriously as an instrument of national development, whatever the risks.[6] In a non-oil-producing developing country it is not sensible (even if easy) to train fewer doctors, engineers, managers or teachers, and it would be downright suicidal not to engage in serious research so as to build up indigenous fact-finding and intellectual analytical capabilities. Otherwise, continuing dependency on the hegemonic developed world is guaranteed. And this is a political choice most developing-country governments would not wish to make, especially if they have attained power on nationalist platforms of self-determination and independence. In any case the loss of well trained skills by the developing world to the developed is a factor that has to be dealt with in practical terms. A surplus of skills has to be produced.

For the industrially and technologically developed countries the monetarist deflationary policy, as a matter of tactics if not of faith, may be plausible in rhetoric if not altogether possible in practice. At least there is in each of these countries a private sector steeped in traditions of risk taking and possessing well honed skills of manipulating the market, if even because that market is usually of their own making and very much under their constant control, whether through multinationals, cartels or joint venture projects. Developing countries, on the other hand, are not blessed with such gifts. Their private sectors are more often than not dependent, powerless, manipulable and remain the commission agents that history has recommended them to be, with no long-lasting traditions of or real experience in innovative risk taking or actual control over world markets. Making the private sector the engine of economic growth is therefore a far more difficult task in developing countries. And the universities, if divested or deregulated by the state power, are not likely to receive competent or willing tenders from among a private sector that, in fairness, has never made the level of profits for Rockefeller-type philanthropic benefactions leading to the founding of universities, which many of their class would probably see as either too nonproductive for serious attention or too much of a nuisance in matters political and ideological to tolerate.

This political dimension of the university's problem, in both developed and developing countries, is often expressed in the charge that universities are inefficient in organization and performance. Hence the need, goes the perfectly sound economic argument, for universities to effect or be *forced* to effect rationalization of structures and economies of scale.[7] Elitist indulgences in irrelevance are said to manifest themselves in the multiplication of departments, each teaching restricted subject areas. But note how, cleverly disguised, an objective concern can be used to conceal subjective prejudice! The inefficiency is said to manifest itself in the inordinate emphasis placed on such *soft* disciplines as arts, general studies, history and the social sciences, with the 'hard' disciplines such as natural sciences, physics and mathematics neglected in the bargain. Here, the deceptively simple words 'soft' and 'hard' carry ominous political meanings; for sociology, which is soft, is bound to be left-wing and dangerous to some, while chemistry and engineering, which are as hard as nails, are bound to be right-wing and somewhat safe. Here, the university sometimes finds itself being hoisted by its own petard when the hard-line commitment to objectivity as a good in itself is invoked by detractors. It is, after all, one value of the Western rationalist tradition that finds legitimate expression in the sometimes exaggerated claims for science and its method, especially among the social scientists whose claims to objectivity can have the dysfunctional effect of dogged attachment to theological dogmas rather than to free and open thinking. And the attraction of Keynes and Marx in many a developing-country university's short-lived traditions of intellectual discourse can be as much a problem for such universities as it has been a means of bringing understanding to the social and economic phenomena in their own societies and the world at large.[8] Latter-day doctrinaire liberalism extolling the virtues of 'the market' without reference to specificities of social or cultural context is hardly the engine to drive intellectual development in the Economics departments of developing country universities or research institutes. There is room for creative scholarship, after all, which is what Commonwealth Caribbean higher education ignores at the region's peril.

Certain assumptions of the university's role and function invite political responses as well. The autonomous principle fosters a liberal morality that claims areas of inviolability in the thinking and behaviour of every human being and logically gives to the individual academic the right to opt out of any obligation that he or she might be expected to have to the service principle that has also guided university action. This claim has been seen by some, especially by political leaders in developing countries but also by inflation-ridden developed-country leaders, as a revolutionary threat to the political *status quo,* since that right to think freely and to pursue truth wherever it leads may indeed lead to founts of knowledge that flow counter to the pet policies, programmes and ideologies of whatever group of men and women may be in power at a given time. Such men and women, faced with the crisis of balancing their budgets, will naturally wish to have the universities that they fund subject themselves as well to budgetary discipline, and will even require them to eliminate waste by less wanton use of telephones, stationery, electricity and the like – stringencies that, admittedly, they are likely to impose as well on the civil service administrations over which they preside. In this, university grants committees (UGCs) are surreptitiously transformed from the buffers they were supposed to be between universities and the political masters into the viceroys (albeit reluctant viceroys) of governments, sending sad tidings of budget cuts, impending penury and the contentious prospect of increase in tuition fees for the students. This, in itself, poses a particular problem for universities in both the developing and the developed world.[9]

The suggested and attempted solutions are themselves common to both developed and developing countries. But some of these in turn present further problems, again contrasting in degree rather than kind. Take the rise in students fees or the limitation of student intake, for example: neither is without political repercussions. The question of elitism versus the commitment to democratic mass education immediately comes to mind. A beleaguered developing country that has acquired political independence and now determines who administers power on the basis of mass electoral competitive politics will want to see the university as an instrument of national development and as a means of spreading social services and other benefits equitably; and not least among these benefits is higher education, which for most in the developing countries remains the surest gateway to recognition and status, to lifelong occupational challenges and lucrative careers. Populist democratic urges vie with aristocratic elitist impulses in developed countries even more intensely. Universities are the arenas of combat for such conflict. They are also the target for questions of autonomy versus service, of pure research versus applied, of excellence and 'quality assurance' versus equality, of ivory tower exclusivity versus populist developmental relevance. But all of these questions are often mere euphemisms for unstated political positions or serve as props to competing power centres that are jealous of their own right to define the parameters of their concern and to be able to follow through with action based on such definition.

The University of the West Indies (UWI) itself has gone a step further by reconceptualizing itself as the hub in a network of tertiary level institutions, by facilitating articulation into its courses by graduates of other tertiary institutions, by franchising programmes to other tertiary level institutions such as community colleges, and by spearheading the establishment of the Association of Caribbean Tertiary Institutions (ACTI) to maximize the benefits from collaboration without prejudice to the maintenance of academic standards.[10] Contributing governments are in this way forced to take the university seriously in its effort to respond creatively to the demands of change.

The intensity of the preoccupations with such problems in developing countries contrasts perhaps with the seemingly matter-of-fact ambience surrounding similar problems in the developed world. But this is an illusion. The phenomenon of power – political power – everywhere threatens the university's survival as a self-determining, self-regulatory, self-directed producer and transmitter of knowledge in the service of humankind.

II

As with politics so with the economic factors, some of which I have made bold to suggest are more 'political' in nature and intent than appears at first on the surface. But budgetary constraints, by whatever name, constitute an economic factor that carries far-reaching implications for teaching, research and outreach work in any university anywhere today. To recapitulate: galloping inflation, especially since the oil crisis of 1973, has rendered Keynesian economics inadequate if not inoperable in most of the Western world. Friedmanesque monetarism, reinforced by the new globalization/ market forces dispensation, has been virtually decreed the substitute. This entails the cutting of public sector expenditure to an irreducible minimum. Since education is a major public utility, universities in their traditional form have become vulnerable at this time. In practice, this has meant the retrenchment of academic staff, the rationalization of organizational structure and equipment supply and utilization, a decrease in student intake and a corresponding rise in students' fees. This is the scenario for most developed-country universities, including those in Britain and Australia. The situation in the developing world is exacerbated by the fact that, even where monetarist strategies still compete with Keynesian or socialist-type development programmes, the fall in market prices for primary agricultural produce, the burdens of debt repayment, the restricted quotas from lending agencies like the World Bank and the policing powers of the International Monetary Fund (IMF) have all forced on developing countries similar policies of cutback on public sector expenditure, leaving developing-country universities with options very similar to those open to their developed-country counterparts, though of a contrasting degree of intensity.

This lack of money, then, challenges all universities in such situations to a wide range of solutions. But these, in turn, lead to a wide range of further problems – from the deprivation of potential groups able to benefit from higher education, through the absence of innovation in both teaching methods and the learning process, to the general degeneration of intellectual and educational activity down the line. The lack of money hits telling blows: first, against the construction, maintenance and geographical distribution of physical facilities in most countries, and especially in developing ones, since many developed countries will have had such facilities well in place following the expansion of educational facilities programmes in the post World War II period; secondly, against the implementation of policy with an orientation towards mass education – again, this is especially true of developing countries where the sons and daughters of the voting electorate must be provided for as part of the pact between the elected and the electors; and thirdly, against the realization of the commitment to a policy which postulates that education must be relevant to socioeconomic development, whether through courses specifically designed to inform public policy initiatives or in the preparation of new instructional material with indigenous content and perhaps in indigenous language(s).

Then there is that cluster of economic problems, common to both sets of countries, relating to the internal and external efficiency of the university system. The internal efficiency factor already dealt with is, admittedly, often within the university's capabilities to achieve, given the will and activation of its survival instincts.[11] But it is not always easy for universities in their traditional form to deal with the proposition that if the output of the schools, universities and nonformal programmes possesses the attitudes, knowledge, skills needed by society, and particularly by the economy, the education system is regarded as efficient in this external sense.[12] This concept of external efficiency clearly turns on cost-benefit analysis, quantifiable variables indicating the clear and present usefulness of the university to society, on straight manpower questions of how many engineers, teachers, agriculturists, nurses, doctors, and other professionals, are to be supplied to service the nutrition, food and agriculture sectors of the economy or to provide good healthcare delivery systems, and of how many managers may be needed for industry and the production process. This has been particularly acute in developing countries where the needs and desires are eloquently articulated, but usually without budgetary support for their realization. Many developed-country universities have at last caught up with their counterparts in the developing world in respect of this dilemma. These are not contrasting problems therefore. Inflation is demanding from both worlds internal and external efficiency in their universities.

A developing world university such as the UWI is unequivocal in its intentions to meet the increasing demands of higher education by making distance education one of its major thrusts into the new millennium. India, China, and several small states of the South Pacific have embarked on the 'open university' or dual/mixed mode type institution to meet the challenges of access and cost. At the time of writing the UWI, which serves some fourteen territories scattered all over the Caribbean, has some twenty-five sites in its telecommunication network system with plans for nearly double that number located in campus and noncampus countries by the year 2000. These are designed to "facilitate the delivery of a much wider array of teaching and learning opportunities enhancing existing University level courses in Social Sciences, Business and Public Administration and Education".[13] Cooperation with contributing governments promises to meet the problem of cost-effectiveness in higher education in the medium and long run.

Perhaps there is some contrast in the effect that population growth has on universities in either world. Indications, according to United Nations reports, are that the world population will increase by about 54 percent between 1975 and the year 2000. But the increase will be some 10 percent in Europe and 104 percent in Africa, while the total population of the developing countries will rise by 70 percent.[14] The need for more school places is implied for developing countries while in many of the developed countries low and declining birth rates will lead to a reduction of the school-age population as well as a general ageing of the population owing to greater life expectancy. This presents a particular challenge for developed-country universities which may find increasing pressure placed on them for continuing education or experiential education programmes, as well as education via distance learning.[15] Such exercises are likely to provide a welcome source of revenue from the offer of short certificate and diploma courses designed for mid career upgrading, skill retraining and personal enrichment. Less hope for this exists in developing countries that must reserve their still meagre intellectual resources for the undergraduate training of their still youthful populations, most of whom are too eager to emerge from their low socioeconomic status through rapid social mobility via education and the acquisition of university qualifications.

Further, economic problems attendant on world population increase are bound to have serious repercussions on developing-country universities in the areas of food supplies, raw materials and energy supplies; for the priorities in curriculum content, research initiatives and service functions are going to be determined by this fact. Ecological problems, too, will take on genuine importance in the thrust towards maximizing scarce resources without irreparable damage to fragile environments. The orientation of research effort in at least one developing country follows from a conscious relationship between research and development problems. Research areas cover the following categories: natural resources and environment, agriculture, forestry and fisheries, mining, industrial technology, energy, housing and development of construction technologies and materials, transportation and telecommunications, health, social development (that is, socioeconomic development problems and issues), basic knowledge.[16] These represent the specifics of developing-country university problems of adapting to express needs. There may be contrasts in details to the problems of developed-country universities, but behind the shopping lists is a common problem of the university's need to respond positively to the economic imperatives of a rapidly changing world.

The spectre of slow economic growth in developing countries points to the persistence of intractable problems and the consequent limiting of resources available to higher education. A key factor in all this is the application of science and technology to resource exploitation. Developing countries are increasingly aware of this.[17] The training of scientific and technological personnel for practical work, the increase in scientific research capabilities through the encouragement of indigenous research potential, the continuous updating of scientific material to keep abreast of new theories and discoveries, will continue to challenge the developing-country universities to new orientations. These may indeed pose problems of perception and definition for traditionalists among university men and women, but they will also offer points of departure for those who see relevance as the touchstone of the university's existence in late twentieth century society.

The developed world is itself obsessed with the continuous application of science and technology to human needs, as can be seen in the acceleration of growth in technology that has transformed industry and communications. Such developments in Japan, Europe and the United States, as well as the Soviet Union, pose problems for the survival of those who are stubbornly attached to traditional forms. They must either transform themselves or disappear, some would say. One is told that the product which is high in skill and brainpower and low in raw material is the best bet for Britain.[18] But the developing world, which is rich in raw materials, is also in need of skills and brainpower to meet, on more equitable terms, the skill and brainpower of the developed world, and to produce the raw materials in greater quantities and better yields at lower costs. Developing-country universities face the same challenge as the farmer, fisherman, forester and decision maker. Post-harvest and storage techniques, marketing and negotiating skills (to command fair prices for primary products), manufacturing and industrializing capabilities, and planning for the rational use of scarce resources – all require the acquisition of skills and fresh bodies of knowledge that may be new to the developing-country citizenry. The universities' role in this is unquestionably one of active advocacy and dynamic responsiveness. For the developing-world universities have the serious problem of the low level of mastery of skills in mathematical, scientific and practical disciplines among the undergraduate populations at the time of admission. The establishment of specialist technology institutes/colleges/universities suggests itself as has been apparent in different Caribbean countries for at least two or three decades.[19]

Closely associated with these and the traditional type of university is the role of what has been termed the *knowledge media* by which the relationship between people and knowledge is being changed in fundamental ways. For, according to a vice chancellor of Britain's Open University, the knowledge media "denote the convergence of computing, telecommunications and the cognitive sciences . . . capturing, storing, imparting, sharing, accessing, creating, combining and synthesizing of knowledge". He was careful to point out further that "[t]he knowledge media are not just a technical format, such as CD-Rom or computer conferencing, but the whole presentational style, the user interface, the accessibility, the interactivity".[20]

III

Technology is, indeed, more than hardware with blinking lights. My own advocacy of the importance of the science and technology factor in coming to grips with the end-of-century problems of universities in both the developed and developing world is not meant to succumb to the unrelieved determinism of a scientific age, whereby the distortions of what is otherwise a perfectly viable rationalist tradition are made to rule out the expression of all human acts of intelligence, of which university activity is but one, variables of *human feeling* and *human culture* manifest in *creative expression,* a *moral sense,* and even *religious faith.*

Some would assert that the biggest problem faced by the university as an institution of growth and development in both worlds surrounds the loss of certitude in these very particulars. Some would blame the loss on the betrayal over time of the original aims of the university in the integrated advancement of human civilization – a claim that developing countries view with some ambivalence, since that 'civilization' is not infrequently defined narrowly in terms of the intellectual, artistic and technological achievements of a Europe that emerged out of the Greek-Christian-Hebraic cultural heritage. The uncertainty of the verities distilled from that civilization among the developed-country citizenries themselves also serves to compound the issue, though there is no shortage in the developing world of inspired imitations of the old Oxbridge, or of the drift to the inherited notions of what a 'proper university' ought to be.[21]

By the same token, the developing world is not short on myths, morality, religiosity, human compassion, feeling and all the things that make metaphor and poetry of reality. Indeed, a major problem lies in the fact that decisions of moment are too often taken on hearsay, intuition and personal feelings rather than on scientific observation and analysis of objective data. Yet, out of loyalty to its intellectual inheritance the developing-world university is very much like its Western developed-country model – "locked into the empirical conception of knowledge".[22] A former professor of higher education at the University of London cries for the re-establishment of longer-term objectives which involve moral and more imaginatively human dimensions in British colleges and universities.[23] But that call will not be heeded as long as the university lecturer, administrator, student and researcher remain the victims of an epistemology that views all human knowledge as the "accumulation of certainties based on observation and experimental evidence"[24] with little or no room for "feeling and being and reflecting on the process"[25] of creating and transmitting that knowledge.

Even hard-boiled programmes of studies, designed to meet pressing contemporary needs, are likely to be the poorer for depriving themselves of the injection of bodies of knowledge long identified as the humanities. Management studies, which is yet to gain the level of intellectual coherence its advocates tend to claim, is a case in point. Heavy doses of information drawn from traditional sociology, economics, politics, history and anthropology may prove critical in the preparation of managers of enterprises and nation-states that have evolved in the Caribbean out of a history of slavery, the plantation and colonialism. Things of moment, so perceived, in taking the planet into the twenty-first century, point to an interdisciplinary approach to both undergraduate studies and graduate research. The fact that the word 'interdisciplinary' is sometimes dismissed as the greyspeak of campus grandees, and therefore potentially nonproductive, offers little excuse for not facilitating the cross-fertilization of knowledge and methodologies to ferret out of lived reality such knowledge where appropriate. The pluralistic nature of modern societies in both the developing and the developed worlds demands no less, hence the growing interest worldwide in something called cultural studies.

The Cultural Studies Initiative in the UWI is clearly an attempt to speak to the creative diversity of the region and of the wider world and to prepare adequately its graduands through acts of discovery of new and appropriate ontologies, new and appropriate cosmologies and, by extension, new and appropriate epistemologies.

As the institution with major responsibility for the human resources of the Caribbean region, the UWI recognizes that it must take the lead in developing a cadre of persons, grounded in a sensitive understanding of their own history and cultural heritage, who can articulate and infuse this understanding into the development of the society at every level. Their research will form the basis of a new approach to education, with changes in the curriculum that can create the building blocks for a just and more humane Caribbean society.[26]

The prevailing empiricism in the academy has indeed reduced research, even in the humanities, to objective and quantitative terms, making of disciplines like philosophy and history 'nondisciplines' among an intolerant and smug clerisy of 'value-free' social scientists. How many are the social scientists in developing-country universities who write tomes of quantitative analyses without the benefit of an historical framework?

Computational skills are vital for twenty-first century existence but they are in no way incompatible with the gift of interpretation and creative imaginative capabilities. The university administrator in both the developed and the developing worlds is wont to define himself or herself as something of a broker among different constituents on a university campus and is therefore free of the responsibility of giving moral leadership in times of crisis. The university lecturer takes refuge in the dry and programmed communication of abstractions devoid, as someone puts it, of "feeling, touch or spontaneity".[27] Small wonder that he usually loses out in many developed countries to the vagaries of daytime television, which prove more provocative, interesting and even profound. The university institutions in many developed countries have been forced to become degree factories producing more run-of-the-mill BAs and unemployable PhDs than is sometimes good for human intellectual progress, since the training merely perpetuates the recycling of abstract, symbolic knowledge without adding significantly to the frontiers of knowledge.[28] An American academic pointedly comments on the university's

peculiar orientation to public relations which leads it to court public support and hence public approval even under circumstances that would clearly favour, instead, a policy of coolly reminding the public that it, too, is dependent on the university as a major source of revenue and employment and that it might well be advised to avoid excessive harassment even of those it does not particularly like.[29]

This is timely advice for a university such as the UWI which has embarked on marketing itself to attract much needed funds for capital and recurrent costs.

Whether universities in the developing world can make bold to defy their constituted authorities in this fashion is a problem not only of politics but of cultural, philosophical and moral significance. For the university must be prepared to be "the intellectual and ethical forum of the lay society" as suggested by an American psychology professor back in 1970,[30] all the more since many feel that the great religions of humanity – Judaism, Christianity, Islam and Marxism-Leninism – have virtually disembodied themselves from their real-life beginnings and have become "dogmatic authoritarian codes of intellectual beliefs and moral behaviours".[31] Yet the revival of Islam is a profoundly significant event against the background of loss of faith in the Western 'isms'; and the developing world's passionate attraction to Marxism-Leninism during the Cold War may be seen in part as a desperate effort to salvage from the West's technology-based ethos the spirituality of man at the centre of the cosmos. Christian fundamentalism offers the same hope for many young people on university campuses all over the Western world. The search for a moral purposiveness in society is, then, a major challenge for technological society – meaning the developed world – as well as for those who hanker after the fruits of technology – meaning the developing world.

A new ethic rooted in the resolve to place humankind at the centre of the development process – which means now what it has always meant, namely liberation from ignorance, fear, disease and hunger – is probably the university's greatest challenge and certainly one of its major problems if it is to survive. Let me quote our British professor of higher education again:

We need to give a profoundly thoughtful consideration to present administrative and academic practices with a view to hooking up the assumptions which lie underneath them. Curriculum content is too confined, with subjects taught in isolation one from the other. The social and moral consequences of applying so many of the skills that can be learned are little attended to – even in medicine and surgery, certainly in economics, agricultural science, [and] the managerial arts. Theory and praxis are too often studied in remarkable isolation . . . History is neglected as if the present could be understood without any real entering in to the past. A greater depth and understanding of humanity is what our higher education is so much in need of.[32]

Seventeen years later, the Dearing Report coming out of the United Kingdom echoed and expanded on this:

Higher Education [it declared] is fundamental to the social, economic and *cultural* health of the nation. It will contribute not only through the intellectual development of students and by equipping them for work, but also by adding to the world's store of knowledge and understanding, *fostering culture for its own sake and promoting the values that characterise higher education:* respect for evidence, respect for individuals and their views; and the search for truth. Equally, part of its task will be to accept a duty of care for the wellbeing of our democratic civilisation, based on respect for the individual and respect by the individual for the conventions and laws which provide the basis of a civilised society[33] (my emphasis).

As with the developed countries, so it is with the developing world. The university institution in both these worlds will need the gifts of adaptability and plasticity – in other words the capacity to tolerate the contradictions and complexity of the human condition and the ability to respond to the demands of fundamental change. This indeed is the essence of the creative spirit stored in abundance wherever people have functioned over time in shaping societies and constructing systems, procedures and strategies for their survival. In the developing world's experience of domination and subjugation this most elusive of human faculties has been thoroughly exercised, and it is this very fact that promises hope when despair should suggest itself. The developed world, for all its self-doubt and current confusion, is in possession of a patrimony of sterling achievements which, when freed from the viler aspects of imperial domination and the scourge of exploitative impulses, remain an ennobling testament to human capacities.

Adaptability and plasticity have been the driving forces of much of that achievement in the past. Why cannot they serve again for the future? Some faith may, indeed, be placed in what a former vice chancellor of the UWI said of universities: "no government or combination of governments, no commercial or trading organisations, no common markets or free trade areas can fulfil what are university functions – the search for knowledge by means of objective and free enquiry and the sharing of that knowledge."[34] The self-criticism and continuing self-revising features of such a task are the true guarantees for long-term fitness and ultimate survival; and the present problems of the university, whether they be political, social, economic, cultural, philosophical or ethical, may be just the kind of test needed at this time for the university to re-establish its indispensability to human growth and development. The question is whether universities are ready for this test. The UWI, in initiating self-reformation on the basis of a Governance Commission, which it set up to review and evaluate its work, clearly means to send the message that it is ready.

Notes

1. See Tyrrell Burgess, "Excellence or Equality. A Dilemma in Higher Education?", *Higher Education Review* (Spring 1978): 43. He defines the autonomous tradition as one that "sees higher education as an activity with its own values and purposes, affecting the rest of society obliquely and as a kind of bonus", while the service tradition is characterized as "responsive, vocational, innovative and open".
2. Juan Manuel Villasuso, "Social Science Research in Central America. Current Situation and Future Perspectives" (paper presented to the Board of Governors of the International Development Research Centre in San Jose, Costa Rica, 1 April 1982 [q v.]).
3. For a long time it has been the practice for West Indian governments' annual economic reports to list education and culture under the 'nonproductive sector'.
4. Cp. Maurice Peston, "Universities: End of the Robbins Era", *The Times Educational Supplement*, 20 March 1981.
5. For example, Jamaica, where the policies of the ruling Jamaica Labour Party were promulgated in declared opposition to the democratic socialism of the ousted People's National Party which governed from 1972 to 1980. The Jamaican government gave a central role to the private sector in the recovery of the economy, but had inherited a number of public enterprises, some of which it found difficult or inadvisable to divest The University of the West Indies is one such public enterprise.
6. For example, in the Commonwealth Caribbean where the Heads of Government declared the UWI a "regional institution indefinitely" on grounds that it is a key instrument of development in the region's plan for growth and Caribbean integration The declaration was made in Grenada in July 1989.
7. See Neville V. Nicholls and Ivan L. Head (co-chairmen), *A New Structure: The Regional University in the 1990s and Beyond Report of the Chancellor's*

Commission on the Governance of UWI (Mona, Jamaica: UWI, 1994). See also Phillip Sherlock and Rex Nettleford, *The University of the West Indies: A Caribbean Response to the Challenge of Change* (London: Macmillan, 1990), 256 ff.

8. The progressive political tendencies of the late sixties and the entire seventies were informed in the region by left-wing ideology on both the Mona and St Augustine campuses, more so on the latter. This brought vigour to intellectual debate but made many a sitting West Indian government uneasy. The ruling revolutionary government of Grenada after 1979 looked to the campuses for support and received it from individual academics. The Workers' Party of Jamaica (the leading communist enclave in Jamaica) operated virtually from the Mona campus. This author has always rued the fact that a School of Caribbean Marxism, comparable to the Frankfurt School, had not developed with greater emphasis on Caribbean history and existential realities. Many felt that the undiscriminating embrace of Bolshevism and the Moscow line left the otherwise laudable movement impoverished with some damage to the university's image in the wider community

9. See Sherlock and Nettleford, *The University of the West Indies: A Caribbean Response,* especially chapter 15.

10. The Association of Caribbean Tertiary Institutions was established in 1990 with the UWI vice chancellor as its first president with a secretariat working out of the office of the UWI's pro vice chancellor for Outreach and Institutional Relations. A Tertiary Level Institution Unit (TLIU) was later established in the UWI as part of a new governance structure to strengthen and deepen the UWI's partnerships with TLIs throughout the region.

11. Compare the ultimate success by universities coping with student pressures for democratization of university administration by allowing student participation in the planning of courses and membership on strategic academic and administrative committees, as well as with the trade union pressures from radicalized academic and senior administrative staff. Joint appointments, interdisciplinary courses, reorganization of teaching schedules, were among some of the responses of the universities since the sixties to effect internal efficiency.

12. See introduction to "The Future of Education", in *Educational Documentation and Information* (Bulletin of the International Bureau of Education), no. 220 (3rd quarter 1981).

13. See *University of the West Indies, Strategic Plan 1997–2002* (Mona, Jamaica: UWI), 126.

14. See note 12 above.

15. The Commonwealth of Learning (COL), a Commonwealth Secretariat initiative of the 1980s, was a response to the clear need. This author and the then principal of the Mona campus, Professor Gerald Lalor, were members of the committees establishing COL. UWI had before experimented with the University of the West Indies Distance Teaching Experiment (UWIDITE), as did the Indira Gandhi National Open University which in 1995 registered 242,000 students. Access, cost and flexibility are criteria used to justify the new outreach type university.

16. Fernando Chaparro, Fereico Vargas, Hernan Jaramillo, "Present Situation and

Characteristics of Research Activities in Costa Rica", IDRC/CONICIT, San Jose, Costa Rica, 1982 (preliminary report, cyclostyled).

17. For a useful discussion of this see Sir John S. Daniel, "Why Universities Need Technology Strategies", *Change* (July/August 1997). "At the end of the millennium in which the idea of the university has blossomed, population growth is outpacing the world's capacity to give people access to universities", he writes. Hence the need for the use of technology and on page 14 he gives a table of what he terms "mega-universities" to be found in developed and developing countries, all utilizing technology to increase access.

18. See "Some Reflections on Education in the Eighties", by the Rt Hon The Lord Glenamara, formerly Secretary of State for Education and Science, UK, in *Education Today* 31, no. 2: 5.

19. So in Jamaica the College of Arts Science and Technology – CAST, a polytechnic type institution – was transformed into the University of Technology in 1995 by the Jamaican government. Ghana long established a University of Technology in the late fifties.

20. Daniel, "Why Universities Need Technology Strategies", 16

21. Burgess, "Excellence or Equality", 46. Burgess reflectively writes: "Unfortunately life is seldom simple. My colleagues and I have noticed one further characteristic of academic life *the world over* – and that is the tendency of institutions founded in the service tradition to move inexorably in the direction of autonomy. We call the process 'academic drift' " (my emphasis).

22. Edgar Z. Friedenberg, "The University Community in an Open Society", *Daedalus* (Winter 1970): 71.

23. Roy Niblett, "Is it Really Enough Just to Be Useful?", *The Times Higher Education Supplement*, no. 425 (26 December 1980). 8.

24. Burgess, "Excellence or Equality", 50.

25. Friedenberg, "The University Community in an Open Society".

26. *University of the West Indies Strategic Plan 1997–2002*, 125.

27. Friedenberg, "The University Community in an Open Society".

28. *The Times* of London dated 16 March 1978 made reference to an ILO report on the employment conditions of professional workers The report estimated that in the United States alone some 420,000 new doctoral graduates would be competing for 200,000 jobs between 1974 and 1985. The number of jobless graduates in India, the report said, rose tenfold between 1966 and 1971. A university degree is "fast becoming a ticket to nowhere", said the ILO in a February 1978 issue of its monthly *Information*. Quoted in "University Newsletter" (internal, from the desk of the UWI registrar), no. 6 (December 1978).

29. Friedenberg, "The University Community in an Open Society".

30. S.E. Luria and Zella Luria, "The Role of the University: Ivory Tower, Service Station or Frontier Post", *Daedalus* (Winter 1970): 77.

31. Ibid.

32. Niblett, "Is it Really Enough Just to Be Useful?".

33. See *Higher Education in the Learning Society 1997,* London (Summary Report, 9).

A National Committee of Inquiry into Higher Education (in Britain) was appointed under the chairmanship of Sir Ron Dearing "with bipartisan support by the Secretaries of State for Education and Employment, Wales, Scotland and Northern Ireland on May 10, 1996 to make representations on how the purposes, shape, structure, size and funding of higher education, including support for students, should develop to meet the needs of the United Kingdom over the next 20 years, recognizing that higher education embraces teaching, learning, scholarship and research". The Dearing Committee reported in July 1997.

34. Phillip Sherlock, *Report of the Secretary General* (Association of Caribbean Universities and Research Institutes, 1972), 3, and quoted in Rex Nettleford, *Caribbean Cultural Identity: The Case of Jamaica* (Kingston: Institute of Jamaica, 1978), 161.

3

Higher Education and Caribbean Identity

Orville Kean

Introduction

Identities in the Caribbean are largely determined by historical trajectories. From the very beginning, cultural and linguistic diversity emerged in the Caribbean as a result of the multiplicity of national allegiances of the populations of the colonies and the mimetic behaviour that the respective allegiances engendered. As the colonization process unfolded, racial and ethnic diversity were added to this milieu. The question of whether or not a Caribbean identity has emerged from this diversity that applies to the region as a whole remains an open question among Caribbean scholars.

Much has been written on this subject, usually from a political, economic or cultural perspective, or from some combination of these perspectives.[1] This examination of the Caribbean identity employs a different method. It presents three different perspectives on the existence of the identity and suggests an approach that might reconcile the differences. The approach provides a framework for an analysis of why the identity survives in regional higher education associations but generally fails to inhere in the daily operations of the universities in the region. The creation of a virtual Caribbean university (VCU) is recommended as a solution to this problem.

The Coherence and Inherence of Identities

In *UNICA Looking to the New Horizons of the XXI Century,* Thomas Mathews asserts that in spite of its diversity the Caribbean has its own strong indigenous traditions that define the region as an entity and bind it together as a whole.[2]

Ralph R. Premdas holds the opposite point of view on the existence of an encompassing Caribbean identity. Premdas begins *The Caribbean: Diversity and a Typology of Identities* with the statement that the Caribbean identity (which he refers to as the trans-Caribbean identity) is an illusion, and ends by calling it "a divided if not schizophrenic identity".[3]

The *Overview of The Report of the West Indian Commission: A Time for Action* occupies the middle ground between Mathews' and Premdas' positions. In the chairman's preface to the report, Sir Shridath Ramphal begins by stating that the West Indian identity is "an identity that is clearly recognizable not only to ourselves and our wider Caribbean but also in the world beyond the Caribbean Sea".[4] He uses his own family history to illustrate the identity:

I am the fourth generation of my family's anguished transplantation. Other West Indians have been here over a longer period, and through systems of greater anguish; yet it was natural for me to remind an audience during the Commission's consultations that 'I am a Guyanese before I am an Indian; I am a West Indian before I am a Guyanese.' Oneness had replaced separateness in four generations. So it is for most of the people of our CARICOM Region. That oneness is the basic reality of our West Indian condition.[5]

This idea of oneness is expanded on later in the *Overview* to include all Caribbean societies. It asserts that although the wider Caribbean lacks the cultural bedrock of CARICOM, its cultural dynamic provides the raw material for achieving oneness.[6]

What then is to be believed about the possibility of an identity that embraces the whole Caribbean? One response is that the three perspectives mentioned above can be viewed as examples of self-fulfilling prophesies. Certainly, it can be argued that each perspective is self-reinforcing in the sense that believing each gives rise to behaviour that supports it and provides evidence for its confirmation. As such, Mathews' long tenure as secretary general of the Association of Caribbean Universities and Research Institutes (UNICA) reflects his view that a single, regional identity already exists, and the West Indian Commission's findings and recommendations illustrate its perspective of the Caribbean identity as a work in progress.

Although the theory of the self-fulfilling prophecy is helpful in understanding why each point of view persists, it provides little insight into how these three points of view might be resolved. Perhaps the most direct approach to enlightenment here is to develop a theory of coherence (and inherence) of identities. For example, Ramphal's declaration of the three identities that inhere in him simultaneously provides an example of the dynamics of the multiple identities that cohere in so many Caribbean people.

Three ideas will be used, the first of which is existential theory building as outlined by Donald Schon in *Beyond the Stable State:*

No theory drawn from past experience may be taken as literally applicable to [the situation in question], nor will a theory based on the experience of this situation prove literally applicable to the next situation. But theories drawn from other situations may provide perspectives or projective models for this situation, which help to shape it and permit action within it.[7]

The idea is that the theories drawn from other situations should serve as metaphors in shaping our understanding of a given circumstance.

The second idea, situation theory, provides a framework for the study of information.[8] According to situation theory, the perspectives of Mathews, Premdas, and the Commission on the existence of a Caribbean identity are not in themselves true or false, rather each may be true or false about a situation. Situation theory is useful because it is existential in nature. It recognizes that although situations cannot always be replicated, the truth values of statements are always situation bounded. This is especially true in cases of identity. Both individuals and groups self-select their identities as a function of the situations in which they find themselves. Simon Peter's denial of Jesus Christ is the quintessential example.

In Peter's case, a situation arose in which a saint suddenly switched his identity and denied his god in the name of self-interest. There are also situations that provide opportunities for mortal enemies to coexist peacefully by forgetting the differences that inhere in their public identities. Rashid Sakher, an Islamic Jihad suicide bomber, sheds light on how this happens in the interview "A Terrorist Moves the Goal Post", in the August 1997 issue of *Harpers Magazine.* The interview is taken from the documentary film *Shaheed,* written and directed by Dan Setton.

Sakher was arrested in April 1996 prior to his planned attempt to blow himself up on an Israeli bus, and is now being held in the Gaza prison. At the beginning of the interview, Sakher extols the virtue of being a Shaheed (witness) and explains that he would blow himself up to help drive Israel from Palestine land in order to ensure a place for himself and his family in paradise. Later on, he admits to being a soccer fan (or perhaps fanatic) and admits to missing soccer terribly while in prison. Here is how the interview ends:

SETTON   Will you allow me to ask you a difficult question?
SAKHER   Go ahead.
SETTON   If [the Islamic Jihad] came to you and ordered you to perform a terrorist attack in a large soccer stadium, where there are Jews and Zionists, what would you do?
SAKHER   No. I couldn't do that. No.
SETTON   But they are Zionists. They are nonbelievers.
SAKHER   Yes, they are nonbelievers. But on a soccer field? I couldn't do that.

Evidently, a passion for sports can unite those whom religions design to divide.

Because identities are determined by situations they may not be reliably captured by observations, conducting interviews, surveys or by other scientific means. Identities are constructed, reconstructed, resurrected and provoked into existence, as the situation demands. They are not immutable or conserved, but are existential in nature.

The third idea is quantum mechanics (QM), a theory that has had unrivalled success in predicting and explaining physical phenomena, but continues to defy the most basic common sense interpretations of reality.[9] Common sense tells us that there is an effective reality that exists independent of whether someone observes it or not. According to QM, however, things have no *unique* physical characteristics until they are observed.[10] This means that a particle may behave as if it is in several different places simultaneously when it is not being observed.[11] During the times that they are not being observed or measured, when particles or systems behave as though they are in several different positions simultaneously, these particles or systems are said to be in a *coherent* state. When they are actually detected as a result of observation or measurement, they are always found to be in one specific place. Evidently, in the act of observation or measurement, the particle or system *chooses* one specific position and the other positions in which it existed simultaneously are said to *decohere* from this chosen position and disappear.

Used as a metaphor, QM might shape our understanding of identities by suggesting that whenever people are not required to declare their identity, most of them are in a coherent state in which several, often contradictory, identities inhere in them simultaneously. For example, Ramphal's admission that he is simultaneously an Indian, a Guyanese and a West Indian expresses such a coherent state. He admits, however, that he is first a West Indian, then a Guyanese and then an Indian. This is the pattern by which his Indian and Guyanese identities decohere and disappear. For Ramphal, his West Indian identity always inheres, it never decoheres and disappears; it persists whatever the situation.

On the other hand, Sakher's Shaheed identity is not as persistent as his initial statement in the interview would lead one to believe. He admits to having another identity, a soccer fan identity, that coheres with his Shaheed identity while he is in jail and presumably in most other instances. Surprisingly, it is the soccer fan identity that seems to inhere in him persistently. At a soccer game, his Shaheed identity decoheres and disappears. It is important to note that Sakher's Shaheed identity is not "a schizophrenic identity" as Premdas claims of the trans-Caribbean identity. Instead it is a single, undivided identity that coheres with and decoheres from at least one other identity in accordance with certain rules of inference in Sakher's head as applied to the situations in which he finds himself.

The same thing can be said about the regional or trans-Caribbean identity. It is not an illusion, a divided if not schizophrenic identity or a work in progress, but a *real* identity that coheres with a number of *other* identities in the heads and hearts of many people in the Caribbean and many people from the region who live elsewhere. It is not readily seen because it decoheres from the other identities so easily. Nevertheless, the continued existence of regional associations such as UNICA, the Caribbean Studies Association (CSA), the Association of Caribbean Historians (ACH), the Association of Caribbean Economists (ACE) and the Caribbean Universities Sports Association (CUSA) reflect that there are situations when the identity continues to inhere in a significant number of higher educators. But the identity does not inhere often enough in the right places to make the contributions that it should be making to the improvement of the quality and robustness of higher education in the Caribbean. Too frequently it decoheres from the other identities in the classrooms, laboratories, libraries, extracurricular activities, research projects and administrative offices.

Dependency and Dynamic Conservatism

There appear to be two principal reasons why this occurs. First, Caribbean higher education is dependent upon the higher education centres in Europe and North America. These centres produce the concepts, governance structures and programmes that are copied in the Caribbean, and they produce the technology and textbooks that are used in the region. This dependence tends to cause the universities to cleave to the higher education communities in the countries in Europe or North America that previously governed or currently govern the territories where the universities are located. Thus, universities in Puerto Rico and the University of the Virgin Islands (UVI) identify themselves as American universities. The Université des Antilles et de Guyane (UAG) is French and the University of the Netherlands Antilles (UNA) is Dutch. The University of the West Indies (UWI) evolved from a British university and continues to be identified with the British higher education community.

The second reason has to do with how universities evolved in Europe and North America and how this evolution shaped their governance structures and operations. The word university is derived from the medieval Latin word *universitas* – meaning guild or corporation. A number of scholars have suggested that universities still maintain a guild culture. The vice chancellor of the Open University in Milton Keynes, England, Sir John S. Daniel, hints that universities are still guilds in his statement that "Higher education is still a craft industry".[12] Gordon Arnold and Janet T. Civian are more direct; they observed that faculty function as members of their guild in debates about general education reform.[13]

In truth, faculty function like members of a guild in most matters because the governance structures used by universities allow faculty members to set standards and protect their interests. These governance structures mediate the process by which universities construct their identities. Unfortunately, these governance structures also contribute to the dynamic conservatism that is so prevalent at universities and that compromises their ability to function effectively as learning organizations. Donald Schon defines dynamic conservatism as the tendency of a social system to fight to remain the same, and Peter M. Senges describes learning organizations as, "organizations where people continually expand their capacity to create the results they truly desire, where new and expansive patterns of thinking are nurtured, where collective aspiration is set free and people are continually learning how to learn together".[14]

The irony of higher education is that universities are not effective learning organizations because they have not learned to practise the things that they teach. A critical case in point is that they have not learned the lessons of the management revolutions taught in their business classes. Of course, it may be said that their self-concept as guilds precludes them from thinking of themselves as being subject to the lessons learned in business classes. This is true, but there is another more significant reason. The way that courses are developed and taught – particularly the practice of individual teaching – lends itself to individual learning rather than team learning on the part of the faculty. Most administrators, being former members of the faculty, also tend to be individual learners rather than team learners. Conferences do offer opportunities for team learning, but they are generally too narrowly focused and punctuated to qualify as meaningful opportunities for faculty, staff and administrators to learn to learn together as teams. Additionally, faculty research generally becomes increasingly narrow in focus; it is seldom expansive in nature. Finally, institutional goal setting is often driven by departmental trajectories. Most departments, however, do not believe that they should be responsible for expanding their capacity to create the results they desire. This is generally left to the administration, particularly in public institutions.

Because of these conditions, it is unlikely that the universities in the Caribbean will become the effective learning organizations that Senges describes; it requires too great a change for institutions that are by tradition so dynamically conservative. It is equally unlikely that a regional identity will inhere in any meaningful way in these institutions if changes are not made to their governance structures that provide incentives to faculty and administrators to collaborate with their colleagues from other Caribbean universities. For public universities that have national missions and are sensitive to the political ambitions of their elected leaders, changing their governance structures to provide such incentives may be particularly difficult. But it is not impossible. What universities in the Caribbean will have to do is to stop carbon copying what universities are doing or have done in Europe and North America. The ideas and products that are borrowed or bought from these centres of higher education must be used as raw material to create new ideas and products that are uniquely Caribbean but have global appeal. The creation of the steel pan serves as a metaphor for this process.

It is no coincidence that the creation of the steel pan was an existential act; that its dual identities as a musical instrument and an oil drum still cohere so beautifully, and that it serves as a metaphor for the Caribbean identity. It *is* the quintessential Caribbean creation and the music it makes is a vector that transmits many of the values that inhere in the region. The higher education community in the Caribbean must become like the community of pan musicians and forge new regional educational instruments that are finely tuned to the prevailing needs and opportunities. Only then will it be possible for the universities to create a regional environment in which a truly Caribbean identity inheres on a daily basis.

A Virtual Caribbean University

The obvious entity that should provide the leadership in this area is UNICA, the organization established in 1967 to foster contact and collaboration between Caribbean universities and research institutes.[15] It comprises a number of universities from the Dutch, English, French and Spanish speaking Caribbean. UNICA has not lived up to the expectations of its founders. Nevertheless, the time may be ripe for the association to surpass their expectations. This can be achieved by the creation of a VCU in which the regional identity is used to mediate the courses and programmes offered, and to propel the region as a force into the global higher education market.

There are four initiatives currently taking place that suggest how UNICA can create a VCU. The first is the UWI Executive Masters of Business Administration (EMBA) programme. The second is the UVI's general education curriculum reform project. The third is the information technology strategies that are being developed and implemented to deliver asynchronous courses; and the fourth is the IBM global campus. Using the existential theory building approach, these initiatives can be 'applied' by UNICA to shape the creation of a new virtual university in the Caribbean that would operate as a regional university on a daily basis. This would allow the universities that comprise UNICA to maintain a Caribbean identity without sacrificing their national identities. The coherence of a national identity *and* a regional identity in its member institutions is critical to the success of UNICA.

The EMBA programme at the UWI is important because it demonstrates how a public university can create a new identity that coheres with its legally mandated identity as a public institution. Essentially the EMBA programme is outsourced. It is administered by the Centre for Management Development (CMD), an independent entity governed by a board of directors. The UWI is represented on the CMD board by the principal of the Cave Hill campus, the dean of the Faculty of Social Sciences and the head of the Department of Management Studies, all of whom serve as ex-officio members. Except for accreditation matters, all the affairs of EMBA are guided by the policies set by the CMD board of directors.

It is easy to miss the innovations embodied in the EMBA programme. First, the UWI created a new entity (the CMD) with its own governance structures (the board of directors), then it created and privatized a new graduate degree programme by asking the CMD to develop and administer the EMBA. Now the UWI functions both as a public university *and* a private university. The coherence of these dual identities enables the university to exploit opportunities that improve its position in the Caribbean higher education market and still fulfil its mandated mission as a public institution.

The creation of a VCU will require similar innovations on the part of the UNICA membership. It will also require changes in their curricula that speak more directly to the region's problems, particularly its precarious position in the global community. The general education curriculum reform project that is currently taking place at the UVI provides an example of how this can be accomplished. The university has begun its reform project by implementing new programmes at the beginning and at the end of its undergraduate programme. It began at the end first, with the UVI Summer Institute for Future Global Leaders in the Caribbean (GSIFLC) that was implemented in the summer of 1995. The institute brings together student leaders from universities in the Dutch, English, French and Spanish Caribbean to learn about each other's ethos as Caribbean people and to begin to explore what is required to be an effective leader in the current global environment.

The programme is both multidisciplinary and interdisciplinary in nature. It examines the problems facing the Caribbean and the opportunities for regional development that these difficulties engender, from the perspectives of business, economics, culture, communication and leadership. Its focus is based on the concept that the greatest strength of Caribbean people is the ability to create new worlds that transcend the old worlds of their ancestors and colonial masters. Examples of these new worlds are provided in art, cuisine, dance, music and literature.

As the following statement from the presidential address given at the 1996 UNICA Annual Meeting illustrates, the GSIFLC serves as a transforming institute in shaping the identities of its students.

An example of the success is the response a participant from Puerto Rico gave to my question about what was of greatest significance to her about the Institute. She said that she learned that she was truly a Caribbean person. I asked what did she think she was before she attended the Institute. A member of the Hispanic minority in the United States, she responded. Of course she will learn that she is both and that by drawing on the strengths of each identity she can create a new synthesis that transcends them both.[16]

The institute serves as a capstone general education course. Its participants are seniors, recent graduates and graduate students. At the opposite end of the higher education journey, first year students at UVI are also required to immerse themselves in the Caribbean identity as part of the university's general education mandate. In fall 1997, the UVI initiated its new Freshman Year Program by introducing a new science course and a new social science course, both of which are rooted in the Caribbean. The title and description of each of these courses is given below:

1. *The Caribbean: The Natural World – 3 credits to be offered by the Science and Mathematics Division.*
   Course Description: A topical examination of the natural world of the Caribbean. Included will be considerations of the elements of Caribbean life associated with the natural world with emphasis on their roots in the natural sciences. The approach is interdisciplinary with a variety of learning strategies employed.

2. *The Caribbean: The Social Dimension – 3 credits to be offered by the Social Sciences Division.*
   Course description: A topical examination of the social dimensions of

Caribbean cultures from the origins of human habitation to the present. Its interdisciplinary approach will emphasize the perspectives of the various social sciences, with attention also given to the arts of the Caribbean. A variety of teaching and learning strategies will be utilized.[17]

In the fall of 1998, the UVI had plans to introduce new sophomore level general education courses and presently the majors are being fine tuned to the circumstances of the region. The UVI's commitment to modify its curriculum and learning environment to enhance its Caribbean identity is based on the belief that its legislatively mandated territorial mission is more easily achieved if its territorial identity coheres with a strong regional identity.

Although the developments taking place at the UWI and the UVI are helpful in enhancing their Caribbean identities, these universities do not have the resources – individually or jointly – to adequately cover the region. Furthermore, the Dutch, French and Spanish universities must be part of every learning environment in which an authentic Caribbean identity inheres in its students, faculty and curriculum. Employing information technology strategies to achieve asynchronous learning and following the example of the IBM global campus that includes a large number of universities that share on-line services, UNICA can create its own VCU in which an authentic regional identity inheres in every detail of its operation.[18]

As it is now being used, asynchronous learning is the buzz word for what is sometimes called distance education or distributive education. It is a learning strategy that makes use of the potential of students to study on their own. It does not require daily contact with teachers, but provides interactive study materials and decentralized educational facilities where students can seek assistance. James Morrison gives the following example of how the Internet is being used to provide asynchronous learning in *On the Horizon*, May/June 1997.

Professor Lev Gonick sent out a message to several listservs to solicit professors and students focusing on global, political and economic issues. Some seventy-five professors and several hundred students around the world responded. After spending the initial part of the semester identifying issues, students were required to team with other students (who had to be in another country) to write papers that were posted to a Web site for critique and discussion by all.[19]

To establish its VCU, UNICA could first create a subsidiary corporation much like the UWI created the CMD. Each member institution that wishes to participate in the VCU would be required to develop courses that could be offered asynchronously throughout the region. Each would also be required to develop a core of courses in which the Caribbean identity inheres. As is the case with the UVI, these courses should not all be social sciences courses. Students could enrol in the VCU by enrolling in one of the participating UNICA universities but take courses on other campuses asynchronously. At graduation, students would receive certificates or degrees from both the university in which they are enrolled and the VCU. Because the present fiscal climate in Caribbean higher education is one of scarce resources and cost containment, the success of the VCU will depend on the participating universities' ability to develop and deliver asynchronous courses without a need for a continuing subsidy from their respective general operations fund. The VCU will have to operate more as a business than as a not-for-profit organization. Its courses will have to have enough market appeal to be bought by enough students to recover the cost of development and cover the cost of delivery.[20]

This may seem to be an outrageously ambitious vision but it must be seriously considered for two reasons. First, it is the only approach that will positively assure the achievement of the UNICA mission, which is collaboration between member universities and institutes. Second, and perhaps of more importance to the region, if UNICA does not do it, someone from outside the region will. The Caribbean higher education market is part of the global higher education market that has become a highly competitive international market. Several universities in North America are already using the Internet to offer asynchronous courses in the Caribbean. Others are sending their faculty to the region with instructional materials. If the region's higher education community is unable to develop its own virtual university, its share of the higher education market will shrink and the universities in the region may become marginalized.

On the other hand, because a VCU offers courses asynchronously, it has the capacity to become competitive in the global market. A strong Caribbean identity can be helpful in this regard. The fact that the identity coheres so successfully with other identities, both within and outside the Caribbean, suggests that the VCU's courses and programmes can be tailored to be compatible with a number of non-Caribbean cultures and identities. This ability to be compatible is critical since most of the increase in demand for higher education will continue to come from the developing countries where cultures and identities often collide when educational innovations are copied from the developed countries. The creation of the VCU will require a lot of time, commitment, human resources and money. But the region may have little choice if it intends to build its future in its own image. There is no time to lose.

Notes

1. See, for example, Ian Boxill's surveys in St Lucia and Jamaica on the main characteristics of a Caribbean identity. Ian Boxill, *Ideology and Caribbean Integration* (Mona, Jamaica. Consortium Graduate School of Social Sciences, UWI, 1993), 74–80.
2. Thomas Mathews, *UNICA Looking to the New Horizons of the XXI Century*, edited by Hector Rodriguez (Santo Domingo, Dominican Republic Association of Caribbean Universities and Research Institutes, 1992), 6
3. Ralph H. Premdas, "The Caribbean: Diversity and a Typology of Identities", *Caribbean Perspectives* (Eastern Caribbean Center, UVI) (December 1997): 3 and 7.
4. *Overview of the Report of the West Indian Commission: A Time for Action* (Black Rock, Barbados: The West Indian Commission, 1992), vii.
5. Ibid.
6. Ibid., 62
7. Donald A. Schon, *Beyond the Stable State* (New York. The Norton Library, 1973), 231.
8. A very abstract, mathematical description of situation theory can be found in Keith Devlin's article, "The Logical Structure of Computer-Aided Mathematical Reasoning", *American Mathematical Monthly* 104, no. 7 (August–September 1997) 639–42.
9. See Arthur Robinson, "Quantum Mechanics Passes Another Test", *Science* 217 (30 July 1982): 435.
10. Arthur Robinson, "Loophole Closed in Quantum Mechanics Test", *Science* 219 (7 January 1983): 40.
11. Bernard d'Espagnot, "The Quantum Theory and Reality", *Scientific American* 241, no. 5 (May 1979). 158.
12. Quoted from John S. Daniel, "Why Universities Need Technology Strategies", *Change* 29, no. 4 (July/August 1997): 13.
13. Gordon Arnold and Janet T. Civian, "The Ecology of General Education Reform", *Change* 29, no. 4 (July/August 1997): 22.
14. Schon, *Beyond the Stable State,* 32, Peter M. Senge, *The Fifth Discipline* (New York: Doubleday/Currency, 1990), 3.

15. A brief history of UNICA can be found in Mathews, *UNICA Looking to the New Horizons.*
16. Orville Kean, "Ananci, Epistemology and Higher Education in the Caribbean" (paper presented at the Association of Caribbean Universities and Research Institutes 1996 annual meeting in Kingston, Jamaica, 12 September 1996), 3.
17. Denis Paul, "New Curriculum Development", a report with general education course recommendations, approved by UVI president Kean, St Thomas, 16 June 1997, 4–8.
18. More about information technology strategies can be found in Daniel, "Why Universities Need Technology Strategies". The IBM global campus is mentioned in James L. Morrison, "Looking Back from 2005", *On the Horizon* 5, no. 3 (May/June 1997): 3
19. Morrison, "Looking Back from 2005", 2.
20. For a better understanding of some of the hidden costs associated with the production and delivery of asynchronous courses, see Kenneth Green, "Think Twice – and Businesslike – About Distance Education", *AAHE Bulletin* (October 1997): 3–6.

4

Academic Travails and a Crisis-of-Mission of the University of the West Indies' Social Sciences: From History and Critique to Anti-Politics

Don D. Marshall

Introduction

Nineteen ninety-eight marked the fiftieth anniversary of the establishment of the University of the West Indies (UWI). More than the symbolism associated with this, it coincided with the historical rise of parvenu neoliberal thinking and entrepreneurial academia. The celebratory and congratulatory tenor of the speeches may have provided succour to those of us committed to the mighty struggle of maintaining the integrity of the university-as-institution. The university has been and still is a state sponsored institution, heavily reliant on Commonwealth Caribbean government financing. Since the late 1980s, budget consolidation measures by the various cash strapped governments have led to a "downward financial spiral".[1] Alleviation is being pursued through alternative sources of funding, private and research grants, extraregional student intake, and the streamlining of UWI operations. This situation is especially worrying for all concerned as the university is expected to do more for the community with less. But while a crisis in university financing is serious enough, there are a range of nonmaterial forces at work that when drawn together may spell a crisis-of-mission of the university itself.

This essay penetrates to the deeper problems facing academe. One relates to the dearth of critical academic research emanating from the social sciences of the UWI (circa 1980 onwards). The other relates to the nature of the state–university relationship in recent times, one where university academics and policy communities are drawn dangerously close. Preoccupied with career and pay, or a naive sense of duty, some have become attracted to and have been encouraged by the university system to join the twilight world of consultancy (that is to say, illuminated less by the intellect than the limits of an officially sanctioned imagination).

How have we arrived at this situation where liberal–positivist enterprise and intellectual service to state power are considered putting our best foot forward as research scientists? Academic and cultural life necessarily require contestation, critique and countercritique for sustenance. When dissent meets orthodoxy, both are mutually transformed, causing paradigmatic ruptures or refinements. Evidence of this was clearly in view at an earlier time where the university was resistant to the colonial project and modes of economic organization. Particularly disturbing is the absence of such strident protest to prevailing orthodoxies and the antipolitics of technical experts and institutional overlords. Indeed it is not excessive to state that the university throughout the 1960s and 1970s became a significant actor in the development debates both in the Caribbean and in the intellectual world. The contest between those who would extol the virtues of Keynesian market planning and externally financed industrialization (for example, Arthur Lewis, William Demas), and those proclaiming a state planning approach (for example, George Beckford, Lloyd Best) inspired nationalist imaginings across the region. Traditional political economy approaches faced vigorous critique from the intellectual 'soft' and 'hard' left of the New World group.[2] In those times, historical and social science research was guided by a moral compass of concern for the problems of the Caribbean: injustice, pain, underdevelopment, unemployment and the agro-commercial model of accumulation; and explicit ideological critique was part of the academic enterprise. But this concern and thrust waned in the 1980s. Social science research in the main has since lost both the critical and emancipatory character of its early years. Indeed, a plethora of 'normal science' research and teaching programmes have since emerged from the UWI, using what were once insurgent concepts. There are two predominant explanations for this. One relates to the end of the Cold War and the notion that it has given way to a postmodern movement in thought that forecloses the left and right cleavage in historical development studies. As the logic goes, the modes of theorizing open to critical intellectuals are in crisis, resulting in a reflexive retreat from the orthodoxies of dissent. The second relates to a 'publish or perish' tarantism at the UWI, one which is increasingly leading to a pretense at occasioning quantifiable scholarly 'travails'.

At the campus level, multiple reasons for the decline in critical research are on offer, ranging from Emmanuel's[3] prognosis to lay suggestions of laziness, ineptitude and an aging staff. Quite often, too, the 'exigencies' argument has been put forward. This view asserts that the university operates on limited resources and hence could not speedily undertake the outfitting of academic offices with a computer, printer, Internet and e-mail access; efficiently fill posts when they became vacant; allow for research assistantship programmes; and could only establish a publishing press in 1994. Most scholarly reviews of the university usually acknowledge these constraints, but guard against overstating these for some academics, particularly historians, have managed to be productive and critical under these difficult circumstances.[4] Emmanuel accounts for "the prevailing mood of quietism and pragmatism" by highlighting the following:

i) the burden of semesterization on an academic staff not bolstered by teaching assistants and delays in the filling of academic posts;

ii) increasing disenchantment among academic staff as a 'cliquist hegemony' takes root at the top – a virtual information-rich coterie of individuals who enjoy full membership status in all the key university committees, especially those determining the three fundamental properties of concern for academics: tenure, rank and office;

iii) and the absorption of academics into administrative positions on the notion that academic ability could easily translate into competent management and planning.

Interestingly enough, the last point made by Emmanuel was a direct counter to Sherlock and Nettleford's[5] plea for academics to run their own institution lest it be run by "insensitive hired hands". Belle,[6] in a review of Emmanuel's essay, concurs with Sherlock and Nettleford but warns against a technicist zeal, a trait that may arise with bad managers or fellow academics in their administrative posts. In another contribution to the wider debate on the state of the university, Belle[7] alluded to the pace of global and hemispheric change, pointing out that once it is greater than that inside an institution of higher learning, crisis looms for that institution. He surmises that the university is caught not only in the swirl of global change, but also the tide of anti-intellectualism that remains a part of the region's colonial heritage. While bemoaning the absence of communication between disciplines and departments, he scores the restructuring exercise within the faculties (that is, social sciences and arts) and university as the creature of "endless thoughtless reorganization". This capitulation to excessive bureaucratism and pragmatism at the UWI, Belle argues, is reflective of poor leadership and a loss of 'mind' (read philosophical anchor).

This discussion will, however, be limited to those tensions felt on an intellectual level, leaving for more appropriate venues discussion of institutional concern. Two lingering problems haunt social sciences at the university and prevent the respective disciplines from developing their potential as frameworks for the theoretical and empirical examination of the Caribbean life space. One stems from the university's struggle for relevance in a community of former colonial, low-accumulation countries, now on the market ideological track. The pressure remains enormous. Indeed, the charge that the university is irrelevant to society unless it could compete or join with other governmental agencies as problem solver for the respective countries' immediate concerns, remains a powerful and dangerously seductive one. It can lead to academics abrogating their intellectual responsibilities by giving identity to the immediate realms of the policy process. The consequence is one that not so much brings an appropriate education to public affairs, as infiltrates the academy with the unreflective imperatives of state bureaucracies.

The second and related observation refers to the pervasiveness and resilience of a liberal, positivist discourse within the university that has survived the paradigmatic clashes of the 1960s and 1970s and is becoming a sort of an entrenched intellectual tradition in the Caribbean. Take the combination of an entrenched intellectual tradition, an intellectual left unprepared to question (or unconscious of their own ontological assumptions), a social environment that is increasingly encouraging pragmatism and conservatism, and the result is a virtual discouragement of dissenting approaches. I argue that intellectual service to state power and enduring modernist fallacies together, place the university in a double jeopardy: by foreclosing on curiosity we lose intellectual legitimacy; and by giving itself in this condition to the purposes of governmental agencies, it becomes the purveyor of advice and succour which is plainly dangerous.

The Early UWI Years and the 'Cartesian Anxiety'

There is a need to revive popularly held conceptions of the university befitting the era of the 1960s and 1970s when social sciences found institutional space at the UWI. Among these are the notions that it is the site of rigorous, unbiased research and analysis. Coterminous with this, the university was seen as the employer of unconventional intellectuals whose theoretical concerns were complemented by a willingness to subject all that passed before them to a radical critique of a type not possible in the media or the bureaucracy. Academic social scientists and professionals are, after all, different animals. And so they should be. Where professionals are governed by imperatives, academics are governed by paradigms. Further, the timescale of academic scholarship and policy practitioners are often very different; the academic can wander over the decades and the centuries, while the professional must act today. Academics usually know a range of interpretations about a particular phenomenon, with each interpretation drawing attention to its various aspects. This is the stuff of epistemological dispassion, of an acute awareness that 'knowledge' is only tentative. Thus, when it comes to policy prescription social scientists will be found on all sides of every question. For the professional seeking advice or guidance from the academic, the question then becomes "Which academic?" or "Which perspective?"

From the outset, the UWI has been beset by the 'relevance problem', a situation especially magnified given its heavy reliance on state subventions. Theoretically, in an aspirant democratic pluralist community, it is not inconceivable that the state would seek to co-opt the institution that is ostensibly the repository of intellectual authority and unbiased analysis, for legitimation of its policies. The proof in the co-option is when we witness the UWI valuing its connections (to government agencies) more highly than the intellectual courage it is popularly thought to possess as a university. But a brief historical account is required.

In 1944, the secretary of state for the colonies established a commission on higher education under the chairmanship of Sir Cyril Asquith. A West Indies committee of the commission recommended the foundation of a University College of the West Indies to be placed in Jamaica. The British government, along with other West Indian colonial governments, accepted the committee's recommendation. Between 1948 and 1950, undergraduates were admitted first in medicine, then natural sciences and finally the arts. The university college prepared its students for the degrees of the University of London in accordance with the proposals of the Asquith Commission. An Extra Mural Department, with a resident tutor in each contributing colony, was soon established to facilitate the spread of education. In 1948, the Institute for Social and Economic Research (ISER) was established under a grant from the Colonial Social Science Research Council. The establishment of a campus in Trinidad (St Augustine) and also Barbados (Cave Hill) followed in 1960 and 1963, respectively.[8] As it was, the emphasis on arts, natural sciences and medicine was in keeping with the designs of the postwar colonial project to prepare a cadre of elites and professionals for self-government and efficient social service distribution. In short, the university was bequeathed to the Caribbean to give its identity to the immediate realms of the policy and governance processes. This of course occurred against the backdrop of a prevailing modernization zeal across the West, of which liberalism was its reigning faith and diffusion of Western institutions its operation.

Even as imperialism was on the defensive after 1945, colonial rule continued to provide the political context for nationalist consciousness in the Caribbean. To be sure, a proto-nationalist consciousness extended back to the 1860s where there was steady opposition by the creolized elite and a small middle strata to the elimination of an elective element in the then introduced crown colony government. Merchants and planters in Trinidad and Jamaica clamoured for greater control over expenditure and revenue; and a more widely based reform movement in the 1880s, inclusive of professional elements seeking political office, advocated an expansion of the franchise. By the time of the birth of the university, intellectual currents varied where units of analysis encompassed the individual, the society and the broader sweep of human history. The progressive intellectual currents ranged from a Ciprianist protest against the autocratic character of crown colony government, a positive Garveyite assertion of West Indian political rights, to a Williams and Jamesian penetrative cultural–historical assault on the foundations of Euro-imperial rule. These competing tendencies clashed with their conservative opposite – from the gradualism of Lord Moyne and the pragmatism of Albert Marryshow, Cecil Rawle and Grantley Adams, to the pro-colonialist posture of sections of the traditional elite.

Debate on the quality of the decolonization project was stimulated considerably by the establishment of the Faculty of Social Sciences at Mona (1959), and the introduction of social science teaching at Cave Hill and St Augustine in the mid to late 1960s. A social science research institute arm (ISER) soon followed for St Augustine and Cave Hill, with degree granting status already conferred on the university in 1963. Under the circumstances of a newly autonomous UWI, a resonance was struck between critical intellectual endeavour in the human sciences and anticolonial currents, both at the diasporic and societal levels. Arthur Lewis had written his seminal article "Industrialization of the British West Indies" over ten years earlier, but popular attention was drawn to it as the postcolonial governments searched for development policy guideposts.[9] While his work was set within the modernization tradition, it did not follow the classical political economy counsel of a minimal state interfering little in the accumulation process. His argument was that, given the absence of developed capital markets, industry and savings in the Caribbean, and the existence of a large jobless labour force, there was a need for the state to play a crucial role in promoting infrastructural expansion, social welfare, deeper regionalization and the rise of branch–plant industry. It was left-Keynesian in character and hence constituted a challenge to the existing agro-commercial model of accumulation allied to microstates. Further support for Lewis' argument later came from William Demas, who pointed to the small size of the island economies as imposing limits on the capacity to achieve growth of the Rostow variety.[10]

By the mid 1960s, as Caribbean governments shaped development policy out of the theoretical positions of Lewis and Demas, UWI (Mona) academic social scientists and others began to subject these perspectives to greater scrutiny. But it was not always the case that dissenting perspectives freely competed in issue spaces of Caribbean life. Garveyite viewpoints and Jamesian thought struggled in the Caribbean of the 1930s and 1940s. Theirs was an attempt at historical self-understanding and addressing public issues of social structure, while prevailing discourse centred on the personal troubles of the milieu. James' *Black Jacobins*[11] and Williams' *Capitalism and Slavery*[12] were later rendered visible through a social science journal entitled *New World Quarterly*, with contributors such as Best, Beckford, Levitt, Girvan, Jefferson, Rodney, Brewster, Munroe and Thomas.[13] These 'New World' writings extended from a challenge to the optimism behind incentive industrialization strategies, to the theoretical roots of traditional political economy. Marxist social analysis was proffered by Thomas and Munroe, while Girvan and Jefferson probed the metropolitan bias within ownership and decision making structures of multinational corporations. Beckford's *Persistent Poverty*, published in 1972, was as much a repudiation of Caribbean development strategies, as a paradigmatic challenge to the liberal fallacy of 'progress'. For him, the mode of accumulation in the region remained a modified plantation economy variant, as dependent investment and aid ties with London and other metropolitan cities persisted. Best, Levitt, and Rodney also challenged the modernist paradigm in areas of diasporic history and political economy, Best himself resistant to Eurocentric restrictive frames.

In world perspective, critical theory has a rich tradition extending from the writings of Horkheimer, Adorno, Marcuse and others of the 'Frankfurt School', to Habermas, the 'dependency' proponents, world systems theorists and neostructuralists. Critical intellectual enterprise at the UWI was nourished by feedback relationships with parallel intellectual currents in Latin America in the thought of Raul Prebisch, Andre Gunder Frank and Osvaldo Sunkel, among others. Two distinct aims emanate from this tradition of criticism: the analysis and critique of particular existing social configurations and oppressions, and the more emancipatory or reconstructive method needed to move beyond current conditions. This has been denounced in some quarters – and perhaps touches a chord with elements in Caribbean society – as a hopelessly academic and abstract enterprise lacking in empirical zeal.[14] But critical theory cannot be judged in terms of its 'application'. It does not produce empiricist–inductivist sets of laws that can be applied neutrally to a supposedly epistemologically independent world. Instead, it helps us to penetrate beyond mere appearances and probe the apparently chaotic. At any rate, discerning academics embrace elements of the critical enterprise to better guide their formulation of a compelling vision. Take intellectual trends of the right, for instance. Neoclassicism features a tension between market ideologues and market rationalists on the pace of liberalization in Third World countries. The former is confident of the catalytic and allocative capacities of the 'invisible hand' of the market; the latter is less so, pays more attention to particularities and is pragmatic on the role the state can play in augmenting the market. Critical theory and leanings, in short, ignite new imaginings, train eyes, exert a pressure on our institutions, moving us closer to the ideal of achieving a better way of life.

It is worth noting that radical scholars in the Caribbean experienced various degrees of hostility. Walter Rodney was banned by the Jamaican government in 1968, officially charged for "engaging in subversive activities" – an act that sparked disturbances in Kingston following a student protest.[15] Critical academics were blamed for the failures of the Manley regime in Jamaica and the February 1970 riots in Trinidad, while C.L.R. James became unpopular with the Eric Williams administration during his stint as an adviser to the government.[16] Indeed, following critiques on governance and economic organization, Williams in 1973 revealed that at a Caribbean Heads of Government meeting his colleagues denounced the UWI Faculty of Social Sciences, suggesting that it be closed down.[17] These were times when UWI academics in the main understood their role as scholars even as some were prepared to work with governments. Lewis, Girvan, Jefferson, Beckford and James, for example, never became tied to policies nor did they adopt the short time-frame of professionals; they instead remained free-floating disputatious wild spirits. They remained independent and true to their way of thinking, following political and intellectual events critically. It was their station to be irritating.

Caribbean consciousness was raised by the sociohistorical and development debates, and the political activism of UWI intellectuals.[18] It brought the university its greatest success, the challenge to orthodox modernist frames for fashioning Caribbean development. These intellectual currents carried well into the crisis filled 1970s as the two oil shocks negatively affected the economic well-being of most of the territories, including Manley's Jamaica, the site of UWI inspired statist experiments. Critical intellectual enterprise in the tradition of Beckford, Best and Rodney thereafter waned.

Given the fervour, the clashes of perspectives, the burgeoning critical tradition and the attention paid by the wider community, the instinct must be to ask, Where are our theories of society today, of crisis tendencies and cultural modernity? Certainly the critiques of the 1960s and 1970s beckon critiques themselves and perhaps partly explain why there is a dearth of research along these lines. The collapse of 'existing socialism' in Europe has paved the way for some reflection among Caribbean writers, but the spectacular crash itself seems at the same time to have clouded the need for far more penetrative critiques of social science and academic endeavour. But further elaboration on the decline-of-the-left thesis is required.

Hutchinson[19] and Lewis[20] affirm that the crisis of the intellectual and political left in the Commonwealth Caribbean relates to the end of the Cold War, witnessed by the collapse of 'existing socialism' in Eastern Europe. Lewis holds that apart from the theme of democratization propagated by James, George Padmore, Rodney, Eusi Kwayana and Thomas, critical discourse was often hijacked by slavish attention to rigid Marxist orthodoxy. The effect was a virtual eschewing of any form of criticism of the Soviet model. Hutchinson's analysis penetrates to the ideological and theoretical premise of Euro-inspired socialism. A crucial feature at work in the collapse of the socialist experiment in Grenada, he argues, was the mechanistic adherence to the Leninist view of the vanguard party, which, in the circumstances, was the ideological legitimation of cliquism and authoritarianism. This dovetails with Munroe's point of the debilitating effect "mechanistic brands of Marxism" have had on the Jamaican left.[21] These appraisals are quite in order but because the focus has been on the state of the left, we seem to miss the acute vulnerability of orthodoxies of dissent once entrapped in the conceptual masonry of liberalism and positivism.

The liberal–positivist edifice divides global social relations into 'national' and 'international' levels and 'political' and 'economic' categories. The Caribbean intellectual left challenges the liberal world view employing Marxian and critical concepts, but do so within the distinctly liberal architecture so described above. Until now, none seemed prepared to challenge this Cartesian division of our social world, or positivist ontologies. Beckford, Girvan and Jefferson often struggled to demonstrate (1) the unity of the assemblage of state (read politics) and national wealth and class relations (read economics), and (2) that the social formation is a moment in the international. For example, Beckford's use of a 'plantation economy' or 'plantation society' construct/metaphor to describe the nature of the Caribbean political economy made for an excessive gaze at the plantation-as-institution even as it was intended to draw attention to the connection to the world economy.

The intellectual 'hard' left like Munroe and Thomas are far more cognizant of the Caribbean's external linkages, and further holism in their work. But ideological attachment to 'capitalism' and 'modes of production' prevent them from asking what has endured over many millennia from what is new in the last 500 years? Thomas speaks of a "colonial mode of production" to describe the Caribbean under slavery and colonialism.[22] This is Munroe's "pre-capitalist mode of production". Together they, along with others, suggest that world capitalism presents limits to Caribbean development. This may be true in certain respects, but in light of recent developments in historicizing the modern world system, is it at all possible that we may have been confusing the world system with its modes of production? Why do we bestow distinctiveness and ascribe blame to this thing called 'capitalism', when development for a few at a time has been a perennial feature of world historical development for many millennia? The paradox can be located in the Marxist project itself: the call for a dialectical understanding of our material world viz. the ideological presentation of world history as an evolutionary typology – primitive communalism, feudalism, capitalism. The political/ideological reason is that adherents are intent on the 'subsequent transition' to socialism. But these categories act as obstacles to the social scientific study of the underlying continuity and essential properties of the world system both in the past and at present.

There has been a complex mixture or articulation of modes of production at all times in the development of the world accumulation process. Consistent with the Marxian framework, Caribbean left intellectuals fixate on modes of production and claim the last 500 years for 'capitalism'. The world system is now identified with its dominant mode of production. Abu-Lughod and Frank and Gills inform us that the world political-economic system long predated the rise of 'capitalism' in Europe and that if there was any transition then, it was a hegemonic shift within the system rather than the formation of a new system.[23] It is strongly argued that it is these analytical categories of 'modes of production' – 'transition', 'feudalism' and 'capitalism' – that prevent us from seeing the real world system. This is not the same as claiming all of world history for capitalism, for the label itself does little to highlight what is fundamentally distinctive about the capital accumulation logic of the present that was not there in the past anyway. The point is that while positivist ontologies were resisted in Caribbean Marxist writing, excessive attention to modes of production and this thing called 'capitalism' represented capitulation to an obsession with categories. The Caribbean moved from a marginal periphery (to civilizations in the Americas) to a contact periphery to technologically superior 'high cultures' by the eighteenth century.[24] But this took place within a world system in which the rise and fall of cultures and geographic shifts in centres of accumulation are constants. The sense in which there is *movement* in the political economy of the world system was not in full view in Caribbean and most other left scholarship. Throughout the various works, the modern hierarchy of First World core and Third World periphery are seen as permanent 'fixtures', at least until the web of capitalist relations breaks down.

Of the three fundamental features of a world view – philosophical foundations (epistemology and ontology), theoretical constructions and normative judgements – Caribbean left intellectuals remain sparked by normative concerns. Neville Duncan and George Belle point to the prospect of 'recolonization', as Caribbean state weakening, increasing indebtedness, urban decay and technological backwardness threaten social cohesion and governability.[25] Munroe and Beckles bemoan the existing 'economic injustices' in the Caribbean corporate world following positive democratic advances in the 'political' sphere. And Herb Addo suggests as a solution to the region's woes, a neo-autarkic strategy of delinking from the capitalist world system, what he calls "dis-engaged cultural transformation".[26] While such analyses provide a call to action, the critical premise and social promise of the work of James, Beckford and Thomas remain unfulfilled because a telling ideological critique is lacking. Without it, the critical studies rest upon unexamined liberal, positivist foundations that do not well support New World's critical, emancipatory aspirations. Of course, neoclassicists at the UWI see no problem here, for it is their version of reality that has been internalized by local society. But their research projects could be better served if there is an intellectual exchange with dissenters.

Liberalism and Positivism

The implicitly liberal foundations of UWI scholarship need to be examined. Over the last two centuries, liberalism has been the outstanding doctrine of Western civilization. Its diverse strands include concern with individual freedoms, the reduction of state power, the right to consent to and participate in political institutions, and a commitment to pluralist politics and society. The human essence is freedom from dependence on the will of others, and the being is seen as proprietor of his or her capacities. Individuals bearing property rights constitute 'society'; the exchange of property rights is the essence of the realm of 'economics'; and the protection of those rights from state usurpation or other infringement is the domain of 'politics'. These elements constitute the 'national' sphere of social relations. The 'international' is a neutral space where countries could all mutually achieve benefits in exchange relations. These normative claims, theoretical premises and practices rest atop deeply embedded ideological assumptions. Social life here is reduced to a scientistic reading. This is not surprising, for Arblaster notes that "the growth of modern science and the emergence of liberalism are overlapping developments".[27] Scientific procedures and methods, the distinction between facts and values, confidence in individual experience and empiricism, rationality, concerns for control, knowledge as a tool, and the analytic reduction of wholes into parts align liberal individualism with the outlook of modern science. This orientation is positivist. Positivism is an ontology identifying for us what is real. The world is understandable once unproblematically conceived of as featuring 'things'. These 'things' can be measured, tested and presented to make 'facts'. And through these 'facts' we know the world positively. Our social world is thus divided into separate domains (economics, politics, sociology) and reality is vertically divided into 'levels of analysis' (that is, individual, state, state system). C. Wright Mills had long warned that social phenomena "are not to be so mechanically and so externally linked".[28]

In the social science faculty at the UWI, the underlying discourse and mental map of economists and management specialists remains a neoliberal one.[29] This must be understood first against a wider backdrop, for it is as much to do with prevailing free market mantras as with the deceleration of liberal theorizing into crude economisms. The classical task was to explain market regularities as the outcome of the rational choices of individuals subject to constraints. The programme has since evolved into a mathematical form with the following research strategy foremost in the minds of US, British and Austrian economists: (a) maximizing behaviour, (b) stable preferences, and (c) market equilibrium.[30] This evolution occurred over the last hundred years, with each successive generation weeding out the use of natural language. Mathematics from the 1950s became the standard language of economic science. And while this was a Western development, it is worth noting that most UWI Caribbean economists of the 1960s and 1970s (for example, Jefferson, Beckford, Best) went against the trend. Their language did not crowd out questions of subjective assessment, institutional context, social embeddedness, knowledge (as opposed to information), judgement, pro- cess and history. But most current practitioners at the university have succumbed to the behaviouralist fallacy that unless an idea could be stated in formal proof, then the idea remained an interesting one but not a contribution to science. Mainstream economists, particularly at the Cave Hill campus, may do well to acknowledge what Pigou had to say about Alfred Marshall, an early twentieth century economist:

Though a skilled mathematician, he used mathematics sparingly. He saw that excessive reliance on this instrument might lead us astray in pursuit of intellectual toys, imaginary problems not conforming to the conditions of real life: and further, might distort our sense of proportion by causing us to neglect factors that could not easily be worked up in the mathematical machine.[31]

Beckford and others limited mathematics to the footnotes, but a reading of recent work by UWI economists in say, the Mona-based journal, *Social and Economic Studies*, reveal that the footnotes have become the text, so to speak. Indeed, footnotes containing Keynes, Galbraith or even Marshall have disappeared from view as instructional articles and books on adjusted mathematical techniques and models proliferate. This reflects a capitulation to positivistic notions of scientific inquiry. Reference is here made to the formalistic demand for mathematical representation, something which some fellow neoclassicists have begun to argue against.[32] The perception at the UWI seems to be: Science is empiricism and formulae; not Arthur Lewis, not George Beckford. Theirs was encyclopedic and made for interesting reading, but this exercise should not be confused with science – "we have moved beyond that".

An entire generation of our brightest students has since been and still are taught how to master these techniques and solve imaginary problems. We no longer train our economics undergraduates in the substantive logic and 'art' of economics. The language of mathematics is largely taught, where it is commonplace to witness students and graduates valuing the grammar of the discipline, rather than its substance. Mastery of technique has supplanted mastery of the kind of intuitive economic analysis of the Lewis strain or New

World type. The flagging postgraduate programme in the economics departments across the three campuses is perhaps mainly for this very reason.[33] Certainly the large menu of mathematically based courses underdevelops and subsequently may weed out a certain type of scholar with skills in history and philosophy. In order to touch an intellectual chord with future generations, the economics departments need to introduce students to the history of economic thought (as theory) and economic history (as empirical touchstone). Mathematical models need to be constrained by an understandability criterion and a return to the research direction of older or newer scholarship.

The point was made earlier that UWI radical scholarship also suffers from inadequate critique. While the structural ontology of New World and current left intellectuals challenge liberalism's individualism, the very identification of the key structures as political – (state centred power politics); and economic (production and trade) actually reinforce a liberal–positivist framework. For them these structures exist positively and they set the context of social relations, but we are not enabled to picture what must be the case in reality, namely the simultaneity of politics and economics. As a result, the separately constituted domains (that is, 'modes-of-production' – politics, economics, national, international and the like) reflect reifications. Would somebody please explain how this multistorey gallery of distorting mirrors is supposed to aid our understanding?

There is a need for an approach that seeks to connect individual agents and social structures into a coherent social theory grounded in an ontology that balances actors, structures and concepts. But this is a deeply reflective enterprise that perhaps does not sit well with a 'publish or perish' tarantism taking root at the UWI. Rational and casual empirical studies thus triumph. Economists especially acquiesce to this tendency, but most UWI social scientists have succumbed to the narrow conception of 'science' that currently prevails. The preoccupation with the analytic realm of postulates, hypotheses, models, theories, categories, taxonomies, explanations, empirical statements and logical rules overemphasizes ontology and method. It demeans the ideological realm of epistemological presuppositions that drive and frame scientific inquiry. We need to ask epistemological questions. The Caribbean as a recreated lifespace – attested by the events following early colonization and the societies thereafter forged – perforce requires a closer look at ideological foundations such as positivism, objectivism, individualism, structuralism, and the like. To challenge positivism and empiricism is to challenge the premise that individuals are the basic elements of social reality. To challenge structuralism is to resolve the dilemma of weighing agency against structure. Individuals create and reproduce social structures, yet such structures create the conditions in which certain kinds of individuals exist. UWI left intellectuals want to be ontologically holistic and structural, yet normatively emancipatory. Clearly, the relationship between individuals and structure is at issue otherwise who or what is being liberated, and from what?

In the absence of an ontological revolution, we engage in a univocal discourse. Critical enterprise in the Cold War context easily took on a normative and emancipatory character, but the free market world order requires more than this; as doublespeak, language and ideology have to be unpacked as well. There may be something after all in the postmodern movement of thought at this conjuncture. They question, among other things, foundations, our vocabulary and the philosophical assumptions of liberalism. But caution is required. There is a pattern that can be discerned if we take note of historical global developments. During phases of economic expansion, universal theorizing occurs. Economic deceleration phases produce their own pattern of thought, one where universal theorizing comes into question and multiple-cause approaches proliferate. The three 'post-' moves in today's intellectual climate are poststructuralism, postmodernism and postpositivism. While radical scholars in the intellectual world warn of a destructive 'bent' in the first two, given their deconstructivist drive and nihilistic conclusions, they generally remain either agnostic or receptive on postpositivist attempts to scrutinize ontologies.[34] As we query our passion for categorization, however, care must be taken not to abandon the search for an inner logic of the international system.

The Rise of 'Normal Science'

The present state of social science scholarship, in the main, reflects a capitulation to hegemonic discourse and vocabulary. UWI political scientists have turned towards a cluster of issues under the themes of governance and globalization. But there is more by way of discussion on *forms* of governance and *inevitabilities* of globalization than a query of these very terminologies. They and others tend to use the term globalization as a kind of conceptual 'trash compactor' into which they dump a list of political, economic and social processes. Some do not even bother to explicitly define the concept.[35] There is not a sense that we need to understand their modes of arrival upon 'our shores', of a need to unpack these concepts and lay bare their ideological content. Sociological inquiry has merged well with cultural studies, with attention drawn to the state of the family, gender, youth, ethnic relations, and rehabilitative infrastructures, but too narrow a state-centric focus restricts its capacity to point to wider global systemic pressures and influences. State-centricity, too, pervades the economics discipline with increasing attention paid to microeconomic issues, tax policy, fiscal controls, credit rationing and firm lending, and the like.

Uncritical macroeconomic attention is drawn to areas such as 'sustainable development', growth of services, human resource management and tourism performance. Questions addressing the political are almost entirely left out in the research and teaching. Such questions are vital: What is the real scope for political action for cash strapped states in a complex world of interdependence and supranational governance structures? Can Caribbean states freely choose an economic system? And surely if they can in the short run, have these choices any chance of being sustainable if they fail to conform to the competitive logic of worldwide capital accumulation? Can human resource management strategies combat authoritarianism and cronyism in family, firm and public sector labour markets? Does a services-development model preclude the need for an industrial policy, and indeed can such a strategy (minus robust manufacturing) lead to graduation in the world system hierarchy? What of the condition of the bulk of the workforce in low paying, mundane services-related jobs? And who benefits, which classes and groups are augmented by current development strategies?

A closer look at the titles in *The Press UWI Catalogue* (1996–97 and 1997–98) reveals that of the 39 (forthcoming and new) titles, 9 are in the critical tradition, 9 are bibliographies and 21 feature normal science approaches. The 1997–98 catalogue from Ian Randle Publishers, a major publisher and distributor of Caribbean academic texts, also reveals a similar dearth of critical research in the social sciences. A reading of departmental reports from 1986 through to 1996 at the UWI reveal that neoclassical diagnosis has become a burgeoning area of research and teaching in economics and management – areas of high student intake.[36] The research agenda, particularly at the Cave Hill campus, has included concerns of both a macroeconomic and microeconomic variety: from public sector financing, labour productivity, export development and employment strategies to monetary arrangements, taxation systems and mathematical models. Most of the research has been policy-focused and linked to fiscal and human resource management questions. And of the 31 economics courses on offer in 1992–93, 16 were mathematically based; the ratio grew exponentially to 20 of 28 by 1995–96.

Its sister institution, the Department of Management, attracts a higher student intake. This is more reflective of the requirements of the services juggernaut of the Barbadian economy and prevailing perceptions than anything innate in the programmes themselves. Auxiliary professionals are required in the areas of tourism, offshore banking, real estate and property development and the message has gone out that problems affecting firms, businesses and parastatals can all be tackled by sound management practice. The research produced and the courses on offer constitute a highly successful affirmative use of positivist and liberal normative categories.[37] With policy applicability being given priority in the last ten years, case studies and analysis have been applied to issues such as equity markets, project management, personal financial planning, decision support systems, workplace relations and gender and entrepreneurship. Apart from the studies conducted in trade unionism and entrepreneurship, course design and research from this department serve as an intellectual apologia that elaborates and justifies the existing model of political economy, even as it reconceptualizes and tidies away problems as issues of management. Not surprisingly, management aspires to the exclusively professional standing of a 'discipline', and it experiences no identity crisis in understanding its project as being multidisciplinary where it is not, more accurately conceived, parasitic upon the established university disciplines.

Regrettably, students are not taught what they need to know. The vast majority of honours graduates from economics and management programmes leave without knowing the standard scholarly definition of capitalism and the logical moral/human implications of it. Nor are they informed about the permeating culture of merchant capitalism, the corporate monopolist trends and family firm norms in the Caribbean. In this way only a neoclassical imagination pervades, as social consciousness is dulled.

The research arm of the social science faculty, ISER, reveals a change of focus away from issues such as poverty, unemployment, positive nationalism (read statecraft) and wealth distribution. It does appear that ISER has succumbed to the view that reality is local and temporal, as its agenda seems shaped by the imperatives of policy and bureaucracy. The main foci of the ISER Mona research programme since 1992 has been human resource development and microeconomic issues. The university director of ISER, Professor Selwyn Ryan, alludes to "an ongoing effort to maintain a clear policy orientation in the analysis and presentation of material and information".[38] More by way of normal science research is in store when we consider the research agenda for the future:

Health Economics and Financing;
Crime and Crime Management;
Migration Policy and the Caribbean Family;
Teacher Preparation Programmes and Student Performance;
Situational Analysis of Injuries Due to Motor Vehicle Accidents and Violence.[39]

Research emanating from the ISER Cave Hill from the late 1980s became decidedly noncritical, policy driven and prescriptive in character. Political integration, entrepreneurship and distributive issues receded as microeconomic, public administrative and social issues received targeted address. In the last five years, completed studies were done in the areas of services, the youth in the Eastern Caribbean, bank lending, human resource management, neoclassical modelling, fiscal policy, gender and reproductive health, and tax policy.[40] But was the work underpinned by involvement in the theoretical debates that characterize the associated disciplines?[41] Increasingly there seems to be a commonality of purpose and interests between the government and the ISER. For example, government-commissioned research on the youth undertaken by the ISER Cave Hill and St Augustine has not led to criticism of development policies at a fundamental level.[42] And the ISER (Mona and St Augustine) project on *Critical Issues in Caribbean Development* has not approached a critique of the populist character of governments and the risk-adverse bias of the region's private sector. To put it bluntly, the ISER is duplicating the policy advice role already extant in government at the same time that it foregoes more seriously reflective enterprises that it is capable of discharging.

It is worth noting that providing public service is one of the criteria for academic promotion. This can serve to extend the realms of government and private enterprise into the academy.[43] Some social scientists, particularly economists and management specialists, serve or have served as chairpersons of statutory bodies, government appointed committees and state-run enterprises. A few serve or have served as directors in private firms. It is little wonder that the research emanating therefrom amounts to hegemony affirming refinement of official or neoliberal thought, the highest form of unintended flattery.

An intellectual rethink within the social sciences at the UWI is necessary. Caribbean civilization needs goals. That is, goals beyond tourism, increased consumption and liberation of the individual to pursue personal aims upon which the society must remain agnostic. We need to structure a genuine alternative to the present aberration, built on an entirely different set of foundations that Lewis was understood to advocate. But an entrenched liberal–positivist ideology and intellectual service to state power stifles imagination. In the absence of interrogation, the suggestion is that the future of the Caribbean is but a linear extrapolation of whatever version of the present is agreed upon. Perhaps the aim is to defer, obfuscate and conceal the inevitable, which is to say, death, in its various manifestations: the island-national option, the economy and the civilization. Conferences, public lectures and a few published essays provide information on the crisis symptoms facing the Caribbean. Fiscal insecurities, apathy and alienation among the youth, gender discrimination, environmental pressures and pending foreclosure on preferential arrangements are usually conflated in overarching narratives of the effects of globalization on the region. Solutions are sought through appeals for enhanced bargaining capacities both at the island-government level and at the regional level (read CARICOM).[44] Yet missing in these appreciations is any sense of context, any sense of causes being more appropriate than effects.

Rigorous interrogation might lead instead to a query of globalization – Does it have a grammar or logic that requires further inquiry? What of the undemocratic global institutionalism of the IMF, World Bank, World Trade Organization, Bank for International Settlements, and the like, which, unless remedied, will displace expressions of national political will as the basis of government policy? At the island-government level, political scientists urge greater democratization and, the much cliched, 'good governance' as though these can be achieved in the absence of a viable economic platform. Moreover, there seems to be little critical comment emanating from the university of the services model of development. This is unfortunate, for our economies continue to offer services at the lowest levels of the value added hierarchy of the capitalist world economy. Indeed, all the many constructive possibilities of our development policy are being frozen by the neoliberal discourse and the fiction of our continued viability as separate island states. The freeze is already so deep that nothing is left at the regional level but plans for market openness. CARICOM is promoted as a vehicle for interest representation, but what of its lack of organic intensity? Meanwhile, Caribbean countries seem to be on an inevitable march to the glorious anomic end-state.

Overall there seems a persistence in using models that are consistent, clear and wrong, or to offer ad hoc counsel at variance both with theory and historical experience. Take the neofunctionalist arguments in support of a dichotomized approach to regional integration, beginning first with the economic and culminating with the political. This ties in with liberal notions of open regionalism and open markets. Of particular interest is the support given for these principles by senior UWI academics and administrators in the *Report of the West Indian Commission*.[45] The idea of political union was dismissed as irrelevant at this time. But the Caribbean situation begs the following question: Can a single market and economy in a region of low-accumulation countries arise in the absence of a state? A regional negotiating machinery, of which the chancellor of the UWI is key negotiator, has been established to undertake post-Lomé and hemispheric free trade negotiations on behalf of CARICOM member states. But this promises *not* to yield much fruit when we consider the historical record of CARICOM and the lack of coherence among the territories. What is likely in the years ahead is a race-to-the-bottom wages and conditions game among the countries. UWI social scientists, in an individual and collective act of cowardice and self-intimidation, opt for silence on these matters. Is there no relief from this bleak landscape?

Conclusions

The modernist fallacy and the Europeanist fallacy are everywhere and must be identified, criticized and expelled from our research projects.[46] The Caribbean and wider Americas were the original sites of modernity and so it is easy to understand how intellectuals slip into the well worn tracks of these two fallacies. But as liberalism continues to triumph in the intellectual firmament, it behoves the academic from the South to seriously weigh the historical and ideological character of his or her work. This harkens back to the attention paid by Gramsci to the class function of intellectual work, including that hiding behind the cloak of scientific objectivity. The university's struggle for relevance in a Caribbean wracked by decay or crisis symptoms, and its sensitivity to budget efficiency make for a climate where conformity to the prevailing common sense seems the best course for research programming. Privilege, wealth and protection are rewards that come from aligning oneself with the dominant order. In short, there is private gain for undertaking such research, not to mention a chance to put an entry in one's curriculum vitae. It takes exceptional people, however, to decide not to side with power or the dominant discourse, a decision made bolder given the Caribbean's small size and easy social contact. The task facing a scholar of this nature is especially difficult given that the very ground upon which orthodoxies of dissent rest is a liberal–positivist one; and the present balance of global sociopolitical forces is with neoliberalism. This reinforcement of liberalism both at the deep philosophical and material levels comes at a time when social science at the UWI has been under pressure to give its immediate address to the policy realm. A publish or perish imperative also set in as budget shortfalls perforce implied possible job cuts. The situation is one where priority of survival continues to be asserted both as an operating principle and as a rationale for the absence of radical critique.

Care must be taken that a "rigorous and independent research" university operation is not undone by these multiple forces. Mainstream development discourse in the Caribbean, unlike the sixties and seventies, is one of collaboration rather than critical dialogue between the policy community and the university. Translated another way, the discourse shared is one of infatuation with detail and the immediate. If we can explicate the role played by earlier UWI scholars in the policy making process we will note a difference.

Lewis, Beckford and others saw that the academic has a valuable social role to play in policy making – one that derives from the strengths of scholarship. They can perform four functions in the policy making process that are congruent with his or her expertise: the provision of alternatives, information, sensitization and criticism. It becomes a matter of keeping one's distance while not disassociating oneself from the policy process. This will be the first step towards really rendering the UWI relevant to the region well into the next century.

Notes

1. As noted in the "Principal's Overview" (Cave Hill campus) in 1996. See the *Annual Report to Council, 1996* (Cave Hill, Barbados: UWI, 1996), 3–11.
2. The intellectual tendencies within the New World group (Walter Rodney, George Beckford, Lloyd Best, Kari Levitt, Clive Thomas, Trevor Munroe, Norman Girvan, Owen Jefferson, H.R. Brewster, Edwin Carrington and Roy Augier) ranged from moderate to 'progressive'.
3. Patrick A.M. Emmanuel, "Academic Relations of Power: The Case of UWI", *Bulletin of Eastern Caribbean Affairs* 21, no. 4 (December 1996).
4. Caribbean historiography, by its turn towards gender, cricket and the dispossessed in recent times reveals a critical bent, one in the direction of understanding the politics of spaces in emancipatory struggles. Some recent examples are, V. Shepherd, B. Brereton, B. Bailey (eds), *Engendering History: Caribbean Women in Historical Perspective* (London: James Currey Publishers; New York: St Martin's Press, 1995); R. Reddock, *Women Labour and Politics in Trinidad and Tobago: A History* (London: Zed Press, 1994); H. Beckles (ed), *Inside Slavery: Process and Legacy in the Caribbean Experience* (Kingston, Jamaica: Canoe Press, 1996); B.L. Moore, *Cultural Power, Resistance and Pluralism: Colonial Guyana 1838–1900* (Kingston, Jamaica: Canoe Press, 1995). Incidentally, Carl Stone, a political scientist based at Mona, remained for a long time during his life a leading researcher.
5. P. Sherlock and R. Nettleford, *The University of the West Indies: A Caribbean Response to the Challenge of Change* (Basingstoke: Macmillan, 1990).
6. G.A.V. Belle, "Commentary Review of Patrick Emmanuel's 'Academic Relations of Power' ", *Bulletin of Eastern Caribbean Affairs* 21, no. 4 (1996).
7. G.A.V. Belle, "Reform: The University of the West Indies and The Emperor's New Clothes", *Bulletin of Eastern Caribbean Affairs* 21, no. 4 (1989): 17–25.
8. It was in 1960 when the Imperial College of Tropical Agriculture situated at St Augustine was incorporated into the University College of the West Indies. A College of Arts and Sciences was sited first near the deep water harbour at the outskirts of Bridgetown in 1963, but a permanent campus was erected in 1966–67 at Cave Hill.

9. See W.A. Lewis, "Industrial Development in the Caribbean", *Caribbean Economic Review* 2, no. 1 (1950): 1–61; and W.A. Lewis, *The Theory of Economic Growth* (London: Allen and Unwin, 1955).
10. See W.G. Demas, *The Economics of Development in Small Countries with Special Reference to the Caribbean* (Montreal: McGill University Press, 1965).
11. C.L.R. James, *The Black Jacobins: Toussaint L'Ouverture and the San Domingo Revolution*, 2nd edition (New York: Vintage Books, 1989).
12. E. Williams, *Capitalism and Slavery* (New York: Capricorn Books, 1966).
13. See G. Beckford, *Persistent Poverty* (Morant Bay: Maroon Publishing House; London: Zed Press, 1972); L. Best and K. Levitt, "Outlines of a Model of Pure Plantation Economy", *Social and Economic Studies* 17, no. 3 (1968): 283–326; N. Girvan, *The Caribbean Bauxite Industry* (Mona, Jamaica: Institute of Social and Economic Research, UWI, 1967); N. Girvan, "The Denationalization of Caribbean Bauxite: Alcoa in Guyana", *New World Quarterly* 5, no. 3 (1971); N. Girvan and O. Jefferson (eds), *Readings in the Political Economy of the Caribbean* (Kingston: New World Group, 1971); H.R. Brewster and C.Y. Thomas, *The Dynamics of Caribbean Economic Integration* (Mona, Jamaica: Institute of Social and Economic Research, UWI, 1967); T. Munroe, *The Politics of Constitutional Decolonization: Jamaica 1944–62* (Mona, Jamaica: Institute of Social and Economic Research, UWI, 1972); and W. Rodney, *How Europe Underdeveloped Africa* (Dar es Salaam: London and Tanzania Publishing House, 1972).
14. This amounts to a veiled attack on cultural criticism as well. For a useful discussion on 'policy application' and critical enterprise, see J. Ruane and J. Todd, "The Application of Critical Theory", *Political Studies* 36 (1988): 533–38.
15. Comments made in a divisive attack on Rodney and the UWI following the Kingston riots. For more on this see A. Payne, *Politics in Jamaica* (Kingston: Ian Randle Publishers, 1994).
16. For a clearer outline of the nature of James' critique of Williams' administration, see his *Party Politics in the West Indies* (Trinidad: Vedic Enterprises, 1961).
17. See E. Williams, *The University of the Caribbean in the Late 20th Century 1980–1999* (Port of Spain: PNM Publishing, 1973), 21.
18. These included Lewis' public lectures, Best's establishment of a democracy challenging community group, Tapia, the emergence of *Abeng* in Jamaica influenced by New World members, and the formation of a pressure group for social change known as Ratoon. For a reading of Rodney's contacts with Jamaican working class communities, see L. Lewis, "The Groundings of Walter Rodney", *Race and Class* 33, no. 1 (1991): 71–82.
19. See M. Hutchinson, "Rastafari in Transition" (PhD diss., UWI, Cave Hill, 1994).
20. L. Lewis, "Socialist Crisis and the Trajectory of Caribbean Politics", *Beyond Law* 6, issue 17 (January 1997): 89–114.
21. See T. Munroe, *The Cold War and The Jamaican Left* (Kingston: Kingston Publishers, 1992), 140–44.
22. See C.Y. Thomas, *The Poor and the Powerless* (London: Latin American Bureau, 1988), 24–28.
23. See two of the more important works, J. Abu-Lughod, *Before European Hegemony*

(New York: Oxford University Press, 1989); A.G. Frank and B.K. Gills, *The World System: 500 or 5000 Years?* (London: Routledge, 1993).
24. 'Contact periphery' here means the systematic political, economic and cultural subordination of an area by a core power.
25. See G. Belle, "Against Colonialism: Political Theory and Re-colonization in the Caribbean" (paper presented at the Conference on Caribbean Culture, UWI, Mona, 1996); N.C. Duncan, "Rise of Mega Trading Blocs and Implications for the Caribbean", in *Global Developments: Caribbean Impacts and Organized Labour*, edited by N.C. Duncan (Barbados: Friedrich Ebert Stiftung, 1995).
26. See H. Addo, "The New World Order and the Prospects for Global Social Justice: A Third World Perspective" (unpublished paper, UWI, St Augustine, 1991).
27. See A. Arblaster, *The Rise and Decline of Western Liberalism* (New York: Basil Blackwell, 1984), 26.
28. See C. W. Mills, *The Sociological Imagination* (Oxford: Oxford University Press, 1959).
29. Basically, neoliberalism emanates from the seedbed of classicism and is expressed in the treatment of privatization and increased capital mobility as in themselves a desirable thing from a broad social viewpoint. It is the ideological complement to present-day global restructuring where emphasis is placed on the need for limited government, open economies and free competition. For more on this see my "National Development and the Globalization Discourse", *Third World Quarterly* 17, no. 5 (1996).
30. For more on this, see G.S. Becker, *The Economic Approach to Human Behaviour* (Chicago: University of Chicago Press, 1976).
31. See A.C. Pigou, *Memorials of Alfred Marshall* (1925; reprint, New York: Augustus M. Kelley, 1966), 84
32. See, for example, R.H. Coase, *The Firm, the Market and the Law* (Chicago: University of Chicago Press, 1988).
33. See *Departmental Reports 1995–1996*, 163. The head of department reported once again a suspension of the MSc programme, and alluded to only six other students involved in postgraduate study (five at MPhil; one at PhD). (There has been some difficulty in obtaining current figures but in 1989–90, only six students entered the MSc Economics programme at the St Augustine campus.)
34. Wallerstein once cast postmodernists and poststructuralists as "marauding irrational warriors", while Peterson speaks of their destructive bent. See I. Wallerstein, "The Challenge of Maturity: Whither Social Science", *Review* 15, no. 1 (1992): 1–7; V.S. Peterson, "Transgressing Boundaries", *Millennium* (Summer 1992): 183–206.
35. For an example of this, see some of the contributions in L. Searwar (ed), *Diplomacy and Survival: Caribbean Development in a World of Change* (Kingston: Friedrich Ebert Stiftung, 1991). Also see the following recent work: A. Wint, *Managing Towards International Competitiveness* (Kingston: Ian Randle Publishers, 1997); W.G. Demas, *Critical Issues in Caribbean Development: West Indian Development and the Deepening and Widening of the Caribbean Community*, no. 1 (Kingston: Ian Randle Publishers, 1997).
36. This is so especially at the Cave Hill campus. Added impetus occurred following

the introduction of a BSc degree in Business, Economics and Social Statistics in 1990–91.
37. The following courses, Industrial Relations, and to some extent Government, Business and Society offer insight into the counter-hegemonic, the terrain of struggle where interests arrayed in class or group form seek compromise or unmitigated advance. Here there has been some space opened for critical discourse. The same could be said of the scholarship of Lawrence Nurse and the research thrust of Maxine McClean. Workplace relations and entrepreneurship issues are respectively treated holistically with culture, politics and history intruding on the inquiry. See for example, L. Nurse, *Trade Unionism and Industrial Relations in the Commonwealth Caribbean* (Connecticut: Greenwood Press, 1992); and M. McClean, "The New Venture Capitalists: The Caribbean Credit Union Movement in the Year 2000", *Caribbean Affairs* 3, no. 4 (1990): 137–49.
38. See Ryan's comments in *Vice Chancellor's Report to Council 1996,* Volume 2 (Mona, Jamaica: Office of the Vice Chancellor, UWI), 51–55.
39. Ibid., 52.
40. For more information on the research trends of ISER Cave Hill, consult the compilation *Activities of the ISER 1963–1997*, produced by the ISER librarians.
41. We may be sure of this in some of the individual research work, but what of the bulk of the commissioned or corporate funded projects of late – namely the Changing International Environment and Impact on CARICOM Countries project (Andrew Mellon Foundation); Youth in the OECS (Government/Ford Foundation); Migration Policy and the Caribbean Family (Ford Endowment Grant) and others?
42. One of the leading researchers is now director of youth affairs in the Barbados government.
43. 'Public Service' first made its entry at Cave Hill as a category in the Departments of Economics and Management report in 1991–92. See *Departmental Reports 1991–92 Cave Hill Campus* (Cave Hill, Barbados: UWI, 1992), 190.
44. I refer to the Caribbean Community (est. 1973) which comprises the thirteen English-speaking territories, along with newcomers Haiti and Suriname.
45. Among the commissioners were chancellor of the UWI, Sir Shridath Ramphal; vice chancellor, Alister McIntyre; pro vice chancellor Professor Rex Nettleford; and senior lecturer and resident tutor (Montserrat) Dr Howard Fergus.
46. The modernist fallacy is the one where social scientists and historians assume that everything important in the Caribbean and contemporary world began at some point after 1492 A D Whether it is 1650, 1815 or 1945, everything that happened before is irrelevant to an understanding of human history. The Europeanist fallacy defines some areas of the world as European or Westernized (different areas at different times) and similarly dismisses all other cultures as irrelevant

5

The Politics of Caribbean Higher Education

Bevis F. Peters

Introduction

In this chapter, it is proposed to examine certain elements and concepts of political processes, actions and decisions and to demonstrate their interrelationship as the basis of an analytical framework for the study of higher education in the English-speaking Caribbean. In making the case for such investigations, that is, the study of the politics of higher education, we might well start with the Platonian and Aristotlean precept that man is a political animal. Political behaviour must therefore be regarded as a basic human condition. In situations where human relationships are in evidence and irrespective of the social and organizational contexts, there will inevitably be manifestations of political behaviour. Aristotle further introduced the idea of the "chief theatre" – the centre stage of life on which the drama of human interaction is played out.[1] In this scenario, mankind strives to achieve 'goodness' as a responsible citizen and an ethical individual; and in the process is obliged to be an active participant in influencing and determining the kind of drama played out in the theatre of life. By Aristotle's definition, this is what constitutes politics – the drama of human beings, who in the process of becoming responsible and ethical citizens, participate in and seek to influence decisions that may affect their lives and well-being.

As a derivation from the above, it can therefore be posited that an investigation of the what, the how and the why of decisions, the structures, activities and human behaviour within the context of a social organization constitutes what is essentially a study of political phenomena; that is to say, the study of political events. In more recent times, Mangham[2] elaborated on the idea of politics as theatre and sought to demonstrate its application within the context of higher education. In such an organizational setting, he observed that there were certain notable aspects of political activities and behaviour that might well be considered as performance, rehearsal and improvisation – all of which can give real meaning to the political dynamics of organizational life and render it as social theatre.

For the purposes of this chapter, we shall adhere to the conceptual principles indicated above and therefore will treat higher education in the Caribbean as the stage on which has occurred some of the most intractable issues, and the requisite decisions and policies in relation to the development, consolidation and change in education in the region. We shall also consider the prevailing socioeconomic conditions that would have provided an appropriate backdrop to these developments.

The analytical framework that will be employed in such a study will of necessity be based on concepts and models adopted from the study of political science and policy sciences; and these will be combined with the relevant historical documentation to reflect the dynamic and progressive nature of the developments under consideration. In setting the stage or context for the analysis of political phenomena in Caribbean higher education, we shall also identify some critical development milestones starting in the 1960s and continuing to the present (1990s). These past four decades represent a period in which some of the most significant policy decisions were formulated and implemented to guide the development of higher education in the English-speaking Caribbean, and which to many observers would have provided the strategic basis, and set in train the emergent policies, new structures, institutional reorientation and programme reforms that we are witnessing today.

Higher Education Defined

In this chapter we define the term higher education in its broadest sense to include all postsecondary or tertiary institutions that may offer degree or sub-degree programmes – full-time or part-time. This effectively includes the non-university sector (community colleges, polytechnics, technical-vocational institutions, teachers' training colleges, and other specialized institutions, as well as universities). In adopting an inclusive approach to the definition, we are in fact recognizing and embracing the diversity and heterodoxy that exist at this level of education in the English-speaking Caribbean. We are mindful too that in countries such as Britain, where higher education used to be synonymous with universities, this has contributed to much confusion.[3] The term tertiary has currency in the region as the concept to denote postsecondary or higher education.[4] Higher education then or tertiary education may include non-university and university programmes, technical and vocational education and training, professional and subprofessional training and continuing education programmes.[5]

In the Commonwealth Caribbean, apart from the regional University of the West Indies (UWI) with campuses in Barbados, Jamaica and Trinidad, the higher or tertiary education landscape consists of three national universities: in Belize, Guyana and Jamaica. Additionally, there is a state/national college in both Antigua and St Kitts and community colleges in the Bahamas, Barbados, Cayman Islands, Dominica, Grenada, Jamaica, St Lucia and St Vincent. Teachers' colleges also exist in many of the countries, as well as technical/vocational institutes, theological colleges, colleges of fine arts and other specialized single purpose training institutions. Students attending these institutions would normally be sixteen years and over and would generally be required to meet certain minimum academic or experiential standards to be eligible for admission. As evidence of successful completion of the programme in which they are enrolled, they would normally be expected to be granted some sort of certification or academic credit. As will be demonstrated in later discussions, this highly diversified nature of tertiary education has provided a unique context for some of the most telling political drama that has been played out over time concerning the promotion of access and the forging of interinstitutional relationships within the region's tertiary education sector.

Political Perspectives in Higher Education

The literature related to the scholarly investigation into the politics of education indicates that up until the 1960s, this particular field of study had not only been relatively late in arrival, but as Layton[6] points out, there was also a certain reluctance in the United States to even use the term 'politics of education'. Similarly in the United Kingdom, such types of studies were almost nonexistent. It was not until the late 1960s and early 1970s that the concern with the political dimension in education was beginning to gain increasing acceptance as a legitimate area for study. And even then, in the studies that were especially undertaken to analyse and critique education decision making from a political perspective, that is to investigate such matters as organizational governance, power, authority and conflict as their primary concern, there was the tendency, particularly in the United States, to avoid the use of the term 'politics of education'. Expressions such as the analysis of educational policy making or similar euphemisms were generally preferred to describe what was definitively the study of the politics of education.

As more and more researchers increasingly accepted and engaged themselves in the study of the politics of education as a field of scholarly activity, this brought with it growing criticism in relation to how the discipline was being developed. For example, one of the main criticisms often cited in the literature is the conceptual diffuseness created by the inclusion of everything approaching 'politics' as being worthy of investigation with little or no delimitations imposed. One article quoted by Layton sums up the critics' point of view of the state of the art as it obtained in the 1970s:

The politics of education is presently without an integrative intellectual identity. Its scope is not well defined or its boundaries firmly fixed. Researchers in the field have shown differing conceptions of the essential core of their studies, whether it be the governance of education, education and the political system, or the policy process in education.[7]

This particular critique is most instructive in that, in considering the major shortcomings that Layton has identified, one can discern how the methodological approach to the politics of education as a field of study might be improved. Perhaps the most important task in undertaking such studies, is that the purpose and scope of the investigation must be clearly defined. Particular care must also be shown in the research in the selection and definition of the concepts to be employed; and importantly, the framework for analysis should be constructed in such a way so as to reflect coherence among the variables selected for their theoretical importance. Where issue perhaps could be taken with this particular critique concerns the basic premise as to what should constitute the 'essential core' of such studies. The inference that is to be drawn would suggest that in order to develop a 'true core', researchers (political analysts) in the field should work within fixed boundaries in their investigations of such matters as governance, or in the treatment of education as a political system, or alternatively to restrict themselves to the policy process in education. But these are not mutually exclusive analytical concepts, and the reality is that in contemporary educational systems with its "power plays, conflicts, and rough-and-tumble politics",[8] we could hardly accept such impositions and choose only to focus on any one particular aspect at the expense of the others. For as Baldridge rightly argues, complex organizations such as universities should be studied as micropolitical systems that are multifaceted and dynamic. Moreover, such systems by definition do embrace the set of political dynamics that may involve conflicts, controversy and the influence of particular interest groups as they struggle to become closely involved in organizational policy formulation and decision making. With all that this entails, it is clear that no one 'core' of studies will suffice if the researcher is to investigate adequately the inherent complexities related to institutional development and change, questions concerning conflict over organizational goals, and the dynamics of the political processes that such matters embrace.

The essential requirement, that the core of political studies in education should embrace a variety of political perspectives, harkens back to the references made earlier to politics as the 'chief theatre' (social organizations) in which conflict, among groups and within and between the various units or departments, is seen as an inevitable part of organizational life. Those who have an interest (interest groups) in influencing what should be played out in the theatre are in a continual struggle that is part of the drama itself. In the area of higher education, political intrigue, controversy and attempts at their resolution are matters of great significance insofar as they relate to decision making and the implementation of decisions. These are some of the elements that can contribute to a broader perspective and more penetrative analysis of the attendant issues.

Indeed, this has been the approach adopted by Baldridge in proposing his basic political model as a framework for analysing decision making within the university and which he treats as a political system. Riley and Baldridge[9] were later to expand on this model to help explain the university's formal structure, the dynamic political processes that are involved in policy formation and decision making including the critical political issues and the various interest group struggles that occur over time within the university.

But coming closer to home in the Caribbean, it is clear from the related literature that the study of the politics of education has been a less than popular field for researchers in the region. As will be shown from a review of the related literature, much work remains to be done in the areas of the politics of education and higher or tertiary education. The development and modernization of education at all levels and the accompanying issues and ensuing decisions have been and will continue to be some of the abiding concerns worthy of accumulative research. Emmanuel,[10] in his *Academic Relations of Power: The Case of UWI,* has suggested that Caribbean academics have somehow avoided this area of study in relation to the UWI for a variety of reasons. For example, he speculates that there may be reluctance to undertake this type of research because of a shared perception among Caribbean academics that the university may well be too valued an institution to have its internal operations subject to scrutiny from a political perspective. A more contentious reason perhaps is his assertion that this reluctance could be based on "fear of internal sanctions".[11] But apart from the reasons cited by Emmanuel, some of which may be of an idiosyncratic nature, and others systemic, there are also hurdles of a methodological nature that may well be part of the problem. We will address this particular aspect in a later section of the chapter.

Emmanuel's own study, as he himself has stated, was "very much a preliminary effort" in which he focused on the governance and power relationships within the university and comes to the conclusion that power at the higher end of the administrative hierarchy was unduly concentrated. He deplores explicitly the effects of such a state of affairs on the working environment of the wider academic community by noting the remoteness, alienation and heightened cynicism that has prevailed among faculty members in particular. He was equally concerned with the ways in which policies were formulated and decisions made, and found them troubling. In the circumstances, his call for increased research activity in the field of higher education with a particular emphasis on the political dimensions would seem most timely and justifiable.

A further observation coming out of the review of the literature in relation to the politics of education in the Caribbean is that even though the research so far conducted has been sparse and quite uneven, there have been a few pioneering works that stand out because of their penetrative and insightful analysis. Nettleford's paper on the UWI[12] – a focus on past, present and future trends, along with the implications of the restructured UWI on its programmes and operations – is a carefully crafted analysis and synthesis of these and related matters of educational policy. A notable feature of this particular study is that it is replete with the important and controversial political issues with which the university as a regional institution had to contend at the time it was going through its restructuring in 1984–85; and although not explicitly stated, it is evident that the study sought to examine and assess regional higher education – that is, the direction, nature and pace of development and the attendant policy issues – within a framework of the politics of education. The result is a fascinating account of the problems, opportunities and threats to the university from the time it came into being in 1948 and up to the time of the restructuring.

Recurring issues of institutional change and policy reorientation are taken up and, in the course of analysis, again and again, Nettleford delves into the important aspects of conflict, controversy and tension in relation to matters of university governance, its administrative structures and processes, and seeks to show how these were inextricably linked to powerful external forces such as the fourteen contributing governments that fund the university. In his discussion on the university's relationship with its sister tertiary institutions, political processes and concepts are clearly in evidence: internal and external interest group conflict, power strategies, the struggle and exercise of dominant authority and control, and legitimacy. Finally, in dealing with another major policy issue such as increased access to university level education and the related implications of costs and funding, Nettleford stressed the need for the UWI to lead the way and to systematically respond to the expressed needs and aspirations of the fourteen contributing governments that support the university. Anything short of this could have the effect of rendering the university dangerously vulnerable. In the investigation of such matters, due recognition should be given to the political dynamics and actions that are integral to the decision making and policy processes of the university.

The book entitled *The University of the West Indies: A Caribbean Response to the Challenge of Change* by Sherlock and Nettleford[13] offers a vivid history of the development of the university; and although this was not a study of the politics of education per se, we are, however, treated with cameos of the external political forces that have had significant impact on the life of the university, starting at the time of its inception and proceeding through the period of growth and consolidation during the 1970s and 1980s. The political issues discussed in this book are wide ranging – some recurring, others of a 'particularist' nature, some requiring immediate attention, and of course there are those that continue to have a wide impact on the organizational and academic structures and processes. The issues include the changing role and function of a university that at its inception was patterned on the traditional British elitist system, access to the university and associated matters of academic quality, the university's relationship with its external constituencies and in particular with the emerging national tertiary level institutions.

The book also captures the dynamic tension between the university community and the contributing governments as matters relating to decision making, control, university autonomy, expansion and decentralization and resource allocation are described and analysed. All this, of course, is set within a period when the region was experiencing political turmoil (federation and the break-up thereof), constitutional changes (national independence), and when the university was itself formulating and implementing major policies in relation to restructuring and decentralization. Altogether these factors represent the dominant environmental influences and political conditions that have shaped and continue to influence the development of the UWI up to the present time.

As already indicated, the two documents identified above are undoubtedly outstanding works for their in-depth historical content, the scope of the research and sophisticated analysis. But since the authors had set out to conduct a historical rather than a political analysis of the matters discussed, this methodological orientation provides only partial answers to the questions of political importance. Indeed, for the most part, we can only speculate on the political processes and the internal dynamics underlying the political activities. And as to the consequences of political actions of significance with their political undertones, we are able only to surmise.

Wellington Friday's doctoral dissertation, "Restructuring Higher Education in the Non-Campus Territories of the British Caribbean as a Strategy for Development", provides a similar comprehensive, historical and, to some extent, political analysis of the relationship between the UWI and the contributing territories, particularly those without a campus (noncampus countries). One of the purposes of his study is to "identify the extent to which 'political forces' in the Caribbean generally and in the non-campus territories specifically, have contributed towards the momentum for restructuring the University so that the University might more adequately meet the needs of the non-campus territories".[14] Relying on historical documentation and using a political frame of reference without explicitly stating so, Friday was able to look at the first four decades of the life of the university through 'political lenses'. As such the problems, opportunities and threats, which together constitute the political issues of that particular period, were treated as the essential focal points of his investigation. In dealing with the wide scope of political activity that was associated with the restructuring of the university, he provides insights into relations of power, authority and influence as the political directorate representing the fourteen national governments sought to impose their own particular views on the role of higher education – including the university – in responding to the development needs of the countries concerned. He further examined the external and internal environments of the university as a political system, particularly in reference to events involved in the determination and implementation of policy decisions concerning student access, university financing by the contributing governments, and the pace and direction of university development in particular and higher education in general throughout the region.

Friday was particularly blunt in his own assessment of the political controversies, conflict and power tactics being exercised by the dominant political forces, and his characterization of the modes of response of the university leadership to what must have been seen then as some of the most exacting political circumstances facing the university was equally unequivocal. Indeed, it was his assessment that "the University is so circumscribed by politics and political considerations that the success of Principals and Vice Chancellors, from Lewis to Marshall depended very much upon their ability to respond with understanding and finesse to the political forces operating both within and without the institution".[15] Further, in his examination and analysis of what he styled the "diverse political processes and complex behaviours and actions", Friday was able to go beyond the mere reporting of the restructuring 'saga' itself by unearthing the underlying political forces, the opposing influences, and the pervasive political dynamics at play. He also sought to document and critique how certain developments in governance occurred and why certain organizational structures, academic processes and organizational arrangements were either transformed or eliminated during the decades of the 1970s and 1980s.

In Paul Parker's dissertation, "Change and Challenge in Caribbean Higher Education",[16] the methodological approach could usefully be described as the forerunner to Friday's work in that Parker also treated elements of development and change within the university as imbued with political processes. Again, Parker's orientation to the study was largely 'historical' and as a consequence could not permit much divergence into the political issues and ramifications that inevitably came to light as part of his historical analysis. As noted, the study was essentially an analysis of development and change of two universities (UWI and University of Puerto Rico) during a thirty-year period. Questions concerning the nature of change, particularly as this relates to whether or not the two universities had become more adaptable to their respective socioeconomic contexts, were not only raised and analysed, he was also able to demonstrate the progressive movement of these two universities from their 'colonial' moorings – the educational model by which they were patterned. And it is in this regard that one could hardly miss the creative tensions brought about by these two distinct concepts of education, one American, the other British, vying for predominance and the resultant influences of these extraregional relations on the pace and direction of change within these two institutions. In his investigation of this particular phenomenon – the developments and influences – Parker, as did Friday, sought to place the analysis of historical events within the broad framework of comparative education as a field of study, and in the process, he was able to compare and contrast fundamental changes within the two universities in relation to governance structures, organizational and academic processes. Like Friday, the matter of change in funding arrangements was raised and treated as one of the major direct consequences of these new arrangements. Among his main conclusions was the fact that external pressures from outside of the two universities, some of which were extraregional, continued to provide the impetus for change within the two universities, not only at the stage of their inception, but throughout their existence.

Perhaps one of the most noteworthy historical developments brought to light in Parker's survey of the evolution of higher education in the region was Guyana's decision to withdraw from the regional UWI. Parker, however, only hints at the political factors concerning this crucial decision as he describes the governance and administrative structures of the new University of Guyana and the financial arrangements that were put in place. He also restricted himself to a description of the academic structures and student characteristics that the then Guyana government thought most suited to Guyanese circumstances, a methodological approach that appears similar to that used later by Fletcher, France and Sukdeo[17] in their study of the development of higher education in Guyana. But theirs is an even more restricted approach, having confined themselves to a general description of the formal organizational structures and the details of the academic arrangements and programmes in place at the University of Guyana. The circumstances and implications of Guyana's withdrawal from the UWI were of such political import, however, that it would seem to be a legitimate area for more in-depth political analysis, beyond the present limited scope of investigation. A study of this nature is warranted, in that it would lay bare the underlying political factors and should fully assess the consequences of the most critical development decisions to be made in higher education in the region. In their introduction, the authors thought it of such import that they quoted the White Paper on Higher Education (1963):

Our national needs cannot be met satisfactorily if we continue to rely on facilities in institutions outside our country. If Governments' objective of providing higher education for the largest number of people who can benefit from it is to be realized, then every effort must be made to create a National university as rapidly as possible.[18]

From this statement we are able to glean the government's official policy position on the establishment of its national university, but clearly such decisive matters of policy would seem to merit closer examination within a political frame of reference. But here again, we can only speculate as to what were the political circumstances and the real reasons why this particular policy decision was taken. Moreover, it is of utmost importance to understand what were the political ramifications of such a decision. In this regard, there are a number of questions that require answers. To what extent did internal political factors within the UWI itself contribute to this outcome? What were the factors – political or otherwise – within Guyana that influenced the decision to withdraw? Was there a consensus on the respective positions of the various interest groups within Guyana (politicians, professionals, students, employers and so on) in relation to the decision to establish a national university? Were the other contributing countries in a position, or were they at all inclined, to bring any influence to bear on the decision? Was the decision in fact a consensus or unilateral position? These are, and will continue to be, questions of political significance, especially since Guyana's decision to withdraw from the regional university has had major financial and policy implications for the development of UWI as a regional university.

Education, more so than higher education per se, also received some treatment as a political system in a major work by Bacchus[19] in which he examined the historical basis of the education systems in the region during the period of colonization and up to 1845. The book, in part, provided a revelation of political conflicts in the context of decisions concerning education during the colonial period. It examined the nature of the conflict among the various interested groups who held opposing views about the role and function of education in the context of development and change. The competing interests included the government elites, the missionaries, public servants and other functionaries, and other powerful key players within the region. Naturally, these powerful interest groups all had their own ideas about the kind of education that should be provided in the colonies and sought through a variety of power strategies to ensure that their particular perspective would hold sway. The effect of all this political action has led Bacchus to conclude that the educational institutions – schools in particular during that period – became "instructional, cultural and political sites all in one". They had come to represent "areas of contestation and struggle among differentially empowered groups".[20]

While Bacchus dealt with issues of the colonial period in the region as a whole, Miller[21] examined a number of contemporary issues in education in Jamaica during the period from 1945 to the 1980s. This particular period, he asserts, represented the 'golden era' of Jamaican education and he sought to place the developments in education within the context of political change and economic development. In doing so, he raised the matter of class interests and conflict – the ruling and upper classes versus the poorer groups of Jamaican society – as the policy of equal access to education evolved to become the government's official policy for education. This resulted in Jamaicans enjoying free secondary and tertiary education starting in the early 1960s. But

Miller was also quick to point out that certain external influences – not the least of which were the adverse changes in the Jamaican economy – conspired to help reverse this policy in a significant way, in that fees were subsequently introduced for tertiary education.

In reference to some of the external influences on the educational system in Jamaica, Miller also introduced the issue of political control and he raised the matter of the vulnerability of the educational system to external influences, and indicated a concern over the "losing battle of sovereignty in educational decision-making". Much of this state of affairs, he concludes, is a consequence of an overdependence on external sources of funding and the effect of the government of Jamaica having to meet "conditions and priorities" of the agency that loans or gives the money. He goes on to state emphatically, that with these imposed conditions, and with the external bodies "now determining recurrent expenditure on the public sector, both capital and recurrent expenditure in education are now under external control. There is now far less control of the educational system by Jamaicans, after twenty-four years of independence".[22] Miller's concern over external influences on decision making in education at all levels echoes that of Parker cited earlier.

While both the abovementioned works of Miller and Bacchus have introduced explicitly the political perspective concerning educational development and change in the Caribbean, their approaches of course vary, as they were dealing with issues of a different time frame and locale. Moreover, it is important to bear in mind that it was not the expressed major purpose of their particular works to undertake a critical analysis of the political aspects of education in the region. In their dealing with the historical and institutional dimensions of education in the region, however, they were able to identify some of the most complex educational issues as areas amenable to more in-depth political/policy analysis. They, like Nettleford, Sherlock, Friday and Parker, whose works have been cited above, have been able to bring to the fore the gamut of political issues facing education in general and higher education in particular in the Caribbean context. Their treatment of higher education – although somewhat partial – as a political system is reflected in these works. Political conflict and controversy, and the associated interest groups also receive partial treatment in the works. The policy decisions that are inherently political and their formulation that arise from political activities are also reflected in these works. So too are other political elements including power, control, authority and influence. We also get glimpses of the dynamic political action and activities, the power strategies utilized, hints on how decision making can be influenced, and comments on the effects of these decisions. These are but examples of the areas that lend themselves to an in-depth political analysis, areas in which the true substance of politics should be unearthed and systematically analysed. But the overall picture so far has been uneven, suggesting that there is still much work to be done to help fill the information gap indicated. For the remainder of this chapter, we shall construct an analytical framework consisting of the relevant concepts and seek to apply this framework in further investigating some of the selected issues that have been identified in the works already cited.

A Framework of Analysis

The conceptual framework to be discussed in this section is intended to provide a model of political science that can aid in a critical analysis and help to attain a better understanding of the major issues in higher education in the Caribbean. At the same time, it should help to make a contribution to filling the void of relevant and appropriate research tools for investigating areas that by definition are political in content and import. This broadening of perspective is not only essential within the field of education as an area of scholarly investigation, it also becomes necessary for those who may wish to venture into the field of comparative educational studies.

In relation to the field of higher education in the Caribbean, the authors cited previously have provided some rich analyses of the emergent policies and the associated changes and new developments in tertiary education across the region. The combined contribution of these works may be taken as providing an important knowledge base of contemporary issues in higher education specifically and education generally. But as indicated earlier these works, for the most part, would appear generally to fall within the sociohistorical–comparative education genre. And as Emmanuel has contended, there is much work to be done to depict more fully the political perspectives and to treat more adequately underlying issues of political significance affecting higher education in the region. Emmanuel has argued that this is a major failing on the part of the Caribbean's researchers in so far as examination of the politics of higher education in the regional university is concerned. And as would seem by the present review of the related literature, there is a case to be made for more researchers in this vitally important area of education. How then to fill the void? It requires essentially purposeful examination of the political structures, processes and political apparatus that are imbued within the region's tertiary education systems: universities, community and national colleges, and the specialized institutions. Particular attention also needs to be paid, from a political perspective, to the dynamic underpinnings of policy formation and policy decisions and their outcomes in higher education in the region. The interest group element in higher education is another principal area for investigation.

The literature reviewed indicates that major decisions concerning development and change in higher education may be better understood with primary reference to these interests. Fundamentally, we need to accept fully the notion that the organization of higher education is essentially that of a social structure circumscribed by a political system. In adhering to such a view, it is clear that within and without the higher educational system there are power relationships at play. Accordingly, in pursuing such investigations, a major task is to be able to define the locales, sources and instruments of power, the conditions under which the use of power is manifested and the political effects of the overt and covert use of power in decision and policy making. Such orientation requires the construction of a model that defines the political system, emphasizes political actions and gives central focus to the major policies and decisions. It also enables us to investigate in a systematic way the conflicts, controversies, and the internal and external forces that have had an impact on the decisions made and offers a more coherent and relatively straightforward approach for explaining political outcomes and effects.

In designing such a model, we can first consider Riley and Baldridge's illustration of a political paradigm that seeks to provide a balance between the organizational dimensions and the critical political elements mentioned above within a broad conceptual framework. The context of Baldridge's model is higher education, for as he contends, such a model is essential if we are to grapple with the power plays, conflicts and the rough and tumble politics to be found in many academic institutions.[23] The assumptions that underpin Baldridge's model include:

1. Universities and colleges (higher education) are complex organizations and therefore should be studied as micropolitical systems. A particular feature of higher education organizations relates to the internal political dynamics always in evidence by virtue of the presence of the varied interests (individuals and groups) and their memberships. Along with this is the influence of powerful external forces on decision and policy making, and the manifest political struggles that may be involved between the 'internals' and the externals as they attempt to control policy and decision making processes. The political analyst should consider such matters as fertile areas for in-depth examination and critique within the sphere of higher education.

2. The model of course recognizes the formulation of major policy and decision making as central concepts and processes for analysis; and hence the decisions and policies in relation to the development, consolidation and change in higher education should be considered as substantive matters worthy of in-depth and systematic study.

   As Riley and Baldridge argue, the internal 'influentials' may overtly, and in some cases, covertly strategically position themselves so they become significant players in policies and decisions; and this becomes quite evident particularly in those situations where "resources are tight, outside pressure groups attack, or other internal groups try to assume command".[24] Of course in higher education, one would expect the senior administrators of universities and colleges to comprise this powerful internal interest group or groups. One would also expect from an analysis of political behaviour in higher education the existence or emergence of other obvious internal interest groups representing faculty, students and other administrative and support staff. Within the UWI, Emmanuel's portrayal of the balance of power among these groups seems to suggest a critical need for redress. In addition to the internal interest groups, Baldridge's model makes allowance to incorporate groups of interests that are external to the organization and as is the case of the internal interest groups, these external interests (individuals and groups) do organize themselves for the purposes of exerting influence on policy and decision making processes. Under the right circumstances, these 'externals' can be powerful shapers not only of broad higher educational policy but they can also bring their influence to bear on decisions in respect of the institutional structures and academic programmes, its governance processes and administrative procedures. It is therefore of utmost importance that in the analysis of political phenomena within higher education that due consideration be given to the political manoeuverings and impact of these external 'power blocs' and other powerful individuals as they seek to make their influence felt on higher education policies and their outcomes. For example, in higher education in the English-speaking Caribbean region, and insofar as the UWI is concerned, the fourteen contributing governments constitute a powerful group of internal interests by virtue of their statutory role as directors of the university. At the same time, because they represent different external constituencies, they can also be included in the category of 'externals'. Such a phenomenon would seem to demand a critical analysis of its implications on the determination of the role and mission of the university, its governance, decision making and financial viability.

3. Beyond those elements already discussed, Riley and Baldridge have suggested that we need also to focus on the organization's change and reform processes and in particular how the organization might respond to various environmental factors that are closely related to its ongoing viability and maintenance. From the perspective of a university, they have argued that the political dynamics of such an institution are constantly changing, and that this is due in no small measure to the impact of environmental factors. Environment, in this instance, can be defined as the conditions and circumstances external to an organization as a political system, and that constitutes demands made upon it and supports for its maintenance and long-term viability. In analysing higher education in the Caribbean from a political perspective, it is again essential that the environmental factors that impinge on the higher educational systems in the region be identified so as to better understand the nature and extent to which they influence directly or indirectly the internal workings of the systems concerned. By investigating and critically analysing these factors, we should be well placed to position our higher education systems to be more responsive and to garner the necessary supports from its significant environs.

As indicated earlier, Baldridge and his colleague Riley have provided us with an analytical approach for examining and assessing political phenomena such as higher education within an organizational setting. But what they have presented essentially are the broad outlines. To complete the analytical construct, we will need to elaborate in some detail on the essential and distinguishing features or elements of this framework and to explain their interrelationship. What follows then is a discussion of a selected list of concepts and suggestions showing how these may be applied to analysing higher education as a political system in the context of the English-speaking Caribbean.

Some Selected Concepts and Their Application

One of the most basic and pervasive concepts in the literature relating to political analysis, irrespective of the context, is the notion of a 'political system' that for present purposes can be defined as relating to the structure – its functions, governance arrangements and decision making apparatus – which when combined creates a social unit of organized human activity. By relating this social vent to the most basic level of political analysis, we are in agreement with Miller[25] that we begin to establish the "main facts of political life" regarding the system. Beyond that, some of the questions posed by Miller in this regard would seem highly relevant to a study of the political dimensions of the system: Who makes decisions about, and who runs the system, by what authority and rules, how is power distributed, and what are the relationships of the system with other similar systems? An examination of such important questions in a particular political system, which in this case is the higher education system that comprises university and nonuniversity institutions, should help to provide insights into the processes of decision making and the implementation of the decisions.

The Emmanuel paper cited earlier largely illustrates this particular perspective in that his thoughtful analysis was not restricted to a mere examination of the formal structures of the UWI. It went beyond this to attempt to emphasize the processes and structures of political life within the system, and the interaction of the university with its sister institutions in the region, adding a decidedly political improvisation to the dynamics involved. This particular brand of micropolitics is borne out by Riley and Baldridge who remind us of the uniqueness of organizational characteristics of colleges and universities, which they argue stem from the concept that institutional goals are, generally speaking, "ambiguous, inconsistent and often contested", and that in relation to the clients they serve, these often demand a voice in the decision making process. Another useful feature is that their technology (method of work) is perceived as problematic in that it is nonroutine, complex, while at the same time requiring flexibility and adaptability to individual needs. Additionally, he asserts, these are professional organizations in which the employees demand a large measure of control over institutional decision processes and in terms of their relationship to their external environments, he finds that such organizations have a tendency to become more and more vulnerable to those elements on which the organization depends for support and sustenance.

In sum, the unique goals that characterize the system, the particular clientele served and technology used, the professional nature of the system, and its vulnerable tendencies are factors that should be of particular relevance in research studies aimed at examining and analysing the political dimensions of organizations. These particular elements not only help to differentiate the design and purpose of higher educational organizations, they also provide the structural and functional domains in which change and reform processes in education may be investigated. And this is well illustrated by Paul Parker, Errol Miller, and Wellington Friday in their treatment of various change processes in which they sought to indicate that politics and the political processes are very much embedded in institutional change processes in higher education in the Caribbean region. Beyond that, these are the elements that can also constitute the basis of a conceptual framework when undertaking educational studies of a comparative nature. They can be particularly fruitful by suggesting certain issues, problems and lines of inquiry in relation to comparative investigations of development, consolidation and change of the various tertiary/higher education institutions in the region.

In earlier discussions, we have alluded to the 'political process' as a central concept for inclusion in any research effort geared to analysing higher education from a political perspective. According to Rogers[26] the manifestation of the political process in social organizations can best be considered in relation to the allocation of power.

The political process is also manifested in superior/subordinate relationships in the organization, and is also evident in relations among peers. Conflict and competition are also inescapable aspects of the political process. And the reasons why these are such vitally important factors in the study of political phenomena in organizations is that they not only provide for a better understanding of the reality and the dynamics of the organization, at the same time they enable the researcher to discern and explain more adequately the causes and consequences of organizational activities under investigation. To paraphrase Rogers, an organization's political processes represent the optimum foundation and framework for analysing political activities. Rogers further contends that it would be too confining an approach were we to limit ourselves only to an observation and analysis of the organization's goals, its functions, and that aspect of the process that is operational within the structure. But in order to understand the political processes in their totality, we must necessarily observe all the activities at play within the organization, in relation to both time and space.[27] What is being suggested in all of this concerns the need for a more comprehensive approach to be taken in the analysis of an organization's political processes. To meet this requirement of broad-scope analysis, we are therefore obliged to give full account in the framework to such concepts as power, authority, control, influence and conflict – all of which are related notions normally included in political analysis frameworks.

In seeking to analyse and critique political processes, political action as a concept is obviously a central concern for investigation and is especially related to the activities involved in policy formulation and implementation. As Rogers puts it, policy is derived from political action, and action is political when it focuses on policy.[28] In other words, in seeking to describe the nature and impact of policy, it becomes essential to take account of the actions inherent in arriving at the policy and the activities entailed in the subsequent execution of the policy. Thomas Dye,[29] in the opening statement of his book on public policy, refers to what he considers to be the primary features of public policy. He summarizes his conception of public policy as "what governments do or choose not to do, why they do it, and what difference it makes".[30] If we are to accept Dye's conceptualization as an appropriate guide to the analysis and explanation of educational politics, we might for present purposes replace the word 'governments' to read higher education systems. In relation to the higher education systems of the region, we need then to concern ourselves with matters related to what these systems choose to do or not to do, and to raise questions as to why they make certain choices, as well as the effects of the choices made.

The literature already cited in this chapter on higher education in the region provides ample examples of the kinds of policies formulated and decisions made in relation to development and change in the region's higher education systems. In Nettleford's paper, and Sherlock and Nettleford's book, a considerable amount of discussion is devoted to the major policy issues regarding the goals and role of the UWI – the regional university. Among the matters raised by the two authors is the important question of increased access to university level education in particular, and access to tertiary education in general. The matter of the role of the university in the development of a more coordinated and articulated system of tertiary education has also been raised by the authors as another central issue, particularly in the context of the amalgamation of a number of single-specialist institutions into state, national or community colleges in all contributing territories. Similarly, when in 1984 the university decided to implement a restructuring process, the resultant governance arrangements also became a major issue, in that it raised serious debates about the need for, and impact of, a decentralized system of governance. Further, with the more recent restructuring exercise that was completed in 1996, the university was forced to rethink its mission and goals in the context of a debate on its future role by its various constituencies, including the supporting governments of the region. All of these issues: access, system efficiency and effectiveness, the university's evolving relationship with its sister institutions in the region, the restructuring of the university, and more recently, the introduction of new governance arrangements, including further decentralization of decision making to the three campuses – Cave Hill, St Augustine and Mona – are by definition and in their manifestations political. And in the process of formulation of policies and decisions to address them, the UWI holds centre stage of political action in which a variety of political processes and strategies can be observed, analysed and critiqued.

The recurring issue of ensuring increased access to higher/tertiary education meets the requirements cited above as an area warranting analysis from a political perspective. It is no secret that there are conflicting views both within and external to the university concerning how this might be achieved and what role the institution should play in achieving this desirable goal. The university's official position on this is unambiguous – the Strategic Plan of the university explicitly commits the institution to increasing access in a significant way. Indeed, the UWI has put in place a number of organizational and academic measures to help achieve this particular objective. These include significant expansion of its distance education thrust, introduction of a semester system to enhance access, the consolidation and strengthening of its outreach capacity, the promotion of articulation arrangements with its sister tertiary institutions in the region, and the introduction of several initiatives such as the reorientation of curriculum to improve flexibility in the delivery of its programmes face to face and at a distance. To the interested observer, however, there is still evidence of controversy and conflict in relation to the policy decision itself and as regards its execution.

As an important and undoubtedly powerful interest group within the university, some members of the faculty are perceived to be not as enthusiastic as the senior administrative officers about the policy decision regarding increased student access. Opposing positions include the problem of insufficient resources – physical, staffing and student supports – to accommodate the increased number of students stated in the policy. In the case of the implementation of the UWI's distance teaching and outreach policies, it was contended that the university continued to reward research at the expense of teaching and therefore distance teaching had little currency where the promotion of staff was concerned. Moreover, some staff members remain adamant that increased access would compromise quality. But dealing with the problem of increased access has not been a new issue. It has been one of much conflict and controversy that has plagued the university since its establishment in 1948. During the 1950s and up to the Lewis years (the period when Professor Arthur Lewis was vice chancellor), there is documented evidence of overt internal resistance to the transformation of the university from its elitist tendencies. And when Lewis himself set about to change this perception, he was forced to engage not only the staff but the students as well in their opposition to moving the system from its 'elitist moorings'. This state of affairs moved Friday to describe it as a product "of academic conservatism perpetuated to a great extent by its faculty".[31]

What seems evident here is that the university has been faced with serious and recurring issues that have eluded closure for close to some fifty years –

over the life of the institution. In relation to such important issues of policy, there is certainly a case to be made for an in-depth analysis of the political dynamics at play. It may well be that one of the fruitful results of such an investigation is a deeper understanding of the political perspectives when decisions to change fundamental policies in an organization such as the university are being contemplated. Such a study might also be instructive particularly with regard to the use of political conflict as a constructive and positive force in the implementation of major university policies related to development and change.

In order to complete the discussion of the major elements of a conceptual framework with which to guide the analysis of the politics of higher education, we need to consider the operational definitions of two related concepts. The first is the notion of political power; when we speak of power, this refers to the power relationships involved in the decision making processes in a micropolitical system. Power also refers to the ability to control and mobilize resources – particularly financial resources – in order to achieve policy aims and to implement policy decisions. The exercise of power can be carried out by sources within the organization or outside of it. In the related literature, power by definition is the ability to control the actions of others so as to produce intended outcomes or effects. There is another important element associated with power; that is, authority that as defined in the context of micropolitical systems (social organizations) is the right to give orders and the power to exact obedience. Authority is the legitimate use of power and carries with it the right of application of sanctions. While power and authority form part of the essential conditions for the management of any social organization, it is important to emphasize that there is an essential distinction between these two concepts. Schein[32] makes the distinction by qualifying power as "pure power" and introduces the requirement of consent on the part of those on whom power and authority are exercised as the distinctive element. According to Schein:

Pure power implies that with the manipulation of rewards or with the exercise of naked strength you can force someone else to do something against his will. Authority by contrast implies the willingness on the part of a 'subordinate' to obey because he consents, that is he grants to the person in authority . . . the right to dictate to him.[33]

The second concept to be introduced here concerns the groups and individuals that compete as organized interests for power to decide policy and make major decisions about the organization's goals and operations. In the related literature, there is the assertion that when individuals of a group share a common belief about choices in policy, and when they seek to become a force to either change or sustain policy then this by definition makes them a politically influential group whose ability to influence decisions will depend to a large extent on the group's own political resources and the other resources (information and expertise, for example) to which it can lay claim or access. The effectiveness of these influential groups is also dependent on the modes of action (strategies or tactics) and inducements they may use in pursuing their particular group interests.

Application of the Framework

The combination of these elements, along with the analytical framework discussed above, should be subjected to a test of their efficacy and appropriateness in the context of higher education in the Caribbean region, especially given the multitude of issues of a political nature that have challenged and will continue to confront those responsible for the development and management of the region's tertiary educational systems. The remainder of this chapter will therefore be devoted to analysis of one particular episode involving the university administration, the political directorate, especially those from the noncampus countries, and the resulting policy decisions and outcomes.

Starting in the 1970s and continuing up to the present, one of the most politically sensitive issues in tertiary education in the region has been the unease in the relationship between the noncampus countries and the university. For some time, the Organization of Eastern Caribbean States (OECS) governments have felt, for a variety of reasons, that the contributions they make to the development and maintenance of the university are at a level much greater than what they perceive to be the actual benefits to their respective countries. As a consequence, they have continued to make insistent demands on the university that it should be more proactive and flexible in responding to the education and training needs of these countries. Moreover, its response needs to be more systematic, deep and broad ranged. Friday[34] summarizes the related issues and expectations of the noncampus country governments as follows:

There is a considerable body of opinion, both from within and without the West Indies, that the University of the West Indies should respond more intimately to territorial needs: for teacher training (both at primary and secondary level), agricultural training (down to village level), middle-level technical and professional training of many kinds, continuing education, and the sort of training which will bring about a psychological conversion and a fundamental change in the traditional value system. Also the University is expected to improve the quality of the secondary education and indeed to bring about a more meaningful articulation among all sectors of the educational system, both within each territory as well as within the region as a whole.

More recently, in 1994, the *Report of the Chancellor's Commission on the Governance of UWI*[35] called attention to similar concerns and cited a number of factors that have contributed to the need for the university to redouble its efforts to expand and deepen its outreach activities to the noncampus countries. The report states categorically that "the impact of the 1984 restructuring initiative especially the financial arrangements which have strengthened the national focus in the campus countries, weakened the Centre and, to a considerable extent, marginalized the Non-campus Countries".

Emmanuel also raised this particular matter and made particular reference to the perceived marginalization of the noncampus countries in relation to the governance administration and programme operations of the university. He also noted some of the controversies surrounding the proposal of measures to resolve what was then a highly politically charged issue. As Emmanuel noted, one such measure was the establishment of the Office of University Services (OUS) at the Cave Hill campus to serve the OECS, Anguilla and the British Virgin Islands. This was intended to be a major organizational response to strengthen and deepen the university's relationship with national tertiary institutions in these countries. All nine countries would be targetted for OUS activities and efforts.

But at the time of the OUS decision, and after it had started its operations in October 1984, and up to the time when the OUS was renamed the Tertiary Level Institutions Unit (TLIU) in 1996, it seemed that the office was destined to be embroiled in political controversy and conflict. It was certainly not surprising that conflicts did arise between the various interest groups concerned, namely the senior university administration and the heads of the contributing governments, given that the noncampus countries were determined "to maximize their own benefits from the regional university and to find the most suitable mechanisms they felt would guarantee them swift and effective delivery of university services wherever they may be generated or reside".[36] This episode not only exemplified the dynamics of internal interests versus external interests in relation to policy formulation and decision making, but all of the ramifications relating to the exercise of power and authority, and the control of resources are also indicated.

The decision by the heads of government in 1983 to accept the proposal of the OECS and thereby direct the university to establish two Offices of University Services to serve the noncampus countries, set in train a series of political events involving some major players, which when seen through the eyes of a political analyst was virtual theatre. Indeed, the decision in itself was political; and from the perspective of the UWI, the manner in which it was made could have been perceived as unilateral, thereby calling into question its legitimacy. The heads of government on the other hand were determined to exact full compliance with their decision on the part of the university authorities.

In March 1985, five months after the OUS came into being, the *Vice Chancellor's Report to Council* drew attention to progress made in respect of the Offices of University Services. The report states, among other things, that:

The establishment of Offices of University Services at Cave Hill and at Mona has provided a mechanism for more effective communication between the campuses and the NCCs, and I am glad to report that as a result the University has a clearer idea of what needs to be done and some misunderstandings which had been with us for a long time are now being cleared up.[37]

There is much in this statement to suggest a willingness on the part of the university for an accommodation – but on its own terms. This is indicated by the apparent delimitation of the role of the office: providing effective communication, clarifying needs and "clearing up misunderstandings". These were hardly what the OECS governments had conceived of the office in their proposal. What was stated explicitly in the OECS Secretariat Report, to which

OECS member governments agreed, was that the OUS would "have the primary executive responsibility for providing University Services to all the non-campus countries".

In addition to the high level of authority and broad scope of responsibility assigned to the OUS, the governments also agreed that the office "should be headed by a full-time Pro-Vice-Chancellor and should be adequately staffed". But they also indicated that this should be accomplished through a redeployment of resources (Development Planning Unit, 1984), an idea that clearly did not find favour with the leadership of the UWI. Moreover, some three years later, Paul Parker observed in his *Report on the Evaluation of the Performance of the Office of University Services (1984–88)* that the idea of the OUS being headed by a pro vice chancellor was vigorously resisted initially by the then vice chancellor.

It is also of some import that when the office at Cave Hill was established, it consisted of a pro vice chancellor, a project officer, an administrative assistant and a stenographer/clerk; and the resources for its establishment were provided by the Ford Foundation to whom the university had applied for financial assistance. As Parker recalls, the reasons for seeking funds from the foundation was that the budget was agreed on before the decision to setup the office, "so there was no provision in the budget for supporting it or to create a PVC to head it".[38] Here again, it was evident that the university was not too disposed to comply with the decision of governments to redeploy existing resources. The Ford Foundation, however, provided a grant of US$450,000 for three years, and this was used mainly to cover all the operating and administrative costs of the OUS during its initial three years.

In 1986 the *Vice Chancellor's Report to Council* noted that the OUS had "performed to expectation". That is, it was meeting the objective of increased participation of the university in the development of tertiary education in the noncampus countries. The report also recorded a number of programmatic details: the OUS was working with the tertiary level institutions (TLIs) in the OECS in planning and programme development activities; that in relation to preliminary university and first year programmes it was collaborating with some of these TLIs to deliver these programmes. The office was also in the process of negotiating for funds from external agencies to support the TLIs, and was helping them to sort out accreditation issues.[39] Then the report goes on to mention the "teething pains" that such an office would normally experience in its infancy and sounded the optimistic note that "they were learning fast". Also contained in the report was a plea for cooperation: "One thing is certain," states the vice chancellor, "OUS effectiveness will come only with support not only of colleagues within the university campuses, but with the fullest cooperation from the ministries of education and policy determinators in the countries the offices are designed to serve." This was undoubtedly a timely plea, for as Parker revealed in his evaluation (1988), there was still much political controversy in the air. But this was mainly in reaction to the decision taken by the university. Some of the issues centred on objections over the appointment of a pro vice chancellor who was not a national of an OECS country. Another contentious issue was that the countries wanted a share of the Ford budget to be allocated to their own local (national) institutions. In fact, there were objections over the university using these funds entirely for running the OUS. There was also expressed dissatisfaction with the office itself; that it was not aggressive enough in demonstrating leadership in development of the new national/community colleges; some even argued that it should be relocated to one of the noncampus countries, perhaps more as a symbol of the university's commitment to the new outreach dispensation than anything else. It was the combination of these matters that led Parker to conclude that "the OUS began amidst a host of misconceptions and unrealistic expectations all the way round". But as Parker contends, perhaps the most controversial issue to have stayed with OUS throughout its existence was the perception by the OECS constituency that the university had not provided the vitally important enabling resources – finance and the necessary power and authority – to carry out its mission in the way the OECS governments and indeed all heads of government had conceived. Staff resources were thin; "PVC Goodridge," suggests Parker, "has been like a general without an army." The OUS had little control over the university's programme and administrative bodies so that whatever it was able to accomplish was generally based on the goodwill of the teaching and administrative staff.

How did Mona (the university) address the issue relating to the lack of enabling resources for the OUS? The answer lies in the fact that throughout its existence, the OUS operated under the same staffing and administrative arrangements until it became one of three executing arms of the new Board for Non-Campus Countries and Distance Education and was renamed the TLIU. As noted in the *Report of the Chancellor's Commission on the Governance of UWI (1994)*, the office during those ten years of operation was able to achieve a "considerable measure of success in negotiating programmes and services on behalf of the OECS Countries". What was actually accomplished included initiatives taken in infrastructural, staff and programme development, along with the arrangements made for smoother institutional articulation among the tertiary institutions and the university. Parker, in his evaluation, was able to come to the same conclusion as the commission that what the office achieved was commendable. Despite the record, it was quite an open secret that some members of the university community continued to hold the view that the office was indeed unnecessary; that in the scheme of things it commanded little operating resources and therefore the impact of its work would be negligible, except perhaps in the performance of its role as a 'post office' – a conduit for communication between the noncampus countries and the university. Those were the perceptions of the 'internals'. The external interests, according to Parker (1988), were of the view that the office could be regarded as "nothing but a political symbol or a 'sop' to assuage the fears of abandonment on the part of the NCCs".[40] Comments such as these do in fact reflect a perverse indifference towards what was intended to be a most crucial outreach mechanism of the university – one intended to strengthen the UWI's relationship with and forge links with its sister tertiary institutions within the region. But perhaps the main lesson to be drawn from this particular episode in political terms is essentially this: when powerful political forces are in conflict over the decisions to address major political issues, and should the ultimate decisions be perceived as unilateral and coercive, questions of legitimate authority, control and autonomy will loom large, so that in the final analysis if these are not sensitively addressed, the results may turn out to be either counterproductive or ineffectual, or both.

Conclusion

As a branch of educational studies in the Caribbean, the politics of higher education has for too long been ignored and needs to be further developed as a discipline in its own right, especially in view of the fact that our higher/tertiary educational systems have assumed more and more importance in the context of the region's human resource development. The politics of higher education, while concerned with the processes of policy and decision making in relation to the development, change and, some would say, restructuring of educational institutions and systems, must by definition also be intimately concerned with the issues confronting these systems, some of which will be unavoidably highly contentious and replete with conflict. The decisions, administrative actions and power strategies engaged in by those responsible for decision making and those involved in their execution, are valid areas for examination from a political perspective. There are too the internal interest groups or groups external to higher education systems but who nevertheless have the means (power) to influence what goes on in these systems. How they position themselves, and the strategies used to influence decisions must also be systematically investigated and analysed.

This chapter has provided the broad outlines of a framework for such types of analysis and the synthesis. It is intended to be a modest contribution to what may be considered to be a relatively new field of study in the region. It is also suggested that the lessons learned from such studies should prove useful in helping to guide important policies and decisions in respect of the development, growth, consolidation and change in higher education – the sector of the education system in the region that is being called upon to assume a greater importance in the development of the region's human resources.

Notes

1. Jonathan Barnes, *The Ethics of Aristotle: The Nicomachean Ethics*, rev. ed. (London: Penguin Books, 1976).
2. Iain L. Mangham, "The Performers: Higher Education as Theatre", in *The Management of Educational Institutions: Theory Research and Consultancy*, edited by H.L. Gray (Sussex: The Falmer Press, 1982), 41–62.
3. Peter Scott, *The Crisis of the University* (London: Croom Helm, 1984).
4. Gem Fletcher, Lynette France and Iris Sukdeo, *Higher Education in Guyana (University of Guyana)* (Caracas: UNESCO Regional Centre for Higher Education in Latin America and the Caribbean [CRESACC], 1987); W.R.C. Friday, "Restructuring Higher Education in the Non-Campus Territories of the British Caribbean as a Strategy for Development – Problems and Prospects" (PhD diss., University of Southern California, 1975).
5. Bevis F. Peters, *The Emergence of Community, State and National Colleges in the OECS Member Countries: An Institutional Analysis* (Cave Hill, Barbados: Institute of Social and Economic Research, UWI, 1993).

6. D.H. Layton, "The Emergence of the Politics of Education as a Field of Study", in *The Management of Educational Institutions: Theory Research and Consultancy*, edited by H.L. Gray (Sussex, England: The Falmer Press, 1982), 109–26.
7. Ibid., 112.
8. Victor J. Baldridge, *Power and Conflict in the University* (New York: John Wiley, 1971), 14.
9. Gary L. Riley and Victor J. Baldridge (eds), *Governing Academic Organizations. New Problems, New Perspectives* (Berkeley: McCutchan Publishing, 1977).
10. Patrick Emmanuel, *Academic Relations of Power: The Case of University of the West Indies* (Cave Hill, Barbados: Institute of Social and Economic Research, UWI, 1993).
11. Ibid., 1.
12. Rex Nettleford, *The University of the West Indies as a Regional University in the English Speaking Caribbean* (Caracas: CRESACC, 1986).
13. Philip Sherlock and Rex Nettleford, *The University of the West Indies: A Caribbean Response to the Challenge of Change* (London: Macmillan, 1990).
14. Friday, "Restructuring Higher Education", 8.
15. Ibid., 382.
16. Paul Parker, "Change and Challenge in Caribbean Higher Education: The Development of the University of the West Indies and the University of Puerto Rico" (PhD diss., Florida State University, 1971).
17. See Fletcher et al., *Higher Education in Guyana*.
18. Ibid., 11.
19. M.K. Bacchus, *Utilization, Misuse and Development of Human Resources in the Early West Indian Colonies* (Waterloo: Wilfred Laurier University Press, 1990).
20. Ibid., 368.
21. Errol Miller, "Contemporary Issues in Jamaican Education", in *Education in Central America and the Caribbean*, edited by Colin Brock and Donald Clarkson (London: Routledge, 1990), 100–137.
22. Ibid., 117.
23. Riley and Baldridge, *Governing Academic Organizations*, 14.
24. Ibid., 14.
25. J.D.B. Miller, *The Nature of Politics* (Harmondsworth: Pelican Books, 1967).
26. Rolf E. Rogers, *The Political Process in Modern Organizations* (New York: Exposition Press, 1971).
27. Ibid., 43.
28. Ibid., 27.
29. Thomas R. Dye, *Understanding Public Policy* (Englewood Cliffs, New Jersey: Prentice Hall, 1972).
30. Ibid., 1.
31. Friday, "Restructuring Higher Education", 389.
32. Edgar Schein, *Organizational Psychology*, 2nd ed. (Englewood Cliffs, New Jersey: Prentice Hall, 1970).

33. Ibid., 13.
34. Friday, "Restructuring Higher Education", 341.
35. Neville V. Nicholls and Ivan L. Head (co-chairmen), *A New Structure: The Regional University in the 1990s and Beyond. Report of the Chancellor's Commission on the Governance of UWI* (Mona, Jamaica: UWI, 1994), 32.
36. Sherlock and Nettleford, *The University of the West Indies*, 219.
37. *Vice Chancellor's Report to Council, 1985* (Mona, Jamaica: Office of the Vice Chancellor, UWI, 1985), 17.
38. Parker, "Change and Challenge", 11.
39. *Vice Chancellor's Report to Council, 1986* (Mona, Jamaica: Office of the Vice Chancellor, 1986), 4.
40. Parker, "Change and Challenge", 10.

6

Access to Tertiary Education in the Commonwealth Caribbean in the 1990s

Errol Miller

Introduction

The purpose of this chapter is to examine some of the pressing issues related to access to tertiary education in the Commonwealth Caribbean in the 1990s. There are seventeen different territories that constitute the Commonwealth Caribbean. They are Anguilla, Antigua and Barbuda, Bahamas, Barbados, Belize, British Virgin Islands, Cayman Islands, Dominica, Grenada, Guyana, Jamaica, Montserrat, St Kitts and Nevis, St Lucia, St Vincent and the Grenadines, Trinidad and Tobago, and Turks and Caicos Islands. Five of these are still British dependencies: Anguilla, British Virgin Islands, Cayman Islands, Montserrat, and Turks and Caicos Islands. The other twelve are independent countries represented in the United Nations. Political status notwithstanding, the seventeen territories are a linguistic and cultural block with a common history and many shared institutions.

Tertiary education is here defined as that level of education that requires, as a prerequisite, a degree of mastery of basic and general education. Formal credentials are only one form of evidence of the mastery of basic and general education, but are not prerequisites in and of themselves. Similarly, age is not a distinctive criterion essential to the definition of tertiary education, although most of the students enrolled in tertiary education are adults. Nevertheless, a degree of mastery of basic and general education is a defining criterion since this level of education is beyond the fundamentals in any field and tends to be focused on specific and not general content. By defining education in this way a distinction is being made apropos adult education which could be directed toward literacy training as well as continuing general education. The gray area that remains is the exact boundary line between secondary and tertiary education. That line has always to be drawn within a specific historical and geographical context.

A broad definition of tertiary education is critical to any discussion of issues related to access from both historical as well as contemporary perspectives. Given the changing nature and explosion of knowledge, tertiary education cannot be defined solely in terms of content. Highly specialized knowledge taught in universities fifty years ago, especially in the sciences, is now routinely taught in general secondary education at the current time. Also open admissions policies, practised in several countries, raise problems for defining tertiary education in terms of credentials obtained at the secondary level. In addition, it is only over the past 200 years that admission to university education has been prescribed in terms of credentials obtained at the secondary level. Performance in entrance examinations, formal or informal, was more contemporary.

Historical Considerations

It is almost impossible to deal with issues related to access to tertiary education without making some reference to the history of schooling. Schools were created probably a thousand years after writing was invented around 3500 BCE. The first schools, the eduba of ancient Mesopotamia around 2500 BCE, operated at a single level which encompassed both the basics of the scribal art of writing and reading and the professional tasks of the scribe in documenting and accounting for the resources of temples and palaces. The purpose of schools was to train scribes to satisfy the administrative and bureaucratic requirements of the temple and palace. This purpose never changed throughout the history of ancient Mesopotamia.[1]

Sjoberg[2] has pointed out that the instruction given to scribes in training included the technical language used by smiths, jewellers, shepherds, master shippers and priests of several classes. It also required that they mastered the terminology and techniques of surveying fields, numerous mathematical and accounting operations including balancing accounts, how to make all kinds of allotments, divide property, and delimit shares of fields. In other words, scribal training involved not only mastery of the basic techniques of writing, but included sound knowledge and understanding of the enterprises that scribes would administer as well as general principles of public administration. Later in history, teaching in the fundamentals of writing and reading was separate institutionally from the professional preparation of scribes, thus creating two levels of schooling.

From a historical perspective, therefore, it is necessary to observe that schooling did not commence at the basic level of primary education or as an institution for children. The historical development of schooling was not from the bottom up but rather from the top down. To put it bluntly, schooling started at the tertiary level and then moved to the basic level, thus creating a two-tiered system of education which lasted for thousands of years. It is only over the last three hundred years that an intermediate level, secondary schooling, was interposed between the elementary and tertiary levels.

In addition, schooling was not established as a universal right but rather as privilege for a very select elite scribes. In the Religious Age, which supplanted the ancient civilizations, schooling became the preserve of priests, prophets and holy men. The broad mass of people were unschooled.

The history of education could therefore be written in terms of two major trajectories. First, the movement from tertiary education and training for a select group of adults to elementary education for all children and early childhood education for most infants. Second, expanding access to education at all levels to the point where elementary education for children, and to a lesser extent secondary education for adolescents, is deemed as the right of all.

Notwithstanding the expansion of education to include adults and children and the trend towards universal education for all children and adolescents, tertiary education cannot be accurately described as being a right of all. Only one country, the United States, enrols more that 50 percent of its young adults in some form of tertiary education. Neither is there any trend towards or call for universal tertiary education.

It is a moot point whether any state could develop the capacity to provide tertiary education for all of its population. But even if that were possible, three principal factors would tend to subvert its attainment. First, there is the question of ability. Not everyone in any reasonably sized population of humans possesses the ability to undertake tertiary education. Physical, physiological, mental and psychological disabilities hamper a significant minority of every generation in almost all populations. Second, many who have the ability fail to achieve the level of mastery of basic and general education that would allow them to qualify for or successfully undertake tertiary education. Third, many who have both the ability and level of mastery of basic and general education choose not to continue to the tertiary level.

In light of the above, any discussion of access to tertiary education must take place within the boundary of less than universal provision or demand, and therefore within the context of limited and selective availability. In this regard, the issue of equity becomes as important as access since there is no capacity to accommodate all. In essence, therefore, the discussion of access rotates around questions of equity between groups in society in gaining entry into the forms of tertiary education that exist in a particular setting.

Brief Historical Sketch of Tertiary Education in the Commonwealth Caribbean

The British thrust to found colonies in the New World resulted in the establishment of colonies in North America and the Caribbean at about the same time in the first half of the seventeenth century. For very different reasons, the West Indian colonies followed very similar patterns to the North American colonies in the establishment of schools and mass schooling at the elementary level. At the tertiary level, however, the patterns in North America and the Caribbean diverge sharply.

In the North American colonies colleges were founded very soon after schools were established. Harvard College was founded in 1636, William and Mary in 1693, Yale in 1701, Princeton in 1746, Kings College in 1754, Pennsylvania in 1755, Rutgers in 1766, Brown in 1765 and Dartmouth in 1769. While nine colleges had been founded in the North American colonies before the declaration of American independence in 1776, up to the end of the eighteenth century not a single college had been established in the West Indian colonies. It was not until 1830, nearly two hundred years after the founding of Harvard, when the Codrington Grammar School was transformed into a theological college, that the first tertiary institution was established in the Commonwealth Caribbean. In other words, schools were founded in the Commonwealth Caribbean and operated for more than 150 years before a single college was established in the region.

During the seventeenth and eighteenth centuries the pattern that had developed in the West Indian colonies was for those who could afford it to send their sons to England to university.[3] Brathwaite, in his study of colonial creole society in Jamaica showed that between 1770 and 1820, 229 Jamaicans went to Oxford and Cambridge. The Jamaican practice mirrored a common pattern throughout the West Indian colonies.

It should be noted that universities were established very early in the settlement of Spanish colonies.[4] Sherlock and Nettleford have noted that in the first half of the seventeenth century the Spanish established the universities of Santo Domingo, Mexico and Lima. In the second half of the seventeenth century, Spain established five more universities in its New World colonies and followed this with the founding of another ten universities over the course of the eighteenth century. Put another way, the pattern of founding schools and colleges in North America resembled the pattern that had previously been established by the Spanish in Latin America. The pattern in the Commonwealth Caribbean, however, differed from both Latin and North America.

Interestingly, the British West Indian colonies always had levels of enrolment at the elementary level that were comparable to North America and Western Europe, and always had higher enrolments at the elementary level than the Spanish colonies, and later the independent countries of Latin America.[5] On the other hand, the British West Indian colonies always had much lower levels of provision for tertiary education.

The most appealing explanation of this enduring difference between the Commonwealth Caribbean on the one hand and North and Latin America on the other, is that the former were mainly colonies of exploitation while the latter were mainly colonies of settlement.[6] The majority of the colonists in the North and in Spanish America planned to make the New World their home. They therefore brought with them the infrastructure of community and intellectual advancement. The West Indian colonies were loci of exploitation in which the majority of the colonists planned to make a quick fortune and return to Britain to enjoy their new found wealth. Accordingly, they made no long-term provisions for either community or intellectual advancement in the West Indies.

Whatever may have been the reason, tertiary education had a late start in the Commonwealth Caribbean. In was only in the first half of the nineteenth century that colleges began to be established. Even then it was only theological and teachers colleges that made their entrance. These institutions were founded to train 'native' teachers and clergy. Codrington in Barbados was the only college to offer degrees, which they did after 1835 in conjunction with Durham University in Wales. An aborted attempt was made to establish a university college in Spanish Town, Jamaica, in the 1870s, but this attempt was short lived. The college lasted less than a decade. Yet another attempt was made at Jamaica College between 1889 and 1901 which graduated thirty persons with bachelor's degrees.[7]

Between 1830 when Codrington was transformed into a college and 1950 when transition to independence had begun, there were no more than about ten small colleges training teachers, five even smaller colleges training ministers of religion, a few schools of nursing and one college training agriculturalists in the entire Commonwealth Caribbean. This very meagre provision constituted almost the entire tertiary level enterprise in the region. The only new type of institutions that had been introduced over this period of 120 years was the Imperial College of Tropical Agriculture (ICTA) founded in 1922 in St Augustine, Trinidad, and a few schools of nursing in Barbados, Guyana, Jamaica and Trinidad.

Heuman[8] explained the lethargy in building an indigenous capacity for tertiary education in Jamaica on the grounds that by restricting its size and structure, the colonial administrators justified the recruitment of British officials, technocrats and professionals. In addition, the recruitment of Europeans was seen by the local elite as one means of bolstering the declining numbers of whites in the colonies. Following emancipation and the decline in the fortunes of sugar and the plantations, there was a noticeable decline in the European segment of Commonwealth Caribbean populations. Colonial control and race seem to have been two of the contributing factors to the neglect of tertiary education provision in the region.

Following the postemancipation period, the pattern of going abroad for tertiary education was institutionalized in the secondary school system that developed in the region in the latter half of the nineteenth century. Island scholarships were granted, for study in universities abroad, to those students who performed best in their island each year in the Cambridge examinations. By this measure, not only those who could afford it went abroad, but the brilliant offspring of those who could not otherwise have accessed this level and type of education.

Developments in Tertiary Education in the Postwar/Postindependence Periods

At the beginning of the postwar period in the Commonwealth Caribbean the provision for tertiary education was still miniscule and restricted to a few fields. The democratization of political power with the advent of adult suffrage and representative government, together with the movement from colonialism to national sovereignty, brought substantial developments within tertiary education in the region. The imperative to expand tertiary education came from the anticipated demand for local leaders, professionals and technocrats in the newly emerging nation states and semi-autonomous dependencies.

The major developments and trends in the transformation of tertiary education in the Commonwealth Caribbean since the mid 1940s can be listed and summarized briefly as follows:

1. The establishment of university education within the region, beginning with the founding of the University of the West Indies (UWI) in 1948, followed by the founding of the University of Guyana in 1963 and continuing more recently in Jamaica with the upgrading of the College of Arts, Science and Technology to the University of Technology in 1995.
2. The founding, in the 1950s and 1960s, of a wide variety of tertiary institutions serving mainly particular occupations. These included teachers colleges, technical colleges, schools of nursing, physical therapy, occupational therapy, pharmacy, radiology, medical technology and other health fields, business colleges, colleges of agriculture, colleges of physical education and sports, and schools of music, art, drama and dance. Invariably these single discipline institutions were small and often served only the students from the countries in which they were located.
3. The founding, in the 1970s and 1980s, of community colleges serving a wide variety of needs including preparation for university study, training for various middle level occupations, continuing education of persons who had not successfully completed high school, and personal development interests. Invariably, community colleges developed strong part-time evening programmes which, in many instances, had

higher enrolments than their full-time day programmes. While the full-time programmes offered by community colleges were premised on an admissions policy that required credentials from the secondary level, their part-time and day release programmes practised an open admissions policy.

4. The amalgamation, in the 1980s and 1990s, of small single discipline colleges into larger multidisciplinary institutions with various labels such as state, national or community colleges.
5. The creation of distance teaching programmes as a means of expanding the reach of some colleges and universities to include students off their campuses.
6. The emergence of a wide variety of articulations, accreditation, affiliation and franchising arrangements linking different colleges with the universities within the region, thereby facilitating movement between college and university.
7. In the substantial expansion of tertiary education in the Commonwealth Caribbean over the last fifty years, only Anguilla is currently without at least one tertiary institution within its borders. In all there are well over 100 tertiary institutions currently operating in sixteen of the seventeen countries within the region. Most are public institutions funded mainly by the governments of the countries. While private institutions have established a niche in this sector of the education system, it is public resources and provision that have driven the postwar and postindependence transformation of tertiary education.
8. The World Bank Study 1993 indicated that enrolment in public tertiary institutions stood at approximately 15,000 in 1970. By 1980 enrolment had doubled to 30,000 and by 1989 it had climbed to 41,000, an increase of approximately 35 percent.

A Footnote on Developments in Secondary Education

Expansion of tertiary education cannot be sustained if there is not a constant flow of students who have attained the required degree of mastery of basic and general education. The main source of such students is the secondary school system. An important question to address is, what were the policies that were implemented in secondary education that contributed to the expansion of the tertiary education provision in the postwar and postindependence periods?

The main thrust of education reform in the postwar and postindependence periods was increased provision of secondary schooling. Mass elementary education had been attained in the Commonwealth Caribbean by the end of the nineteenth century. By the mid twentieth century approximately 80 percent of primary school-age children were enrolled in schools. Universal primary education was therefore not a particularly challenging task. On the other hand, the provision for secondary education was very modest. No more that 10 percent of adolescents received five years of secondary schooling.

Governments, therefore, focused their attention on two aspects related to access and equity relative to the provision of secondary education. First, merit was introduced as the basis for moving from the primary to the secondary levels, particularly into those secondary schools that were in greatest demand. Throughout the region Common Entrance Examinations were introduced in the 1950s to ensure that it was merit and not money or connections that determined which children would move from primary to high school.

Secondly, governments throughout the region embarked on policies and projects to expand the secondary education provision. By the mid 1990s, eight countries had achieved universal secondary education. These were Anguilla, the Bahamas, Barbados, British Virgin Islands, Cayman Islands, Montserrat, St Kitts and Nevis, and the Turks and Caicos Islands. In the other nine Commonwealth Caribbean countries more that 50 percent of adolescents between the ages of twelve to seventeen years receive some type of secondary education for five years.

The postwar and postindependence periods have therefore witnessed substantial and impressive increases in the provision of secondary education throughout the region. The problem that some countries have been experiencing, particularly the larger countries of Guyana, Jamaica and Trinidad and Tobago, is the low level of achievement within the expanded system of secondary schooling. In the 1990s several countries have embarked on reforms and projects designed to improve the quality of secondary schooling and consequentially the quality of student performance.

The general enrolment picture of schooling below the tertiary level within the Commonwealth Caribbean can be summarized as follows:

- Approximately 80 percent or more of children four to six years are enrolled in some type of preschool offering early childhood education.
- Primary schooling is universal. All children between the ages of six to twelve years are enrolled in either public or private primary schools.
- Secondary schooling is universal in eight countries and more than half the children of secondary school age are enrolled in schools in the remaining nine countries.

Access to Tertiary Education in the 1990s

The CARICOM prime ministers, in their Montego Bay Declaration of 1997, set as one of their major goals in education, substantial expansion of provision in tertiary education. The target set was that of providing tertiary education opportunities to 20 percent of the 18- to 24-year age group over the next decade. It is therefore appropriate to examine the existing levels of provision and participation at the tertiary level in the Caribbean. Student enrolment in national and regional tertiary institutions, as a percentage of the 20- to 24-year age group, ranges from 2.9 percent in St Vincent and the Grenadines to 21.0 percent in Barbados. The average enrolment for the region is 6.4 percent. Table 6.1 shows student enrolment in fourteen of the seventeen Commonwealth countries in 1990.

Viewed in the context of the Montego Bay Declaration, Barbados has already achieved the target set; Montserrat and the Bahamas would appear to be within striking distance. For the rest of the region, however, achieving the target would represent substantial achievement. In the case of Antigua and Barbuda and Trinidad and Tobago, it would mean doubling their current provision. For the others the challenge would even be greater.

When tertiary enrolment is compared with primary and secondary enrolment within the region the picture that emerges is a broad base at the primary and secondary levels but a very narrow apex at the tertiary level. The apex narrows even further if only university education is considered. Only 2 to 4 percent of students within the region are enrolled in university education.

Table 6.2 shows rates of enrolment at the tertiary level within Latin American countries. Compared to the Commonwealth Caribbean, enrolments are much higher in Latin American countries although the Caribbean enjoys somewhat higher levels of enrolment at the primary and secondary levels.

Table 6.1: Enrolment Ratios in Public Tertiary Institutions in the Commonwealth Caribbean, 1990

Country	Tertiary	Tertiary and Higher
Antigua	9.6	10 5
The Bahamas	12.7	13.7
Barbados	14.1	21.0
Belize	6.4	6.4
British Virgin Islands	4.8	6.1
Dominica	4.3	4.9
Grenada	3 4	3.9
Guyana	4.9	8 0
Jamaica	4.9	6.6
Montserrat	14 0	17 8
St Kitts & Nevis	7.3	8 4
St Lucia	4.1	4.8
St Vincent & Grenadines	2 4	2 9
Trinidad & Tobago	7 3	10.7
Overall Average	6 1	7 8

Source: World Bank, 1993.
Note: The enrolment ratios are calculated on the basis of students enrolled in national and regional institutions as a percentage of the 20- to 24-year age group in the population These figures do not include students studying outside the Caribbean.

Table 6.2: Enrolment Ratios in Tertiary Institutions in Latin America, 1985

Country	Enrolment Ratios
Argentina	36.4
Bolivia	19.5
Columbia	13.0
Costa Rica	23.0
Dominican Republic	13.8
Ecuador	33 1
Mexico	16 0
Panama	25.9
Uruguay	31.7
Venezuela	26.4

Source: World Bank, 1993.

The point to note is that up to the beginning of the 1990s, the historic differences that have marked the patterns of enrolment between the Commonwealth Caribbean and Latin and North America still remain, despite the expansion and development that took place in the postwar and postindependence periods. Also, even the goals set by the Montego Bay Declaration are well below the level of tertiary provision in Argentina, Costa Rica, Ecuador, Panama, Uruguay and Venezuela.

Access to Tertiary Education Abroad

There is evidence to support the proposition that, by only reviewing enrolments in national and regional institutions, the access to tertiary education opportunities of Commonwealth Caribbean nationals is underestimated because significant numbers of Caribbean nationals go overseas to access tertiary education opportunities. Table 6.3 shows the numbers of student visas issued by the United States and Canada immigration authorities to nationals of ten Caribbean countries during different periods of the 1980s.

Table 6.3 shows that on average more Caribbean students study in the United States than Canada. These data would seem to indicate that during the decade of the 1980s more than 3,000 Caribbean nationals were granted student visas to study in North American institutions. Trinidad and Tobago leads Commonwealth Caribbean countries in the number of its nationals going to North America for tertiary education. Given that enrolment in public tertiary institutions increased from 30,000 to 41,000, and that most programmes are for two to three years, it would appear from a back of the envelope calculation that Caribbean nationals studying in North America constitute no less than 30 percent of public tertiary enrolment within the region.

Table 6.3: US and Canadian Student Visas Issued to Caribbean Nationals in the 1980s

Country	US Visas 1980–84	Canadian Visas 1980–90
Barbados	1350	998
Guyana	not available	1707
Jamaica	8951	1461
Trinidad & Tobago	9293	7344
Antigua	724	403
Dominica	531	229
Grenada	323	214
St Kitts & Nevis	605	205
St Lucia	303	296
St Vincent & Grenadines	299	156

Source: Adapted from Alan B. Simmons and Dwaine E. Plaza, "International Migration and Schooling in the Easter Caribbean", in *OECS Consultation on Education Reform* (Antigua: OECS Secretariat, 1991), 52; see also Alan B. Simmons and Dwaine E. Plaza, "International Migration and Schooling in the Eastern Caribbean", *La Educacion* 34, no. 107 (1990): 187.

The point is, however, that the majority of Caribbean nationals going abroad to study do not return to the region after completion of their courses.

Hence, study abroad results in a net loss to the region, although this avenue is yet another route through which Caribbean nationals access tertiary education.

Simmons and Plaza showed that Caribbean nationals migrating to North America in the decades of the 1970s and 1980s had higher levels of education than average for the population in their homelands. Further, they found that educational opportunities ranked among the highest motives for emigration to North America. Moreover, many Caribbean nationals enrolled in college or university programmes within two to three years after emigrating and had a good record of successfully completing their programmes.

Simmons and Plaza made the observation that the relationship between schooling and migration in the Commonwealth Caribbean has to be understood within the context of the major changes in migration patterns that emerged after the 1960s compared to previous migrations. One noticeable shift was that North America became the principal destination of migrants. In this regard, both United States and Canadian immigration policies favoured better educated persons through the explicit priority given to skilled workers and professionals. For example, in the Canadian Points System used to assess applications, education, specific vocational training and occupation accounted for 32 points out of the 100, where 70 points constituted the 'pass mark'. Table 6.4 shows the percentage of adults with at least a basic university education in some Caribbean countries compared with Caribbean immigrants

Table 6.4: Percent Adults with some University Education: Comparing Recent Caribbean Immigrants to Canada and the United States with Populations in their Countries of Origin

Country	Adults in Country of Origin	Adult Immigrants US 1975–80	Adult Immigrants Canada 1975–81
Females			
Barbados	2 0	37 5	8 8
Guyana	0.7	17.9	7.2
Jamaica	1 1	26.4	8 0
Trinidad & Tobago	1.5	23.8	9.9
OECS countries	0 7	16 2	9 7
Males			
Barbados	3.8	29.8	13.0
Guyana	2 0	31 3	15 1
Jamaica	1.9	21 4	14 8
OECS Countries	1.6	24.9	18.9

Source: Simmons and Plaza, 1991

in the United States and Canada as revealed by the 1980–81 census data in those countries.

If the US and Canadian immigration policies favoured the better educated and trained applicants from the Commonwealth Caribbean, the expansion of secondary and tertiary education that took place in the region in the postindependence period facilitated Caribbean nationals in satisfying the education and training criteria. Caribbean education has always been integrated into the international labour market as Caribbean nationals have used migration as a means of accessing job opportunities not available in the region. The immigration policies of the United States and Canada over the last twenty-five years and the expansion of secondary and tertiary education provision within the region have both contributed to the strengthening of this link.

Issues Related to Equity in Access

Bearing in mind that universal access to tertiary education does not exist anywhere and that access to tertiary education is more limited in the Commonwealth Caribbean than in other parts of the hemisphere, and indeed in many other parts of the world, the critical question becomes: What are some of the factors that appear to be related to who gets access to the available opportunities for tertiary education in the region? In this regard, equity becomes as important as access and cannot be treated separately from the latter. Factors that are usually related to issues of equity in access to educational opportunity are cost, class, residence and gender. It is important to examine each of these in turn.

Cost and Affordability

The expansion of tertiary education opportunities within the Caribbean in the postwar and postindependence periods has increased access to this level of education principally because it has made it more affordable, when all the costs are considered. Having to go abroad to study severely limited access to tertiary education during the colonial period largely because of the cost involved.

Even in the postindependence period, however, the relationship between cost and access to overseas tertiary education remains. Simmons and Plaza found that there was a significant relationship between the buoyancy of a Caribbean country's economy and the number of students who went to study abroad. They illustrated this relation with reference to both Jamaica and Trinidad and Tobago, where there was a substantial fall-off in the numbers of students studying abroad after downturns in the economies of these two countries. The relative strength of Caribbean economies appears to be one of the factors explaining why nationals of Trinidad and Tobago lead the region in going overseas for tertiary education and why there was a decline when the Trinidad and Tobago economy experienced a downturn in the latter half of the 1980s.

Within the Caribbean, cost is also a factor related to equity in access to tertiary education. To address this issue several Caribbean governments in the 1970s instituted policies that provided their nationals with free tuition along with loan assistance for the other costs involved, including accommodation and books. The criterion for receiving free tuition and other assistance was acceptance by the tertiary institutions. Once admitted, the students became eligible for the free tuition and loan assistance. Academic merit and not money predominated as the primary criterion for access to tertiary education. Some countries, for example Barbados, Jamaica, Trinidad and Tobago, and St Lucia, applied this policy to their national institutions as well as the UWI, the regional institution. Others, such as St Kitts and Nevis and Dominica, restricted the policy to their national institutions but excluded the UWI. The result was that nationals from countries that implemented policies of free tuition that included the UWI had greater access to university education within the region than the nationals of those countries that did not.

In the 1990s several governments have reversed their policies of free tuition at the tertiary level. For example, both the governments of Jamaica and Trinidad and Tobago have implemented policies that require their nationals to pay 15 percent of the economic cost of their programmes at the UWI. With respect to national institutions, cost sharing schemes have been implemented that vary by type of institution and programme. For example, lower levels of cost sharing have been applied to teacher and nursing education programmes than to say business and technical education. Governments implementing cost sharing policies have maintained that no student will be denied access to tertiary education because of their inability to pay. Accordingly, these governments have expanded and provided capital replenishment to their student revolving loan programmes.

Barbados is the exception to this trend away from free tuition at the tertiary level. The Barbados government has maintained its free education policies at all levels of the education system. Probably it is not a coincidence that Barbados leads the region in providing access to tertiary education. Governments implementing cost sharing schemes have justified them in terms of expanding access and improving quality. Barbados has maintained its free education policy on grounds of both equity and access. It is too early to assess the empirical outcomes of these different policy positions. What is needed are studies that would establish baseline positions that would facilitate careful evaluation in the future.

Class and Status

While several empirical studies have been done on the social background of secondary school students, there are very few studies that have addressed this aspect of tertiary education. Miller[9] and Gordon[10] have produced data to show that most teacher trainees come mainly from a peasant or emerging middle class background. Only a small proportion of teacher trainees come from the higher socioeconomic categories.

Several studies – Cross and Schwartzbaum,[11] Baksh,[12] Miller,[13] Miller,[14] Gordon[15] and Layne[16] – have shown that secondary school students, enrolled in those sections of the school system where access is gained through the Common Entrance Examinations, or admission to the more prestigious high schools, are drawn mainly from the middle and higher socioeconomic groups in the various Caribbean countries. Students from the lower socioeconomic categories are concentrated mainly in the types of secondary schools that allow very limited access to tertiary education either through not being articulated with the GCE/CXC examination systems or through poor performance if they are so articulated.

Given the social biases evidenced in the structure of opportunity at the secondary level, and seeing that access to tertiary education is determined by successful completion of secondary education, it is not unreasonable to assume that tertiary education is similarly biased since the vast majority of students entering tertiary institutions in the 1990s have completed secondary schooling. Indeed, it is possible that tertiary education, on the whole, could be even more biased towards the higher socioeconomic categories, given the fact that several studies have found a strong positive correlation between social class and performance in the GCE and CXC examinations.

Within the tertiary education system it would appear that students from the higher socioeconomic categories are more concentrated in the universities, while those from the lower socioeconomic categories are more frequently found in the other types of tertiary institutions. Put another way, the establishment of university education within the Caribbean has significantly expanded access, but most of the expanded opportunities have gone to children from the middle and upper socioeconomic categories. While establishment of university education within the region would also have expanded access to the lower classes, in that they had little or no access previously, the actual number and proportion of those categories that have benefited have been very modest.

It would appear that even in the 1990s teachers colleges and theological colleges have continued to be the tertiary institutions that provide the greatest access to students from the lower socioeconomic categories. Moreover, they constitute an important route through which these social segments gain access to university education. In other words, while the sixth form is the main path to university education by students of the middle and higher socioeconomic categories, the teachers and theological colleges are the main avenues for students from the lower socioeconomic categories, although no route exclusively serves any particular social category. While there has been no study of the social background of students enrolled in community colleges, it may well be that this type of tertiary institution has also expanded access to the lower socioeconomic categories. This, however, is speculation that would need to be corroborated by empirical findings.

Race and Colour

Apart from Baksh,[17] there are no studies on tertiary education in the Commonwealth Caribbean that have provided data on the race or colour of tertiary students. Cognizant of the strong correlation at the secondary level between race/colour and class, as shown by Gordon,[18] Miller[19] and others, it can only be inferred that similar relationships would be found at the tertiary level. The point to note is that prior to the mid twentieth century, race was the preeminent criterion on which Commonwealth Caribbean societies were organized. Class operated within racial categories. Since then, class has displaced race/colour as the preeminent criterion. As Gordon[20] has shown, race/colour currently operates as a facilitating factor within class. Hence, the lighter skinned members of any social stratum appear to have an advantage in accessing opportunities when compared to the darker skinned members of that stratum.

By casual observation it would appear that Caribbean nationals going abroad to obtain tertiary education would on average be of lighter skin colour than those studying at tertiary institutions within the Caribbean. It would also probably be true that those going abroad would on average be from the higher socioeconomic categories. What is indicated is that the social legacies of the past have not been eliminated within the context of contemporary access to tertiary education.

Location and Residence

Invariably, colleges established in the postwar and postindependence eras have been located in urban centres. During this period also there has been a tendency for institutions to move away from providing residential accommodation for students. Both of these developments have favoured urban residence and have been disadvantageous to rural residence. In the Caribbean where there are several multi-island states, tertiary institutions are almost always located on the island on which the capital is located. In these instances not only rural but also out-island residents are at a disadvantage.

Given that, with the exception of Guyana and Belize, almost all Commonwealth Caribbean countries are relatively small states, the distance between urban centres in which colleges are located and rural villages, and between main and out-islands, is usually not that great in absolute terms. The location of colleges and the residence of students should not pose an overwhelming problem with respect to equity in access. The transportation system in most countries, however, with the possible exception of Barbados, leaves much to be desired. In many instances rural and out-island residents have to relocate, at least for the duration of their period of study, in order to access tertiary education opportunities. While this situation is by no means unique to the Commonwealth Caribbean, combined with other socioeconomic factors like income, it is not to be dismissed.

Gender

The general pattern for many so-called developing or Third World countries is that women are disadvantaged in gaining access to education at all levels, but in particular to tertiary education. As Miller[21] has shown, this picture is not true generally of the Commonwealth Caribbean. In the region, on the whole, girls start schooling earlier, attend school more regularly, repeat fewer grades, are less likely to drop out and therefore more likely to stay in school longer, and achieve higher standards of educational performance than boys. In the adult population more women are literate than men. Girls are more highly represented in those sections of the secondary and tertiary levels of the education system that enhance the prospects of upward social mobility. In a real sense girls and women constitute the first sex in Caribbean education. The Caribbean is one of the few areas of the world in which this is the case. The data to support these assertions are not in question. They are routinely reported and confirmed by the annual education statistical reports of all the countries in the subregion. Probably, it is most appropriate simply to provide some illustration of this general pattern as it applies to access to tertiary education. The pattern is best outlined by looking at output of graduates from the UWI in 1995–96.

Table 6.5 shows that on all three campuses of the university there were more females than male graduates in 1995–96. This pattern was most pronounced at the Mona campus in Jamaica and least marked at the St Augustine campus in Trinidad. Of the graduates from the Mona campus, 71.2 percent were female compared to 57.6 percent at St Augustine. Cave Hill in Barbados occupied the middle position. For the university as a whole, 34.9 percent of the graduates were male and 65.1 percent were female.

Table 6.5: UWI Graduates by Campus and Gender, 1995–96

Campus	Male		Female		Total	
	Number	Percent	Number	Percent	Number	Percent
Cave Hill	235	37.7	389	62.3	624	100
Mona	611	28.8	1508	71.2	2119	100
St Augustine	623	42.4	845	57.6	1468	100
Total	1469	34.9	2742	65.1	4211	100

Source: University of the West Indies statistics, 1995

Table 6.6 shows that the only faculty from which there were more male than female graduates was engineering, where 76.4 percent of the graduates were men. In the other faculties the majority of the graduates were females including the science-based faculties of natural science, medicine and agriculture. The proportion of female graduates was highest from the faculties of arts and general studies, and education.

Table 6.6: UWI Graduates by Faculty and Gender, 1995–96

Faculty	Male Number	Male Percent	Female Number	Female Percent	Total Number	Total Percent
Agriculture	44	48.9	46	51.1	90	100
Arts & Gen. Stud	162	23.1	540	76.9	702	100
Education	83	22.1	292	77.9	375	100
Engineering	184	76.4	57	23.6	241	100
Law	49	31.8	105	68.2	154	100
Medical Sciences	140	42.0	193	58.0	333	100
Natural Sciences	267	48.7	281	51.3	548	100
Social Science	539	30.4	1229	69.6	1768	100
Total	1469	34.9	2742	65.1	4211	100

Source University of the West Indies statistics, 1995-96.

Table 6.7 shows that among graduates earning master's and doctorates females outnumbered males for the university as a whole. Fifty-five percent of master's and doctorates went to females. At the Mona campus female graduates significantly outnumbered male graduates while males outnumbered females at the Cave Hill and St Augustine campuses.

Table 6.8 shows that it was only in engineering and natural sciences that men earning higher degrees outnumbered females. In the other faculties, including agriculture and medicine, females outnumbered males.

When the UWI pattern is examined in its entirety the salient points to note are:

- While women hold an overall advantage in access to educational opportunities at the UWI, this does not obtain to the same degree in all countries and all disciplines.
- Men still hold a considerable advantage in engineering and at the higher degree level in some countries.
- The pattern of female dominance is most marked in Jamaica.
- While women were once predominant in the Arts-based faculty, in the mid 1990s their predominance has extended to include some of the science-based faculties.

Table 6.7: Higher Degrees Awarded by Campus and Gender, 1995–96

Campus	Male		Female		Total	
	Number	Percent	Number	Percent	Number	Percent
Cave Hill	44	61.6	28	38.9	72	100
Mona	89	35.2	164	64.8	253	100
St Augustine	69	55.6	55	44.4	124	100
Total	202	45.0	247	55.0	449	100

Source: University of the West Indies statistics, 1995–96.

Table 6.8: Higher Degrees Awarded by Faculty and Gender, 1995–96

Faculty	Male		Female		Total	
	Number	Percent	Number	Percent	Number	Percent
Agriculture	6	35.3	11	64.7	17	100
Arts & Gen. Stud	6	26.1	23	73.9	29	100
Education	6	23.1	20	76.9	26	100
Engineering	19	76.0	6	24.0	25	100
Law	6	54.5	5	45.5	11	100
Medicine	29	38.2	47	61.8	76	100
Natural Sciences	29	55.8	23	44.2	52	100
Social Science	101	47.4	112	52.6	213	100
Total	202	45.0	247	55.0	449	100

Source: University of the West Indies statistics, 1995

It is necessary to examine gender patterns in access to tertiary education, not only with respect to students studying within the region, as exemplified by the analysis of the UWI situation, but also with respect to students studying outside the region. Reference has already been made to the fact that the Commonwealth Caribbean has had a long tradition of the wealthy families within the region sending their offspring, especially their sons, to study in metropolitan countries. While the circumstances in the 1990s suggest that not only wealthy families access education outside of the region, the question that arises is: what are the gender patterns that obtain relative to students who study abroad?

There are not a lot of studies that provide data on students studying abroad disaggregated by gender. Simmons and Plaza provide some empirical evidence with respect to Caribbean students attending Canadian universities between 1980 and 1984 and on the proportion of males per hundred females among Caribbean university students granted visas to Canada between 1980 and 1990. These data are shown in Tables 6.9 and 6.10, respectively.

Table 6.9 shows that for the region as a whole slightly more Caribbean male than female students were enrolled in Canadian universities between

Table 6.9: Caribbean Students Issued Visas to Study in Canadian Universities by Gender, 1980–84

Country	Female Number	Female Percent	Male Number	Male Percent
Barbados	212	43.4	276	56.6
Guyana	439	35.1	810	64.9
Jamaica	493	56.9	373	43.1
Trinidad & Tobago	2047	49.9	2052	50.1
OECS Countries	352	41.7	492	58.3
Total	3543	47.0	4003	53.0

Source: Simmons and Plaza, 1991

Table 6.10: Caribbean University Students on Visas in Canada: Ratio of Males per 100 Females

Country	1980	1985	1990	Overall
Barbados	164	118	94	117
Guyana	203	152	185	177
Jamaica	84	76	67	72
Trinidad and Tobago	110	92	117	101
OECS Countries	128	147	119	139

Source: Simmons and Plaza, 1991.

1980 and 1984. The pattern was most marked for Guyana. In the case of Jamaica, however, the situation was the reverse, more Jamaica females than males were enrolled in Canadian universities.

Table 6.10 shows that the gender pattern observed for Caribbean students enrolled in Canadian universities from 1980 to 1984 obtained throughout the decade. More Caribbean males were enrolled than Caribbean females. The exception to this pattern was Jamaica, where more Jamaican females than males were enrolled. The point to note, however, in Table 6.10 is that the proportion of males to females declined between 1980 and 1990. This was most marked in the case of Barbados, where the male to female ratio was close to 5:3 in 1980, but declined to less than 1:1 by 1990. In the case of Jamaica the ratio of male to female declined even though females were at an advantage in 1980. What these data in Tables 6.9 and 6.10 seem to indicate is that while the traditional pattern is of more males than females leaving the Caribbean to study abroad, that pattern is shifting in a similar direction to the shifts already noted within the Caribbean. In this regard, the pattern is most marked with respect to Jamaican students where the shift had already taken place prior to 1980.

It is considered that in access to tertiary education opportunities one would expect that Caribbean students studying outside the region are likely to be from a somewhat higher socioeconomic background; however, the observed gender pattern would suggest that the pattern favouring females is more marked among students from a relatively lower social background while the traditional male bias is more evident among students from the higher social categories. In other words, gender is interacting with other social criteria, particularly class, to produce the observed pattern. Miller,[22] in his study of high school students, showed that there was a clear interaction between class and gender. Among students from the lower socioeconomic categories it was mainly the girls who gained access to the coveted high school places through the Common Entrance Examination. As the social ladder was ascended, however, this bias was reduced and disappeared among the highest socioeconomic categories. Gordon,[23] studying intergenerational mobility through high schooling, noted that boys were more likely to inherit their social status while girls from the lower socioeconomic classes were more likely to change their social position through upward social mobility. While there are no comparable studies done at the tertiary level, these analyses of secondary data sources would indicate that a similar pattern is likely to exist at the tertiary level.

Conclusion

In the foregoing analysis it has been shown that tertiary education within the Commonwealth Caribbean represents an area of historic underprovision. While substantial progress has been made to correct this deficit since the 1940s, the gains made are comparatively modest when compared to the rest of the Americas. Even the recent targets set by the CARICOM heads of government do not reach the norm for the hemisphere. Access to the existing provisions of tertiary education within the region is influenced, and to some extent determined, by cost, residence, class and gender. The inequities in the existing provision favour the higher socioeconomic categories, urban residence and females. Bearing in mind that these factors interact, the most disadvantaged by the existing structure of opportunity would be lower class males who reside in rural areas. Bearing in mind that strong correlation still exists within the Caribbean between race and class, the persons with least access to tertiary education would be lower class black and Indian men resident in rural areas and out-islands in multi-island states. The policies and programmes that would need to be implemented to address the observed inequities in access to tertiary education within the Commonwealth Caribbean are, however, beyond the scope of this chapter.

Notes

1. Samuel Noah Kramer, *The Sumerians: Their History, Culture and Character* (Chicago: University of Chicago Press, 1963).
2. A.W. Sjoberg, "The Old Babylonian Eduba", in *Sumerological Studies in Honor of Thorkild Jacobsen on his Seventh Birthday*, edited by Stephen J. Lieberman (Chicago: Oriental Institute of the University of Chicago, University of Chicago Press, 1975), 159–79.
3. Edward Brathwaite, *The Development of Creole Society in Jamaica: 1770–1820* (Oxford: Clarendon Press, 1971).
4. Phillip Sherlock and Rex Nettleford, *The University of the West Indies: A Caribbean Response to the Challenge of Change* (London: Macmillan Caribbean, 1990).
5. Aaron Benavot and Phyllis Riddle, "The Expansion of Primary Education, 1870–1940: Trends and Issues", *Sociology of Education* 61 (1988): 191–210.
6. Lloyd Best, "Outlines of a Model of Pure Plantation Economy", *Social and Economic Studies* 17 (1968): 283–326
7. Hopeton Gordon, "University and Nation-Building in the Commonwealth Caribbean. Early Commitments", *Caribbean Journal of Education* 11 (1984): 184–201.
8. Gad J. Heuman, *Between Black and White: Race, Politics and the Free Coloreds in Jamaica, 1792–1865* (Westport, Connecticut: Greenwood Press, 1981).
9. Errol Miller, *Marginalisation of the Black Male* (Mona, Jamaica: Institute of Social and Economic Research, UWI, 1986).
10. Derek Gordon, *Class, Race and Social Mobility in Jamaica* (Mona, Jamaica: Institute of Social and Economic Research, UWI, 1987).
11. M. Cross and Allan M. Schwartzbaum, "Social Mobility and Secondary School Selection in Trinidad and Tobago", *Social and Economic Studies* 18 (1969): 189–207.
12. Ishmael J Baksh, "Education and Equality of Opportunity in Trinidad and Tobago", *Caribbean Journal of Education* 13 (1986): 6–26.
13. Errol Miller, "Education and Society in Jamaica", *Savacou* 5 (1971): 51–70.
14. Errol Miller, *Jamaican Society and High Schooling* (Mona, Jamaica: Institute of Social and Economic Research, UWI, 1990).
15. Derek Gordon, "Access to High School Education in Post-War Jamaica", in *Education and Society in the Commonwealth Caribbean*, edited by Errol Miller (Mona, Jamaica: Institute of Social and Economic Research, UWI, 1991), 181–206.

16. Anthony Layne, "A Review of Research on Access to Education and Educational Achievement in Barbados", in *Education and Society in the Commonwealth Caribbean*, edited by Errol Miller (Mona, Jamaica: Institute of Social and Economic Research, UWI, 1991), 75–101.
17. Baksh, "Education and Equality", 506.
18. Gordon, "Access to High School".
19. Errol Miller, *Men At Risk* (Kingston: Jamaica Publishing House, 1991).
20. Gordon, "Access to High School".
21. Miller, *Men at Risk*.
22. Miller, *Jamaican Society and High Schooling*.
23. Gordon, "Access to High School".

7

Higher Education and Agricultural Development in the Caribbean

Carlisle A. Pemberton, Sarojini Ragbir and Rita Pemberton

Introduction

The dependence on agriculture varies widely among CARICOM states as is evident by the contribution of this sector to their gross domestic products (GDPs). In Belize, Dominica, Grenada and Guyana this contribution is more than 30 percent; it is between 10 to 25 percent in St Lucia, St Vincent and the Grenadines, and St Kitts and Nevis, while in Jamaica and Trinidad and Tobago the contribution is less than 7 percent. There is no doubt that the tropical environments of the Caribbean have contributed to the diversity of the crops that have been grown and the animals that have been reared. Good soil and climatic conditions have also facilitated agricultural development in the region. Success in agricultural production, however, is also in part due to the contribution of higher education. What this paper will attempt to do is highlight this contribution of higher education to agricultural development in the Caribbean. For the purpose of this paper, higher education is defined as tertiary (including university) level education and the paper focuses on the contributing territories of the University of the West Indies (UWI).

Education of agriculturalists exists in most of the contributing territories, through tertiary level institutions (TLIs) and the UWI. While the main function of the TLIs is to train primary producers, technicians and teachers, the role of the UWI, apart from educating students, is to conduct research to solve problems in the agricultural sector with the ultimate aim of increasing food production on a sustainable basis, for the benefit of Caribbean people. The paper will first give a description of the TLIs and their contribution to

Caribbean agricultural development. A description of the School of Agriculture of the UWI's Faculty of Agriculture and Natural Sciences and its contributions to agricultural development follows. The paper ends with a look at future directions in agricultural development in the region and the potential contributions of higher education.

Tertiary Level Institutions in Agriculture in the Caribbean

Several TLIs exist in the contributing territories. The descriptions of the major TLIs that follow are based on two documents, their submissions to a workshop on *Articulating TLI/UWI Programmes in Agriculture* held in Castries, St Lucia in April 1997,[1] as well as a report by Wilson, Timothy and Crichlow.[2] In the Bahamas, the College of the Bahamas offers associate degrees in agriculture, agriculture and biology, and agribusiness, which can normally be completed over two years. The main objective of this programme is to provide fundamental background knowledge and lay the foundation for specialized knowledge and technical skills in agriculture.

The Barbados Community College offers an associate degree in agriculture designed to provide students with a sound base in agricultural production, management and marketing and to prepare them to undertake careers in these areas, as well as to provide a basis for further studies in agricultural sciences and agro-industries. This programme was launched in 1996. The Belize College of Agriculture offers an associate degree programme that aims to develop a well rounded, functional individual who is nationally and internationally competitive, by imparting relevant knowledge, teaching skills and technology and developing character attributes so as to facilitate the sustainable development of Belize's natural resources on an economically and environmentally sound basis.[3] The programme has a duration of two years and there has been an average output of approximately twenty-three graduates over the period 1989 to 1993.

The Clifton Dupigny Technical College in the Commonwealth of Dominica offers a two-year certificate programme at the technician diploma level and in agriculture. The certificate programme is designed to expose students to issues, practices and knowledge critical to a full understanding of agriculture. The programme also seeks to adequately prepare students to adapt to the rapid technological changes that are constantly occurring within the field of agriculture. This programme was restarted in 1992. The Grenada National College offers a two-year and a one-year certificate programme in agriculture. The aim of the one-year certificate is to train farmers in new and improved technology. The College of Agriculture, Science and Education (CASE) in Jamaica is a multidisciplinary institution established in 1995, through the merger of the former College of Agriculture and the Passley Gardens Teachers' College. The mandate of the college is to provide residential instruction, research, outreach activities and leadership in the fields of agriculture, science and education. The college offers a three-year programme of study leading to the associate of science degree in general agriculture. This programme is offered through full-time study to prepare students for careers in agriculture and allied industries. The college has articulation arrangements with the UWI, Ohio and Louisiana State Universities in the United States, and Nova Scotia and McGill Universities in Canada. In the existing UWI/CASE articulation arrangement, CASE's associate degree programme graduates with cumulative grade point averages (GPAs) of 2.9 or more earn normal matriculation as well as exemptions from and credits for some Level I and Level II UWI courses. The students are therefore able to complete the bachelor's degree in two additional years.[4]

The Sir Arthur Lewis Community College in St Lucia offers three programmes in agriculture: an associate degree, diploma and certificate. The associate degree programme is designed to instruct students in the fundamental principles of agricultural and related disciplines. It prepares them for jobs at the levels of senior technicians, middle management, agricultural science teachers, commercial farmers and farm managers and provides a base for advanced agricultural studies at the bachelor's degree level. The diploma programme is designed to instruct students in the fundamental principles and disciplines relevant to the agricultural sector. It prepares them to work as teachers, commercial farmers and assistant managers. The certificate programme is designed to instruct students in the principles of crop and livestock production, and it prepares them to be commercial farmers and workers at agricultural institutions.

In Trinidad and Tobago, the School of Agriculture of the Eastern Caribbean Institute of Agriculture and Forestry (ECIAF) was established in 1954, the School of Forestry in 1969 and the Agricultural/Teacher Education Centre in

1983. Three separate diplomas are offered in agriculture, forestry and teacher education. ECIAF has a 40-hectare farm and about 50 percent of student time is devoted to farm practice and field visits, an arrangement that is achievable because of the college's residential status. The objective of the diploma in agriculture offered by ECIAF is to educate and train persons in agriculture at the subprofessional or teaching level. Roberts reports that: "There are currently fifty-five (55) students in Years One and Two of the Agricultural Programmes which have a capacity to accommodate sixty-four (64). Additionally there are fifteen students in Forestry and twenty in Agriculture Education."

Contributions of the TLIs to Agricultural Development

The contributions of the TLIs to Caribbean agricultural development have been as follows:

1. *Preparation of graduates for entry into UWI*
   Students graduating from the TLIs with associate degrees or technical diplomas can qualify for entry into the UWI. Such entry into UWI can be into the year one. Also, year one can be exempted and entry can take place into year two. Several workshops have been held recently to address the issues of matriculation and UWI accreditation with respect to graduates from the TLIs.

2. *Technology transfer*
   Some TLIs offer programmes for farmers to improve their practical skills and at the same time introduce them to new and improved technologies. Training of extension officers also focuses on solving farm level problems and allows the opportunity to introduce new and improved technologies to the extension officers for onward transmission to farmers. This transfer of technology allows farmers the opportunity to improve their farm efficiency and profitability.

3. *Training for the workplace*
   The TLIs offer several programmes that allow graduates to work as extension officers or assistants, teachers, commercial farmers, managers and supervisors, thereby contributing to the provision of trained human resource in agriculture in the Caribbean.

4. *Agribusiness development*

Graduates are also trained to enter the agribusiness subsector in industries and institutions such as credit banks, agro-industry, chemical shops, small enterprise processing, cooperative development and rural development projects. Such entrepreneurial activity serves to expand business opportunities in the agricultural sector and contributes to the experiences and diversification of agriculture and the GDP.

The University of the West Indies, School of Agriculture

The Imperial College of Tropical Agriculture (ICTA) was founded as the West Indian Agricultural College in 1921. In 1924 the name of the college was changed to the ICTA with the aim to provide general instruction in tropical agriculture, to give opportunities for thorough training in science and practice of the subject to those intending to become tropical planters, investigators or experts in different branches of agricultural science or technology, and at the same time to provide facilities for the study of tropical agricultural subjects, on the part of graduates from other universities and colleges, who desire to acquire knowledge of these subjects in tropical surroundings. Pemberton reports that the main contributions of ICTA were more to the British Empire than to the Caribbean itself. As she states:

... though located in the region, ICTA was neither of or for the West Indies. Rather, it was the Caribbean leg of an imperial system ... Its main function was to assist imperial development and it saw its commitments to West Indies as marginal and at times something of an encumbrance.[5]

Its primary function was postgraduate training in tropical agriculture of young graduates for the colonial service. Thus the academic programme was closely tied to that of the University of Cambridge. Nevertheless, training was also offered to prospective planters, administrators, extension workers and teachers in the West Indies. Its research activities that contributed most to tropical agricultural development included research in cotton at the Empire Cotton Station, the Low Temperature Research Station that did the seminal experimental work on the cool storage of bananas and other fruits, the Cocoa Research Unit (CRU; to be discussed in more detail later) and its Sugar Technology programme.

In 1960 the ICTA was merged with the UWI to become the Faculty of Agriculture. The faculty inherited (as part of the ICTA) the Regional Research Centre (RRC) for the British territories in the Caribbean. The RRC came into being on 1 September 1955. Its nucleus was formed from the staff of the three research schemes for bananas, cocoa and soils that were wound up on 31 August 1955.[6] In May 1975, the Caribbean Agricultural Research and Development Institute (CARDI) was established as a successor organization to the RRC and has among its objectives to provide for the research and development needs of agriculture of the region as identified in national plans and policies, and to provide an appropriate research and development service to the agricultural sectors of member states. CARDI is now an autonomous organization, which is affiliated to the UWI and serves the contributing territories as well as Guyana and the British Virgin Islands.

In 1996, as part of a change in its governance structure, the UWI merged the faculties of agriculture and natural sciences to form the Faculty of Agriculture and Natural Sciences, with a School of Agriculture and a School of Natural Sciences. The School of Agriculture comprises the Department of Agricultural Economics and Extension and the Department of Food Production, and it is closely associated with the Department of Life Sciences of the School of Natural Sciences. The School of Agriculture also has a Cocoa Research Unit, a Biotechnology Unit and operates the University Field Station (UFS), which consists of a 90-hectare farm with a dairy herd of 118 cows, and extensive buildings and equipment including a feed mill and an abattoir. Also falling under the portfolio of the School of Agriculture are the Continuing Education Programme in Agricultural Technology (CEPAT), the journal *Tropical Agriculture* and the Herbarium. These will be described in detail later.

Description of the School of Agriculture

The School of Agriculture offers undergraduate degrees in agriculture (a general degree as well as degrees with specialization in livestock production and agronomy), human ecology (home economics, nutrition and dietetics) and agribusiness management. The BSc (agribusiness management) degree, a joint programme with the Faculty of Social Sciences and its Department of Management Studies, replaced the agricultural management option in the BSc (management) degree in 1990. The BSc (human ecology degree) started in

1993 and produced its first set of twenty-two graduates in 1996, all specializing in nutrition and dietetics. The school also offers a diploma in agricultural extension that provides professional training to practitioners in agriculture, fisheries and forestry extension, cooperative development and rural development.

The School of Agriculture's wide range of postgraduate degrees contain a strong disciplinary and departmental focus. MPhil and PhD degrees are offered in the Department of Food Production in Soil Science, Crop Science and Livestock Science and in the Department of Agricultural Economics and Extension. An MPhil and a PhD in Plant Science are also offered in the Department of Life Sciences, and MSc degrees are offered in agricultural economics, tropical commodity utilization, and crop protection. In conjunction with Wye College of the University of London, a diploma and MSc in agricultural and rural development by distance is also offered by the school's External Programme in Agriculture.

The Contributions of UWI to Agricultural Development

This section highlights some of the major contributions of the School (Faculty) of Agriculture of UWI to agricultural development in the Caribbean. The areas highlighted are research, training, extension, conferences, the journal *Tropical Agriculture* and the Herbarium. The paper then deals with the contribution of UWI to policy formulation in the region.

Research

Cocoa Research Unit

In 1930, the CRU was established at the ICTA with funding from the British government, British cocoa-growing colonies and chocolate manufacturers. Wild germplasm was collected on various expeditions to the South American forests, initially by F.J. Pound, particularly for obtaining material resistant to Witches' Broom disease, which had arrived in Trinidad in the 1920s. This collection, called the International Cocoa Germbank, Trinidad, formed the basis of the cocoa genebank, and is recognized by the International Board for Plant Genetic Resources Institute (IPGRI) as a global centre for cocoa germplasm. The distribution of germplasm to other research centres is a major contribution to the global effort to improve cocoa culture.[7]

The CRU is now recognized internationally as an important resource to the world cocoa industry, as the custodian of a valuable collection of cocoa germplasm, and for its functions as a research unit for characterization and evaluation of cocoa germplasm. Currently, the collection consists of 2,500 accessions. In addition, 600 accessions are under quarantine in Barbados. While the activities of the CRU deal mainly with conservation, evaluation and distribution of the germplasm, part of its mandate also includes training of scientists at the postgraduate level and the offering of facilities to visiting scientists, particularly those who wish to utilize the collection.[8] In 1990, as part of a Canadian Development Agency funded project, the unit assisted farmers in Grenada in controlling black pod disease by using a 'single application' spraying programme. The CRU also collaborated with the Tropical Agricultural Research and Training Institute (CATIE) in developing improved cocoa varieties in Grenada.[9]

Tissue Culture Research
The Department of Life Sciences' Biotechnology Unit carries out tissue culture research on various crops. Protocols have been developed for mass production of breadfruit, aloe vera, carambola and yambean. Also developed were protocols for the improvement of techniques used in the production of bananas. Currently, through genetic engineering, the Biotechnology Unit is working on developing resistance to bacterial wilt in anthuriums and reducing the level of abscission of flowers in pigeon peas. The unit has benefited Caribbean agriculture by its supplies of anthuriums and bananas, as well as training regional personnel in the techniques of plant tissue culture.

Livestock Science Research
The research programme in Livestock Science concentrates on feed formulation and nutrition with specific relevance to small ruminants, rabbits, pigs and broilers. Research has also been undertaken on production systems with particular reference to rabbits, small ruminants and dairy animals. In addition, rabbits have been sent to some territories to enhance production in the region. In order to address a number of livestock reproductive problems that exist in the Caribbean, databases on the reproductive performance in cattle as well as reproductive diseases of livestock are being established. Another interesting area of research has been wildlife farming, which has as its goal

satisfying the demand for meats of exotic species and assisting in the conservation of these species.

Soil Science Research

The contribution of soil science research to the region began under the ICTA. The Soils Research Scheme was initiated in May 1947 and provided for the undertaking of systematic soil surveys, together with related research into the chemistry and physics of the main soil types, including an investigation of the possible role of trace-elements in West Indies agriculture.[10] Beginning in 1958, *Soil and Land-Use Surveys* of the former British territories in the Caribbean area were published by the ICTA and later by the UWI. These surveys include parts of Guyana and the former British West Indian islands with the exceptions of some of the Grenadines and Anguilla. Land capability surveys of Trinidad and Tobago were published between 1965 and 1968. Profile and analytical results were published for many of the islands.

In 1965 and 1966, soil surveys were published for additional parts of British Guiana by the Food and Agriculture Organization of the United Nations (FAO), Rome. Soil surveys of Puerto Rico and the US Virgin Islands have been published by the United States Department of Agriculture and the classification of the soil series of those islands was published in 1972.[11] The studies on soil classification led to further studies on the optimization of fertilizer use (primarily nitrogen) in cash crops, mainly sugar cane. From 1985 to present, studies have been conducted on the behaviour of fertilizer nitrogen when applied to a range of soils in various cropping systems. Commenting on this research Ahmad states:

The various soil processes affecting fertilizer nitrogen are not well understood, yet knowledge of these is most important in improving nitrogen efficiency. The availability of nitrogen to plants can be influenced by manipulation of the soil and crop biological systems and an understanding of the processes by which it becomes available in this system is critical in the development of sustainable agriculture. These problems have been engaging the Department of Soil Science of the University of the West Indies for some time and with the support of the GTZ we have been able to utilize advanced fertilizer research techniques such as the use of isotopically labeled nitrogen to provide solutions.[12]

With the thrust in environmental protection, the department has started to conduct research on soil and environmental conservation, and a study is currently being done on reducing or breaking down petroleum hydrocarbons present in sludges.

Root Crop Research

The Faculty of Agriculture implemented a root crop programme in 1967. The aims of the programme were to develop cultivation practices that would result in immediate yield increases as well as reduced cost of production, and to study the range of genetic material available with a view to increasing the yields potential of these crops through understanding of the mechanisms of yield. The programme concentrated on sweet potatoes and yams. The policy of the programme was, according to Wilson, "the achievement of a better understanding of the cultivation of different cultivars (sweet potatoes) and species (yams) of the crops, in a single ecosystem, prior to investigating production under different climatic conditions". Wilson foresaw a major contribution of the research in root crops. He wrote:

the experience gained in the last four years with the two crops studied can now be easily expanded to a third crop with available staff and expertise. It is, therefore, envisaged that work on aroids will in future be included in the Root Crop Programme. Preliminary investigations in the agronomy and crop physiology of the aroids have already been started in the Faculty of Agriculture and processed products (soups) have been produced in Barbados. Fresh tubers (dasheens) are also being exported to the UK.[13]

Education and Training

Degree Programmes

The ICTA's mandate from inception was research and teaching. The undergraduate diploma (DICTA) – Diploma of ICTA – was initially for West Indian students and the associateship (AICTA) for graduates with first degrees or DICTA. In 1984, a one-year postgraduate diploma course in tropical agriculture was started (DTA). Students came from the British West Indian colonies and also included agricultural recruits of the Empire Cotton Growing Corporation. After 1950, all graduates recruited to serve as agricultural officers in the Departments of Agriculture in British colonies had to spend a year at ICTA. With the formation of the University College of the West Indies (UCWI) in 1948, in Jamaica, and its degree granting arrangements with the University of London, many West Indian students went to UCWI in preference to ICTA, though the latter continued to attract postgraduate students. It is in this area of training that ICTA really excelled.[14]

The Faculty of Agriculture has made major contributions to the CARICOM agriculture sector over the last thirty-five years, through its undergraduate and postgraduate programmes. Ministers of government, permanent secretaries, successful entrepreneurs, farmers, bankers, researchers, extensionists and educators of the Caribbean have been graduates of the faculty. The Faculty of Agriculture graduates have also occupied (and continue to occupy) key positions in regional and international agencies such as the Work Bank, the Inter-American Institute for Cooperation on Agriculture (IICA), the FAO, international research centres and universities. The Faculty of Agriculture has established a worldwide reputation for postgraduate training in research in tropical agriculture, as evidenced by the awarding of over 532 diplomas, MSc, MPhil and PhD degrees to individuals from thirty-five countries in Africa, Asia, Latin America, the South Pacific, Australia, Europe and North America. Table 7.1 gives the number of undergraduate and postgraduate students registered in the Faculty of Agriculture, by gender and type, for the academic years 1993–94 to 1996–97.

Table 7.1: Number of Undergraduate and Postgraduate Students Registered in Agriculture by Gender and Type for the Academic Year 1993–94 to 1996–97

Period	Undergraduate			Postgraduate		
	Male	*Female*	*Total*	*Male*	*Female*	*Total*
1993–94	160	86	246	70	57	127
1994–95	140	147	287	56	51	107
1995–96	144	162	306	62	46	108
1996–97	125	168	293	78	55	133

Source: UWI Statistics, 1993–94, 1994–95, 1995–96, 1996–97.

CEPAT

The Continuing Education Programme in Agricultural Technology (CEPAT) represents one initiative of the Faculty of Agriculture towards meeting the changing agricultural education and training needs of the region. The primary objective of CEPAT is short-term training and the provision of a mechanism for the rapid introduction of new and improved technologies in agriculture in the Caribbean. CEPAT has trained 1,864 persons during the period 1990 to 1995 by conducting 93 courses in the regional states.[15]

The External Programme in Agriculture (EPA) is administered by CEPAT and started in January 1994 for advanced training in agricultural and rural development. The EPA offers course certificates, a postgraduate diploma and an MSc degree in agricultural and rural development by distance teaching. It is a collaborative programme with Wye College, University of London. Fourteen students registered for the MSc in the academic year 1995–96, seventeen for the diploma programme and thirty-one for the course certificate programme (UWI, 1996). This programme produced its first MSc graduate in 1997.

In-Service Training

The Department of Agricultural Extension introduced its first in-service training courses for extension officers in 1966 in Barbados and St Lucia with the aim of retraining and introducing them to new technologies, which could then be disseminated to farmers. Subsequently, annual courses were run by the department, both in the Leewards and Windwards in accordance with its policy of assisting in the development of the agricultural extension services.[16]

Extension

The Caribbean Agricultural Extension Project and the Agricultural Research and Extension Project

The Caribbean Agricultural Extension Project (CAEP), a collaborative project of the UWI and Midwest Universities Consortium for International Activities (MUCIA), conducted from 1980 to 1989, was funded by the US Agency for International Development (USAID). The goal of CAEP was to improve the economic and social well-being of small farm households in the Eastern Caribbean and Belize by increasing the effectiveness of the national extension systems in the region. The project also sought to increase the capacity of the Department of Agricultural Extension at the UWI to support the region's extension services.

CAEP had two phases. Phase I involved the establishment of a National Extension Improvement Planning Committee in each of the eight participating territories. The National Extension Improvement Plans coming out of Phase I constituted the basis for a Phase II proposal and were based on each country's analysis of its situation and the changes required if its extension service was to become a viable entity. The major focus of Phase II, carried out in the Windward and Leeward Islands, was the implementation of the National Extension Improvement Plans. Additional activities included the forging of better linkages between research and extension and the development of better communication capabilities, both within countries and in the region as a whole. To support and facilitate implementation of the national plans, the project provided technical assistance, training and equipment.

CAEP was externally evaluated by Alkins, Adams and Cuthbert[17] and the following review of its achievements is based on their report. One major achievement of CAEP was the Excellence in Extension Award. This award was given to the best extension officer in each participating country. Each winner travelled to the UWI at St Augustine, Trinidad to attend a three-day conference on 'Excellence in Extension'. At this conference, the winners from each country selected the overall winner, who was awarded a trip to the United States. The award served a valuable purpose, both in motivating extension officers and in improving the image of extension service. Because of the award, extension officers became more professional and responsible in their jobs. Many sought out training and professional improvement.

Under CAEP, the Department of Agricultural Extension implemented a one-year diploma in agricultural extension. This programme was developed in response to long-standing requests from regional governments for training opportunities for experienced extension staff. The diploma programme includes studies in needs assessment, planning, programme development and project evaluation, and it is designed, not exclusively for agricultural extension officers, but also for other professionals who serve the development of the rural sector in areas such as adult education and nutrition.

Another problem that CAEP addressed was the inability of extension officers to reach farmers living in remote areas. To deal with this situation, CAEP implemented a vehicle revolving loan programme. Also, heavy four-wheel drive vehicles were procured for the Department of Extension. This increase in mobility led to a greater number of farmer-extension contacts. Farmers reported increased production and were able to set up markets for their produce with the assistance of the extension officers. CAEP has had considerable impact on UWI by increasing the Department of Agricultural

Extension's ability to operate its academic and outreach programme. It also gave academic and technical staff opportunities to travel throughout the region and to participate in training sessions, thereby expanding their awareness and understanding of the agricultural extension needs of the region.

The Agricultural Research and Extension Project (AREP) developed out of CAEP, also with funding by USAID. This was a joint project of CARDI and the UWI through the Department of Agricultural Extension. It started in 1989 with the aim of strengthening the institutional capability of national extension services and regional research and extension organizations to generate, adapt and disseminate continuing streams of improved agricultural technologies which were responsive to the needs of participating countries and were widely adopted at the farm level.[18]

A final evaluation was conducted to review the overall achievements of the project with regard to its original objectives.[19] The evaluation team found that AREP had been relevant in addressing the need to strengthen the regional and local research/extension institutional capabilities and linkages. Numerous extension activities were effectively continued under AREP such as: the diploma in agricultural extension at the UWI (completed by ten extension officers), the Excellence in Extension annual awards, annual in-service training courses for the Leeward and Windward Islands, three meetings of the Regional Agricultural Research and Extension Coordinating Committee (RARECC) and the creation of five island professional agricultural extension associations. The evaluation report recommended a continuation of the Farm and Home Management Programme through the development of a "small farmer friendly record and analysis system" and continuous sample surveys "to develop a data base for monitoring and evaluation across Ministries".[20]

The Regional Extension Communications Unit
Under CAEP, the Regional Extension Communications Unit (RECU) was established within the Department of Agricultural Extension. RECU has served the region by providing training and information via various media: radio, newsletters, videos, bulletins and fact sheets. The *Extension Newsletter* which started in 1970 was, according to the dean of the Faculty of Agriculture:

an important addition to the many media employed by the Faculty of Agriculture of the University of the West Indies to communicate the results of agricultural research ... *Extension Newsletter* will provide summaries of research results, reports on agricultural developments and information on extension education. It will be circulated to staff members of government departments in the several territories supporting the University and to associations of farmers and progressive individual farmers in the area. The Department of Agricultural Extension of the University of the West Indies, Faculty of Agriculture is to be commended on successfully launching this *Extension Newsletter*.

According to the editor of the first issue:

The publication of this newsletter by the Department of Agricultural Extension of the University of the West Indies is in keeping with the objectives of the Department which, *inter alia*, is specifically charged with the responsibility for ensuring the staff of local Departments of Agriculture, at different levels are kept aware of the knowledge available from research conducted at the Faculty of Agriculture and of the problems for which solutions are being sought there. The newsletter will provide one means for maintaining close relations and providing regular opportunities for exchange of views and information between research workers at the Faculty, staff members of government departments in the several territories and associations of farmers and progressive individual farmers in the area.[21]

Initially the newsletter was produced quarterly, now two issues are produced yearly having over 2,000 subscribers. RECU has also published a number of books which are used by students, farmers and agriculturalists throughout the region. These include the *Soil and Water Conservation Methods for the Caribbean* by F.A. Gumbs,[22] and the *Farm and Home Management Business Record Book* by C.A. Pemberton,[23] which introduced farmers to holistic farm record keeping, planning and budgeting under AREP's Farm and Home Management Programme.

RECU has produced a number of videos for the region, including one on the Hibiscus Mealybug, others on the management of fisheries resources in St Lucia, Grenada, Dominica, Guyana and Trinidad and Tobago. Other videos have featured the *Amblyomma Variegatum* tick in the Caribbean, intestinal parasites in the region and banana production. RECU has also produced a number of fact sheets and bulletins on crops, livestock and ornamentals, all with the aim of servicing the agricultural community.

Outreach Offices

Three UWI Outreach Offices were established in Phase I of CAEP in St Lucia, Antigua and Belize. The offices in St Lucia and Antigua have continued to function since. They are managed by outreach lecturers and provide agricultural services to the Leeward and Windward Islands, in the areas of administration, organization and in-service training.

Recognition

The extension work of the Faculty of Agriculture has been recognized in many ways, including the presentation in 1997 of an award to the faculty by the Ministry of Finance, Agriculture, Lands, Fisheries, Planning and Co-operatives, Antigua, "In appreciation for its invaluable contribution to the development of Agricultural Extension in Antigua and Barbuda".

Conferences

Conferences arranged by the UWI have contributed to the development of agriculture in the region and the tropics by the communications of research findings, as well as by the formation of professional and international societies. These societies themselves have had a significant impact on agricultural development in the region. The West Indies Agricultural Economics Conference series has become the premier forum for the discussion of matters pertaining to the agricultural development and the economics of agriculture in the region. The first such conference was organized by the Department of Agricultural Economics and Farm Management of the UWI in 1966 and held at the St Augustine campus. Twenty-one other conferences have since been held. The twenty-second conference was held in Barbados in August 1997 with the theme "Trade and Economic Liberalization: Implications for Agriculture and the Environment in the Caribbean and Latin America". The conference series led to the formation of the Caribbean Agro-Economic Society (CAES) in April 1974, at the Ninth West Indies Agricultural Economics Conference, and this society took over the organization of the conferences from then on.[24] The secretariat of the CAES has been housed in the Department of Agricultural Economics and Farm Management (now Department of Agricultural Economics and Extension) since 1982 and members of the department have continued to hold most of the society's executive positions.

The proceedings of the West Indies Agricultural Economics Conference have formed the bulk of the literature on the economics of agriculture in the region. As such they are widely distributed throughout the world and are used extensively in teaching and research. The first symposium of the International Society for Tropical Root Crops (ISTRC) was held in 1967. According to Wilson:

The Faculty of Agriculture, founded seven years earlier in 1960, had taken the decision to eschew research on the traditional export crops of sugar, coconuts and bananas in favour of the food crops, long neglected in the recently concluded colonial era, as food for the poor and feed for livestock. The decision was unanimously acclaimed neither within nor indeed without the University walls. And, perhaps it was in an attempt to justify this decision, and, in so doing, to canonize research on tropical root crops in the Caribbean and worldwide, that the first symposium was mounted. The symposium which was supported by the UWI and the Rockefeller Foundation achieved these objectives and many others.[25]

The eleventh symposium of the ISTRC was again held on the St Augustine campus in October 1997, hosted by the Faculty of Agriculture and Natural Sciences. The theme was "Tropical Root Crops Staples for Sustainable Food Security into the Next Millennium". Papers and posters were presented on the tropical root and tuber crops: cassava, yams, sweet potato, aroids, potatoes and minor carbohydrate storage root crops.

The first International Conference on Leucaena was organized by the Faculty of Agriculture in July 1989.[26] This conference reported on the agronomic evaluation of a number of indigenous Caribbean accessions of Leucaena carried out at the UFS to determine its use for forage, green manure, wood, windbreak and erosion control. The conference also featured papers from all over the tropics on the agronomy and use of Leucaena. The International Symposium on Nitrogen Economy in Tropical Soils was held in Trinidad from 9 to 14 January 1994. According to Ahmad:

Nitrogen is the most important of all major nutrients and its low inherent status in the soil is probably the major cause of poor crop yields in the developing world. The nitrogen pool can be increased through fertilizer use; however, there are associated problems . . . These problems have been engaging the Department of Soil Science of the UWI for some time . . . with the support of the GTZ . . . This symposium is an integral part of this collaboration with the main aim being to communicate a state of the art in several important scientific areas which affect nitrogen economy in tropical soils.[27]

Some of the topics addressed at the conference were: interactions of important nitrogenous fertilizers with different soils; the influence of soil type and cropping system on the losses of applied nitrogen by volatilization, denitrification, leaching and run-off; increasing the persistence of fertilizer nitrogen in the soil system; the importance of nitrogen recycling in conservation and efficient use of the nutrient; possible environmental hazards in the Third World from an increased nitrogen fertilizer use. The proceedings of this symposium have been published.[28]

In 1994 a special conference on Advances in Tropical Agriculture in the Twentieth Century and Prospects for the Twenty-first: TA 2000 was held in Trinidad to commemorate the seventieth anniversary of the journal *Tropical Agriculture*. The goal of the conference was to point to new directions for tropical agriculture in the next century that would allow agriculture to make a more meaningful contribution to the development of tropical countries. A selection of forty-one of the papers presented at the conference, along with abstracts of thirty-four other papers, have been published in a special issue of *Tropical Agriculture*.[29] This publication covers the full range of topics associated with tropical agriculture, including tropical crop and livestock production and utilization, research and education for the development of tropical agriculture, economic issues in agricultural development, tropical soil management and the environment, women in tropical agriculture, agriculture in small island states and plant genetic resources.

Tropical Agriculture

The journal *Tropical Agriculture* was founded in 1924, as a publication of ICTA. According to the editor of the first edition:

The journal should display in broad yet exact terms understandable by all classes of readers what tropical agriculture means, the latest discoveries of research and the many problems that await scientific solution. It should in time become a connecting link between country and country by indicating one another's progress or difficulties. It should also become a bond of union between past students, some of whom are already at work in the tropical world.[30]

Four issues of the journal are published each year and continue to document tropical agricultural research that could contribute to the development of agriculture in the region. According to Gumbs,[31] *Tropical Agriculture*:

> has made a significant contribution to tropical agriculture development through the publication of research results on the many constraints to tropical agriculture development. Many of these findings have been implemented in the tropics and the journal continues to be a source of information to researchers in tropical, subtropical, and temperate regions. In the early years of the journal most of the articles were in the areas of crops and soil science but today the coverage has increased substantially to include other technological areas, for example, livestock production and mechanization, and topics in the social sciences, for example, economics of agricultural production and agricultural extension methodologies. Significant contributions have been made in these areas. The journal recognizes the need to address both the technological and sociological constraints if tropical agriculture is to develop. Technology must be relevant to the social context in which it is to be applied if it is to be successfully adopted and sustained ... The policy of the journal is to address the practical aspects of tropical agricultural production and improvement. It is concerned with the applications of science and technology to the understanding and removal of constraints to tropical agriculture and not the results of basic science research on topics that pertain to agriculture.

The contribution of the journal to agricultural development was also endorsed by the UWI chancellor, Sir Shridath Ramphal,[32] in his message on the occasion of the seventieth anniversary of *Tropical Agriculture* in 1994. He stated: "The journal and the UWI Faculty of Agriculture have made significant contributions to agricultural development in the region and therefore to the general economic and social progress of its people." One such contribution noted by Ramphal was that the "agro-ecological approach to tropical farming was espoused in Trinidad as long ago as the 1930s by the late Professor Frederick Hardy, the first scientist on the staff of the Department of Chemistry and Soil Science of the Imperial College of Tropical Agriculture".[33] Ramphal also stated that this approach should be the one to guide the sustainable development of tropical agriculture into the next century.

The Herbarium

The Herbarium was established in Port of Spain, Trinidad, in 1887 to service the agricultural needs of the colony. In 1960 it was moved to the UWI campus as part of the Faculty of Agriculture. The Herbarium is a national archive that houses a collection of preserved, dried plant specimens. The services of the Herbarium include teaching and research; and the identification of plants for biological control programmes, local medicines, as well as plants that are toxic to livestock and domesticated animals.

According to Pemberton,[34] the Herbarium in its 110 years may be described as one of the "lesser known scientific institutions of Trinidad and Tobago . . . [and one that is] unique to the English speaking Caribbean . . . The Herbarium enjoys the status as the oldest institution on the St Augustine Campus of the UWI".

Agricultural Policy Formulation in the Region

The UWI, through the School (Faculty) of Agriculture, has played a distinct role in policy formulation in the Caribbean region, with particular regard to CARICOM. The faculty has been invited annually to participate in the Meetings of the Standing Committee of Ministers of Agriculture (SCMA) of CARICOM and to present a report on its activities. This avenue allows the faculty to advise the ministers on matters of regional policy and also allows an input from the ministers on the directions that the university should take to improve its contribution to agricultural development of the region.

One example of such direction to the university was the suggestions to upgrade the UWI BSc degree programme in agriculture. These suggestions came out of debates at the SCMA meetings over the period 1986 to 1989, on the need for more hands-on training for agriculture undergraduates. Accordingly, at the 1989 SCMA meeting in Roseau, Dominica, the UWI Faculty of Agriculture presented proposals for three science-based and technology-oriented BSc degrees: crop production, livestock production and a general agriculture. The university did not quite accept the notion of a Bachelor of Technology degree, but it did establish CEPAT and the BSc degree in agribusiness management.

The faculty and its members have also been called upon to provide specific inputs into regional agricultural development. Important examples have been the contributions to the Regional Food and Nutrition Strategy that was put forward by CARICOM, the establishment of the Common External Tariff (CET) of CARICOM and more recently the formulation of the CARICOM Agricultural Regional Transformation Programme (RTP).

Conclusion

Parasram[35] has labelled the ICTA, UWI, CARDI continuum – spanning 1921 to the present time – as a centre of excellence based in Trinidad. He states:

St Augustine has been the site of the centre of excellence – many of the buildings of ICTA are still there; the streets of the town around the campus bear the names of ICTA principals and teachers; for example Watts Trace, Cheesman Avenue, Hardy Drive, Evans Street, Baker Street. Milner Hall is still here, the Frederick Hardy and The Sir Frank Stockdale buildings still stand. CARDI is headquartered there and so too is the St Augustine Campus of the University of the West Indies. The continuing vitality of agricultural research and education at CARDI and the Faculty of Agriculture of the UWI is a tribute to the patience, understanding vision and wisdom of all those persons who ensured that the research did not die, despite changes in control, financing and direction. It must be a proud record. Given the support of government, a strong demand and support from producers, and a broadened regional focus, small developing countries can indeed sustain centres of excellence.

Higher education is poised to continue to make a substantial contribution to agricultural development of the region and, in this regard, it is clear that this must take place through joint and integrated programmes and collaboration by the TLIs and the UWI's School of Agriculture. With respect to collaboration, in the first instance, the UWI is committed to the strengthening of its relationships with the TLIs. As mentioned earlier, several discussions have been held to further the collaboration between the UWI and the TLIs. With respect to agriculture, the aim is to ensure that there is a seamless transfer of students from the TLIs to the UWI's School of Agriculture. This will entail the streamlining of course programmes and syllabuses, so that students graduating from the TLIs would be accorded automatic matriculation to UWI. At the second level, there should be collaboration between the TLIs and the UWI in research and postgraduate supervision. The TLIs and CARDI can provide the facilities and local supervision for UWI postgraduate students.

The TLIs could also allow the opportunity for UWI students to get involved in teaching, as part of their training. As well, the collaboration will allow student research to be more targetted to the problems of the particular territories of the university.

The UWI is also targetted to make a substantial contribution to agricultural development in the region in the area of agricultural policy formulation. One way in which this role will be fulfilled is through the CARICOM Agricultural Regional Transformation Programme (RTP). This programme was endorsed by the Heads of Government of CARICOM at their meeting in Bridgetown, Barbados in August 1996. Its aim is to revitalize and re-equip the agricultural sector of the Caribbean to play a more proactive role in economic development, notwithstanding the changes that are due to overtake the regional agricultural sector with the directions provided by the Uruguay Round of GATT and the rulings against certain provisions of the European Union's preferential banana trading arrangement by the World Trade Organization (WTO).

The UWI has been given the chairmanship of two of the RTP's sub-programmes – human resource development and agribusiness development. The human resources subprogramme has as its objectives:

1. to identify, on an ongoing basis, the demand for agricultural training, and assess the ability of existing programmes to provide required training;
2. to plan and implement training programmes for private and public sector businesses interested in pursuing agricultural investments as elements of their expansion and diversification strategy;
3. to build a cadre of high quality, trained human resources at the national level, to focus particularly on problem solving and farm/fisheries management for farmers, fishers and their organizations within the agricultural sector.

The objectives of the agribusiness development subprogramme are:

1. to stimulate high levels of investment within agriculture;
2. to strengthen agribusiness enterprises in the region; and
3. to promote the expansion and diversification of agribusiness activities in the region.

Through the RTP, therefore, higher education has an important role in the future development of agriculture in the region. In the future, however, the main contribution of higher education to regional agricultural development will remain in the areas of teaching and research. Nevertheless, the role for the university in the area of advice on policy formulation will become increasingly important. The changes that are likely to regional and international agriculture will call for improved capability in the region in policy formulation and negotiation, and the ability to quickly commission and execute studies that will form the basis for advice to establish negotiating positions as well as to formulate policy responses. The university must be prepared to play an increasing role as a consultant and resource to regional governments. This is important, since while there are a number of agencies, international and hemispheric, that can also assist regional governments in this process, the nature and sensitivity of these matters requires that Caribbean states consolidate an appropriate *regional capacity* under the auspices of the CARICOM secretariat. It is hoped that this will be one of the major outputs of the Regional Transformation Programme.

Notes

1. V. Roberts, *Report on Workshop on Articulating TLI/UWI Programmes in Agriculture* (Cave Hill, Barbados: Tertiary Level Institutions Unit, UWI, 1997).
2. L.A. Wilson, E. Timothy, and E.C. Crichlow, "Report on the Technical and Vocational Training Programmes in the Eastern Caribbean States" (paper, UWI, St Augustine, 1994).
3. Roberts, *Report on Workshop*, 38.
4. Ibid., 18.
5. R.A. Pemberton, "The Evolution of Agricultural Policy in Trinidad and Tobago 1890–1945" (PhD diss., UWI, St Augustine, 1996), 159.
6. K.C. Vernon, *Soil and Land-Use Surveys, No. 1. Jamaica: Parish of St Catherine* (Trinidad: Regional Research Centre, Imperial College of Tropical Agriculture, 1958).
7. A.F. Posnette, *Fifty Years of Cocoa Research in Trinidad and Tobago* (St Augustine, Trinidad: Cocoa Research Unit, UWI, 1986).
8. J. Spence, "History and Present Activities of the Cocoa Research Unit", *Extension Newsletter* 26, no. 2 (1997).
9. Cocoa Research Unit, *Report for 1995* (St Augustine, Trinidad: UWI, 1995).
10. K.C. Vernon, *Soil and Land-Use Surveys, No. 10. Jamaica: Parish of St Mary* (Trinidad: Regional Research Centre, Imperial College of Tropical Agriculture, 1960).

11. D. Smith, *Correlation of the Soils of the Commonwealth Caribbean, Puerto Rico, The Virgin Islands and Guyana. Soil and Land-Use Surveys, No. 27* (St Augustine, Trinidad: Department of Soil Science, Faculty of Agriculture, UWI, 1983).
12. N. Ahmad, *Nitrogen Economy in Tropical Soils* (The Netherlands: Kluwer Academic Publishers, 1996), ix.
13. L.A. Wilson, "Report Root Crop Programme 1967–1971" (paper, Faculty of Agriculture, UWI, 1971).
14. S. Parasram, *Centre of Excellence Based in Trinidad, West Indies: A Historical View,* ISNAR Staff Notes, no. 90-85 (The Hague: ISNAR, 1990).
15. CEPAT, *Review of CEPAT's Activities 1990–1995 and Strategic Plan 1996–2000,* vol. 1, *Main Report* (St Augustine, Trinidad: CEPAT, 1996).
16. M.C. Alkin, K.A. Adams, and M. Cuthbert, *External Evaluation Report of the Caribbean Agricultural Extension Project Phase II* (St Paul: Department of Agricultural Extension, University of Minnesota, 1984).
17. Ibid.
18. J. O'Donnell, A. Coutu, and V. Malone, *Evaluation of the USAID/RDO/C Agricultural Research and Extension Project (AREP)* (Winrock International Institute for Agricultural Development, 1991).
19. J. Chapman, J. Lancini, and B. Greene, *CARDI/UWI Agricultural Research and Extension Project: Aid Grant No 538-0164. Final Evaluation Report* (United Kingdom: Cargill Technical Services, 1994).
20. Ibid.
21. *Extension Newsletter* 1, no. 1 (1970).
22. F.A. Gumbs, *Soil and Water Conservation Methods for the Caribbean* (St Augustine, Trinidad: Department of Agricultural Extension, UWI, 1987).
23. C.A. Pemberton, *Farm and Home Management Business Record Book* (St Augustine, Trinidad: Regional Extension Communications Unit, UWI, 1990).
24. C.A. Pemberton, "Address of the President", *Proceedings of the Seventeenth West Indies Agricultural Economics Conference* (St Augustine, Trinidad: Department of Agricultural Economics and Farm Management for the Caribbean Agro-Economic Society, 1986).
25. L.A. Wilson, "Reflections of the First International Symposium on Tropical Root Crops, April 2–8, 1967", address at Eleventh Symposium of the International Symposium on Tropical Root Crops, 19–24 October 1997.
26. T.U. Ferguson and G.W. Garcia (eds), *Leucaena in Agricultural Development: Proceedings of the First International Conference on Leucaena, 10–13 July 1989* (Port of Spain, Trinidad: Faculty of Agriculture, UWI, 1989).
27. Ahmad, *Nitrogen Economy in Tropical Soils,* ix.
28. Ibid.
29. C.A. Pemberton, Foreword, *Advances in Tropical Agriculture in the 20th Century and Prospects for the 21st,* Special Issue of *Tropical Agriculture* (1997), vii.
30. *Tropical Agriculture* 1, no. 1 (1924), 2.
31. F.A. Gumbs, "Message from the Editor-in-Chief on the Occasion of the 70th Anniversary of Tropical Agriculture", *Tropical Agriculture* 71, no. 1 (1994), v.

32. S. Ramphal, "Message from the Chancellor on the Occasion of the 70th Anniversary of Tropical Agriculture", *Tropical Agriculture* 71, no. 1 (1994), iv.
33. Ibid.
34. R.A. Pemberton, "The Trinidad Botanical Gardens and Colonial Resource Development, 1818–1899" (paper presented at the 29th Annual Conference of the Association of Caribbean Historians, 1997).
35. S. Parasram, *Centre of Excellence Based in Trinidad, West Indies: A Historical View*, ISNAR Staff Notes, no. 90-85 (The Hague: ISNAR, 1990).

8

A Vision of Transformational Leadership for the University of the West Indies

Glenford D. Howe and Earle Newton

Introduction

In today's postmodern and rapidly changing societies, the principal challenge facing educational leaders and administrators is that of creating and maintaining effective and excellent institutions. This is of crucial importance to the Caribbean with its limited financial and material resources and in the light of the significant role education must inevitably play in regional development. The University of the West Indies (UWI), as the 'designated regional university', has publicly acknowledged its obligation to support the growth and development of the region and its people.[1] In this way the UWI is in step with the thinking that as the twenty-first century approaches, organizations may be well placed to effect unanticipated advances for society, and to resolve the most complex problems by virtue of their ability to mobilize resources and transcend, to some degree, political boundaries.[2] The constraints under which the UWI operates notwithstanding, we believe that it is well poised and capable of meeting this demand.

In light of this, our vision of educational leadership is one which has as its objective the engaging and transformation of the malaise and lack of effectiveness and excellence found in many of our schools and educational institutions. Mitchell and Tucker observed that because we have defined leadership as the capacity to take charge and get things done, we have overlooked the importance of teamwork and comprehensive improvement. They further warned that we must avoid seeing leadership as aggressive action and envisage it as a way of thinking about ourselves, our jobs and the nature of the educational process.[3] This is the essence of transformational leadership.

Burns, with whom the theory of transformational leadership originated, defines it as "a relationship of mutual stimulation and elevation that converts followers into leaders and may convert leaders into moral agents",[4] and later in the same text he states that it "occurs when one or more persons engage with others in such a way that leaders and followers raise one another to higher levels of motivation and morality".[5] Bass, who further developed the theory, observed that leaders are truly transformational when, through their beliefs, words and actions, they create or increase awareness of what is right, good, important and beautiful, when they help followers to fulfil their needs for achievement and self-actualization, and when they foster in followers high moral maturity and inspire them to go beyond their own self-interest for the good of the group, the organization, and the society. Bass then warns against pseudo-transformational leadership which also motivates and transforms but does so in support of special interests and self-interest at the expense of the collective good. He concludes:

If leadership is truly transformational, its charisma or idealized influence is characterized by high moral and ethical standards. Its inspirational motivation provides followers with challenges and meanings for engaging in shared goals and undertakings. Its intellectual stimulation helps followers to question assumptions and to generate more creative solutions to problems. Its individual consideration treats each follower as an individual and provides coaching, mentoring and growth opportunities.[6]

In practical terms what does all this mean? We feel constrained to elaborate these general characteristics of transformational leadership as they apply to professionally staffed educational institutions. In educational institutions, transformational leadership is guided by a powerful vision and purpose that emphasizes the importance of learners, parents and the community as a whole in the schooling process and, holding high expectations for all learners, is especially sensitive to the special needs of the disadvantaged. It is dynamic, reducing the difference in status between leader and follower, boss and manager, and emphasizes participative decision making based on consensual or facilitative power that manifests itself through, rather than over, other people, as Leithwood observed.[7] It is moral, mature and inspirational, grounded in a firm knowledge of the law and the mores of the community, sensitive to the needs and circumstances of the environment and rooted in a flexible inclusive knowledge base which incorporates gender, class and race issues. Transformational leadership provides intellectual stimulation and fosters the development and acceptance of group norms and values, while respecting and valuing individuality. It is reflective, professional and supportive of the growth and development of each individual. It is conscious of the role and significance of, and actively promotes, traditions, symbols and rituals in the life of the organization.

We believe that a transformational approach to educational leadership is not only desirable but, indeed, imperative and appropriate if schools and universities such as the UWI are to respond effectively to the multiple problems, challenges and opportunities with which they and the region are currently faced. While transactional leadership (often placed at the other extreme of the continuum), which emphasizes management and doing things right, is important for organizational maintenance, it is our view and that of Leithwood[8] and others, that it is transformational leadership, comprising the components we indicated above and which is more focused on doing the right thing, that is the crucial factor in achieving organizational change and excellence. This multifaceted or multidimensional vision of transformational educational leadership, which we are articulating for the UWI, is the outcome of our dialogue during the course ED61 C: Effective Leadership in Education and other related courses taught in the Master's of Education programme offered by the School of Education, Cave Hill campus, our reading of the literature on excellent schools and dynamic leaders, as well as our experiences as teachers, observers and administrators at the UWI. The public debates on radio, television and other public fora on the weaknesses and strengths of the educational system in Barbados and other Caribbean countries also helped to shape our vision of educational leadership. In other words, it is a vision grounded in, and emerging out of, theory, practice, dialogue and reflection on the debates about leadership, which reflect multiple, even competing, assumptions and emerging from different paradigms.

Our vision of educational leadership is also premised on the belief stated earlier that leadership, which we regard as a dynamic "social relationship, a social dyad, involving both leaders and followers",[9] is a major factor in the creation and maintenance of effectiveness and excellence in schools, even though the nature and degree of the leadership effect remains a moot point among academicians, not least because the relationship is complex and not easily subject to empirical verification.[10] Even though educational institutions have been seeking primarily to improve schools through retraining, restructuring or strategies of empowerment, increasingly educational theoreticians and practitioners alike are coming to recognize the vital role effective leadership plays in the process of change and improvement in schools.

The subject of educational leadership, as many authors have recognized, is a particularly difficult and illusive one to deal with and not only because people perceive the notion of leadership, and more particularly effective leadership, from multiple perspectives. More fundamentally, the question of leadership raises numerous methodological and conceptual issues, provokes value judgements and dilemmas, and is affected by many social, political, cultural and psychological forces. The high level of dissonance in the debate about leadership is, in other words, rooted in underlying epistemologic and ideological differences; differences reflected and rooted in broader controversies over the political nature of the construction and representation of knowledge, morals and values, and the purposes of education, among other issues. It is against this background of turmoil and lack of clarity in the field that we will seek to articulate a new type of leadership and administration for the UWI which, it is hoped, will provide the institution's leadership with a fresh and proactive way of thinking about and doing their tasks. This leadership that we envision represents what Starratt calls, "leadership of substance – a leadership of ideas, of vision, of commitment to deeply held human values that can be translated into farsighted educational programmes and humane institutional structures".[11] It is leadership diametrically opposed to that articulated by the dominant positivistic philosophies, paradigms and practices current in the field of educational administration and leadership.

UWI and the Quest for Excellence

Since our vision of leadership is inextricably linked to the creation of excellence and effectiveness in educational institutions, it is necessary that we describe what we mean by an effective or excellent school. While the epistemologic and ideologic differences that characterize the leadership debates make it difficult to define definitively the meaning of effectiveness and excellence in schooling, it is nevertheless possible to identify some main characteristics. According to Beare et al., and Dufour and Eaker, the concept of effectiveness has to do with the achieving of some predetermined goal(s),[12] but we would add, achieving these goals in an eminent degree. They believe, as we do, that effective or excellent schools are characterized by strong administrative leadership; a climate of expectation which serves to lift and motivate students to better performance; an orderly but not oppressive environment; a strong emphasis on instruction; a strong commitment to staff and student development; a clear vision of what students are attempting to accomplish and what they are trying to become; a core of important values; a commitment to a moral vision; the monitoring of what is important and a commitment to continued renewal.

While cognizance of the attributes of the effective school is of utmost significance in order to embark on school renewal and improvement, equal attention also needs to be given to the social, cultural and political contexts within which the schooling process takes place, for as Kimbrough and Nunnery assert, the school (and by extension colleges and universities) often mirrors the problems, concerns and successes of the society in which it exists.[13] Thus, while acknowledging there are alternative conceptual frameworks that may be used to analyse educational institutions, it is our view that schools are fundamentally open systems, in perpetual interaction with the external environment, and consequently are faced with the numerous moral and value dilemmas that may characterize that external environment. For example, skewed economic policies that attempt to reduce every aspect of life to cost-benefit analysis have generated great stress and anxiety about job security and other issues among all workers, not least teachers and university lecturers.

Likewise, during the 1980s International Monetary Fund (IMF) and World Bank instigated structural adjustment programmes had negative effects on education throughout the Caribbean and other developing parts of the world. During the period from 1977 to 1987 in Jamaica, for instance, expenditure on primary education declined in real terms by approximately 30 percent, teacher–pupil ratio increased, there was a persistence of low attendance patterns, and a decline in performance levels.[14] As in the case of escalating crime, drug abuse and other social ills, the school is often severely affected.

This conceptualization of educational institutions that emphasizes their dynamic and interactive relationship with the external environment most adequately reflects the reality of most Barbadian and West Indian educational institutions even though most, like the UWI, may have a highly bureaucratic mode of operation, or reflect in varying degrees the attributes of alternative models or conceptualizations of schools.

In the following section of this paper we will be focusing primarily on the UWI, but will also make references to other educational institutions. Our approach will be to try to show how the various components or aspects of the leadership we envision (as indicated in our opening section) can transform and enhance the overall quality and effectiveness of the UWI in terms of meeting the needs of its stakeholders and achieving its overall aims. To this end, we will seek to demonstrate how the vision we articulate can be imbued in the structures, policies, programmes and processes at the UWI. In so doing, we will, to some extent, highlight those organizational arrangements currently in place at the UWI that can frustrate the realization of our vision, and further suggest how these arrangements may be reconfigured to "carry the vision into the routines of everyday school life".[15]

In this paper, the term vision is used to mean "a dynamic source of leadership that imbues other aspects of leadership with a special energy and significance".[16] It is our belief and that of Dufour and Eaker[17] as well, that excellent schools have a vision that provides a sense of purpose, direction and ideal future. It involves, as Greenfield[18] asserts, the exercise of moral imagination and is focused on, as Sergiovanni[19] argues, the building of a shared covenant, or binding and solemn agreement between principals, teachers, students and parents to honour certain values, goals, and beliefs.

Part of the difficulty of articulating a vision of transformational leadership for any institution is that there is always the implicit (sometimes explicit) suggestion that something is fundamentally wrong with the institution, that something is broken and needs fixing. In addition, doubts may be cast on those within the organization who are responsible for its leadership and management. What is usually not so well recognized is that transformational leadership is also about improving, enhancing, making things better – even those things considered to be already of good quality. Thus, when we speak of transformational leadership within the context of the UWI, we are speaking not simplistically or necessarily of fundamental reforms, or getting rid of, or abandoning, but essentially of adding quality and value to what exists (such as the level of academic discourse and writing) and is regarded by the university's stakeholders and others as being of good quality.

Nevertheless, it seems appropriate to begin with the acknowledgment that in spite of its significant achievements, all has not gone well at the UWI since its establishment in 1948. For example, the UWI has evolved an elaborate, burdensome, bureaucratic structure; there is an enormous amount of red tape; there is inadequate interaction and dialogue between staff and students on the one hand, and senior administrators on the other; and there is a problem of low morale and a problem with collegiality. In addition, there is inadequate integration of the individual's needs, interests and potential with the goals of the organization; many staff feel that they have little control over their job situation as a result of, among other things, the overcentralization of power; many noncampus stakeholders feel they have been short-changed, if not ignored by the UWI; and many students feel that there is an absence of adequate congeniality on the campuses.

The recognition of these difficulties has been the basis of two major efforts on the part of the university to initiate and implement changes throughout its system. The first effort in 1984, aimed to restructure the university to give the campuses greater autonomy so the university could respond and contribute more effectively to the perceived national needs of its contributing members.[20] This attempt achieved some success but might more accurately be described as a failure.[21] The second major restructuring exercise at the UWI began in 1993–94 with the *Report of the Chancellor's Commission on the Governance of the UWI*. The commission had been requested to review the governance of the university in light of its current and prospective developmental role in the region, and relevant developments in university administration and practice elsewhere. It was asked to pay particular attention to the need to:[22]

1. Achieve the greatest possible cost effectiveness in the operations of the university.
2. Speed up the processes of decision making.
3. Assign well defined lines of responsibility to the principal officers and organs of the university.
4. Further clarify the relationship between the UWI Centre and the campuses.

5. Achieve greater transparency in, and accountability for, the university's operations, including specific identification of the financial implications of decisions made and projects being undertaken, as well as more adequate and timely financial reporting.
6. Improve communications between central administration and other parts of the university community.
7. Make provision for the increasing importance of outreach activities in the work of the institutions.
8. Provide for greater participation in the management of the university, particularly by outside persons.
9. Deal with any other major matters pertaining to governance.

The identification of these areas for special consideration clearly suggests that the university's officials had now come to realize that the UWI was not performing as efficiently and effectively as it could because of the dysfunctions of its bureaucratic structures and relations. Unlike the recommendations of 1984, which focused on structural reform, those of the vice chancellor's commission recognized, in addition, that "human action and intention" are, as Greenfield and Ribbins put it, "the stuff from which organizations are made".[23] Recognizing the need for a qualitative shift in the management of the university, the commission stressed the need for clarity, competence, accountability, cost-effectiveness and integrity.

As part of its efforts to transform itself, the UWI has developed a strategic plan for the period 1997–2002 (in part, a continuum of the exercise initiated in a previous Ten-Year Development Plan) which postulated that the UWI must introduce important changes in its methods of operation and discard the 'business as usual' syndrome.[24] The plan outlines the following four objectives for the UWI:

1. To enhance its role as a development resource for the peoples and the countries of the region by training more of its young people in disciplines critical to achieving international competitiveness and helping to improve socioeconomic conditions in the countries, alleviate poverty, improve the quality of life and sustain the cultural values that characterize the people of the region.
2. To cooperate closely with the region's tertiary level institutions to respond more effectively to the human resource needs of the region

and satisfy the aspirations of the citizens to equip themselves to achieve improving standards of living in the face of the highly competitive conditions that the technological revolution and the globalization process have created.
3. To be a student friendly university that provides high quality instruction and a congenial atmosphere for students to pursue their academic and other university activities.
4. To make the university more financially self-reliant by increasing its internal efficiency, among other things.

Conscious of the changing international economic and political environment and the need for the countries of the region to respond to these challenges, the plan seeks to articulate a vision for the UWI whereby it assists the countries and the peoples of the region to make an effective response. Thus, for example, the plan is predicated on the need for the university, through its research and training, to assist in devising solutions to the economic and social problems of the region; it articulates the imperative for the university to improve its image among its students, benefactors and financiers, and it seeks innovatively to improve the all-round ability of its graduates to work as leaders in their environment and contribute meaningfully to the amelioration of social ills.[25]

The plan also articulates a vision for the university that involves among other things:

1. enhancing the standing of the people of the region in international fora by contributing meaningfully to the world stock of knowledge on development issues and to the arts and literature; and
2. providing a congenial atmosphere for its on-campus and off-campus students and maintaining a friendly and mutually beneficial relationship with its alumni.

To these ends, the overall vision of the Cave Hill campus, for example, is to create a friendly and stimulating intellectual environment and maintain the highest standards of teaching, research and service to the region.[26] It is against the background of these attempts at change at the UWI, as reflected in the 1984 and 1994 reports, and the *Strategic Plan*, and the articulation of a powerful and refreshing vision, that we now turn to illustrate how the transformational type of leadership we envision may help in the process of people improvement and the quest for excellence at the UWI.

Transformational Leadership for the UWI

It seems appropriate to begin this section of the paper with the observation that in many institutions, not least universities, it is possible for the interests of the people who make up the organization, including the various stakeholders, to be frustrated by the bureaucratic mode of operation. For example, students of the UWI frequently complain of the impersonal manner in which they are treated by some staff, but part of the problem has to do with the fact that the university's bureaucracy has frustrated and demoralized many staff members. In light of this, we believe leadership that privileges the value of the human person and provides personalized or individualized support, would significantly enhance the quality of student and staff life on the campus. A more congenial atmosphere would certainly make the student feel more a part of university life and would help to achieve the campus' vision of providing a friendly learning environment. On the other hand, emphasizing collegiality and fostering a "relationship of mutual stimulation and elevation" would go a long way to enhancing staff experience in the work place. Emphasizing collegiality, which has to do with the extent to which teachers, lecturers, and top administrators and principals share common workplace values, engage in specific conversation about their work and help each other to participate in the work of the institution, would also have the spin-off effect of enhancing congeniality and making student life easier and more rewarding. Leadership that emphasizes collegiality and the collaboration involved could also further enhance the level of academic discourse and writing at the UWI, and its international competitiveness.

Emphasis on collegiality and congeniality could also be the basis for creating an atmosphere in which teachers convey expectations of high performance to the students since much of the staff behaviour associated with demotivation of students (for example, showing a lack of interest in them as persons or in their views, asking for questions but never answering them, using concepts and classification categories that students are unfamiliar with, grading in a manner that is not transparently fair, coming to class late or unprepared) would be significantly reduced.[27] In other words, leadership which encourages collegiality would simultaneously encourage professionalism among staff. Professional behaviour would mean that staff would display elements of peer judgement or self-policing and, among other things, adhere to a code of ethics.

In this quest to enhance staff–student relationships and experiences, the issue of strong instructional leadership, both direct and indirect, acquires much importance. Direct instructional leadership refers to the principals, deans and heads at the campuses working closely with their lecturers and other staff on matters pertaining to the classroom, staff development, student performance and curricula. Such activities would include curriculum planning, teacher observation, informal feedback sessions with teachers or selection of instructional material.[28] Indirect instructional leadership activities or types of behaviour that deal with the school's internal and external environment, the physical and cultural contexts surrounding the classroom, teaching and curricula, and the effect that the actions of top administrators have on teachers, are emphasized in our vision of leadership for the UWI. Indirect instructional activities are critical because they can constrain or create opportunities for what teachers do, and can also influence what teachers want to do and how they respond to constraints and opportunities.

One implication of our vision of strong instructional leadership at the university is that it may mean that some leaders may require further training so they can engage in more meaningful instructional leadership which could, in turn, help in achieving the goals of the UWI we alluded to earlier. Another implication or requirement is that for strong instructional leadership to be fruitfully implemented, teachers and others at the UWI will need to be enabled. As mentioned previously, the bureaucracy of the UWI has had a disempowering effect on many staff. Our view on the issue of the enabling of teachers is supported by much of the recent literature which argues that school improvement must be based on giving teachers the discretion, the support, the preparation and guidance necessary to get the job done.[29] At the UWI, the adoption of school-based or site-based management could be effectively utilized to enhance staff participation in the decision making process. It is now imperative that the UWI go further than merely attempting to devolve power to the campuses and reducing the influence of central administration.

What is now required is for the campus leadership to give the faculties and departments greater authority to respond to the needs and challenges they are encountering. Thus, for example, faculties need to be given more say in the matter of admittance of 'mature' students since the Registry, which operates according to strict matriculation guidelines, has tended – in spite of UWI policy to increase the number of mature students – to be hesitant about those who do not meet the stipulated matriculation requirements. More emphasis on site-based management, as well as a team approach to leadership, would also allow individual staff and departments to more effectively engage in initiatives beneficial to the UWI and its stakeholders. The departments would be able to more effectively respond in terms of curriculum change, staff appointments, the securing of needed resources and the rewarding of productive staff. This would also assist in bringing about a 'bottom up' rather than a 'top down' approach to management, as currently exists at the UWI.

In spite of its decisive advantages, however, the benefits of site-based management can easily be subverted if one level of UWI bureaucracy is simply juxtaposed to another. Sackney and Dibski have pointed out that organizations can maintain control over the actions of those in the lower levels by decentralizing decision making but prescribing the "rules of the game".[30] Accountability mechanisms that are imposed under school-based management can, they argue, result in power remaining decidedly in the hands of those at the top of the organization. This could, for example, result if the newly created Board for Undergraduate Studies, Board for Graduate Studies and Research, and the Board for Non-Campus Countries and Distance Education are overzealous in carrying out their stated and perceived duties.

In our vision of transformational leadership for the UWI, we see emphasis on accountability as being the flip side of staff, faculty or department empowerment. As noted before, the issue of accountability was regarded by the chancellor's commission as being of utmost significance. We see true accountability as transcending mere monitoring of the activities of staff, department or faculty. It does not require these parties to follow rigidly specified regulations and requirements. As teachers and administrators at the UWI, we agree with Starratt that rather than a mindless obedience to the authorities, the response to the call for educational reform requires from staff – be they lecturers, principals or other persons – moral imagination and leadership that fosters the acceptance of group norms but respects and appreciates individuality. This moral leadership, as Starratt rightly suggests, interprets policy in the light of local circumstances and implements policy that encourages local understanding of the meaning and values behind the policies. This brings us to another critical aspect of our vision of leadership, namely, that it should be rooted in morals and values since we regard all educational institutions as 'moral institutions' and senior administrators as 'moral agents'.

It is crucial that leaders at the UWI, as in other schools, be competent to take action and make decisions in a distinctly moral manner. According to Greenfield, distinctly moral conduct means that a leader's or administrator's behaviour is grounded in deliberate reflection upon, and consideration of, the moral consequences of his or her decisions, actions, school policies and practices.[31] Educational leadership at the UWI and elsewhere should be based on morals, values and ethics in light of, among other things, the fact that the leaders face moral value conflicts on a daily basis. Through our experience on the job, we have come to realize that the leaders and other administrators at the UWI are often faced with the dilemma of acting in the face of competing and often conflicting moral values associated with such issues as good pedagogical practice, compliance with organizational rules and regulations, political expediency, educational outcomes, another's needs, organizational efficiency and effectiveness, and the use of power and influence to persuade others to a particular point of view or course of action. These issues, as we have seen, are central concerns of both the chancellor's commission and the *Strategic Plan*. For example, the UWI leaders are constantly faced with the dilemmas raised by competition from questionable offshore institutions, as well as by the distinction between achieving effectiveness and subscribing to economic determinism that privileges economic efficiency. Likewise, moral dilemmas are raised in the debates over greater public access to higher education and the maintenance of 'high academic' standards at the UWI, and the various quota systems presently imposed on, or in any case used by, certain faculties.

In the formulation and articulation of a vision for the UWI, moral issues such as whose vision is it, in what standards of good practice is the vision rooted and how is the vision to be achieved, are of utmost importance and demonstrate the complexity and importance of the moral dimension of educational leadership. The many moral and ethical dilemmas that arise on a daily basis also make it imperative for the leaders to have a fairly good grasp of the law, especially provisions relating to the fundamental rights of the individual. The issue of moral and legal competence can, in fact, be regarded as being of crucial importance to the successful implementation of change, improvement and reform at the UWI.

The issue of visioning or purposing is also worthy of independent consideration because it is at the heart of our vision for educational leadership at the UWI. As we have seen, the UWI has a clearly articulated vision on paper. The bulk of the educational literature indicates that emphasizing visioning is a critical and central aspect of dynamic leadership and the creation of excellent schools. Successful schooling is regarded as being premised on the use of purposing in the creation of a binding and solemn agreement between principals, teachers, students and parents to honour certain values, goals and beliefs. It has been our observation both as teacher and administrator at the UWI that inadequate effort has been given to visibly and powerfully conveying the written vision of the UWI to staff, students and the wider community, and seeking reaction and commitment to it.

It is also likely that a more systematic effort at emphasizing purposing at the UWI can help to give its stakeholders a clearer sense of the direction of the university, and help to alleviate problems of staff and student alienation resulting from an overbearing bureaucracy. Indeed, we should be cognizant that, as Gronn asserts, antecedent to both efficiency and effectiveness is some overall abiding purpose or end, a moral economy that provides people's willingness to cooperate with its justification.[32] To effect this, however, the top administrators must recognize the importance of interacting with students and other stakeholders on a regular basis. Emphasizing visioning is also important if the UWI is to achieve its goal of enhancing the standing of the people of the region internationally. Leaders at the UWI can more effectively articulate and implement their vision for the institution if they pay more attention to the use of symbols and meaning. Bolman and Deal have argued that leaders, in order to better fulfil the psychological needs of their followers and other stakeholders, should emphasize the symbolic and cultural aspects of leadership, that is, ritual, ceremony and other symbolic forms.[33] This is essential to the effort to create a moral order that binds the leader to his followers. In addition, emphasizing symbols also has potential spin-off benefits.

For most universities, the presence of an active and visible student alumni association is generally regarded as being of utmost importance, not least because it helps to raise funds and promote the interests of the university in the broader society. At the Cave Hill campus of the UWI, however, it is generally acknowledged that there is an absence of a strong alumni association. Part of the reason for this is that there is little evidence of emphasis on symbols, ritual and meaning at the campus. Thus many students leave the campus without any sense of affiliation or loyalty to the institution. This in part explains the continued very poor response to membership calls from the Guild of Graduates. By emphasizing symbols and meaning it might be possible to create a stronger and more lasting bond between students and the campus, and help make a reality the desire of many past students to be affiliated to the university. This in turn could also help to get rid of the university's 'ivory tower' or elitist image by engaging the wider society in a more meaningful and collaborative way. The effective use of symbols, ritual and purposing is, however, only likely to be the result of a dynamic and proactive approach on the part of the university's leaders and administrators.

According to Newton, principals in effective schools are assertive leaders who are willing to act independently in the interest of the institution, are committed to school improvements, emphasize instructional leadership and communicate their wishes to the staff, and stress academic standards.[34] In his study of the secondary headship in Barbados, Newton found that the head teachers' conception of the headship involved participatory leadership and good interpersonal relationships, but also assertive, proactive leaders with initiative and enthusiasm for the post, and the ability to guide and motivate their staff in the accomplishment of whatever tasks they undertook.[35]

Achieving all the criteria of excellence in today's turbulent schools and societies obviously requires a special type of leadership. Sergiovanni calls this type "Leadership by Outrage". According to him, leadership by outrage "is a symbolic act that communicates importance and meaning and touches people in ways not possible when leadership is viewed entirely as something objective and calculated".[36] It emanates from the notion that the leader cares deeply and passionately about the school and, thus, is determined to achieve excellence in the classroom by whatever means necessary. Sergiovanni is supported by Peters and Waterman who argue that successful companies exhibit a "bias for action".[37] Likewise, Peters and Austin argue:

Courage and self-respect are the lion's share of passion: It's hanging in long after others have gotten bored or given up; it's refusing to leave well enough alone; it means that anything less than the best you can imagine really bothers you, maybe keeps you awake at night. It usually means sticking your neck out: daring to give your best shot to something you care about and asking others to do the same is self-exposing. It asks you to pick sides, to wear your passion on your sleeve, to take a position and remain true to it even under the scrutiny of an audience, when the wish to please, to be accepted, welcomed, can compromise the clearest inner vision. Passion opens you to criticism, disappointment, disillusionment and failure, any one of which is enough to scare off all but the bravest souls.[38]

Thus, as they rightly conclude, the adventure of excellence is not for the faint of heart.

Caution must, however, be taken in exercising leadership by outrage as, more so than for other forms of leadership styles, issues of justice and fairness, and ethical and moral dilemmas are prone to arise in a most problematic way. The recent resignation of the controversial Barbadian, Hallam King, principal of Coleridge and Parry school, clearly illustrated the dangers of practising leadership by outrage. King may have been right to condemn the few teachers who were failing to perform well, but in the end angry trade unions and teachers, and an indecisive Ministry of Education, led to his demise in spite of his popularity with the students. Similarly, the experiences of former principals of other schools, such as the dynamic Charles Pilgrim who was responsible for bringing significant change and improvement to Combermere school during the 1980s, and his eventual resignation in frustration, bear testimony to the risks of practising leadership by outrage.[39] Thus, to be successful, the principal needs to be politically astute and to be able to achieve his or her vision for the school without alienating the institution's multiple constituents and stakeholders, especially those who may be antagonistic to aspects of the vision or his or her mode of operation. Sergiovanni has articulated a strategy he calls "Building in Canvas", which could enable schools to transcend and overcome the constraints of bureaucracy that frustrate the achievement of excellence in schools.

Adopting the "Building in Canvas" approach means that the leader must get his school to reflect the images and values of its bureaucratic sponsors on the one hand, but on the other decisions must be made that count for excellence in schools. This strategy allows school leaders to provide the right public face and thereby achieve the freedom to interpret, decide and function in ways that may have a positive impact on these learning institutions.⁴⁰ It could well be argued that both principals King and Pilgrim might have stood a greater chance of realizing their goals for their respective schools had they adopted the strategies of "Building in Canvas". This is a reasonable point to advance since the adoption of such coping strategies is a reality in other schools. At least one study has shown that in response to insecurity, powerlessness and ambiguity, teachers and principals will tend to ignore or bend the rules, or ensure that in their public performances and statements they keep within the rules and philosophy, as they perceive them, coming from administration.⁴¹ As a result there can be a real dichotomy between what actually happens in schools and what appears to be happening from the outside. The increasing public scrutiny of schools and their politicization, it can be argued, make the adoption of such strategies of utmost importance. School leaders need to be aware of, and know how to handle effectively, the various social, cultural and political forces that impact upon the school.

Conclusion

Clearly, the realization and implementation of the vision of educational leadership outlined above will require as a prerequisite, the retraining of many of the leaders and administrators of the UWI. The new training will inevitably need to be rooted in a knowledge base that is expansive, inclusive, and heavily biased in the recognition of the importance of values and morals. More fundamentally, some UWI leaders may have to come to the realization that leadership is something qualitatively different from management; that there is an urgent need to shift from the present transactional mode of leadership and embrace transformational leadership. We believe, however, that by force of circumstance and the inadequacies of some current practices, many UWI leaders and administrators will eventually have to pay more attention to providing leadership of substance. That is, a type of leadership which privileges innovative and creative ideas, adheres to a clear and powerful vision, and exhibits a commitment to deeply held human values that can be translated into farsighted educational programmes and humane institutional structures, and the achievement of individual and institutional effectiveness and excellence.

Notes

1. *The University of the West Indies Strategic Plan 1997-2002*, rev. ed. (Mona, Jamaica: UWI, 1997), 9.
2. Gill Hickman, *Transforming Organizations to Transform Society* (Richmond: Jepson School of Leadership Studies, 1995).
3. J. Mitchell and S. Tucker, "Leadership as a Way of Thinking", *Educational Leadership* 49, no. 5 (February 1992): 30–35, as cited in L. B. Liontos, "Transformational Leadership", *ERIC Digest*, no. 72 (August 1992).
4. J.M. Burns, *Leadership* (New York: Harper and Row, 1978), 4. Burns uses both transformational and transforming to describe his leadership concept although the latter is more common.
5. Ibid., 20.
6. B.M. Bass, *The Ethics of Transformational Leadership* (New York: Center for Leadership Studies, School of Management, State University of New York, 1996), 4
7. K.A Leithwood, "The Move Toward Transformational Leadership", *Educational Leadership* 49, no. 5 (February 1992): 8–12.
8. Kenneth Leithwood, "Leadership for School Restructuring", *Educational Administration Quarterly* 30, no. 4 (1994): 498–518.
9. Robert O. Slater, "The Sociology of Leadership and Educational Administration", *Educational Administration Quarterly* 31, no. 3 (August 1995): 995.
10. Philip Hallinger and Ronald Heck, "Reassessing the Principal's Role in School Effectiveness: A Review of Empirical Research, 1980–1995", *Educational Administration Quarterly* 32, no. 1 (February 1996): 5
11. Robert Starratt, *Leaders With Vision: The Quest for School Renewal* (California: Corwin Press, 1995), 11.
12. See Headley Beare, Brian Caldwell and Ross H. Millikan, *Creating an Excellent School* (London and New York: Routledge, 1989); Richard Dufour and Robert Eaker, *Creating the New American School: A Principal's Guide to School Improvement* (Indiana: National Educational Service, 1992).
13. Ralph B. Kimbrough and Michael Y. Nunnery, *Educational Administration An Introduction* (New York and London: Macmillan, 1988), 81.
14. Elsie Le Franc, *Consequences of Structural Adjustment: A Review of the Jamaican Experience* (Kingston, Jamaica: Canoe Press, 1994), 46–48.
15. Ibid., xi
16. Ibid., 14.
17. Dufour and Eaker, *Creating the New American School*, 5
18. William Greenfield, "Articulating values and ethics in Administrator preparation", in *Educational Administration in a Pluralistic Society*, edited by Colleen A. Capper (Albany: State University of New York Press, 1993), 279.
19. See Thomas J. Sergiovanni, *Value-Added Leadership: How to Get Extraordinary Performances in Schools* (New York: Harcourt, Brace, Jovanovich, 1990), 55–71.
20. See Sir Roy Marshall (chairman), *The Marshall Report on the University of the*

West Indies (Cave Hill, Barbados: UWI, 1986).
21. See Neville V. Nicholls and Ivan L. Head (co-chairmen), *A New Structure: The Regional University in the 1990s and Beyond. Report of the Chancellor's Commission on the Governance of UWI* (Mona, Jamaica: UWI, 1994), 12
22. Ibid., 3.
23. Thomas Greenfield and Peter Ribbins, *Greenfield on Educational Administration Towards a Humane Science* (London and New York: Routledge, 1993), 1
24. *The University of the West Indies Strategic Plan 1997-2002*
25. Ibid., 5-6.
26. Ibid., 78
27. George B Vaughan and associates, *Dilemmas of Leadership* (San Francisco: Jossey-Bass Publishers, 1992), 90.
28. See Sister Paula Kleine-Kracht, "Indirect Instructional Leadership. An Administrator's Choice", *Educational Administration Quarterly* 29, no. 2 (May 1993): 187-212; Samuel E. Krug, "Instructional Leadership A Constructivist Perspective", *Educational Administration Quarterly* 28, no. 3 (August 1992). 430-43.
29 See, for example, Sergiovanni, *Value-Added Leadership*, 21
30. Larry E. Sackney and Dennis J. Dibski, "School-Based Management: A Critical Perspective", *Educational Management and Administration* 22, no. 2 (April 1994). 104-5.
31. Greenfield, *Articulating Values and Ethics*, 268
32 Peter Gronn, "From Transactions to Transformations: A New World Order in the Study of Leadership?", *Educational Management and Administration* 24, no. 1 (1996). 24
33 Lee Bolman and Terrence Deal, "Leading and Managing. Effects of Context, Culture and Gender", *Educational Administration Quarterly* 28, no. 3 (1992): 314
34 Earle H. Newton, "The Secondary Headship: Perceptions, Conceptions, Performance and Reactions of Head Teachers in Barbados", *Journal of Educational Administration* 31, no 2 (1993): 24.
35 Ibid, 28
36. Sergiovanni, *Value-Added Leadership*, 25.
37 Thomas J Peters and Robert H Waterman, *In Search of Excellence: Lessons from America's Best-Run Companies* (New York: Harper and Row publishers, 1982), 119 and 154
38 Thomas Peters and Nancy Austin, *A Passion for Excellence. The Leadership Difference* (New York: Random House, 1985), 414
39. Keith Sandiford and Earle Newton, *Combermere School and the Barbadian Society* (Kingston, Jamaica: The Press UWI, 1995), 122-33.
40. Sergiovanni, *Value-Added Leadership*, 27
41 Newton, "The Secondary Headship", 40.

9

Managing the Academy: Aspects of the Law Relating to University Administration

Jeff Cumberbatch

Introduction

In the preface to the publication of papers from a symposium held at the University of Manitoba,[1] Dale Gibson, the chairman of the university's Legal Research Institute, observes:

> Life becomes more legalistic by the day and the phenomenon seems even more pronounced within the University than elsewhere. Hostile confrontation is displacing rational discussion. Faculty members who once were willing to leave the determination of their rights and responsibilities to administrative discretion, guided by unwritten customs and understanding, are increasingly insistent on demanding their strict legal rights and are accordingly seeking the assistance of lawyers and courts to an unprecedented extent. Administrators, in response, are also turning to legal advisors with increased frequency. University solicitors, previously consulted on little more than infrequent commercial transactions, are now called upon almost daily . . .[2]

Over two decades later, even if it cannot be definitively stated that these words accurately portray the existing state of affairs at the University of the West Indies (UWI), it must be conceded that they do bear some relation to a likely future. The regional university is not immune to the influences of its environment, and the growing litigiousness of our people, the frequent challenges to the traditional, an increase in lawyering and a heightened awareness of one's rights are all ingredients in a recipe for legal disputes in future pertaining to the administration of the university. That these have not yet occurred in any substantial quantity may owe much to the skills of the incumbent officers, but the signs are clear. The university would do well to be prepared for this development.

What adds substantial complexity to this matter is that the university existence is *sui generis*. Dr Patrick Emmanuel[3] has described it as a plantation whereby the university engages overseers, in the form of deans and heads of department, to superintend the work of staff. Alternatively, he argued, it may be seen as a craft guild with the 'craft' people (lecturers) supplying academic services to the entrepreneur (the university).[4]

Its legal obligations are no less diffuse than its nature. Essentially, there are two sets of applicable laws. First, the local laws to which, as a corporate citizen, it is subject. Given the transjurisdictional nature of the university, these may, and do, vary from one campus to the next. Second, it is subject to its own set of internal laws, contained in the charter, statutes and ordinances. As we shall see, *infra*, these internal laws, their application and interpretation, fall squarely within the jurisdiction of the university visitor.[5] Further, most relationships and procedures within the university are rather loosely defined, based, to a great extent, on tradition and compromise and formed without any contemplation that legal proceedings would arise therefrom. Consider, for example, the relation between a head of department and a member of the department in respect of the latter's academic duties. Would a refusal, even an unreasonable one, by the member to teach a course after being instructed to do so by the head of department be sufficient to constitute a serious breach of the member's contract of employment?[6]

When the clinical scrutiny of the law is ultimately brought to bear on these matters, it is not unusual to find that legal advisers themselves are unclear as to the legal solution. For instance, what is the legal effect of the grant of indefinite tenure? Does it confer a lifetime appointment or is the grantee as easily dismissable as his nontenured colleague? Does the legal recognition of a union other than marriage[7] entitle the spouse to such a union to be included in the university study and travel grant? Is the university responsible if a lecturer/administrator/student is injured or his property damaged while on the university's premises? Who owns the copyright in books produced by staff members with assistance from the university?

In a recent extract from the *InfoTimes* home page on the Internet,[8] Edward Fennell, in a column entitled "A Lawyer for Every Lecturer?", asks "Is 'Education, education, education' going to be followed by 'Litigation,

litigation, litigation'?" According to Fennell, students and their parents are increasingly going to regard themselves as 'customers' of the further and higher education system and he posits that unless educational managers clarify exactly what they are offering to students, the field will be wide open to litigation. Fennell argues, "One possible scenario feared by many institutions is that if students fail their courses, they will sue on the grounds of negligent or incompetent teaching . . . To protect themselves, colleges need to start defining what they want from students in terms of attendance at lectures..."[9] Further, he quotes one solicitor who comments that his education client now publishes exam results against the background of threats of action from students with low grades, and asserts that academic failure is not the only ground for litigation since "cases of sexual harassment and sports injuries are also heating up the legal atmosphere on campus".[10]

It is possible to treat only some of these issues in this study. It attempts to discuss relevant aspects of the professorial contract of employment and the nature of the visitatorial jurisdiction. Generally, I have sought to restrict analysis to the Barbadian law, though, where necessary, I have also included references to the other campus jurisdictions. In any event, apart from, in a limited way, the employment contract, the law is basically common to all relevant jurisdictions. At this stage, the writer seeks to issue the traditional caveat that the material contained herein is not intended for use as legal advice in any form and purports merely to be a theoretical examination of the general legal issues.

The Professorial Contract[11]

Status

So far as academic employment at the UWI is concerned, it would not be entirely accurate to state that "there is nothing mysterious about a professorial contract" and that "in dealing with a professorial contract we are dealing with a relationship of master and servant exactly like that which arises when one person is employed by another in any other capacity, be it street cleaner or manager of a business".[12] Not only the nature of the professorial contract of employment, but its terms, the assessment of the validity of its termination and, probably, the remedies available to the unlawfully dismissed academic, may all vary substantially from those in the ordinary employment contract. The relevant law appears to be an eldritch brew of common law contract, convention, administrative law, rules, statute and tacit understandings.

First, it appears from the Charter of the University of the West Indies that the academic appointment is to an office. According to Article 3, paragraph 1, the university is empowered "to institute Professorships, Readerships, Lectureships and such other academic *offices* as may be required by the university and to appoint such *offices*" (emphasis added). It should be noted, however, that according to the statutes, the academic qua academic is not regarded as an *officer* of the university.[13] To my thinking, the conflict here is more apparent than real. For purposes of construction, the statutes are to be read subject to the charter,[14] though it could be argued that the general words of the article in the charter should not take precedence over the specific words of the statute.[15] The better view, however, would seem to be that, while the officers of the university are those charged with its general administration, its offices are concerned with the academic function. Thus, there is still the possibility of being appointed to an office in, without being an officer of, the university. In other words, a distinction is to be drawn between those in an academic office and those who are administrative officers. This argument is reinforced to some extent by Statute 17, section 1(w), under which the council is entitled "to exercise powers of removal from *office* and other disciplinary control over the academic staff".

The importance of determining whether or not an academic is appointed to an office is directly related to the security of tenure that the academic might enjoy in his job. The most widely cited definition of an office is that given by Rowlatt J. in *Great Western Railway v. Bater*:[16] ". . . a subsisting, permanent, substantive position which has its existence independently from the person who fills it, which continues and is filled in succession by successive holders . . ."[17] The relevance in employment law of a finding that someone is an office holder is that he is entitled to public law remedies, in that the rules of natural justice must be observed before any disciplinary or dismissal decision, thereby rendering it subject to judicial review[18] and that the dismissal might be declared void rather than merely unlawful.[19]

Second, it is clear that an academic appointment confers membership of the university on the appointee.[20] This continues for so long as the appointee continues to possess the qualification for membership listed in the statutes.[21]

The effect of this is, similarly, that the university must follow the rules of natural justice in expelling or dismissing the member, otherwise the action will be declared null and void.[22] Thus in *Gray v. Allison*,[23] it was held that the plaintiff was entitled to a declaration that a resolution of a club which sought to expel him was a nullity. He was also entitled to an injunction to restrain interference with him as a member, since no notice of the charge preferred against him had been given. The purported expulsion was thus contrary to natural justice.[24] These principles also apply to the membership of trade unions and similar organizations.[25]

Both of these instances of the professorial contract of employment were in issue in the relatively recent decision of *Pearce et al v. University of Aston in Birmingham*.[26] In this case, the plaintiffs were employed as lecturers at the defendant university and were among those members of staff whom the university was proposing to dismiss on grounds of redundancy. The plaintiffs objected to the university's proposals on the ground that the institution's statutes made no provision for dismissal for redundancy but only dismissal for good cause. After the issue of jurisdiction had been resolved,[27] the question for the determination of the visitor[28] was whether the university had power to breach the plaintiffs' contracts without at the same time terminating their rights as members and office holders of the university under its charter and statutes, a power which the university admitted it did not have, except for good cause, under the statutes. Sir Nicholas Browne-Wilkinson, vice chancellor (as he then was), on behalf of the visitor, held that the university had no power to breach the respondents' contracts of employment by issuing redundancy notices. Under its charter, he reasoned, the university only had power to undertake those acts which complied with the terms of its internal laws. Its proposed action would be in breach of that statute which provided that academic staff could only be dismissed for good cause. According to his Lordship:

The sole question therefore is whether, assuming the separate existence of a contract of employment, the university has power to breach such contract without purporting at the same time to terminate the [plaintiffs'] rights as members and office holders of the university under the charter and statutes. I have no doubt that as against persons not enjoying rights under the charter and statutes the university has power, if it thinks fit, to commit a breach of contract. But as between the

University and its members, such breach of contract may also constitute a breach of the members' rights under the charter and statutes. If so, . . . the university has no power under its domestic law to commit such breach of contract since . . . the charter provides that all its powers are expressly made exercisable only subject to the other provisions of the charter and statutes.[29]

In his view, the termination of membership and removal from office of the lecturers could not be effected through the back door by the proposed breach, but had to be in conformity with those provisions of the statutes designed to ensure the security of tenure of the academic staff member.

In relation to the UWI, the actual decision that a member of staff could not be legally dismissed on the basis of redundancy has now been affected, to some extent, by the provisions of the new Ordinance 8, clause 16(a):[30] "The University Appointments Committee, or the Campus Appointments Committee, may terminate the employment of a member of the academic or senior administrative staff on grounds of redundancy . . ."[31] Clearly, this clause permits the university to dismiss a member of the academic staff on the grounds of redundancy. However, given that the consequence of such a dismissal would be to terminate the academic's membership of the university and would also constitute a removal from office, it may be argued that a dismissal on the grounds of redundancy should also comply with the rules of natural justice, so far as these are applicable. Thus it would seem that the staff member should be given adequate notice of the dismissal,[32] that he or she should have a right to be heard and that the terms of any industrial relations agreement affecting the staff member should be complied with.[33]

Finally, the fact that the university is a regional, publicly financed institution may also be relevant to an analysis of the status of those employed under a professorial contract. The first issue is whether this element of public employment brings the staff member within the category of those entitled to protection by the rules of natural justice in accordance with Lord Wilberforce's formulation in *Malloch v. Aberdeen Corporation*:[34]

One may accept that if there are relationships in which all requirements of the observance of the rules of natural justice are excluded . . . these must be confined to what have been called 'pure master and servant cases' which I take to mean cases in which there is no element of public employment or service, no support by statute, nothing in the nature of an office or a status which is capable of protection. If any of these elements exist, then in my opinion, whatever the terminology used, and even though in some inter partes aspects the relationship may be called that of master and servant, there may be essential procedural requirements to be observed, and failure to observe them may result in a dismissal being declared to be void.[35]

It would seem that the professorial contract of employment satisfies both the first ("element of public employment") and third ("in the nature of an office . . .") elements of his Lordship's proposition, even though there is no statutory provision for such employment. In the earlier case of *Vidiodaya University Council v. Silva*,[36] however, Lord Morris of Borth-y-Gest for the Privy Council did not consider that the respondent's contract of employment there went beyond the ordinary contractual relationship of master and servant. The facts were that Mr Silva, who had been appointed as a lecturer in the Department of Economics and Business Administration, was dismissed by the council of the appellant university for misconduct. He applied to the Supreme Court of Ceylon (as it then was), for orders of certiorari and mandamus to quash the decision of the council, contending that he had not been told of the nature of the accusations against him nor had he been afforded the opportunity of being heard in his own defence. The university contended that these circumstances were irrelevant since the council was not acting in a judicial or quasijudicial capacity but in a purely administrative capacity. However, the Supreme Court ruled that the council was under a duty to act judicially at the stage of ascertaining objectively the facts as to incapacity or misconduct and, since it had not done so by its failure to give a hearing after notifying the grounds of complaint, the order terminating the respondent's appointment would be quashed. On appeal to the Judicial Committee of the Privy Council, the university adopted the argument that the relationship between the university and the respondent was simply that of master and servant and that in the circumstances it was not competent for the Supreme Court to issue an order of certiorari. This argument succeeded. For Lord Morris, it was important to consider whether the respondent had any status other than that of a servant of the employer, and, in this respect, after finding that the respondent was not an officer of the university[37] and that his employment was not regulated by statute,[38] his Lordship concluded, "It seems . . . that a 'teacher' who has an appointment with the University is in the ordinary legal sense a servant of the University ..."[39]

Even though this decision seems, with respect, to be correct on its facts, for at least two reasons it would appear not to represent the position of those employed as academics with the UWI. Not only does this employment, as argued earlier, place the academic in an office, unlike the respondent in that case, but, given the essentially public nature of university employment in the region, it may be submitted with some force that the professorial contract of employment entitles the academic to have the rules of natural justice observed.[40]

In any event, as can be gleaned from the discussion in A(iii) *infra*, the issue is not a live one, since the internal laws of this university relating to discipline, including matters of dismissal, appear to make at least adequate provision in this regard.

Terms of the Professorial Contract

The terms of a contract serve to delimit the legal rights and duties of the parties. These terms, or incidents of the contract, may be either express or implied. In the context of the professorial contract, the express terms will be those contained in the letter of appointment, a notoriously stark document. These include any assertions made by the university administration prior to or contemporaneously with the formation of the contract, for example during an interview, and reasonably relied upon by the staff member in order to enter the contract[41] and those terms which are timeously incorporated into the contract, whether by reference to documents or other sources. The main source of this last type of express term is the so-titled Blue Book[42] which, *inter alia*, treats with such matters as retiring age, consultancy, leave, allowances, among others.

Ultimately, however, every employment under a professorial contract is subject to the internal laws of the university.[43] It might be considered, therefore, that these are also incorporated into the contract of employment since they provide the legal basis for that institution.[44]

An interesting issue which might arise in this area is whether the member of staff would be legally bound by a subsequent (postcontract formation) alteration, to his detriment, of the incorporated document. Clearly, such an alteration would not be in keeping with good industrial relations practices[45] if effected unilaterally without reference to the relevant West Indies Group of University Teachers (WIGUT),[46] but it seems that even if the matter has been agreed to by the teachers' union, technically the member of staff would still not be bound. In principle, this is so because the contract is an individual one between the academic and the university and not a collective one between WIGUT and the university. In consequence, any subsequent amendment or variation of the terms would require the consent of the staff member rather than that of WIGUT. Even if it might be argued that WIGUT should be treated as the agent of the individual member of that body for the purpose of settling subsequent terms of the contract,[47] this would not satisfactorily explain the position of those professors, lecturers and others bound by the professorial contract who are not members of WIGUT.

Nevertheless, this proposition is subject to at least three qualifications. In the first place, the incorporated document may itself provide for its unilateral variation. This is certainly the case with the internal laws of the university. According to Article 22(1) of the charter:

The Council may at any time alter, amend, add to or revoke any of the provisions of this Our Charter by a Special Revolution in that behalf, and such alteration, amendment, addition or revocation shall, when allowed by Us, Our Heirs or Successors in Council become effectual so that this Our Charter shall thereforward continue and operate as though it had been originally granted, and made as so altered, amended, added to or revoked in manner aforesaid.

Similar prescriptions also exist in respect of the statutes[48] and of the ordinances.[49] To this extent, the staff member would be bound by any variation of these instruments, it is submitted.

Secondly, it is generally accepted that a unilateral variation, even though technically a breach of contract, may be ratified or accepted by the subsequent conduct of the parties.[50] This would be the position where, for example, the staff member treats the variation as effective by complying with it without any protest. In such a case, the academic would have waived the breach by conduct. The courts are, however, generally loath to find a waiver in these contexts where the only other alternative is for the employee to leave or be dismissed.[51] Further, the nature of the varied clause may be relevant to the determination of waiver by conduct. While a unilateral variation that takes immediate effect, for example, a reduction of pay, would probably be waived by continuing to work after having received the reduced wage,[52] a similar finding might not obtain where the purported variation is to take effect at some date in the future and the staff member makes no protest until that date.[53]

Thirdly, it is possible that the court might view the variation not as a breach of contract but as permissible either under the employer's power (managerial prerogative) to determine the rules which operate at the workplace or as an aspect of the implied term (discussed *infra*) that the employee will adapt to necessary changes in his work. The former proposition may be gleaned from the decision in *Rogers v. Discovery Bay Inn Ltd.*[54] At issue in that case was whether a catalogue of provisions known as staff rules were binding on the plaintiff employee, it having been accepted that these rules did not exist at the formation of the contract of employment. Because of this, counsel for the plaintiff argued, the rules could not apply to him. Chase J. agreed with this initial proposition, holding that there was no evidence to show that the plaintiff had notice of the rules at the time of commencement of his employment and thus the rules had not been incorporated into the contract as express terms. Relying on the decision in *Secretary of State for Employment v. ASLEF (No. 2)*,[55] however, his Lordship was of the view that the rules were also to be treated as lawful orders of the employer, unilaterally imposed instructions that were instances of the managerial prerogative. To the extent that the matter in issue is classifiable as a work rule therefore, it may not be treated as an unalterable (without mutual consent) term of the contract but rather as part of the managerial command structure, an element of the custom or culture of the workplace into which the employee must fit.[56]

What appeared *ex facie* to be a unilateral variation of the terms of the contract in *Cresswell v. Board of Inland Revenue*[57] was, however, not regarded as a breach of the employment contract, Walton J. holding that the employee had a duty to cooperate with the employer by adapting to new methods and techniques introduced in the course of his employment.[58] The Inland Revenue Board had introduced a new computerized system that replaced the traditional manual method of tax coding. The plaintiff and some other employees sought a declaration that the employers were acting in breach of contract in requiring them to operate the computerized system. Walton J. was not persuaded:

In an age when the computer has forced its way into the school room and where electronic games are played by school children in their own homes as a matter of everyday occurrence, it can hardly be considered that to ask an employee to acquire basic skills as to retrieving information from a computer or feeding such information in a computer is something in the slightest esoteric or, even nowadays, unusual . . .[59]

As these dicta indicate, the employee's duty to adapt to new techniques is not an unqualified one. Walton J. rightly noted, in a proper case, that the employer must provide any necessary training or retraining, but there might be a stage reached when the retraining "involved the acquisition of such esoteric skills that it would not be reasonable to expect the employee to acquire them". In any event, there must not be such an alteration that the content of the job is put "outside the original description of the proper functions of the grade concerned".[60]

Overall, nevertheless, there would seem to be few circumstances in which a unilateral change of terms and rules could be resisted. One solution might be to include in the university's statutes a provision that recognizes WIGUT and its collective bargaining rights in such a way that any proposals to seriously alter the terms of the professorial contract of employment must first be negotiated.[61] Ultimately, however, much is left up to the nature of industrial relationship between the staff member, the university and WIGUT. This seems to have worked well, so far.

Concerning the implied terms of the professorial contract, these would appear to fall into three basic categories. These are (1) terms implied into the contract by statutory provision; (2) terms implied into the contract to ensure the business efficacy of the relationship, and (3) terms implied as being normal incidents of a contract between an academic staff member and the university.[62] Those terms implied by virtue of statute would bind the parties by virtue of both of them being subject to the general laws of the relevant jurisdiction. To the extent that the statutory provision is capable of exclusion[63] and unless excluded, either expressly or by a term which gives better accommodation to the employee, the professorial employment may entitle the staff member to holidays with pay,[64] maternity leave and benefits,[65] national insurance protection, trade union membership rights,[66] protection of wages[67] and the right to severance or redundancy payments in the appropriate circumstances.[68]

It is less easy to identify with a sufficient degree of specificity those terms that must be necessarily implied into the contract in order to give it business efficacy.[69] There is a quaint formulation of the test which must be satisfied in order for a term to be implied in this context given by Mackinnon L.J. in *Shirlaw v. Southern Foundries (1926) Ltd*:[70]

Prima facie that which in any contract is left to be implied and need not be expressed is something so obvious that it goes without saying; so that, if, while the parties were making their bargain, an officious bystander were to suggest some express provision for it in their agreement, they would testily suppress him with a common, 'Oh, of course!'[71]

On this basis, there would be very few matters in the professorial employment beyond those either expressly covered or otherwise accepted, as a matter of practice, to be terms of the contract. It is argued here, with some understandable tentativeness, that terms which might be regarded as implied under this category are: (1) the professor's right to undertake consultancy in his area of expertise, including the right to practice a profession, serve on public bodies and to undertake research assignments, such right being limited, of course, by a corresponding right of the university to have first call on the academic's time. It may be assumed that the university would bear the evidential burden of proving that the extra-curricular activity would prove a hindrance to the academic's primary obligations under his contract. Further, it would probably be required that any permission necessary for the academic to exercise this right should not be unreasonably withheld by the university administration;[72] (2) that the professor would be permitted the necessary flexibility to deliver the material in his course in the manner he considers most effective and, subject to deadlines, within the time frame he considers appropriate; and (3) to the extent that it is not otherwise expressly covered under the contract, that the professor would be reasonably afforded the means, financial, temporal, facilitative and otherwise, to carry out research in his discipline and to maintain contact with colleagues globally who share his research interests.[73] An interesting matter for reflection, if this last point is accepted, is whether each UWI academic should not be supplied with an Internet-ready computer or be assisted with its purchase, by the university.[74]

The professorial contract of employment, though it has not often been the subject of litigation, would seem to satisfy the criterion of 'common occurrence' which is necessary for a term to be implied into it as a normal incident of such types of contract: "... [T]he first requirement is that the contract in question should be a contract of a defined type ... The second requirement is that the implication of the term should be necessary ..."[75] On the other hand, there are dicta to the effect that the relevant contract must be of the ordinary type and not be of a 'one-off'.[76] Clearly the professorial contract, as indicated earlier, is not your ordinary contract of employment, even though so far as the category of professorial contracts of employment goes, those at the UWI would not, *ex facie*, appear to differ substantially, if at all, from those that exist elsewhere.[77] It is submitted that the present considerations should relate to whether the UWI professorial contract falls within the subset of professorial contracts of employment rather than to whether it falls within the subject of 'ordinary' contracts of employment or the background set of all contracts of employment, a notoriously wide category.[78]

Once the category has been settled, it is a test of necessity[79] that must be satisfied in order for the term to be implied as a normal incident of the contract. In relation to the professorial contract, the incident that is most deserving of analysis is that of academic freedom. This shorthand expression, often used but rarely detailed, is generally recognized to be essential to the proper functioning of the academic environment. It has been defined[80] as "that freedom of members of the academic community, assembled in colleges and universities, which underlies the effective performance of their functions of teaching, learning and research".[81] According to that writer, it rests mainly on three foundations in the United States:

(1) the philosophy of intellectual freedom which originated in Greece ... and came to maturity in the Age of Reason;
(2) the idea of autonomy for communities of scholars; and
(3) the freedoms guaranteed by the Bill of Rights ...[82]

This brief study is not the place for any extensive commentary on the concept of academic freedom and its progeny, academic due process,[83] but most writers seem to appreciate its importance to the pursuit and acquisition of knowledge. As Fuchs[84] argues

... the freedom of individual Faculty members against control of thought or utterance from either within or without the employing institutions remains the core of the matter. If this freedom exists and reasonably adequate academic administration and methods of faculty selection prevail, intellectual interchange and pursuit of knowledge are secured. A substantial degree of institutional autonomy is both a usual prerequisite and a normal consequence of such a state of affairs . . .[85]

Clearly, under the professorial contract, the university can assume no liability for extra-institutional infringements of academic freedom for which it is not responsible. It would seem, however, that the censure of staff for espousing views not seen as 'politically correct'[86] or advocating radical solutions to societal problems, for example, the legalization of currently criminal activity, changes in the politico-economic system and, perhaps two suggestions of recent foreign vintage – that blacks (or whites) are genetically intellectually inferior to other races and that pedophilia is not morally reprehensible[87] – would constitute encroachments on the professorial academic freedom by the university.

Finally, since it also falls within the general category of employment contracts, the professorial contract will include those terms that are usually implied in these relationships. Among these is the requirement that "the employer [UWI] would not, without reasonable and proper cause, conduct itself in a manner calculated or likely to destroy or seriously damage the relationship of confidence and trust between the parties".[88] This duty, known as the obligation of mutual trust and confidence, and therefore also relevant to the employee, may be broken by a failure on the part of the employer to provide proper working environmental conditions, the unwarranted reduction of an employee's status or failure to provide an overworked employee with reasonable support.[89]

On the employer's side there would also be an implied obligation to take reasonable steps to bring to the attention of employees the existence of any right pertaining to the employment that the employee may take advantage of,[90] an obligation to reasonably and promptly afford a reasonable opportunity to the employee to obtain redress of grievances[91] and a duty to take reasonable care for the safety of employees.[92]

The professorial employee will, *inter alia*, be bound to obey *all lawful and reasonable* instructions of the university with regard to the subject matter of the employment.[93] The courts have also established a duty of capability and competence on the part of the employee as well as a duty of fidelity that would include an obligation to act honestly and not to make secret profits from the employment,[94] an obligation not to compete with the employer during the course of employment[95] and an obligation to desist from illegally disclosing any confidential information of the employer, acquired during the course of employment and classifiable as a trade secret.[96]

Of course, the precise nature and extent of these general obligations will vary from contract to contract and from employment to employment, but it appears clear that the unique nature of the professorial contract of employment makes it a fruitful source of dispute as to the term which should be implied, accepted or imposed in such a relationship.

Termination of the Professorial Contract

In his recent novel, *The Third Twin*,[97] Ken Follet puts it in the mind of Professor Bennington Jones concerning his protégée, Assistant Professor Jeannine Ferrami, a biogeneticist at the fictitious Jones Fall University: "A college could not fire faculty the way a restaurant could fire an incompetent waiter."[98] Professor Jones was right. Owing to his status and the terms of the professorial contract, the academic staff member may not be dismissed in a summary fashion.

It should be noted, however, that dismissal is only one, though perhaps the most important, of the modes of termination of a contract of employment. A contract may be terminated (1) by performance – where the purpose for which it was formed has been achieved;[99] (2) by expiry or lapse of time – where a contract for a fixed term expires[100] or a compulsory retirement age is reached;[101] (3) by frustration – where a change in circumstances or the law would render continued performance of the contract fundamentally different from what was originally contemplated by the parties;[102] (4) by agreement – where the parties agree to bring the contract to an end either by substantial variation or rescission;[103] (5) by repudiation – where either party does an act that manifests an intention to be no longer bound by one or more of the essential terms of the contract;[104] and (6) by operation of law – where there is, *inter alia*, death or dissolution of one of the parties.[105]

In respect of these modes of termination other than by dismissal, an interesting point is raised by Ordinance 8, Clause 34, which provides that

A Disciplinary Committee may recommend to the University Appointments Committee or the Campus Appointments Committee, as the case may be, the termination of the appointment of a member of staff if it is satisfied that he or she has become physically or mentally unable to perform the duties of his office, either permanently or for so extended a period as to make it necessary to make a permanent appointment to carry out those duties . . .[106]

Ordinarily, these circumstances would present a classic case of frustration of the contract. Indeed, in *Marshall v. Harland and Wolff Ltd*,[107] Sir John Donaldson P. laid down, as factors to be considered in determining whether or not a contract of employment has been frustrated, the following: "the nature of the illness, how long it has continued and the prospects of recovery" and "the nature of the employment . . . whether the employee was in a 'key post' which had to be filled permanently if his absence was prolonged or whether it was such that it could be held open for a considerable period". In *Egg Stores (Stamford Hill) Ltd v. Leibovici*,[108] the Employment Appeal Tribunal added the factor "whether in all the circumstances a reasonable employer could be expected to wait any longer".

It may be that, by making an express provision for the recommendation of termination in Clause 34(a), the university is acting *ex abundanti cautelae*, choosing not to rely on the vagaries of the law of frustration in this context.[109] It may be, however, that a termination in these circumstances is to be treated as a dismissal of the staff member by the university. In such a case, the requirements of notice would have to be observed. Even though the incapacity of the academic may itself provide a justifiable reason for the dismissal, the university could have treated the matter as a simple frustration of the contract. By providing for termination, however, the university would appear to have put it out of its power to rely on the doctrine of frustration, at least in the context of illness.[110] The doctrine would not apply in a circumstance where the contract adequately provides for the frustrating event.[111]

With respect to termination by dismissal, the internal laws of the university make extensive provision. Before attempting an analysis of those provisions relating to dismissal for misconduct, it is important to remark that the usual professorial contract includes an express provision for termination by six months' notice on either side. Prior to the decision in *R. v. Hull University, ex parte Page*,[112] it seems to have been generally assumed that this was merely the period of notice required when the contract of employment was being terminated for misconduct. In that case, however, the Court of Appeal confirmed a decision of the visitor of the university that the institution was entitled to dismiss the lecturer, either without notice for good cause as defined in the statutes, or by three months' notice, the period of notice prescribed by the letter of appointment in that case. There, Page was appointed to a university lectureship in 1966 on the usual terms that his appointment was subject to the statutes of the university, that his retirement age was 67 and that his appointment could be terminated by either party by three months' written notice. In 1988, he was given three months' written notice terminating his appointment on the ground of redundancy. Page petitioned the visitor of the university, claiming that the institution was not entitled to dismiss him on the ground of redundancy since he could not, under the statutes, be dismissed before retirement except for good cause, which related to immoral conduct of a disgraceful nature or to incapacity, *and* by giving him three months' notice thereof. The visitor, as stated above, rejected Page's petition. Page then applied for judicial review of that decision.[113] The Divisional Court held that judicial review could be granted to challenge the decision of the visitor as to the construction of the statutes of the university and granted a declaration that on the true construction of the statutes the university did not have power to dismiss the application on the ground of redundancy. On the appeal of the university and the visitor, the Court of Appeal disagreed with the holdings of the Divisional Court on the issue of construction of the statutes, upholding the construction placed on them by the visitor.

Each of their Lordships considered that the relevant provision to be construed was that in Section 34(3) of the university statutes which read:

Subject to the terms of his appointment, no member of the teaching research or administrative staff of the University ... shall be removed from office save upon the grounds specified in paragraph 2 [good cause] and in pursuance of the procedure specified in clause 1 of this section [Joint Committee to examine complaint].[114]

Lord Donaldson M.R. adopted the view of the visitor, Lord Jauncey of Tullichettle, that this showed "clearly that section 34 contemplated that individual contracts would contain provisions for termination in circumstances other than those set out in section 34(2)",[115] namely the good cause provisions. For them, it was an inescapable conclusion that Page's contract provided for two situations, removal from office without notice for good cause and "termination of employment by three months' notice . . ."[116] Staughton and Farquharson L.J.J. were of a similar view. For the former: "if the good cause provisions [were] of no practical effect in Mr. Page's case, that [was] because a period as short as three months [had been] inserted in his terms of appointment . . ."[117] and for the latter, section 34(3) was not to be construed as merely auxiliary to the earlier provision in section 34(1) which dealt with removal for good cause. For him, section 34(1) was an enabling clause "giving the University the power of dismissal in the specified circumstances; while section 34(3) describe[d] those entitled to benefit from the protection against dismissal given by the statues"[118] subject, of course, to the terms of their appointment.

The extent to which this decision is applicable to the UWI academic is not immediately clear. There are no provisions in the UWI internal laws identical to those in issue in *ex. p. Page*. The statutory provision governing removal from office at UWI is to be found in Statute 17 – *Powers of Council*. There, subject to the charter and the other statutes, it is specifically declared that the council has the power "To exercise powers of removal from office and other disciplinary control over the academic staff . . . Provided that . . . this power shall be exercised for the reasons, on the grounds, in the manner and pursuant to the procedures set out in the Ordinances . . ."[119] In consequence, once the academic staff member has been appointed to an office,[120] his removal therefrom is to be effected on the basis of the ordinances. The provision there that treats this matter generally is Ordinance 8, more particularly clauses 13(h),[121] 16(a)–(c)[122] and clause 35(a).[123] It appears that none of these permits a removal from office by a mere giving of notice and without the need for an examination of the existence of good cause.[124] It may be argued, and is therefore submitted, that a person in an academic office at the UWI cannot be dismissed simply by reasonable notice. Nor does the further express power given to the council to cancel contracts on behalf of the university[125] appear to be relevant here since, as earlier noted, any purported cancellation of that staff member's contract would also involve a termination of her rights as a member[126] and officer of the university.[127] It may be submitted that the effect of the notice provision for termination in the professorial contract therefore, if it is to serve any purpose, is to designate the period to which the staff member is entitled, once it has been determined, in accordance with the ordinance, that his employment should be terminated.[128]

Under the internal laws of the university, it appears that apart from termination by the UAC or CAC on medical grounds,[129] the professorial contract may also be terminated at the initiative of the university on the grounds of redundancy,[130] unsatisfactory performance[131] or breach of contract[132] by a member of staff with indefinite tenure,[133] by nonrenewal of contract or for good cause. These may be discussed in turn.

Redundancy The ability to terminate on the grounds of redundancy is made expressly subject to "the payment of any superannuation benefits by means of a pension and/or gratuity or such other benefits to which the member of staff may be entitled under any applicable law governing termination of employment by reason of redundancy".[134] Redundancy, in the ordinance, is defined in the traditional way, relating either to a cessation or intended cessation of the enterprise or activity[135] or to the circumstance where the employee is surplus to requirements.[136] It is far more likely that the latter scenario will assume relevance, and, in the present climate of downsizing and financial stringency, the university might increasingly consider a termination for redundancy as an administrative option. It is generally accepted that it is for the employer, exclusively, to define the requirements of the business and once it is determined that a staff member is not needed, any dismissal must be for redundancy.[137] Clearly, the issue of redundancy would loom largest where the university closes a department or faculty, but it may also arise where the course for which the academic was appointed is no longer being offered or, less likely, where a change in the nature of the tasks that the lecturer is appointed to do amounts to a change in the nature of his work and the lecturer is unable to cope with the new allocation.[138] Even in such circumstances, however, the university has statutorily committed itself to "making every effort both *before* and after redundancy, to assist in the retraining and relocation of staff". Further, it is submitted, the express subjection of the ordinances to the statutes[139] would seem to require that there should be some investigation into the redundancy, since a dismissal for this reason might involve a removal from office and thus be governed by Statute 17(1)(w).[140]

Unsatisfactory Performance and Breach of Contract Dismissal for unsatisfactory performance or for breach of contract is applicable to members of staff on indefinite tenure, a matter dealt with under Ordinance 8, Clause 13. It is expressly stated there that tenure "shall be a mark of distinction which signifies the University's desire and commitment to retain a person in indefinite employment . . ."[141] This is recognized as being "consistent with the promotion of academic freedom and the protection against arbitrary decisions or political or other bias guaranteed to all staff . . ."[142] Patrick Emmanuel[143] has described it even more graphically:

Tenure and its forerunner, indenture, are cornerstone ingredients of any realistic theory of university power. The grant of tenure admits staff to permanent secure membership of the university community . . . the status of indenture involves the absence of tenure, and the expectation of its conferment. It is the functional equivalent of candidate [quaere *associate*?] membership in other types of organisation.[144]

He subsequently concluded that "tenure shifts the status of staff from labourer to free holder".[145] Emmanuel's analysis might have been much too benevolent to the tenured academic in terms of dismissability however. It has long been recognized that employment for an indefinite period is terminable by reasonable notice on either side[146] and this is expressly stipulated in the Ordinance which provides for the termination of the tenured appointment if (1) after a second supplemental formal evaluation[147] the Appointments Committee recommends termination on grounds of "the [sic] unsatisfactory performance by the member of staff,[148] or (2) the University exercises its rights arising from breach of contract[149] by the member of staff". The academic may also be dismissed by virtue of any other provision of the internal laws of the university.[150]

Since such dismissals would also constitute removals from office it should follow that the affected staff member would be entitled to the rights guaranteed under the statutes;[151] namely, to appear and be heard by the council or any person or body to whom the council has delegated[152] this function [of removal from office]; to be represented by a person of his choice from among the members of the academic and senior administrative staff; to call and examine witnesses; and to appeal to the chancellor.[153] The ordinance, however, merely affords the staff member a right of appeal[154] and a right to appear before the

Appeals Committee.[155] The question therefore arises as to whether these procedures purport to limit the rights under the statute or whether, for example, a member of staff might still avail himself of the right to appeal to the chancellor, since this is not expressly excluded.

Nonrenewal of Contract   Clause 12(a) of Ordinance 8 states:

The appropriate Appointments Committee shall not renew the contract of a member of the staff completing the first three years of service, unless that member of staff has shown evidence of diligence, competence and integrity.

The clause further provides for the areas of activity to be taken into account in assessing the case for renewal of contract.[156] Under normal circumstances, the expiry of a fixed term contract does not impose a duty on the employer to renew it and is not to be regarded as a dismissal.[157] However, recent developments may suggest that in the context of the professorial contract of employment, nonrenewal of contract may also involve considerations of justification and, perhaps, acting in accordance with natural justice.

First, section 16(1)(5) of the Severance Payments Act of Barbados[158] deems an employee to be dismissed by his employer if "where under that contract he is employed for a fixed term, that term expires without being renewed under the same contract . . ."[159] Since such a dismissal is expressly stated to be "for the purposes of [that] Act", it would seem that any failure to renew would be treated as a dismissal for redundancy unless the contrary is established by the employer.[160] Hence, there would be a duty placed on the university to negative the presumption that the employee was dismissed for redundancy.

Second, the fact that members of the academic staff, even those on three-year contracts,[161] may claim more than a purely contractual right to employment either by way of an office or membership of the university[162] might infuse the nonrenewal with far more significance than ordinarily. In *Perry v. Sindermann*,[163] Sindermann had been a teacher in the state college system for ten years at three different institutions. He was employed under a series of one-year contracts, as the junior college had no formal tenure system. During the 1968–69 academic year, he indulged in public criticism of the administration and his contract was not renewed. He was given no reason for the nonrenewal of his contract. Part of his claim[164] was that the failure to provide him with official reasons for the nonrenewal and to allow him an opportunity for a hearing violated his constitutional guarantee of procedural due process. The Supreme Court of the United States held that a teacher employed for a number of years at the same institution should be permitted to show that he enjoyed a de facto tenure even though no explicit tenure system existed and if he were able to show this he would be entitled to a hearing.[165] While it seems clear that the UWI lecturer cannot claim the benefit of 'de facto tenure' if he has been employed under a three-year contract, there might be room for an argument that by that appointment he acquires a property in the 'office' and that he ought not to be deprived of this without a hearing. It must be conceded, however, that the right of appeal and of appearance before the Appeals Committee might constitute a sufficient academic hearing as is required under the statutes,[166] together with the right of further appeal to the chancellor.

Good Cause – Misconduct   According to the ordinance,

The University Disciplinary Committee or the Campus Disciplinary Committee, as the case may be, may recommend the dismissal of a member of staff if the Committee considers that the misconduct of the member of staff is of such a nature as to warrant dismissal.[167]

Part 3 of Ordinance 8, within which this provision is contained, provides extensively for the constitution of the University Disciplinary Committee and the Campus Disciplinary Committee,[168] together with their respective jurisdictions. There is also a stated procedure for the institution of proceedings for misconduct,[169] provision for suspension (with pay) of the staff member by the vice chancellor or campus principal,[170] for the procedure of the hearing,[171] and, in conformity with the statutes, for the staff member to have a right to appear before the committee,[172] to have legal representation of his choice[173] and to question witnesses.[174]

As to the nature of the dismissal itself, the relevant disciplinary committee is empowered to recommend whether the dismissal should be either with due notice, summary with salary paid in lieu of notice or summary without salary paid in lieu of notice.[175] It has already been argued that the notice periods stated in the UWI professorial contract serve to indicate the amount of notice which ought to be given even if the dismissal is for good cause.[176] On this basis, it might be queried whether it is 'constitutional' to effect dismissal by the other two methods. In any event, the university should be careful to distinguish between a summary dismissal followed by a payment of a sum of money that is to be treated as a payment in satisfaction of damages if the dismissal is not warranted, and the following situations where the payment in lieu of notice might serve to effect a lawful dismissal: (1) the employer gives proper notice of termination to the employee, tells the employee that he need not work until the termination date and gives him the wages attributable to the notice period in a lump sum; and (2) the contract of employment provides expressly that the employment may be terminated summarily on payment of a sum in lieu of notice.[177]

It may be submitted that to the extent that there is a seeming inconsistency between the terms of the professorial contract, which, according to the earlier argument, would require six months' notice of termination for good cause and the ordinances, which would permit a summary dismissal in an identical circumstance, this must be resolved in favour of the academic staff member and *contra proferentem*, or against the university, which is responsible for the preparation of those contractual terms which must be taken to have varied the position in the ordinance.[178] The result of this would be that even after he had been found guilty of misconduct, the staff member might still be entitled to work out the notice period or be paid a sum in lieu of notice. This was foreseen by Fridman:[179]

It seems hard to accept that a professor could commit an act or acts which justified dismissal and yet be entitled to remain on faculty while he worked out his notice, or was given salary in lieu thereof, when, ex hypothesi, he had forfeited all rights to be considered a professor. Yet that might be the conclusion.[180]

As is statutorily prescribed, the academic is given a right of appeal in these cases to the principal officers of the university.[181]

Finally, in this context, the university maintains its right to dismiss the staff member for breach of contract, though it is difficult to see when this would not also come within the generous definition of misconduct in the ordinance.[182]

It may be then that the observations of Professor Jones referred to at the start of this section[183] hold equally true for UWI faculty members. No dismissal except for good cause and, even then, with some notice of termination. Far better off than an incompetent waiter.

Dispute Resolution – The Visitor

An interesting feature of university administration is the manner in which internal disputes are ultimately resolved. This resolution is effected through the medium of the visitatorial jurisdiction, whereby the university is subject to supervision and regular inspection by a person or authority standing outside it with an authority to make orders binding on the foundation. The visitor, as this authority is called, is a creature of the common law and his primary duty is to see that the internal laws of the university are observed. Out of this comes "a jurisdiction to hear and determine any disputes which may arise within the foundation concerning the enforcement or interpretation of [these internal] laws".[184]

The University of the West Indies Charter provides in Article 6 for the visitation of the institution:

We, [Royal] Our Heirs and Successors, shall be and remain the Visitor and Visitors of the University and in the exercise of the Visitorial [sic] Authority from time to time and in such manner as We or They shall think fit may inspect the University, its buildings, laboratories and general work, equipment and also the examination teaching, and other activities of the University by such person or persons as may be appointed in that behalf.

This makes it clear that the visitatorial power in relation to the university remains vested in Her Majesty though, by convention, in England, she does not exercise the function in person but rather entrusts it to one of her judges.[185]

In the relevant West Indian jurisdictions of the regional university, it is not immediately clear to whom it might be held that Her Majesty has entrusted her visitatorial powers. In Barbados and Jamaica, where Her Majesty has been retained, after independence, as the repository of executive authority,[186] it is further provided that the governor general shall be Her Majesty's representative.[187] Since this is not expressly limited to any specific purpose or purposes, it may be presumed that the governor general is competent to act in a representative capacity so far as the visitatorial jurisdiction is concerned.[188] In Trinidad and Tobago, which has republican status, the executive authority of the State is vested in the president,[189] who is not to be treated as the representative of Her Majesty. In that circumstance, the president of Trinidad and Tobago would not be competent to exercise visitatorial authority over the UWI.

In any event, the federal transjurisdictional nature of the institution makes it extremely difficult to state with any degree of certainty precisely which individual would act as visitor of the university. Had the university existed within a federal jurisdiction, then there would seem to be little doubt that the head of state of that federation, whether republican or monarchical, would be treated as visitor. In the existing state of affairs, it would appear that the visitor must vary from campus to campus and that his authority will derive from the jurisdiction in which the visitation or dispute occurs.

There is another possible formula for determining the identity of the visitor, though this might also involve the concept of a jurisdictional visitor. However, it has the added benefit of including the Trinidad and Tobago jurisdiction of the university. As argued above, it would be difficult to ascertain precisely who should act on behalf of Her Majesty in that republic.

However, this formula is based on the thesis that since the lord chancellor traditionally exercises the visitatorial powers on behalf of the crown in England, it might be argued that the person competent to exercise these powers at the university in the absence of any provision to the contrary would be the officer who stands in the equivalent position of the English lord chancellor in the respective jurisdictions. As a result of the legislations constituting the relevant Supreme Courts, which legislations transferred to such courts the powers of the Court of Chancery in the United Kingdom,[190] the chief justice in each jurisdiction would be the proper person to exercise the visitatorial powers on behalf of Her Majesty. It might be preferable if the university, with the gracious consent of Her Majesty, could appoint a single distinguished individual to be a regional visitor rather than to permit the present, unclear and jurisdiction specific visitatorial process to obtain.

In a comprehensive article in 1981,[191] Peter Smith states that the overall supervisory jurisdiction of the visitor may be broken down into five constituent parts. These are (1) to ensure that the statutes of the [university] are enforced and that those who have duties to perform under the statutes are fulfilling their duties; (2) to expel and deprive members; (3) to supervise the administration of the property of the [university]; (4) to hear appeals from members concerning the [university]; and (5) to interpret the statutes in the event of any dispute as to their meaning.[192]

One consequence of this assessment is the exclusive role of the visitor as the principal method of dispute resolution in the university, what Smith describes as the visitor providing "a *forum domesticum* to determine any dispute which may occur within the [University]".[193] For the purposes of this essay, we shall explore the nature of the visitatorial jurisdiction with special reference to the exclusivity of the jurisdiction, the exercise of that jurisdiction and the circumstances in which the visitor's decision is amenable to judicial review.

Exclusive Nature of the Jurisdiction[194]

It seems that any dispute that might be classified as domestic, that is pertaining to the internal governance of the university, falls within the sole jurisdiction of the visitor, with the consequence that the court will strike out any such claim brought before it for want of jurisdiction. In *Vanek v. University of Alberta*,[195] the issue of what constitutes a 'domestic dispute' was treated. The court there drew a distinction between "whatever relates to the internal arrangements and dealings with regard to the government and management of the house" and "rights of property or rights as between the university and a third person *dehors* the University or with regard to any breach of trust committed by the [university], not being matters related to the mere management and arrangements and details of the *domus*".[196] It is in respect of the former that the visitor will have exclusive jurisdiction. Thus, in *R. v. Dunsheath, ex parte Meredith*,[197] a decision not to renew a teaching appointment was exclusively a matter for the visitor and in *Thomson v. The University of London*,[198] the court held that the existence of the visitor was an insuperable barrier to the proceedings. In that case, the plaintiff had been given a gold medal for the highest marks achieved in a university examination for the degree of doctor of laws. Subsequently, it was alleged that the marks had been incorrectly assessed and a second gold medal was offered to another candidate. The plaintiff sought an injunction to restrain the university from awarding this second gold medal. This was refused on the basis that the case was "clearly within . . . the exclusive cognizance of the Visitor".[199] Also held to be within such cognizance are the issues of whether examination marks have been properly assessed,[200] whether a student should be required to withdraw from the university for failure to pass exams[201] and whether a student ought to be allowed to return to a university college.[202]

So far as English law is concerned, the position appears to be fairly well settled that the presence of a common law contractual relationship of employment between the university and the academic does not *ipso facto* derogate from the exclusivity of the visitor's jurisdiction. The issue arose in *Hines v. Birkbeck College,*[203] where a professor had been dismissed from his post for refusing to carry out teaching duties assigned to him. The plaintiff argued that the internal laws and procedures of the defendant college had been incorporated into his contract of employment and that by its failure to observe these in effecting his dismissal, the college was in breach of contract and had committed the tort of wrongful interference with contract. The college was successful in its motion to strike out the claim. Hoffman J. held that this was a domestic dispute within the exclusive jurisdiction of the visitor. So too was the question of whether the senate of the university could lawfully initiate proceedings for the removal of his title and status as professor.

Some doubt, however, was cast on this position by the Court of Appeal in *Thomas v. University of Bradford,*[204] where views were expressed that the enforcement of a contract of employment was primarily a matter for the courts, even if the claim involved an application of the internal laws of the university. According to Fox J.A., the claim was an ordinary one based upon a contract and prima facie justiciable in the courts.[205] In his article in the *New Law Journal*, Peter Smith disagreed with this reasoning, arguing that it was ahistorical and based upon a misconception of the nature of the visitatorial jurisdiction. This, he argued, was not derived from any contract,[206] but from the law itself. Indeed, Kelly L.J. had dealt with the matter earlier in *Re Wingslang's Application:*[207] "... matters may well be in breach of a contract of employment, yet within visitatorial jurisdiction, if those matters are of an internal domestic character or touch upon the interpretation or execution of private rules and regulations of the University ..."[208]

Smith's opinion was subsequently supported by the House of Lords.[209] There, it was held that if a dispute between the university and a member of its staff over his contract of employment involved questions relating to the internal laws of the university *or* rights and duties derived from those laws, the visitor had exclusive jurisdiction to resolve the dispute. Lord Griffiths considered that this jurisdiction was however subject to the supervisory, as opposed to appellate, jurisdiction of the High Court[210] and, further, he found himself unable to accept that if, in the course of a court hearing, a question should arise concerning the interpretation of university statutes and the like, the case should be adjourned pending a decision by the visitor.[211] In any event, he considered the visitatorial jurisdiction far more advantageous to an academic who seeks to be reinstated in his job, a remedy available under the law in Jamaica[212] and Trinidad,[213] but not in Barbados.[214] Further, for him, it was not a disadvantage that the visitor's decision was nonappellable since:

... Today the [V]isitors of universities either are or include persons of the highest judicial eminence. Would not most people consider it better to accept the decision of such a person rather than face the risk of the matter dragging on through the years until the appellate process has finally ground to a halt? There is also the advantage of cheapness, lack of formality and flexibility in the visitatorial appeal procedure which is not bound by the intimidating and formalised procedure of the court of law.[215]

While this decision appears to have settled the law in England, there is no denying that the word 'exclusive', which is used to describe the jurisdiction of the visitor, is used in a special sense to mean "exclusive so far as appeals on the merits are concerned".[216] However, it is generally conceded that the visitor's exercise of his jurisdiction is subject to judicial review by the courts.[217] It is this that might make the holding in the headnote to *Norrie v. Senate of the University of Auckland*,[218] to the effect that a visitor did not have an exclusive jurisdiction over disputes between a university and one of its members, seem inconsistent with the views expressed in *Thomas* above. However, a close reading of the judgment of Woodhouse P. demonstrates that, in the first place, he saw a distinction between the visitation of New Zealand and English universities[219] generally and, secondly, he noted that the university in question was a creature of statute.[220] Most important, Woodhouse P. would not consider the visitor's jurisdiction as exclusive since any exercise of it would be subject to judicial review:

... I do not regard the jurisdiction of the Visitor as exclusive but rather as subordinate to the Courts; and, of course, that the exercise by the University itself of its statutory powers and discretions will be open to challenge in the Courts whether on grounds of mistake or in terms of natural justice or fairness.[221]

At the same time, it must be conceded that even though the English position also recognizes the judicial reviewability of a visitor's decision in certain circumstances,[222] an issue more fully discussed *infra*, Woodhouse P. appears to suggest that because of the relative infancy of the visitatorial system in New Zealand, the courts' supervisory rule there would be even wider or stronger than in England.

> . . . it is not yet possible to know how well this kind of jurisdiction will work within the modern New Zealand or whether it is likely to provide any great advantage or indeed whether it is needed at all except to handle those internal or non-justiciable issues . . . until the system had proved itself in practice in this country, it would be unwise for the Courts, I think, to take the position that University grievances would need to be taken first to the Visitor.[223]

It would seem, therefore, that the exclusivity of the visitor's jurisdiction in New Zealand relates only to certain limited issues such as the "actual marking of examination papers", the awarding of prizes and the choice of fellows.[224]

With regard to the UWI, there is no immediately obvious reason why the position should differ substantially from that in England. While there has not been, so far as I have been made aware, any issue on which the visitor has had to adjudicate, an understandable fact given the relative infancy of the institution and the harmonious existence that it has enjoyed up to now, it is a fact that UWI, established by Royal Charter, differs in legal status from, say, the University of Auckland which has its origins in an Act of Parliament.[225] Further, the person exercising the jurisdiction of visitor or advising the visitor is likely to be a person holding judicial office[226] and the visitatorial process possesses certain characteristics, as itemized by Lord Griffiths above,[227] that would conduce to a less stressful resolution of any dispute than would a trial. Finally, the availability of judicial review in some instances, a point more closely examined below, should provide an adequate safety net of justice for the disputants. In light of these considerations, it could be submitted that the visitatorial jurisdiction over the UWI is, and ought to be, analogous to that over the English universities as expressed in the authorities.

Exercise of the Visitors' Jurisdiction

As stated, *supra*, the visitor's jurisdiction extends over the interpretation, application and administration of the internal rules of the university.[228] His jurisdiction covers all persons who are (or were at the relevant time) members of the institution,[229] at least so long as there is a claim to a right enjoyed under its internal laws.[230] An issue arises, however, as to the manner in which that jurisdiction is to be exercised.

According to Smith,[231] the visitor is acting judicially when hearing a matter.[232] It seems that he has a discretion as to the manner of proceeding in the dispute,[233] described as "[summary, simply,] according to mere law and right". The visitor must, however, observe the rules of natural justice, thus obliging him not to be a judge in his own cause – *nemo debet judex in re sua*[234] – and to hear both sides of the issue – *audi alteram partem*.[235]

These points have been borne out by the recent case law. In *R. v. University of London, ex parte Vijayatunga*,[236] the applicant, a PhD student, had her thesis refused for this degree and was offered an MPhil instead. She challenged this on two occasions before the visitor of the university, but was unsuccessful each time. She then sought an order of certiorari to quash these decisions, contending that the visitor had to act as a court would and not merely as a supervisor. This too did not succeed. It was held that since the powers of a university visitor fell to be exercised in an almost infinite variety of situations, the mode in which the visitor exercised his powers had necessarily to be left to his discretion, subject to his acting judicially. Kerr L.J. found himself unable to accept the submission of counsel for the applicant that "it was incumbent on [the visitor] to investigate all contested issues to the full . . .",[237] since the visitor was the direct and only judge of all grievances within his jurisdiction:

> . . . [I]t seems to me that in some cases [the exercise of the supervisory jurisdiction] may well be the only proper exercise of visitatorial powers. In many situations, for example, it might be an abuse of power, and a justifiable source of grievance on the part of the institution, if the visitor entered on matters which, by the statutes of the foundation, were expressly left in the discretion of specially designated officers or members.[238]

Simon Brown J., while he did not interpret the submission of counsel for the applicant in the same way that Kerr L.J. did,[239] agreed that the visitor's jurisdiction was as protean as was necessary for a particular situation:

> In my judgment, the decision in *Thomas,* determining as it does the exclusivity of visitatorial jurisdiction where it arises, underlines also the need for such

jurisdiction to assume whatever breadth and character will best enable the [V]isitor to discharge his ultimate function . . .

I conclude therefore that the visitor enjoys untrammelled jurisdiction to investigate and correct wrongs done in the administration of the internal law of the foundation to which he is appointed: a general power to right wrongs and redress grievances. And if that on occasion requires the visitor to act akin rather to an appeal court than to a review court, so be it. Indeed there may well be occasions when he could not properly act other than as an essentially appellate tribunal.[240]

Later, in *Pearce v. University of Aston in Birmingham* (No. 2),[241] Browne-Wilkinson V.C. would also see a 'proactive' or interventionist role for the visitor. In his view, "if there is a threat to do an act in breach of the charter or statutes, it is the visitor's function to prohibit such breach".[242] On this basis, the visitor would be entitled to enjoin any action he considers in breach of the internal laws, such as a purported dismissal other than for good cause, as provided for in the statutes in that case.[243]

So far as the specific issue of the dismissal of academic staff members for good cause or misconduct is concerned, it has been stated that the jurisdiction of the visitor in this context is similar to the supervisory jurisdiction that the High Court exercised by way of judicial review. Once the council or the delegated body has made its decision and the member has referred it to the visitor, the function of the latter is not to hear an appeal by way of a full rehearing from the decision of the body, but to ensure that the decision has been properly reached in accordance with the laws of the university. The visitor is thus limited to considering whether, on the facts before the hearing body, the conduct complained of is capable of being held to be good cause or sufficient misconduct by a reasonable body, whether there was any misdirection in law in reaching that conclusion, whether the body has taken into account irrelevant matters or has failed to take into account relevant matters or whether the conclusion reached by the body was so unreasonable that no reasonable committee could have reached it.[244]

The visitor's jurisdiction includes also the power to make any order to redress the grievance and to effect justice between the parties. In *Thomas v. University of Bradford*,[245] it was argued by the plaintiff that the visitor had no power to award damages, a view which was contrary to that expressed in a case from Western Australia[246] where the judge could "see no reason why an action for damages if brought upon the breach of such a contract [one which fell within the visitatorial jurisdiction] would not equally be a matter within the exclusive jurisdiction of the Visitor".[247] Lord Griffiths did not accept the plaintiff's argument:

I can see no reason why the [V]isitor as judge of the laws of the foundation should not have the power to right a wrong done to a member or office holder in the foundation by the misapplication of those laws. The [V]isitor would be a poor sort of judge if he did not possess such powers.[248]

His Lordship thus considered that if a visitor had concluded that there was no good cause for the dismissal of a staff member and had ordered the reinstatement of the member, "the [V]isitor would have power to order payment of arrears of salary between the date of dismissal and reinstatement".[249] Even if the circumstances did not warrant an order of reinstatement, Lord Griffiths was of the view that the visitor could "proceed to right the wrong done to the member by ordering that a mandatory recompense should be paid by the University in lieu of reinstatement".[250] He concluded that "to deny a [V]isitor such a power is to deny him one of the fundamental functions of a judge which is to right a wrong, in so far as money can".[251]

Lord Ackner was of like mind:

As regards the [V]isitor's jurisdiction to award 'damages' I can see no practical problem. The [V]isitor in the course of his supervisory jurisdiction must be entitled, in order to ensure that the domestic law is properly applied, to redress any grievance that has resulted from the misapplication of that domestic law. Such redress may involve ordering the payment of arrears of salary in the case in which the [V]isitor decides that the employment has not been determined, or compensation where the complainant has accepted the wrongful repudiation of his contract of employment . . .[252]

Judicial Review of the Visitatorial Decision

As suggested earlier, the decision of the visitor may be subject to judicial review in some circumstances. In *Thomas v. University of Bradford*,[253] Lloyd

L.J., in the Court of Appeal, was in no doubt that a concession by counsel to that effect was rightly made:

> ... it was conceded by counsel for the defendants that decisions of the [V]isitor would, nowadays, be subject to judicial review. If, for example, the [V]isitor were to exceed his jurisdiction or if, acting within his jurisdiction he failed to observe the rules of natural justice, then an application would lie on normal principles ... as it would in respect of any other subordinate tribunal ...[254]

The issue was dealt with more directly in the later case of *Page v. Hull University Visitor*[255] – a decision of the House of Lords. In that case, the facts of which are identical to those in *R. v. Hull University ex parte Page*[256] the plaintiff was, in 1966, appointed to a university lectureship on the usual terms. The university subsequently purported to terminate his appointment on the grounds of redundancy. It will be recalled that Page's petition to the visitor was dismissed, the visitor holding that the university could dismiss either without notice for good cause or by three months' notice.[257] When Page subsequently sought judicial review of this decision, the House of Lords, by a three to two majority, held that the court had no jurisdiction to do so, even though they were unanimous that the visitor's decision was correct. For the majority, the decision of the visitor on questions of either fact or law, whether right or wrong, were not reviewable – provided his decision was made within his jurisdiction and in accordance with the rules of natural justice. Judicial review would, however, be available if the visitor abused his powers in a manner which would be wholly incompatible with his judicial role and in breach of the rules of natural justice.

A central issue for resolution here was whether the visitor's decision was susceptible to judicial review for an error of law, especially since, as Lord Browne-Wilkinson affirmed, certiorari normally lies to quash a decision for error of law.[258] After an exhaustive review of the authorities, his Lordship found that the courts' inability to determine what are the internal laws of the institution and the proper application of those laws to those within his jurisdiction extends so as to prohibit any subsequent review by the court of the correctness of a decision made by the visitor acting within his jurisdiction and in accordance with the rules of natural justice. In spite of the general rule that decisions affected by errors of law made by tribunals or inferior courts can be quashed, Lord Browne-Wilkinson identified two reasons why that rule does not apply in the case of visitors. First,

... the [V]isitor is applying not the general law of the land but a peculiar domestic law of which he is sole arbiter and of which the courts have no cognisance. If the [V]isitor has power under the regulating documents to enter into the adjudication of the dispute (i.e. is acting within the jurisdiction in the narrow sense) he cannot err in law in reaching his decision since the general law is not the applicable law. Therefore he cannot be acting ultra vires and unlawfully by applying his view of the domestic law in reaching his decision. The court has no jurisdiction either to say that he erred in his application of the general law (since the general law is not applicable to the decision) or to reach a contrary view as to the effect of the domestic law (since the visitor is the sole judge of such domestic law).[259]

Secondly, his Lordship argued, if there were a statutory provision that the decision of a visitor on the law applicable to internal disputes of a charity was to be final and conclusive, the courts would have no jurisdiction to review the visitor's decision on the grounds of error of law made by the visitor within his jurisdiction. He could see no relevant distinction between a case where a statute has conferred such final and conclusive jurisdiction and the case where the common law has for 300 years recognized that the visitor's decision on questions of fact and law are final and conclusive and are not to be reviewed by the courts.[260]

Nor, in his Lordship's opinion, did the anomalous position of the visitor or the artificial distinction between the peculiar domestic law he applies and the general law justify the 'sweeping away' of the principle of immunity from review on the grounds of error of law. He concluded:

If it were to be held that judicial review for error of law lay against the [V]isitor I fear that, as in the present case, finality would be lost not only in cases raising pure questions of law but also in cases where it would be urged in accordance with the *Wednesbury* principle that the [V]isitor had failed to take into account relevant matters or taken into account irrelevant matters or had reached an irrational conclusion. Although the [V]isitor's position is anomalous, it provides a valuable machinery for resolving internal disputes which should not be lost.[261]

Lord Slynn of Hadley, who dissented on this point, could see no reasons in principle for limiting the availability of certiorari to the situation where a visitor has decided something that was not within his jurisdiction and excluding review on other grounds recognized by law:

> If it is accepted, as I believe it should be accepted, that certiorari goes not only for such an excess or abuse of power but also for a breach of the rules of natural justice there is even less reason in principle for excluding other established grounds. If therefore certiorari is generally available for error of law not involving abuse of power ... then it should be available also in respect of the decision of a [V]isitor.[262]

His Lordship was not persuaded that the visitor's jurisdiction was of such an exceptional nature to justify different treatment in respect of judicial review nor was he impressed by the argument that there would be a flood of applications for review of such decisions if the view of the minority was to be followed. In the first place, many of the references to the visitor "do not involve questions of law at all" and, further, where the issue was one "of esoteric university 'lore', the courts are unlikely to override the decision of the visitor, informed as he will be by the university authorities". For Lord Slynn, in matters of law, the visitor should not be held to be in a position of special knowledge and individuals should be entitled to protection by the courts:

> ... issues of law may be referred to the [V]isitor which are wholly analogous to questions decided by the courts. The present is such a case in which, if there had been no referral to a [V]isitor, the matter would have come before the tribunals and Courts on a clearly recognisable employment law question ... If there is a real question of law, particularly if it involves matters analogous to or the same as issues of the general law, I can see no reasonable justification for refusing judicial review. If the individual's rights are affected he should be entitled to the same protection by the courts as he would be in respect of the decision of a wide range of other tribunals and bodies to whom decisions involving a question of law are assigned.[263]

The argument that it would be *infra dig* for the decision of a visitor, advised by an eminent judge, as is the modern practice in England,[264] to be subject to judicial review, given its possible chilling effect on the readiness of senior judges to give advice, did not detain Lord Slynn:

> In most cases, their advice will either be right in law or be in an area where the courts will wish to leave alone the exercise of the [V]isitor's discretion. If there

is an important and difficult question of law, however, I do not anticipate that senior Judges will either feel 'demeaned' or take umbrage at the possibility of the courts looking at the question again on fuller argument.[265]

He concluded therefore that certiorari did lie to "review the construction placed upon the statutes by the Visitor".

In the West Indian context, it is easy to be persuaded by the views of the minority in this case. First, there is nothing in the internal or domestic laws of the University of the West Indies readily identifiable as "peculiar domestic law" of which the ordinary courts have no cognizance.[266] Second, given that the visitor or adviser to the visitor in the regional context would most likely be the chief justice or president/chancellor of the judiciary, it seems overly reductionist to argue that the visitor possesses any knowledge of the internal workings of the academy superior to that of the courts. Third, nor is it strictly accurate to assert that, for 300 years, the visitor's decision on questions of law have been regarded as final.[267] In most cases, this 'law' was not the ordinary law of the land and, in any event, the notion of judicial review in its present form is of relatively recent vintage.[268] Finally, it appears repugnant to our system of justice that the academic should be compelled to acquire the benefit of having his dispute speedily resolved in consideration for the cost of surrendering his legal rights in respect of the procedural and substantive propriety of the hearing.

On the other hand, in regard to those matters of a truly esoteric nature in the university context, there is no true issue of domestic law involved and so the present debate would not arise. So far as ordinary legal matters are concerned, the decisions of a judge sitting alone are subject to overview by the process of appeal. There seems to be no obvious reason why, by assuming the role of visitor, his decision should thereby become imbued with freedom from question, even if given on an identical point of law, for example, wrongful or unfair dismissal.[269]

Some practical examination of the issues pertinent to natural justice is afforded by the decision of the Alberta Supreme Court, though not in the context of the visitatorial jurisdiction, in *Elliott v. Governors of University of Alberta and Allen*.[270] In this case, the applicant, an associate professor of sociology at the defendant university, sought to quash by way of certiorari a decision of the tenure committee denying him tenure, and sought, in addition, to prohibit any further proceedings on his appeal to the tenure appeals committee. He alleged a denial of natural justice in that (1) the acting chairman of his department had recommended that tenure be denied and had thereafter sat as a member of the tenure committee; (2) that the committee held discussions in his absence; and (3) that he was denied the right of cross-examination. In support of the application for prohibition, he alleged a real likelihood of bias and that the appeals committee refused to hear his appeal on the merits. Lieberman J. dismissed both applications. It could not be said that the chairman, as a member of the tenure committee, was sitting on appeal from his own judgment simply because he had made a recommendation. In any event, the appellant had agreed to be bound by the regulations that provided for the chairman's membership of the tenure committee. Further, the applicant knew fully the case he had to meet, was afforded an opportunity to make a written reply and was allowed to be personally present and take part in the deliberations of the tenure committee. In the circumstances, the refusal of the right to cross-examine was not a denial of natural justice. In this context, Lieberman J. adopted the words of Johnson J.A. in *Strathcona No. 20 v. Maclab Enterprises Ltd*:[271]

It does not follow that the refusal of or the placing of limitations upon the right of cross-examination will always require that the court quash an order made in proceedings in which these restrictions are enforced. If he is afforded an equally effective method of answering the case made against him, in other words[,] is given 'a fair opportunity to correct or controvert any relevant statement brought forward to his prejudice' . . . the requirements of natural justice will be met.[272]

In respect of the application for prohibition, the court found that the applicant had failed to show *a real likelihood* of bias; according to Lieberman J., a mere suspicion of bias by people is not sufficient.[273] The test was "whether a reasonable man in all the circumstances would consider there was a likelihood of bias".[274] His Lordship also offered some comment on the nature of natural justice in the present contexts:

First, I think that the person accused should know the nature of the accusation made; secondly, that he should be given an opportunity to state his case; and, thirdly, of course, that the tribunal should act in good faith. I do not think that there really is anything more.[275]

Other instances of the operation of the concept of fairness in the academic setting may be seen in *Re Ruiperez and Lakehead University*.[276] There it was held that an executive committee did not act fairly where it failed to advise a candidate for tenure of the information considered by the tenure committee in denying him tenure, and where, despite his request, he was not given an opportunity to become acquainted with the substance of the material considered by the executive committee nor to make representations to it. According to Grange J., "Obviously, there must have been information detrimental to him which they considered. He ought to have been given the opportunity either orally or in writing to respond to it."[277] A similar conclusion was reached in *Re Giroux and the Queen*,[278] where the Divisional Court of Ontario held that Laurentian University of Sudbury did not meet the required standard of procedural process because it failed to give the applicant an opportunity to respond to a charge that his thesis in progress did not meet the standard of minimal relevancy to the needs of the university.

In *Bezeau v. Ontario Institute for Studies in Education*,[279] however, the point was made that judicial intervention into the affairs of a university would be exercised only if there was 'manifest unfairness' or 'flagrant injustice'. In this case, the applicant was denied tenure. He alleged unfairness on the basis that he could not give an adequate response to the report of the tenure committee since it was insufficiently explicit to permit him to do so, that he had not been made aware of a minority view of a member of the committee, and, finally, that he was not allowed to appear in person but only to make written submissions. The Divisional Court dismissed his application. Reid J. identified the question he had to ask himself as whether this was ". . . the exceptional case in which there is manifest error on the part of the appeal tribunal [or] a flagrant case of injustice at any level of the proceedings which demands that the court interfere . . ."[280] His Lordship did not find either in this case.

Such injustice was, however, found in the case of *Julus Kane v. Board of Governors of the University of British Columbia*.[281] There, after a hearing, Professor Kane was suspended from his post by the president of the university for three months without pay on the grounds that he had made improper use of the university computer facilities for personal purposes. It appeared that at the hearing the president had given evidence against Professor Kane in Kane's absence. The Supreme Court of Canada, by a majority of six to one, held that this amounted to a breach of natural justice and stated the following general principles, *inter alia*:

1. A high standard of justice is required when the right to continue in one's profession or employment is at stake. A disciplinary suspension can have grave and permanent consequences upon a professional career.
2. The tribunal must listen fairly to both sides, giving the parties to the controversy a fair opportunity for correcting or contradicting any relevant statement prejudicial to their views.
3. Unless expressly or by necessary implication empowered to act *ex parte*, an appellate authority must not hold private interviews with witnesses or, a fortiori, hear evidence in the absence of a party whose conduct is impugned and under scrutiny.
4. The court will not inquire whether the evidence did work to the prejudice of one of the parties, it is sufficient if it might have done so.

It is not the purpose of this study to provide a detailed examination of when the university or its organs would be held to be acting in breach of the principles of natural justice. It is urged, however, that the authorities referred to do provide some indication of what is and what is not regarded as consistent with fairness by a university tribunal.

Conclusion

It is hoped that this essay will engender further serious study of, generally, the nature of university employment, and, specifically, the legal rights and obligations of the parties thereto, including students. The past fifty years have been, in the main, incident free; there seems to be no reason to suppose that the next fifty or, indeed, the next fifteen, will be of similar ilk. The challenges for the university administration are considerable. As two of our more insightful Caribbean scholars have observed: "Creative management of the University requires high intellectual skills . . . especially in the conditions of a yet developing system of public administration in the form of operating a multinational university . . ."[282] It can hardly be disputed that the intellectual, and practical, skills are there, in abundance. It is my view that, in addition to these, the administration will require careful guidance through the legal minefield referred to at the outset that attends the management of the university. This study would seek to be regarded as the first tentative step.

Notes

1. *Universities and the Law* (Winnipeg: Legal Research Institute of Manitoba, University of Manitoba, 1974).
2. Ibid., 5.
3. Patrick Emmanuel, "Academic Relations of Power: The Case of UWI" (unpublished paper, May 1993).
4. Ibid., 8.
5. See, generally, Peter M. Smith, "The Exclusive Jurisdiction of the University Visitor", *Law Quarterly Review* 97 (1981): 610; also per Megarry V.C. in *Patel v. Bradford University Senate* [1978] 1 W.L.R. 1488; and J.W. Bridge, "Keeping Peace in the Universities: The Role of the University Visitor", *Law Quarterly Review* 86 (1970): 531.
6. As to the legal position in the 'ordinary' contract of employment see *Laws v. London Chronicle (Indicator Newspapers) Ltd* [1959] 2 All E.R. 285; *Wilson v. Racher* [1974] ICR 428. See further Ordinance 8, Clause 40 (Right of university to terminate services of academic staff member for "breach of contract"). *Hines v. Birkbeck College* [1985] 3 All E.R. 156; *Thomas v. University of Bradford (No. 2)* [1992] 1 All E.R. 964.
7. See Family Law Act 1981 (Barbados), section 39: ". . . the relationship that is established when a man and a woman who, not being married to each other, have cohabited continuously for a period of five years". Section 50 confers a mutual right of maintenance on the parties "to the extent that [either party] is reasonably able to do so".
8. http://www.sundaytimes.co.uk/news/pages/tim/97-09-23/timfealog/01001. Copyright 1997, The Times Newspaper Ltd.
9. Ibid.
10. Ibid. See further Caroline Forell, "What's Wrong with Faculty-Student Sex?: The Law School's Context", *Journal of Legal Education* 47 (1997): 47.
11. This includes the contracts of all members of the academic staff, both teaching and research, of the university. The term "lectorial contract" might have been equally apt.
12. G.H.L. Fridman, "The Nature of a Professorial Contract", in *Universities and the Law* (Winnipeg: Legal Research Institute of Manitoba, University of Manitoba, 1974), 7.
13. See Statute 3 – The Officers of the University. These include the chancellor, the vice chancellor, the pro vice chancellor, the campus principals, the university registrar and the university librarian.
14. Article 23 of the charter: "In the case of conflict, the provisions of this Our Charter

shall prevail over those of the Statutes, Ordinances and Regulations . . ."
15. By virtue of the principle of statutory interpretation expressed in the maxim *"generalia specialibus non derogant"*. See, generally, Dr John Bell and Sir George Engle (eds), *Cross, Statutory Interpretation,* 2nd ed (London: Butterworths 1987), 75.
16. [1920] 3 K.B. 266.
17. Ibid., 274. See also per Browne-Wilkinson V.C. in *Pearce v. University of Aston in Birmingham (No. 2)* [1991] 2 All E.R. 469, 473 ("Persons appointed to the academic staff are office holders of the University . . .").
18. *Ridge v. Baldwin* [1963] 2 All E.R. 66.
19. *Malloch v. Aberdeen Corporation* [1971] 2 All E.R. 1278. But see also Statute 26(7) – ("Appointment for a period of less than twelve months not an appointment to an office . . .").
20. See Statute 2(1)(g).
21. Statute 2(2).
22. See, generally, J.F. Josling, *The Law of Clubs,* 3rd ed (London: Oyez Publishing, 1975), 41–48.
23. [1909] 25 T.L.R. 531.
24. See also *John v. Rees* [1969] 2 All E.R. 274 (". . . a club or other body where exercising the powers conferred by its rules must act in accordance with the principles of natural justice unless these were expressly excluded by the rules themselves . . ."). But see also *Edwards v. S.O.G.A.T.* [1970] 3 All E.R. 689 which held that a rule itself may be contrary to natural justice. And see Statute 2(2) – withdrawal of membership by Senate at request of member.
25. *Annamunthodo v. O.W.T.U.* [1961] 3 All E.R. 621 P.C.
26. [1991] 2 All E.R. 461, [1991] 2 All E.R. 469.
27. *Pearce et al v. University of Aston in Birmingham* (No. 1) [1991] 2 All E.R. 461.
28. See Part B *infra*.
29. [1991] 2 All E.R. 469, 475–476b. But cf further *R. v. Hull University Visitor ex.p. Page* [1991] 4 All E.R. 747 discussed *infra*.
30. The new Ordinance 8 was approved at the Finance and General Purposes Committee meeting on 23 July 1996.
31. This is expressly made subject to the payment of any superannuation benefits or redundancy payments under applicable local law – see section (iii) *infra*.
32. See, for example, Severance Payments Act, Cap. 355A (Barbados) – section 20; Employment (Termination and Redundancy Payments) Act 1974 (Jamaica) – section 3; Retrenchment and Severance Benefits Act 1985 (Trinidad and Tobago) – sections 4, 6 and 7.
33. Clause 16(c) of Ordinance 8 makes express reference to *"The relevant staff industrial relations agreement"* for negotiation of *"overall redundancy arrangements . . ."*. Further, this clause appears to require the university to make every effort, *"both before and after redundancy, to assist in the retraining and relocation of staff"*. (Emphasis added.)
34. [1971] 2 All E.R. 1278.

35. Ibid., 1294.
36. [1965] 1 W.L.R. 77.
37. Ibid., 90E.
38. Ibid., 87C–88B; See *Vine v. National Dock Labour Board* [1957] A.C. 488.
39. Ibid., 90B–C.
40. And see also per Lord Wilberforce in *Malloch v. Aberdeen Corpn.* [1971] 2 All E.R. 1278, 1295 commenting on *Vidiodaya*. ("I could not follow it . . . insofar as it involves a denial of any remedy of administrative law to analogous employments . . . [the employment] was one of a sufficiently public character or one partaking sufficiently of the nature of an office to attract appropriate remedies of administrative law.") The law in this area is hopelessly complex, perhaps mainly because of its still evolving nature. While the earlier cases tended to look at the status of the applicant – *Ridge v. Baldwin* [1963] 2 All E.R. 66 and, perhaps, the functions of the dismissing body – *Vidiodaya University Council v. Silva* [1965] 1 W.L.R. 77 (in the Supreme Court of Ceylon), yet in *R. v. East Berkshire Health Authority, ex. p. Walsh* [1984] ICR 743, the court regarded the nature of the complaint as crucial.
41. *Heilbut, Symons & Co. v. Buckleton* [1913] A.C. 30; *Thake v. Maurice* [1986] 1 All E.R. 497.
42. *Rules for Academic and Senior Administrative Staff* (November 1988) and *Appendices to Rules for Academic and Senior Administrative Staff* (November 1988). *Sed quaere* as to whether this document is properly incorporated into professorial contracts at Cave Hill since it is not always supplied at the time of appointment, but cf. the text to notes 52–54 *infra*.
43. See, for example, Statute 17(1)(a) – empowering council to make the appointments authorized by the charter and the statutes "subject to the Charter and the Statutes"; also Statute 26 – appointment to Academic and Senior Administrative Staff and Ordinance 8, Clause (2) – University Appointments Committee to exercise powers of council under Statutes 17 and 26 to make certain appointments.
44. See *Pearce v. University of Aston* (No. 2) [1991] 2 All E.R. 469.
45. See, for example, Labour Relations Code, 1976 (Jamaica), section 19 – "Communication and consultation are necessary ingredients in a good industrial relations policy as these promote a climate of mutual understanding and trust which alternately [sic] result in increased efficiency and greater job satisfaction . . ." Also Industrial Relations Act 1972, (Trinidad and Tobago), section 13(3)(b) – Court in exercise of its powers shall ". . . act in accordance with equity, good conscience and the substantial merits of the case before it, having regard to the principles and practices of good industrial relations".
46. West Indies Group of University Teachers, a registered trade union for the academic, including library, staff. There is a branch on each campus.
47. This is not necessarily the case – see *Burton Group v. Smith* [1977] IRLR 351 per Arnold J.; *NUGSAT v. Albury Bros.* [1979] I.C.R. 84 but cf *Edwards v. Skyways Ltd* [1964] 1 All E.R. 494.
48. See *Charter*, Arts 20(3), (5) and (8).
49. Ref. *Charter*, Arts 21.

50. *Anglia Regional Co-operative Society v. O'Donnell* [1994] unreported. c.f. *Burdett-Coutts v. Hertfordshire C.C.* [1984] IRLR 91.
51. *Sheet Metal Components Ltd v. Plumridge* [1974] ICR 373 per Sir John Donaldson: "... the courts have rightly been slow to find that there has been a consensual variation where an employee has been faced with the alternative of dismissal and where the variation has been adverse to his interests..."
52. *Rigby v. Ferodo Ltd* [1988] ICR 29.
53. *Jones v. Associated Tunnelling Co.* [1981] IRLR 477.
54. *Rogers v. Discovery Bay Inn Ltd* (No. 888/86, High Ct., Barbados, 19 December 1986, unreported).
55. [1972] 2 Q.B. 455.
56. Note, however, in this context, the duty of the employer to treat the employee with respect – see *Woods v. WM Car Services (Peterborough) Ltd* (1981) IRLR 347.
57. [1984] 2 All E.R. 713.
58. His Lordship was of the view that the officer "ha[d] no right to remain in perpetuity doing one defined type of work in one particular way..." Ibid., 722g.
59. Ibid., 721 d–e.
60. Ibid., 722g.
61. Fridman, "The Nature of a Professorial Contract", 11.
62. G.H. Treitel, *The Law of Contract*, 9th ed (London: Sweet & Maxwell, 1995), 185–95, divides implied terms into three categories as well but these are (1) terms implied in fact – which includes those terms in category (3) above; (2) terms implied in law – which includes those terms in categories (1) and (3); and (3) terms implied by custom or trade usage – not really applicable to the professorial contract but the terms of collective agreements may become incorporated into contracts of employment as crystallized custom so long as there is an intention to introduce them – O. Kahn-Freund (ed), *Labour Relations and the Law* (London: Stevens, 1977) 26–27; *Young v. Canadian Northern Railway* [1931] A.C. 83.
63. See Unfair Contract Terms Act 1985 (Trinidad and Tobago) ss. 5–12; *Johnstone v. Bloomsbury Health Authority* [1991] 2 All E.R. 293.
64. Holidays with Pay Act, Cap. 348 (Barbados); Holidays with Pay Act (1973 Rev. Jamaica).
65. Employment of Women (Maternity Leave) Act, Cap 345A (Barbados); Maternity Leave Act 1979 (Jamaica); National Insurance Act, Cap. 32:01 (Trinidad and Tobago); See also "Blue Book" – note 42 *supra*, para. 115 and Appendix XIII.
66. Trade Union Act, Cap. 361; section 40A (Barbados); Trade Union Act (Jamaica); Trade Unions Act, Cap. 88:02 (Trinidad and Tobago) – see also Industrial Relations Act, Cap. 88:02 (Trinidad and Tobago) sections 42 and 71.
67. Protection of Wages Act, Cap. 351 (Barbados); Truck Act Cap. 88:07 (Trinidad and Tobago).
68. Severance Payments Act, Cap. 355A (Barbados); Employment (Termination and Redundancy Payments) Act 1974 (Jamaica); Retrenchment and Severance Benefits Act 1985 (Trinidad and Tobago).
69. *The Moorcock* (1889) 14 P.D. 64, 68; *Reigate v. Union Manufacturing Co.*

(Ramsbottom) [1918] 1 KB 592, 605.
70. [1939] 2 K.B. 206.
71. Ibid., 227.
72. *United Bank Ltd v. Akhtar* [1994] IRLR 460.
73. See the provisions in the "Blue Book" (note 42, *supra*) paras. 124–38.
74. See D. Galligan "Research Facilities: Legitimate Expectations", *Society of Public Teachers of Law Newsletter* (Winter 1990): ". . . all academics should have their [computer] machines on their own desk and should not be expected to share a central facility. Training in the use of these systems should also be available . . ."
75. *El Awadi v. Bank of Credit and Commerce International SA* [1989] 1 All E.R. 242, 253 per Hutchinson J.
76. *National Bank of Greece SA v. Pintos Shipping Co.* [1989] 1 All E.R. 213.
77. Fridman, "The Nature of a Professorial Contract", 10 refers to the Canadian experience of the terms of the professorial contract being negotiated by unions on behalf of university academic staff. It might be considered that, in some respects, WIGUT serves a similar purpose.
78. The background set of employment contracts would include *inter alia* those of apprenticeship, directorship, public service, those with outworkers, independent contractors, those which create offices and agency employment contracts. See further *El Awadi v. BCCI* [1989] 1 All E.R. 242 (sale of travellers cheques by bank to customer treated as a contract of common occurrence).
79. *Tai Hing Cotton Hill Ltd v. Liu Chong Hing Bank* [1985] 2 All E.R. 947 (PC); *Shell UK v. Lostock Garage* [1977] 1 All E.R. 481, per Lord Wilberforce.
80. Ralph R. Fuchs, "Academic Freedom: Its Basic Philosophy, Function and History", *Law & Contemporary Problems* 28 (1963), cited in Louis Joughin (ed), *Academic Freedom and Tenure* (Madison: University of Wisconsin Press, 1967), 242.
81. Ibid. See also Ordinance 7, Clause 13(a) for the assertion that the conferral of tenure "enhance[s] the promotion of academic freedom".
82. Ibid., 243.
83. Louis Joughin, "Academic Due Process", *Law & Contemporary Problems* 28 (1963), cited in Louis Joughin (ed), *Academic Freedom and Tenure* (1967).
84. Martin Edwards, *Understanding Dismissal Law* (London: Waterloo Publishers, 1984).
85. Ibid., 246.
86. It might be that the university owes a constitutional obligation not to stifle freedom of expression; Barbados Constitution – section 29(1), Jamaica Constitution – section 22(1) and Trinidad and Tobago Constitution – section 4(1). See also *Perry v. Sinderman* 408 US 593 (1972).
87. See also the Charter, Art. 5(1) (no religious, political or racial test to be required of any person in order to entitle him to "occupy any position in or on the staff of the University").
88. *Woods v. WM Car Services (Peterborough) Ltd* (1981) IRLR 347.
89. Martin Edwards, *Understanding Dismissal Law* (Waterloo, 1984), 21; *Post Office v. Roberts* [1980] IRLR 347 (EAT) (breach of implied term where senior officer

without adequate grounds described an employee as wholly unsuitable for promotion).
90. *Scally v. Southern Health and Social Services Board* [1991] IRLR 522.
91. *Goold Ltd v. Connell* [1995] IRLR 516.
92. Generally *Wilsons and Clyde Coal Co. v. English* [1938] AC 57.
93. *Laws v. London Chronicle (Indicator Newspapers) Ltd* [1959] 2 All E.R. 285 (CA)
94. *Boston Deep Sea Fishing & Ice Co. v. Ansell* [1988].
95. *Hivac Ltd v. Park Royal Scientific Instruments Ltd* [1946].
96. *Faccenda Chicken Ltd v. Fowler* [1986] ICR 836.
97. Ken Follet, *The Third Twin* (New York: Ballantine Books, 1996).
98. Ibid., 248.
99. *Ironmonger v. Morefield Ltd t/a Deering Appointments* [1988] IRLR 461.
100. *Brown v. Knowsley Borough Council* [1986] IRLR 102. See further the discussion *infra* concerning the treatment of expiry of a fixed term contract without renewal as a dismissal.
101. See Statute 28 and para. 31 of the "Blue Book".
102. *Davis Contractors Ltd v. Fareham UDC* [1956] AC 696.
103. *Strange (S.W.) Ltd v. Mann* [1965] 1 All E.R. 1069; c.f. *Birch and Humber v. University of Liverpool* [1985] I.C.R. 470.
104. *Western Excavating (ECC) Ltd v. Sharp* [1978] Q.B. 761. Such an act by the employer may be treated by the employee as a constructive dismissal – *Woods v. WM Car Services (Peterborough) Ltd* [1982] ICR 693.
105. *Glenboig Union Fireclay Co. Ltd v. Stewart* [1971] 6 ITR 4; *Fox Bros. (Clothes) Ltd v. Bryant* [1978] IRLR 485.
106. Subclause (a). There is also a proviso that where any medical (sic) question is involved, the Committee cannot act except on the advice of a committee of "not less than three medical advisers" – clause (b). Where an appointment is terminated under this provision, the Appointments Committee is required to consider the making of *ex gratia* payments in addition to any other payments due to the member of staff or his/her dependents – clause (c).
107. [1972] 2 All E.R. 715.
108. [1977] I.C.R. 260. See also *Williams v. Watsons Luxury Coaches Ltd* [1990] IRLR 164.
109. See the discussion in I.T. Smith and J.C. Wood, *Industrial Law*, 4th ed (London: Butterworths, 1989), 197–202.
110. See *F.C. Shepherd & Co. Ltd v. Jerrom* [1986] ICR 802 where Mustill L.J. accepted that the existence of a disciplinary procedure covering the event in question might militate against a finding of frustration.
111. *Achille Laura v. Total Societa Italiana per Azioni* [1969] 2 Lloyd's Rep. 65; generally Treitel, *The Law of Contract*, 810 et seq.
112. [1991] 4 All E.R. 747.
113. As to the resolution of this issue see *Page v. Hull University* [1993] 1 All E.R. 97 (H.L.) and the discussion in Part B *infra*.
114. [1991] 4 All E.R. 747, 755f.

115. Ibid., 756j.
116. Ibid., 756j–757b.
117. Ibid., 758j.
118. Ibid., 761d–f.
119. Statute 17(1)(w).
120. Ref. notes 13–19 *supra* and text accompanying.
121. Termination on grounds of unsatisfactory performance of appointment of member of staff with indefinite tenure – see discussion at (b), *infra*.
122. Termination on grounds of redundancy – see (a), *infra*.
123. Dismissal on grounds of misconduct – see (d), *infra*.
124. Cf. *R. v. Hull University, ex parte Page* [1991] 4 All E.R. 747, analysed in text *supra*.
125. Statute 17(1)(q).
126. Ref. Statute 2(2).
127. See *Pearce v. University of Aston (No. 2)* [1991] 2 All E.R. 469.
128. Cf. Ordinance 8, Clause 35(b), which treats the manner of dismissal with regard to notice and payment of salary in lieu. See also *Orr v. The University of Tasmania* [1957] 100 C.L.R. 526.
129. Ordinance 8, Clause 34.
130. Ordinance 8, Clause 16.
131. Ibid., Clause 13(h).
132. Ibid., Clause 40.
133. Generally, ibid., Clauses 13 et seq.
134. Ordinance 8, Clause 16(a).
135. Ibid., Clause 16(a).
136. Ibid., Clause 16(b).
137. *AUT v. University of Newcastle-upon-Tyne* [1987] I.C.R. 317.
138. *North Riding Garages v. Butterwick* [1967] 2 QB 56, but cf *Creswell v. Board of Inland Revenue* [1984] 2 All E.R. 713, discussed *supra*.
139. Charter, Article 23.
140. *Sed quaere?*: The text of this provision, with my emphasis: "To exercise powers of removal from office and *other* disciplinary control . . ." could be narrowly interpreted to include only a dismissal for reasons of discipline. However, the redundancy procedure, which would doubtless also entail a removal from office, is of recent vintage; it became part of the ordinances in 1995. In such circumstances, the obligation to comply with the rules of natural justice would arise from the basic common law (see *supra*) and not the statute.
141. Ordinance 8, Clause 13(a).
142. Ibid.
143. Emmanuel. "Academic Relations of Power".
144. Ibid., 6.
145. Ibid., 8.
146. *Richardson v. Koefod* [1969] 1 WLR 1812, 1816 per Lord Denning M.R.;

Michaels & Finn v. Red Deer College [1974] 2 WWR 416, 423 per Sinclair J.A. ("I do not view tenure . . . as implying, for instance, any abstract right to security of employment for the balance of one's academic career").

147. See Ordinance 8, Clause 13(e)–(g).
148. Ibid., Clause 13(h).
149. Ibid., Clause 40. The provision simply states "breach of contract". However, since the right to terminate for breach is not absolute, depending primarily on the effects of the breach – see *Hong Kong Fir Shipping Co. Ltd v. Kawasaki Kishen Kaisha Ltd* [1962] 1 All E.R. 474 – and since the university does not expressly provide elsewhere in its laws for a right to terminate for *any* breach whatsoever, it must be presumed that the right to terminate in this clause is exercisable only for recissive breaches.
150. Such as the dismissal for misconduct – Ordinance 8, Part III, see *infra*.
151. Statute 17(1)(w).
152. In this case the relevant Appointments Committee, ibid., subs.(i).
153. Ibid., subs. (ii)–(iv).
154. Clause 15(a).
155. Clause 15(b).
156. For the academic teaching staff (Clause 12[b][i]) and the academic research staff (Clause 12[b][ii]), these are research, publication, teaching, contribution to university life, public service, and scholarly and professional activity.
157. Ref. note 100 *supra*. As to the nature of a fixed term contract see *BBC v. Ioannu* [1975] ICR 267; *Wiltshire C.C. v. National Association of Teachers in Further and Higher Education* [1980] ICR 455 per Lawton L.J. (". . . A 'fixed term' means a term with a defined beginning and a defined end . . .")
158. Cap. 355A, Laws of Barbados [1986]. Cf. section 8, Employment (Termination and Redundancy Payments) Act 1974 (Jamaica).
159. It is possible to contract out of similar provisions in the United Kingdom (section 197, Employment Rights Act 1996), in the Turks and Caicos Islands – (section 58, Employment Ordinance 1988) and in Jamaica – (section 8[2] Employment [Termination and Redundancy Payments] Act 1974).
160. Section 38(2)b, Severance Payments Act (Barbados).
161. But not those appointed for a period of not more than twelve months – see Statute 26, section 7.
162. Ref. discussion under A(1), *supra*.
163. 408 US 593 (1972).
164. He also alleged that he had not been rehired because of his criticism of the board's policies and that this was an infringement of his right to free speech. The majority, per Stewart J., agreed that "the government may not deny a benefit to a person on a basis that infringes his constitutionally protected interest in free speech . . ."
165. 408 US 593, 594.
166. Statute 17(1)(w) (i)–(iv).
167. Ordinance 8, Clause 35(a). Misconduct is defined to include "(a) conduct of a nature which shows that a member of staff is unfit to hold office; (b) wilful

contravention or violation of, or non-compliance with, the Statutes, Ordinances or other rules or regulations for the governance of the university; and (c) conduct likely to bring the reputation of the university into disrepute". Ordinance 8 Clause 38(a)–(c); *Re Slavutych and Board of Governors of the University of Alberta* (1974) 41 D.L.R. (3d) 71 (malicious confidential opinion of colleague treated as misconduct).
168. Ibid., Clause 22, 23.
169. Ibid., Clause 26.
170. Ibid., Clause 27.
171. Ibid., Clause 28–33.
172. Ibid., Clause 30.
173. Ibid., Clause 30(a)(b)
174. Ibid., Clause 31(a).
175. Ibid., Clause 35(b).
176. Ref. notes 112 – 128 *supra* and text accompanying.
177. *Delaney v. Staples* [1992] 1 All E.R. 944, 947 e–g.
178. For the *contra proferentem* principle, see generally G. Dworkin, *Odgers' Construction of Deeds and Statutes,* 5th ed (London: Sweet & Maxwell, 1967), 95–105.
179. Fridman, "The Nature of a Professorial Contract".
180. Ibid., 17.
181. Ordinance 8, Clause 37.
182. Given the statutory breadth of the concept of misconduct – ref. notes 167 and further, note 149, *supra.*
183. Ref. note 97 *supra.*
184. Peter M. Smith, "Visitation of the Universities: A Ghost from the Past", *New Law Journal* 136 (1986): 484 and 519.
185. For the United Kingdom position, see *Patel v. University of Bradford Senate and another* [1979] 2 All E.R. 582, 584 per Orr L.J.: (". . . on the authorities, subject to any appointment that the Crown might make but had not made, the Crown is the Visitor and the Lord Chancellor the proper person to exercise on the Crown's behalf the Visitatorial powers . . .").
186. Barbados Constitution (1966); section 63, Jamaica Constitution (1962); section 68.
187. Barbados – section 28, Jamaica – section 27.
188. See, for other attempts to identify visitors in other Commonwealth jurisdictions, W. Recquier, "The University Visitor", *Dalhousie Law Journal* 4 (1978): 647 and 652; T.G. Matthews, "The Office of the University Visitor", *University of Queensland Law Journal* (1979–80): 152.
189. Trinidad and Tobago Constitution (1976) – section 74.
190. See Supreme Court of Judicature Act, Cap. 117, (repealed) – sections 14(1) and 14(3) (Barbados); Judicature (Supreme Court) Act; section 4 (Jamaica); Supreme Court of Judicature Act, Cap. 4:01, section 9 (Trinidad & Tobago).
191. Smith, "The Exclusive Jurisdiction of the University Visitor"; see also Bridge, "Keeping Peace in the Universities"; Recquier, "The University Visitor"; R.J.

Sadler, "The University Visitor: Visitatorial Precedent and Procedure in Australia", *University of Tasmania Law Review* 7 (1981–83): 2.

192. Smith, "The Exclusive Jurisdiction of the University Visitor", 612.
193. Ibid., 613. Note that apart from resolving disputes the visitor may, on his initiative, hold a visitation of the foundation if any of the officers behave(s) with a disregard for the internal laws or the aims and objects of the university – *Phillips v. Bury* (1694) Holt K.B. 715, 720, 90 E.R. 1294, 1297, *Patel v. University of Bradford* [1978] 1 WLR 1488, 1493.
194. Ref. note 184 *supra*, 485–86.
195. [1974] 3 W.W.R. 167; [1975] 5 W.W.R. 429.
196. See Fridman, "The Nature of a Professorial Contract", 20.
197. [1957] 1 K.B. 127; See also *Thorne v. University of London* [1966] 2 Q.B. 237.
198. [1864] 33 L.J. Ch. 625.
199. Ibid., 634.
200. *Thorne v. University of London* [1966] 2 Q.B. 237.
201. *Patel v. University of Bradford Senate* 1978] 1 W.L.R. 1488.
202. *Oakes v. Sidney Sussex College* [1988] 1 All E.R. 1004.
203. [1985] 3 All E.R. 156.
204. [1986] 1 All E.R. 217.
205. Ibid., 222.
206. But cf Lloyd L.J. in [1986] 1 All E.R. 217, 232 ("It seems to me that the sole . . . basis on which the [visitatorial] jurisdiction can be justified today is that of implied contract . . .").
207. [1984] N.I. 63.
208. Ibid., 81A
209. [1987] 1 All E.R. 834.
210. Ibid., 849j.
211. Ibid., 849f.
212. Section 12(5)(c)(1), Labour Relations and Industrial Disputes Act, 1975 (Jamaica).
213. Section 10(4), Industrial Relations Act, Cap. 88:01 (Trinidad and Tobago).
214. The remedies for wrongful dismissal in Barbados are still governed essentially by the common law – See J. Cumberbatch, "Without Just C[l]ause: Unfair Dismissal in Barbados", in *Commonwealth Caribbean Legal Studies* (P.K. Menon and G.A. Kodilinye eds., Butterworths 1992) 267 – which does not provide for reinstatement or re-engagement through an order for specific performance – cf *Hill v. C.A. Parsons Ltd* [1972] 1 Ch. 305.
215. [1987] 1 All E.R. 834, 849h–j.
216. [1986] 1 All E.R. 217, 233c per Lloyd J.
217. See notes 246–47 *infra* and text accompanying it.
218. [1984] 1 N.Z.L.R. 129 (C.A.).
219. Ibid., 135, ll. 30 et seq.
220. Ibid., 134–35.
221. Ibid., 136 *ll.* 6–10.

222. *Page v. Hull University Visitor* [1993] 1 All E.R. 97 (H.L.).
223. [1984] 1 N.Z.L.R. 129, 36, *ll.* 15–26.
224. Ibid., 134, *l.* 36; See also *Thomas v. University of Bradford* [1986] 1 All E.R. 217, 227 per Fox L.J.
225. University of Auckland Act 1961.
226. See per Lord Griffiths at [1987] 1 All E.R. 834, 849h. See discussion at text to note 215, *supra*.
227. Ref. note 207 *supra*.
228. *Green v. Rutherforth* (1750) 1 Ves Sen. 462, 27 E.R. 1144.
229. *Hines v. Birkbeck College* [1985] 3 All E.R. 156.
230. *Oakes v. Sidney Sussex College* [1988] 1 All E.R. 1004.
231. [1981] 97 L.Q.R. 610, *R. v. Bishop of Ely* (1788) 2 Term. Rep. 290, 336, 100 E.R 157, 181.
232. Ibid., 631.
233. *Attorney-General v. Atherstone Free School* (1834) 3 Myl & K. 544, 40 E.R. 207.
234. *R. v. Bishop of Chester* (1728) 2 Stra. 797.
235. *Local Government Board v. Arlidge* [1915] A.C. 120.
236. [1987] 3 All E.R. 204.
237. Ibid., 212j.
238. Ibid., 213 c–d.
239. Ibid., 219g.
240. Ibid., 220 h–j.
241. [1991] 2 All E.R. 469.
242. Ibid., 475g.
243. Ref. note 29 *supra* and text accompanying.
244. *Thomas v. University of Bradford (No. 2)* [1992] 1 All E.R. 964.
245. [1987] 1 All E.R. 834.
246. *Murdoch University v. Bloom* [1980] W.A.R. 193.
247. Ibid., 198.
248. [1987] 1 All E.R. 834, 849 a–b.
249. Ibid.
250. Ibid., 849c.
251. Ibid., 849d.
252. Ibid., 852j–853a.
253. [1986] 1 All E.R. 217.
254. Ibid., 233 c–d.
255. [1993] 1 All E.R. 97.
256. [1991] 4 All E.R. 747.
257. Ref. note 112 *et seq.* and text accompanying.
258. [1993] 1 All E.R. 97, 103b.
259. Ibid., 108 d–e.
260. Ibid., 109 b–c.

261. Ibid., 109h.
262. Ibid., 114b.
263. Ibid., 114 e–h.
264. See also per Lord Griffiths in *Thomas v. University of Bradford* [1987] 1 All E.R. 834, 849h (". . . Today the visitors of universities either are or include persons of the highest judicial eminence . . .").
265. [1993] 1 All E.R. 97, 114j.
266. In *Page*, counsel for the appellant had termed the concept of a "peculiar domestic law" artificial "since in practice the charter and statutes of a university are expressed in ordinary legal language and applied in accordance with the same principles as those applicable under the general law . . ." [1993] 1 All E.R. 97, 109d. Lord Browne-Wilkinson chose incorrectly to treat this as a proposition that the distinction is artificial "where the visitor is, or is advised by, a lawyer", ibid., 109f.
267. Per Lord Browne-Wilkinson in *Page*, loc. cit., 109b.
268. Generally *Amisminic Ltd v. Foreign Compensation Commission* [1989] 1 All E.R. 208.
269. Especially if the proposition is accepted that the academic enjoys a superior tenure in employment than the ordinary employee. See A(iii) – Termination of Professorial Contract, *supra*.
270. [1973] 4 W.W.R. 195 (Alberta Supreme Court).
271. [1971] [1971] 3 W.W.R. 461, 20 D.L.R. (3d) 200.
272. [1973] 4 W.W.R. 195, 202–3.
273. Ibid., 204.
274. Ibid., 205 citing McDermid J.A. in *R. v. Walker* (1968) 63 W.W.R. 381, 383.
275. Ibid., 201–2.
276. (1981) 130 D.L.R. (3d) 427.
277. Ibid., 431.
278. (1984) 430 R. (2d) 552.
279. (1982) 36 O.R. (2d) 577.
280. Ibid., 580f citing Mackinnon A.C.J. in *Paine v. University of Toronto* (1981) 34 O.R. (2d) 770.
281. [1980] 1 S.C.R. 1105.
282. Philip Sherlock and Rex Nettleford, *The University of the West Indies: A Caribbean Response to the Challenge of Change* (London: Macmillan, 1990), 275–76.

10

Changing a University: Reconciling Quantity with Quality – The Case of the University of the West Indies

Don Robotham

The concern of this paper is with the dilemma of reconciling quantity with quality in higher education. There is a special aspect of this dilemma facing universities in the developing world generally and the University of the West Indies (UWI) in particular. In most of the developing world outside of the newly industrializing countries of Asia, the tertiary enrolment ratios (TER) are extremely low; in the case of the English-speaking Caribbean, approximately 4 percent of the relevant age group has tertiary education. How to increase our TER and enhance quality at the same time is the critical dilemma.[1]

Background

It is now firmly established that, in today's highly competitive global economy, no nation, developing or developed, will long sustain its existing living standards or for that matter its social cohesion, with such a small technical and professional cadre. It is now a cliché to point out that in Singapore, Taiwan, Malaysia and other rapidly advancing economies, the TER is over 15 percent and in some cases as high as 35 percent. In Japan, in cities such as Osaka and Tokyo, it can reach as high as 60 percent, such is the huge so-called hidden competitive advantage of Japan, the economic consequences of which, of course, are now plain for all to see. It is important to state the nature of this problem correctly and not to fall victim to numerical fallacies. The difference between Singapore's situation and say, that of Jamaica, is not primarily the *quantitative* difference of 30 percentage points separating their TER from ours. It is that the TER is an attempt at a numerical shorthand measure of *qualitative* differences between the two systems. Or, to put it more crudely, Jamaica could conceivably close the gap and have a TER equal to that of Singapore *without there being any positive impact on our economic and social problems.* It is quantity of a high quality that counts and not quantity by itself.

Given this situation, the UWI would have been derelict of its responsibilities to the region if it had not immediately embarked on a programme of rapid expansion of its student enrolment. Thus in 1990, we developed a ten-year plan that set out targets for the rapid expansion of the undergraduate student population. These targets have been met and, in fact, easily exceeded; the Faculty of Social Sciences, Mona, for example, surpassing its enrolment target for the year 2000 from as early as 1993. This rapid expansion in numbers, however, has brought to the fore a problem that actually existed prior to the ten-year development plan. This is the problem of the *quality* of our graduates and the extent to which the UWI educational experience is fostering those qualities in our students that fulfil the needs of the community and the individual, broadly conceived.

On paper, there is little hard evidence of deteriorating standards. For example, the numbers in the Faculty of Social Sciences indicate that, if anything, the percentage level of students obtaining first and upper second class honours is increasing. Our graduates continue to be admitted to some of the most prestigious universities in the world, including those in the United Kingdom and North America, and routinely excel. The same is probably true of the graduates in other faculties. Yet those of us with some experience in the field of social investigation have long learned not to wait on statistics before we grasp a problem and begin to develop solutions; for the simple reason that statistical trends, by definition, take time to develop. Unfortunately, by the time the data emerge, fully crunched, the crisis will also have emerged, fully blown. One may rightly ask, however, if the numbers of first class honours are up and our students seem to be getting on in life, what is the cause for concern?

First, we have the persistent complaints from employers about our graduates: that they are not sufficiently practical; that they are opinionated and have false expectations; that their command of the English language and other communication skills leave a lot to be desired; that they lack vision and leadership qualities. Common sense should tell us that, contradictory as some of these complaints may be, they are trying to point us to some really serious issues that it is our duty to address. Moreover, we have the whispered reservations of faculty colleagues about the pressures on teaching and examination generated by the semester system; on the de facto abolition of the tutorial system in some departments; about growing plagiarism and grade hunting among our students; about the serious deficiencies in English; even about the unmistakable decline in the conduct of some students and faculty. It would be the height of folly to disregard what our customers and colleagues have been saying to us, sometimes not so politely, on the ground that the numbers show the percentage of first and upper second class graduates increasing!

It must be emphasized, however, that the main evidence for me is more visceral: it is the state of our economies and societies in the region. Few of us can doubt the evidence of deep and broad stagnation across a wide range of our institutions that is now before our eyes and is felt deeply, to the point of despair, by broad sections of our population from all walks of life. In the case of a country like Jamaica, for example, the 1995 United Nations Development Programme (UNDP) *Human Development Report* confirms what most people feel, that between 1992 and 1994 the country's human development ranking slipped from 69 to 88. It is plain that the cause of this social deterioration finds its immediate cause in economic stagnation and that this is related to political stagnation, among other things. In other words, whatever else is happening, for various reasons (many outside of the control of the university) our graduates are not giving the leadership in our economy and other social and political institutions as is required. We are not rising to the challenge.

My judgment, therefore, is that we have enough qualitative evidence to conclude that a serious problem has developed as regards the quality of our graduates. This problem existed prior to the rapid expansion of enrolment, but the programme of expansion has aggravated it. We are addressing this problem calmly but we need some new approaches. It needs to be understood, however, that the root cause of this problem is not, as the numbers make plain, the result of a decline in UWI standards. On the contrary, the UWI faculty, students and staff have performed miracles of achievement with pitifully limited resources. It is rooted more in the unrelentingly higher demands that global economic and social processes now place on the shoulders of the average citizen in general and those of us with tertiary education in particular. It needs also to be stressed that these demands are not solely to be understood in purely technical, economic and quantitative terms: they have very strong *moral, social and qualitative* dimensions as well.

The quantity/quality dilemma is not peculiar to universities in the developing world. In recent years it has been a major subject of public policy concern in the United Kingdom. In the United States, it expresses itself in the acute concern around the well-known disinclination towards undergraduate teaching in the famous research universities and the entrenchment of the system of allocating this as a chore to graduate students.

In the developing world, however, the dilemma has a particular dimension that it does not have in Europe and North America. There, it seems to me that the elements of a solution are more to hand in that, especially in the United States, there is such a wide range of institutions of higher education, it is perfectly possible for some institutions to specialize in one particular niche of the higher education market and other institutions in another, with the system as a whole satisfying both the quantity and quality needs of the society. In the United Kingdom, the Thatcher government was able to develop an approach of classifying universities into various segments of the higher education market. Controversial though this undoubtedly was, even this approach is not available to us in the developing world. Here, we have few universities that do not have the luxury of filling niches either up- or down-market. We have to be all things to all persons, with the same institution required to excel at undergraduate and graduate education, teaching and research, elite and mass higher education; in a word – quantity and quality. How can this dilemma be resolved?

Some Old Approaches: Entrance and Exit

Let us immediately make clear that the nature and dimensions of this problem place it beyond the solution of quality audit mechanisms. These mechanisms, of course, are critically important in their standard setting, staff and curriculum development, inspection, monitoring and corrective functions. Quality audits are necessary in either a mass or an elite system, but do not by themselves help us in the resolution of the quantity/quality dilemma.

Moreover, audits have major disadvantages. These include potential enormous costs relative to what they can claim to achieve, raising serious questions about their cost-effectiveness. Another related drawback is the possible development of an 'audit industry' – a bureaucracy of inspectors with a self-interest in devising more and more elaborate evaluation procedures of spurious generality and precision.

Further, audits (unless they are customer audits and part of a relational contract) do not connect an institution organically to its customers, a measure that is universally regarded today as a critical step in the search for quality. Instead, it establishes a quasi-customer in the form of a committee of audit experts, often drawn from within the very profession whose performance is in need of qualitative improvement. While there is good reason to believe that the audit mechanism can raise substantially the quality of academic performance, it is by no means to be assumed that this is the appropriate quality required by the true customer. Another way of putting this point is to refer to the evidence that suggests, notwithstanding the introduction of these reforms by the Thatcher government and the improvement in the quality of British academic life which may have ensued, the traditional human resource weaknesses of the British economy, for example, the so-called boffin culture – the ability to invent but not to innovate – continue as before.[2]

Perhaps the biggest weakness of the audit methodology for the concerns being addressed here is that, in true British style, its aim is to identify and set apart an elite, but on meritocratic rather than on the traditional aristocratic grounds. But as has been pointed out at length in the United Kingdom itself, where there are winners there are also bound to be losers, likely, in this quasi market mechanism, to be sent into 'bankruptcy'. The notion that the aim is to raise all to a high standard (indeed, that such a goal is viable at all) is easily lost sight of in the course of this competitive quasi market process.

The conclusion from all this is not that audits are a waste of time. It is instead that they achieve specific and useful purposes when the other truly critical processes are in place. Audits cannot themselves institutionalize such processes. With the introduction of the best audit system in the world, therefore, our quantity/quality dilemma could be more clearly highlighted and measured, but not resolved.

One school of thought is that the dilemma cannot be resolved at all and that, in our long-term national and regional interest, the UWI must return to the elite strategy on which we were founded and on which our reputation was built. The clearest most recent statement of this viewpoint with which I am familiar is that in the *Eckaus Review* of the Faculty of Social Sciences, UWI. In an invaluable report, Professor Richard Eckaus, Ford International Professor of Economics at the Massachusetts Institute of Technology, emphasizes as his first recommendation, the following:

Undergraduate admissions and enrollments should be reduced in order to raise the quality of the educational process . . . In addition, since this would be a significant change in the University's public role, the changes should not be made without public explanation and opportunities for discussion.[3]

Over many intense discussions and with great force, Professor Eckaus argued this point of view. Time and again, he pointed out to me that, politically incorrect though it may be, such a shift in strategy was in fact in the true long-term interest of the region. Its advantages are fairly clear. We would be able to focus on building a strong professional elite who could revive the national and regional development process in the Caribbean. The steady decline of the tutorial system could be reversed. The possibility of combining the best qualities of the British undergraduate tutorial system with the emphasis on graduate studies, as in the US system, would now more clearly emerge. Most enticing of all, the real possibility of the UWI thereby entering the network of elite US institutions as a kind of offshore Caribbean feeder university could become a reality.

The prospect would be that of our undergraduates moving smoothly from the UWI system into the Massachusetts Institute of Technology (MIT), Harvard and the University of Chicago as a matter of course. The irony of this proposal should not be lost, because it is essentially a return to the original model of the UWI as a kind of Caribbean version of the Oxbridge system, but modernized with the elements of a US graduate school programme. This, if you wish, compelling vision of the UWI becoming a kind of Reed or New England College is heady stuff and by no means unachievable. To some extent, aspects of the redesign of our new Economics graduate programme in Mona, heavily influenced by the thinking of young North American trained PhD graduates, seeking to duplicate that strategy with every prospect of success. Yet I reject such a strategy for the

UWI system as a whole, not because it is politically incorrect, but because it surrenders too easily to the idea, all too typical of North America, that quantity and quality are irreconcilable. The weakness of this view is that it accepts out of principle rather than from experience and logic that the horns of this dilemma must, by definition, remain separate and distinct.

The full model of this approach, strongly advocated by some faculty trained in North America, is that, having converted ourselves into an elite school, the UWI would then set up an institutionally distinct evening college. Here we would go for numbers and attempt to satisfy the apparently insatiable demand for university education among the Caribbean people. The model is that of Harvard Extension or of the older external degree programmes of the British universities. A 'softer' version of this approach to the quantity/quality dilemma is one that I myself have, from time to time, advocated. This is the development of a true honours programme of the US type in the UWI system, alongside a standard general degree programme. Thus, in this model, the student masses and the student elite would rub shoulders in the 'same' institution and even be in some common courses together. The elite, however, would have a fundamentally different educational experience from the mass. This group would be in small classes, with the tutorial system, without the constraints of the semester system, educated and examined in a more analytically rigorous manner and probably over a longer period of time. The masses would be put through the kind of programme (by no means of a low standard) characteristic of a respectable US state university.

Those who find such ideas repugnant and who would reject such a model cannot do so convincingly on social, ethical and political grounds alone. If this model is to be rejected, sentiment is not enough. It has to be shown, on intellectual and educational grounds, that it is inadequate and defective. Since its strength is that it frontally recognizes the quantity/quality challenge and seeks to develop a real solution, it is necessary for those who reject this strategy to say what they would propose as an alternative solution to the dilemma. My view would be that the 'soft' 'approach suffers from the same fatal flaw as its 'hard' cousin: it takes as gospel the necessity of a quantity/quality trade-off. There is, however, an objection that is even more fatal to the elite strategy to which I now turn. Such a strategy assumes that the quality of a higher education system is solely determined by processes *internal* to the university itself.

A New Approach: Voice and Loyalty

Without the benefit of research, I wish to put forward the unremarkable proposition that the quality of a higher educational institution is as much, *if not more*, determined by the quality of the students entering the institution and the quality of the forward links to the labour market. Likewise, the quality of our teaching and research is a function of the quality of the institutions from which our staff originate and the forward linkages that faculty develop with the institutions in the economy and wider society. If we accept these premises, then a different solution to the quantity/quality dilemma suggests itself. That is (confining the quality issue to the students for a moment), if the UWI could form a structural partnership with the pre-university level institutions *from which* its students graduate and link these forward with the institutions *to which* our students are employed, then the possibility of resolving the dilemma would arise. In the parlance of modern management, this amounts to a strategy of relational contracting between the pre-university and university elements of the system and the labour market.

In practice, the adoption of such a strategy would require many profound changes in the culture, structure and processes of the UWI system. In particular, it would require that the UWI moves radically away from its current arm's-length admissions practices and procedures. Currently, what is done is fairly traditional, although important new elements, which provide a platform for the system I am suggesting, have recently been added. In the past, the various admissions registrars on each campus would, at the appropriate time, simply place advertisements in the media setting out the programmes of study of the university, the qualifications for entry and invite applications from suitably qualified persons before a stated deadline. These applications would then arrive in the Registries, be classified and ranked according to the standard and nature of the entry qualification and then directed to the various faculty admissions committees for processing. Faculties would then do the actual admission using the agreed qualifications for entry. This is, of course, a classical entrance/exit, as opposed to the voice/loyalty, strategy that I am proposing.[4]

Of late, this system has been improved by analyses at the faculty level of the comparative performance of students with varying types of admission qualifications, for example, 'A' level graduates versus teacher training college graduates. The analysis in the Faculty of Social Sciences, Mona, suggests that possession of even one 'A' level is a reliable predictor of good performance in that faculty. Such a finding, must, of course, be regarded with the greatest caution, as it may only be an indication of the biases and inadequacies built into our system.

Another important improvement in our system in recent years, is the visits to high schools to promote the university, the credit for which must go to the admissions registrars. Academics from the various faculties and departments are combined into teams that go out to the sixth forms of high schools and explain and promote their various programmes of study. By means of this process, a whole new set of applications to the system has been stimulated, especially from students in rural high schools who hitherto would not have considered themselves as having much chance for admission to the UWI. Yet such a system has been primarily inspired by social justice rather than quality considerations. The idea has been to increase access to the widest social strata who can acquire the stipulated qualifications for admission. It is in no way concerned with the quality of our applicants and, indeed, it is possible for an argument to be made that it lowers quality. While the latter assertion is likely to be false, it has to be recognized that such measures do not address the quality issues before us.

Another very important innovation is the development of the Association of Caribbean Tertiary Institutions (ACTI) and the steady effort being made for the articulation of all Caribbean tertiary institutions into a single coherent system. While it is of the utmost importance that the ACTI initiative be pursued with even greater vigour than at present, again, it must be recognized that the current approach emphasizes securing easy and smooth passage from one phase of the tertiary system to the other and on eliminating redundancies and duplication of effort. As I understand it, the main focus is on the possibilities of achieving economies and efficiencies across a more harmonious system. It is not focused on the resolution of quality issues. But, as we shall see below, it is precisely in the context of resolving the quantity/quality dilemma that ACTI takes on very great and special importance for the tertiary education system of the region.

For, if we are to resolve the quantity/quality dilemma, then it is fairly clear that we must go beyond current initiatives, important though all of these undoubtedly are. We must, first of all, identify clearly the institutions from which our students come. Having done so, we must set up a structure in which these institutions and all universities are forged into a permanent partnership. The purpose of this partnership will be for all sides to familiarize each other with their objectives, processes and requirements and for the universities in particular to develop a medium- and long-term programme to work with the other institutions to steadily raise the quality of their educational processes over a definite period of time.

Again there are various ways in which this could be done, some of the elements of which already exist. For example, the George Beckford Foundation in Jamaica and the Department of Economics currently operate a programme of lectures in economics for 'A' level high school students. In 1993 over 1,000 students attended and in 1994 over 900. They also operate annual workshops for teachers of economics which includes the participation of a majority of the teachers of high school economics in Jamaica. The National Association of Teachers of English has, for a number of years, had a similar programme in operation, and, from time to time, lecturers in other fields – sociology and Spanish – have addressed groups of high school students and teachers in the various subject areas. In the Faculty of Natural Science, various summer workshops have been conducted in collaboration with the Ministry of Education to raise high school performance in the sciences, especially as it relates to the faculty's N1 programme.

Yet these efforts, important as they are, consist of bits and pieces that can by no stretch of the imagination be mistaken for the kind of coherent programme for raising the quality of the pre-university system being advocated here. They retain, as a rule, the arm's-length approach to articulating institutions characteristic of our Challenge programmes and to current efforts divesting certificate programmes to other tertiary institutions. The approach is that the UWI should be simply a franchiser of these programmes: that is, our duty stops once we have set the quality standards of curricula and staff, and examination papers have been set and marked. Where we go beyond these measures, our approach is *subject*-focused. But significant improvements in quality cannot be achieved and sustained by improvements on a discrete, course-by-course, basis. It is how these courses and other institutional systems come together for a total experience in a particular institution that is decisive. My proposal is, therefore, for an institutional focus on entire schools and colleges. Nevertheless, these programmes, especially

ACTI, constitute an important fund of experience and an essential platform from which the approach being advocated can be launched.

It was this line of reasoning that led me to take a cursory look at the data available in Mona on the institutions of origin of persons admitted to the university. Looking at the data for the 1995 academic year alone, a striking surprise presented itself, which was quite a revelation. Contrary to stereotype, the single largest source of students is not the secondary schools (as was assumed); it is the ever expanding system of community colleges (essentially sixth form colleges), public and private. For example, in 1995 Excelsior Community College supplied 75 admissions to UWI, Mona. Putting it together with similar institutions, in 1995 community colleges, teacher training colleges and various evening institutes in the Kingston area supplied a total of 279 admissions. The only high school which is remotely close is Wolmers which, boys and girls together, supplied 47 students. Whereas, as mentioned above, the first ten colleges supplied 279 applicants, the first ten high schools supplied only 203 applicants in 1995. Together, these twenty institutions supplied about 20 percent of our admissions for the academic year 1995–96.

Before we rush to new policy conclusions based on these fascinating data it must be pointed out that they are flawed. Currently, UWI application forms do not require applicants to state accurately their institution of origin, so deep are the arm's-length entrance/exit assumptions of our entire education system. Only if the applicant declares his or her occupation to be 'student' is there a field on the form for the student to fill in their 'place of employment'. In such cases, it is assumed that this usually refers to the institution of origin. What is available therefore, due to the kind efforts of the computer section of admissions at Mona, is these 'place of employment' data for those admissions who state 'student' as their occupation for 1995–96![5] This unreliability of the statistics is itself an apt measure of how far off target our present approach to quality is. The analogy would be that of a modern business that had no idea who its specific suppliers were and what their internal processes were, but who merely relied on inputs meeting some general technical specifications for them to be acceptable.

Nevertheless the data are suggestive. If true, they open interesting and important avenues for us to jointly devise an approach to resolving the quantity/quality dilemma that is the subject of this paper. Clearly, if this is the trend, then ACTI takes on a special importance. For it now becomes the natural forum in which, in a strengthened form, we can begin to develop a new approach to the quantity/quality dilemma, upstream so to speak. How would such an approach work?

The first step would be to shift our focus from subjects to a definite set of feeder colleges and schools, possibly some subset of the 'top twenty'. A group from UWI would come together with a group from these institutions and constitute themselves into a permanent body. They would then begin the work jointly of examining the design and quality of courses and programmes at both levels and the extent to which they were mutually supporting. Assistance for upgrading needed by either side would be identified and steps taken, especially by the university, to assist on an ongoing basis with raising the quality of programmes. Over time, the chain would be extended to other institutions until a broad, tightly integrated system from pre-university to university was established. Clearly the intention would be to have a section of the secondary system likewise link backwards to the primary system and to have the whole system linking forward to *specific institutions* in the labour market.

Using ACTI as our point of departure and then moving to other parts of the system, the focus can be on quality. In this model, we tackle the vexed articulation issues by attacking the quality issues for the system as a whole on the basis of new structural relationships. By this means, I wish to suggest that it will be possible to ensure that the level of the 'average' student *entering* any level of the tertiary system, over time, will be raised *prior* to entering. The possibility of maintaining and enhancing high real standards in our tertiary system, while expanding enrolment, can then be met. Of course, none of this is intended as a panacea. It will not work without the institution of all the various elements of a quality system, including the more systematic development, expansion and application of our Staff Development Unit that has taken more than a year to get off the ground with its miserly 'half' staff member allocation. A vital element of this solution lies in enhancing and redesigning internal UWI processes. Absolutely critical for success would be the building of very strong structural relations with employing institutions, downstream if you wish, of an equally close, intimate and long-term kind. What we must seek is a single seamless system of external education/internal processes/labour market relationships that are closely focused on quality, broadly and deeply conceived. None of this will be easy.

Conclusion

In conclusion, I wish to emphasize one point. The above solution is by no means motivated, as some may think, by technocratic concerns that subordinate the university as a simple tool for the achievement of economic and technical ends. I hope that I do not seem sententious or mysterious when I say that resolving the quantity/quality dilemma is, first and foremost, a *moral* issue. By that I mean that the chief consequence of the failure of a society to develop a large professional cadre of high technical *and ethical* quality is moral and social, even more than it is economic and technical. Failure leads inevitably to economic stagnation with political stagnation not far behind. In the scramble for survival, a socially destructive individualism is let loose, moral degradation necessarily follows, leading to the further collapse of social cohesion. An inexorable vicious downward spiral runs from the moral and social to the economic and technical and back again. In the end it becomes a single issue. When I raise the necessity of resolving the quantity/quality dilemma, therefore, I mean, first of all, developing large numbers of persons who have high moral qualities. For to put technical and economic expertise in the hands of persons of dubious morality is not only pointless but dangerous as well. None of these dangers need ensnare us, if we approach our problems in a collaborative partnership with our eyes firmly fixed on the long-term interests of the people of our region.

Notes

1. For excellent readings on dilemma resolution methodologies see Charles Hampen-Turner, *Charting the Corporate Mind* (Oxford: Basil Blackwell, 1994); and Charles Hampen-Turner and Fons Trompenaars, *The Seven Cultures of Capitalism* (London: Piatkus, 1993).
2. For a telling analysis of the unabated decline of the British economy, see Hampen-Turner and Trompenaars, *The Seven Cultures of Capitalism*, 304–20.
3. Richard S. Eckaus, Michael P. Hottenstein, James Midgley and James Snyder, *Report of the Faculty Review Team for the Faculty of Social Sciences, The University of the West Indies (1988/99–1992/93)* (Kingston, Jamaica: UWI, 1994).
4. Albert O. Hirschman, *Exit, Voice and Loyalty: Responses to Decline in Firms, Organizations and States* (Cambridge: Harvard University Press, 1970).
5. See Ms Bandara, "Schools from Which Students Were Admitted to UWI for the

1995/1996 Academic Year". I am extremely grateful to Ms Bandara for her Herculean efforts at data recovery on my behalf at short notice, in the midst of the many more important calls on her time.

11

Future Directions for Research in Caribbean Higher Education Institutions

Roger Prichard

Introduction

Perhaps the most critical ingredient for development in the region is an ability to access and import the rapidly growing body of knowledge in the world. Ideas and innovation are critical to developing new products and services, and improving existing ones, that can compete globally. Higher education institutions in the Caribbean need to take the lead in promoting the connections between Caribbean society and industry and the knowledge economy that is now driving development in the world.

It is critical that higher education institutions in the region become actively involved in research, for a number of reasons. Educational institutions represent the most comprehensive advanced learning and research organizations in the region. Few other bodies have a research mandate. Educational institutions must address their research mandate so that Caribbean countries are better connected with advances in knowledge that are taking place in the world. They must act as conduits for new ideas and develop their abilities as organizations that transfer knowledge: to students through teaching and to business, government and the wider community through technology transfer, informed policy development, commentary and publication.

Those of us who work in higher education institutions need to know what is going on in our disciplines, in order to enrich our teaching and to inform our writings and commentaries. We must therefore be actively engaged in research. This was recognized in the report of the Chancellor's Commission on Governance of the University of the West Indies (UWI) in 1994.[1]

The Chancellor's Commission on Governance

The Chancellor's Commission on Governance of July 1994 called on the university to play an enhanced role in postgraduate training and research, and proposed the establishment of a School of Graduate Studies and Research (SGSR). As part of the implementation of that recommendation, the university established the SGSR in September 1996, with a dean of Graduate Studies responsible for the development of postgraduate training. Also established was the Office of the Pro Vice Chancellor (Research), to assist in the development of research in the university.

The Commission on Governance recommended a SGSR based on the belief that the university occupies a special position in the region to provide research leadership and advanced training to meet the development needs of the countries of the region. The commission felt that, in the long term, the reputation of the university and its ability to support the development needs of the region and in turn be supported by governments and the private sector would be assessed in terms of the relevance of the research and postgraduate training that the institution provides. Furthermore, the ability of the university to attract high quality academic staff and students at both the graduate and undergraduate levels would be dependent on its reputation for research and advanced training.

Some of the responsibilities of the SGSR are:

- to increase the level of research activity in the university;
- to assist researchers in obtaining financial support for their research;
- to stimulate the development of multidisciplinary research and intercampus cooperation focused on the development needs and priorities of the countries in the region.

Research in the Context of Development in the Region

Globally, economic growth now is fuelled primarily by technological and knowledge-based inputs. Startling levels of growth are being achieved in new technology-based industries, with the fastest growing sectors broadly related to (1) information technology, (2) biotechnology and (3) the environment. It is interesting to note that the United States, still the leading manufacturing nation in the world, now has more of its labour force working on computers than on assembly lines and that the return on investing in a company information network is approximately 83 percent per annum.[2]

What are the implications of the new global information economy for the macro environment of Caribbean countries? First, the major economies of the world will behave less cyclically because, as a result of information technology, economic policy makers can now command an enormous amount of information. This will allow policy makers (whose decisions have global impact) to better understand and take corrective actions when there is disequilibrium. This increase in knowledge should also make overall economic growth more sustainable and reduce fluctuations for commodities that come from Caribbean countries.

However, there is a general trend towards reducing tariff and import barriers, to phasing out import preferences – except within the growing number of trading blocks – to greater regulation and enforcement of intellectual property protection and to quality and environmental standards. Thus, on the one hand, the information economy will promote longer term world economic stability and increased access to knowledge; on the other hand, the adjustment of trading relations will increase competition and produce short- to medium-term economic instability in agricultural and manufactured exports from Caribbean countries.

Caribbean countries must embrace the world information economy. Access to the rapidly changing knowledge base in the world comes about through research and a research culture in industry, government and the higher education institutions. The UWI and other higher education institutions must play the role of primary research trainers for the whole region and utilize their ability to integrate information, both fundamental and applied, in the fields in which they have expertise.

Leaders in the region need to recognize the importance of ideas in the transformation of the economy, of innovation in developing new industries and of international networking to transfer experience and knowledge. The most important dividend from research is not the new information that is created directly, but rather the ability of people engaged in research to access and integrate information from around the world on a sustainable basis. This is not the case when 'experts' are flown in for short-term consultancies. The greatest value of research is that it provides a cadre of people who can gather information and help with its import into the economy. To be able to recognize and import new information from wherever it originates, however, people need to be involved in research. Research provides the inspiration for developing new niche products and markets and should be integrated as much as possible across our educational institutions, the private sector and government, provided that integration does not stifle originality and enquiry.

In addition to its essential role in the region's economic development, research is people intensive and, directly and indirectly, creates employment. Expansion of research and graduate research training is an efficient way of creating employment. A high level of research activity will bring investment into the region by drawing development assistance and by attracting capital investment by industry.

The Economy of the Region

Regionally, the strongest industry is tourism, but there is room for expansion of tourism in the Caribbean and world economic stability should assist in this expansion. The growth of tourism in the Caribbean in recent years has been assisted by the deregulation of the North American airline industry. The positive effects of this deregulation on traffic to the region has been almost fully realized. However, deregulation of airline industries in other parts of the world (for example, Europe, Asia and North Africa) could draw tourists away from this region.

Tourism, now the biggest industry in the world, will become increasingly competitive, reducing its profitability in less desirable locations. The quality of the environment (including the location, safety and service) and good communications technology will have a major impact on competitiveness. Even countries with high labour costs can be competitive for tourists if the quality of their total environment and their communications technology (which directly impacts on marketing, sales, financial services and the environment itself) is of a high standard. Thus, in order for the tourism industry of the region to expand and remain competitive, greater attention must be given to the environment and to information technology. This will be contingent upon research in these areas. Another important factor in expanding tourism in the region will be diversification of the tourist product, adding culture and ecotourism to enhance the basic product of sun, sea and sand. Again, thoughtful research is needed to realize an expanded potential.

Besides tourism, the economies of the countries of the region have been dependent on the export of bulk agricultural and extraction industry products. The products of agricultural and extraction industries have had little added value and are mostly low cost commodities that have suffered from high transportation costs and competition from the export of identical commodities by other developing countries. While these products have enjoyed a niche market advantage when tariff and import concessions prevailed, this situation is unlikely to continue much longer, resulting in these industries becoming more marginalized. Technological inputs, particularly those emanating from biotechnology (in the case of agriculture) and from the application of information technology (in all cases), may help Caribbean states to remain marginally competitive.

The Jamaican economy has not realized its full potential for many years. The reasons for this are many and this paper will not analyse them, but rather will look briefly at what needs to be done to develop long-term economic growth and address some of the social issues. The economy at present is dependent on tourism, overseas remittances, bauxite extraction, traditional tropical agriculture, and manufacturing and service industries that produce mainly for the domestic or regional markets. Jamaica's tourist industry is similar to that of the other Caribbean countries and the factors likely to influence its growth are outlined above. Some thought should be given to how the traditional practice of family remittances can be transformed, in some cases, into investment into new industries in Jamaica and to the repatriation of skilled Jamaicans. The bauxite industry is a mature industry and the potential for added value is severely limited by energy costs in Jamaica. It does, however, carry some environmental impacts that require research and follow-up action. Jamaica has potential for agricultural diversification. This should be linked to the tourist industry, diet improvement in the region, in light of the very high incidence of chronic diseases (for example, diabetes, hypertension) related to diet, and to niche agricultural exports. Perhaps Jamaica's greatest unrealized potential is in the manufacturing and service industries. It has a manufacturing and service (including culture) industry base, but has not addressed niche products for international markets. These industries have the potential of having the greatest impact on unemployment and on the incomes of the poorest sectors of the society.

The economic development of Trinidad and Tobago has been based on oil and gas; the manufacture of base chemicals (ammonia, urea, methanol, iron and steel) dependent on the gas and oil industries; agriculture, now largely for domestic consumption; food processing for domestic and regional markets; the production of limited ceramics, glass, electronics, health and personal care products, primarily for the domestic market; and tourism (largely confined to Tobago). The products of the extraction and agricultural industries have had only limited value added by downstream processing and are mostly low cost commodities that depend on the abundance of natural gas to be competitive against exports of identical commodities by other countries. Very few of these products have enjoyed a niche market. The extraction of oil and gas is a rather mature industry, with the necessary research being done in the major petroleum companies around the world. However, the development in Trinidad and Tobago of downstream industries and the manufacture of products that will enjoy niche markets will be dependent on strengthening the research and development infrastructure, particularly the human resources, with research training and the funding of a research culture.

Barbados and many of the smaller states in the region have successfully exploited their natural environment to develop strong tourist industries. Expansion of tourism has been addressed briefly above. In addition, a number have financial service industries and most are dependent on traditional tropical agricultural exports. These agricultural industries have little room for expansion and most, such as bananas and sugar, are under severe threat. Manufacturing in Barbados and the smaller Caribbean states is minimal and almost entirely for domestic markets. However, there is potential for developing selected manufacturing and service industries for niche export markets.

Strengthening the research and development infrastructure, including human resources, is essential if the governments of the region want to address the problem of unemployment. The extraction industries, traditional agriculture and the manufacture of base chemicals alone will not generate the large numbers of jobs required and lead to long-term sustainable economies. It is necessary for the economies to diversify into added value products and services that can create niche markets in the international arena. This requires the integration of knowledge, innovation, marketing and capital. The richest economies in the world are now all dependent on the integration of knowledge, innovation and marketing. Research is fundamental to these activities. Capital will follow them.

Higher education institutions, particularly university level institutions, can make a major contribution to the development of the region. However, research and postgraduate training activities need to be better supported than they are at present and to be well linked with industry and government, and relevant to the requirements of the countries of the region.

Priority Areas for Research

Environmental research is vital to the future of Caribbean economies. The most robust industry in the region as a whole, tourism, is critically dependent on maintenance of the natural environment and remediation of blemished locations. Research aimed at addressing the environmental consequences of the bauxite industry in Jamaica and the problem of harbour contamination in Kingston are examples of only a few projects of current interest. In Trinidad, there is ongoing research into many aspects of remediation, such as restoration of parts of the Caroni Swamp affected by urbanization and effluents, and the decontamination of waste sites affected by heavy metals, such as lead from car batteries. Trinidad's most important industry is related to the extraction and utilization of gas, oil and asphalt. These industries must be managed to ensure their sustainability and minimize their impact on the natural environment. UWI is working with the Environmental Management Authority (EMA) and petroleum companies to develop assays and standards relevant to contamination from the petroleum industry. In Barbados, the Ministry of Health and Environment's Coastal Zone Management and the Environmental Units have worked with higher education institutions to ensure that a South Coast sewage outlet has minimal environmental impact in the waters of Barbados.

Environmental research should be viewed as encompassing the natural environment (involving inputs from biology, geography, chemistry, engineering, agriculture and the medical sciences), as well as the social environment (encompassing economics, politics, the law, sociology, education, management sciences, criminology and communications). In addition to environmental research addressing the needs of tourism and industrial contamination, new products arising from the unique Caribbean environment and new markets should also be pursued. These will add to economic activity and enhance the value of the natural flora, fauna and the inanimate environment within the seas and land spaces of Caribbean countries. Environmental research, including the search for new natural products, will enhance the likelihood that the natural environment will be valued and protected.

While the future of traditional agricultural exports may not be bright, there is room for some agricultural diversification into nutritional fresh produce and consumer crops, such as spices and flowers, for domestic and export markets. Alternative/renewable energy is another aspect of environmental research that is relevant to the region. This includes natural gas and methanol, as well as solar and wind energy. The University of Technology (UTECH) in Jamaica and the UWI Faculty of Engineering in Trinidad should play a key role in developing alternative and renewable forms of energy for the Caribbean. Industry in Barbados and UWI have played a leading role in the utilization of solar energy for water heating, distillation and drying of food products. The UWI Engineering Faculty is working with the National Gas Company of Trinidad and Tobago on the use of natural gas for air conditioning and refrigeration. A major effort should be focused on research that will contribute to the more effective utilization of natural gas, solar and wind energy for the region, and assist with the development of an added value petrochemical industry for Trinidad.

Information technology is the new cornerstone of economic competitiveness but is weak in the Caribbean region. The higher education institutions are weak in information technology research, inadequate in teaching in this area, and their administrations are suffering from insufficient use of management information systems and good communications based on information technology. Although the development of new industries based on information technology and the revamping of established industries through research and development of information technology is revolutionizing the world economy, it has not been adequately embraced in Caribbean countries. Yet, economic activity based on the utilization of information and communication technologies and on researching and developing new information technology niches offers enormous advantages over traditional Caribbean industries. Information technology does not suffer from significant transportation or distance costs; it is exempt from tariff and nontariff constraints under the World Trade Organization provisions on information technology; it has a rapidly expanding global market; is high in added value; does not depend on natural resources except intellect; is people intensive with the potential to create much employment (as it has in the United States); uses English, the language of the Commonwealth Caribbean; and, surprisingly, is not capital intensive. The Indian economy has benefited greatly from embracing information technology and this will also be important to the continued vitality and expansion of the financial services industry in the Caribbean.

Financial data and educational services are very amenable to information technology. Strongly embracing information technology research, development and training could place Caribbean countries in a very favourable position to service the vast and proximate North American market, which, on the whole, shares a common language and has few restrictions on import of goods or services in the information technology domain. Although Caribbean institutions are relatively weak in this area and the governments and the public may not be fully conversant with the importance and potential for developing this sector, it is imperative that we significantly increase research in information technology and more fully embrace it in education.

Sound macroeconomic, trade, social and education policies are preconditions for investment, training and economic development and are an integral part of the region's infrastructure. Such policies must be informed by appropriate research and higher education institutions in the region must play a more active role in research on policy issues such as trading arrangements, investment and taxation policies, constitutional reform and regional integration, education, social assistance and health care reform. There are institutes and research centres in the region focusing on health care economics, monetary policy and a variety of relevant economic and social policy issues. In addition to studying the Caribbean situation, we must also examine and learn from the experiences of other countries of the world, while of course drawing lessons relevant to the Caribbean situation.

In response to demand, much emphasis is being given in the region to training students in management and business. While this is important, the ability of higher education institutions to study and offer solutions to economic, trade and social policy issues through their research has perhaps suffered because of this emphasis. Furthermore, students involved in business and management programmes would subsequently contribute more to economic and social development if they were also exposed to studies in information technology and the sciences, the natural and social environments as well as important economic, trade and social policy issues.

Provision of schooling has been a high priority in most Caribbean countries. Nevertheless, literacy and communication skills – oral, written and now electronic – remain problems for a significant section of the population. Research directed at methods for making improvements in these areas of education, as well as at the tertiary level, must be a high priority. Poverty and associated crime need to be addressed from a social perspective as well as from the perspective of economic growth based on new industries and enhanced competitiveness of existing industries. The higher education institutions must emphasize research into the many facets of economic, trade, social and education policy, and this will have the most relevance and greatest impact when done in association with public and private sector partners.

A third sector leading economic growth in the world is biotechnology. The Caribbean is weak in this important new field. However, UWI has made some efforts to stimulate research into aspects of biotechnology; it has established a biotechnology centre in Jamaica and also has some activities on its St Augustine campus. Activities in the region are focused mainly on agriculture, in plant tissue culture and the selection of disease resistant varieties of plants. In the Caribbean context, the role of biotechnology in medicine, the environment, food processing and adding value to natural products and products of the extraction industries should not be overlooked. Biotechnology is beginning to have a massive impact on the world economy and on health and welfare issues. Typically, biotechnology products are high value, low volume products which do not suffer from the high transportation costs of bulk products. They usually qualify for intellectual property protection and so can readily find niche markets and usually do not suffer from tariff and nontariff barriers. The Caribbean countries and the seas around us are blessed with natural products, many unexploited. When combined with biotechnology research, these could produce novel niche products for export. Biotechnology is almost inherently applied in its orientation and is too important in world economics not to be more strongly embraced by research in some of our higher education institutions.

UWI, particularly in Jamaica and Barbados, although less so in Trinidad, is relatively strong in its epidemiological research of chronic diseases, such as diabetes, hypertension and central nervous system diseases, and infectious diseases, such as the viral diseases human T-cell lymphotropic virus (HTLV), acquired immune deficiency syndrome (AIDS), and dengue, which have high prevalence in the region. Case studies and epidemiological research form the first and second stages in trying to address these chronic diseases and can provide solutions or means of prevention when they are primarily environmentally induced. When, as is very often the case, the chronic diseases have a genetic component, they need to be linked with studies employing biotechnology to find cures and improve diagnosis of predisposition. The strength in epidemiological research needs to be maintained but, if it is to have a major impact on disease control and the quality of life of many citizens of the region, it should be strengthened by being coupled to more research employing biotechnology.

The institutions of the region should be preeminent in the field of Caribbean culture. There is particular institutional strength in Caribbean history, literature and cultural studies such as Caribbean music. Institutions of higher education should play a leading role in research in these areas. The study of the arts and culture is an important contribution to the region's identity and Caribbean literature, history, music, sports and other arts and cultural disciplines should be given a place of priority in our research. It also has considerable potential as an export industry and in support of the development of tourism.

At the same time, the Caribbean has to be part of, and compete with, the rest of the world and we must know the rest of the world well if we are to become better able to compete, to take what lessons we want from it, to inform it of Caribbean culture and to influence it. Caribbean arts and culture, particularly its literature, history, music and sports, should be a major axis of research in the region, but higher education institutions should not neglect the arts and culture of other parts of the world. For the sake of our teaching programmes, for training students to live in and compete in the wider world and to support the economic and social development of the region, attention must also be given to the research and teaching of the arts and cultures of other parts of the world.

The future direction of research in Caribbean higher education institutions should take account of the role of gender in shaping society and affecting the outcome of research and development efforts. Many different, important areas of research need to be addressed by the research of individuals or research teams. Nevertheless, some attention should be given to building research networks in the region that focus our efforts on selected areas that are considered of major importance for the region.

Support of Research is a Precondition for Sustainable Development

The support for research activity that does exist in the region has been overwhelmingly dependent on demand-pull. That is, governments or the private sector have identified a need to solve a problem in an existing activity and have been prepared to fund short-term research projects to address that perceived need. After that immediate need is addressed, research funding typically ceases. Furthermore, the economic base of the region has not been significantly dependent on technology and knowledge, so the demand for research by governments and the private sector has in itself been weak.

This is no basis for the countries of the region to participate in the new global knowledge economy. Research does not fare well if it is maintained on a shoestring or, at best, if it is subject to feast and famine. Research is long-term sustainable development and cannot survive if it is expected to be turned on and off constantly. The virtual total dependence of support for research on (weak) demand-pull is fundamentally flawed. Mowery and Rosenberg, in their review of literature on demand-pull versus technology-push in the creation of industries based on innovation, noted that many officials have concluded that

> the governing influence upon the innovation process is that of market demand; innovations are in some sense 'called forth' or 'triggered' in response to demand for the satisfaction of certain classes of 'needs' . . . Yet, whatever the merits of this questioning of earlier assumptions and goals of science and technology policies, the notion that market demand forces 'govern' the innovation process is simply not demonstrated by the empirical analyses that have claimed to support that conclusion . . . Our purpose, obviously, is not to deny that market demand

plays an indispensable role in the development of successful innovations. Rather, we contend that the role of demand has been overextended and misrepresented, with serious possible consequences for understanding of the innovative process and of appropriate government policy alternatives to foster innovation. *Both the underlying, evolving knowledge base of science and technology, as well as the structure of market demand, play central roles in innovation in an interactive fashion, and neglect of either is bound to lead to faulty conclusions and policies.* [my emphasis][3]

In fact, in the United States only about 19 percent of university research is fully dependent on industry,[4] although even in that technologically developed society the need to better connect university research and graduate training to industry has been well recognized.[5]

The Caribbean region suffers in its research competitiveness and development because there is no significant competitive peer-reviewed funding agency to support a research culture that can interact with industry and government to foster innovation. In order to be more competitive for international funding, we need to have an agency that will provide modest, but sustained, funding for research, provided that, by international standards, the research is of high quality. This need has been identified by the National Institute of Higher Education, Science and Technology (NIHERST) in *A National Policy on Science and Technology for Trinidad & Tobago.*[6]

A criterion of general relevance to the needs of the region should also pertain. In view of the importance of research as outlined above, Caribbean leaders need to realize that the establishment of such an agency would be a very important instrument for economic development and an essential component in second generation reform in the country. In a recent report on Trinidad and Tobago by the International Monetary Fund (IMF), it was concluded that: "The major part of unemployment is structural . . . a strong reduction in real wages that took place over the same period – by more than 50 percent since 1986 (to 1995) – had so little impact on the unemployment situation."[7] Monetary policies alone will not transform the economies of the region and create employment. The region must begin to invest in research on a sustained basis.

A research support agency could be established by the governments of the region. It should have an independent chair and its governing board comprise representatives of the governments, the private sector, groups interested in the support of research and development, and research institutions. The research support agency would function at arm's length from the governments, the higher education institutions and other research bodies. The governing board would determine the overall criteria for eligibility for support under different funding programmes, oversee the administration of the research support agency, determine the distribution of funds between different support programmes – including technology transfer – and report annually to the governments and other sponsors. The governing board would also be involved in seeking funds from sponsors other than the governments.

In the past, what little research funding has been provided has either arisen to meet an immediate need of industry or government, or has been provided as a result of particular projects being 'sold' to government decision makers or development agencies by advocates with appropriate connections. These latter projects have not been adequately evaluated in the context of competing demands for research funding in a project evaluation system. A rigorous and competitive project evaluation system is an aid to good decision making. Decisions on funding individual research applications would be taken by a committee of peer reviewers made up in a majority by researchers, but with members also from the private sector and government who have had research experience. These committees would assess the quality of the application, the track record of the applicants and the relevance of the proposed work to the region. The assessment of the quality of the application and the track record of the applicants would be assisted by each application being submitted to independent international referees, experts in the broad field of the proposed research. Twiss, in analysing the management of technological innovation, points out that, wherever possible, several independent evaluations should be requested to minimize effects of personal bias.[8]

The administration of the research agency would be responsible for holding annual competitions for awards, providing administrative support to the board of governors and the committees of reviewers, and organizing the international review process. Administration costs should not exceed 5 percent of the funds provided. The establishment of a research support agency would greatly stimulate research activity in the region, encourage greater links between researchers in higher education institutions, industry and government, increase the competitiveness of our research community for external research support and indicate to the world that the region is serious about embracing the knowledge economy and stimulating economic development. The return to the community at large from investment in research has been estimated to be close to 50 percent per annum.[9] We cannot afford to pass over such a valuable investment.

Notes

1. Neville V. Nicholls and Ivan L. Head (co-chairmen), *A New Structure: The Regional University in the 1990s and Beyond. Report of the Chancellor's Commission on the Governance of UWI* (Mona, Jamaica: UWI, 1994).
2. Lawrence H. Summers, "Leading a Truly Global Economy", *Newsweek* 129, no. 25 (1997): 17; "Wiring Corporate Japan: Doing it Differently", *Economist*, 19 April (1997): 62–64.
3. David C. Mowery and Nathan Rosenberg, *The Influence of Market Demand upon Innovation: A Critical Review of Some Recent Empirical Studies* (1982).
4. Wesley Cohen, Richard Florida and Richard Goe, *University Industry Research Centers in the United States* (Pittsburgh: Carnegie-Mellon, 1994).
5. Nathan Rosenberg and Richard R. Nelson, "The Roles of Universities in the Advance of Industrial Technology", in *Engines of Innovation: US Industrial Research at the End of an Era*, edited by Richard S. Rosenbloom and William J. Spencer (Boston: Harvard Business School Press, 1996).
6. NIHERST, *A National Policy on Science and Technology for Trinidad & Tobago. Into a New Era of Industrial Competitiveness and Human Development* (Port of Spain: NIHERST, April 1997).
7. International Monetary Fund, *Trinidad and Tobago - Selected Issues*, Staff Country Report No. 97/41 (May 1997).
8. Brian Twiss, *Managing Technological Innovation*, 4th ed. (London: Longman, 1992).
9. "The World Economic Survey: An Acknowledged Trend", *Economist*, 28 September (1996): 43–45.

12

The University of the West Indies Press and Academic and Textbook Publishing in the Caribbean: An Oral History

Wenty Bowen

Introduction

The University of the West Indies (UWI) turned fifty in 1998, and it is useful to reflect on some of the milestones in the life of some of the individual structures that collectively give form to the very idea of what a university is. One such structure is the entity called the University of the West Indies Press or, more simply, the Press.* What is the Press? It is the embodiment of a dream that burned in the hearts and minds of West Indian scholars for almost as many years as there has been a UWI. It is the university's own publishing house, with a mission – itself a part of the university's mission – "to publish research aimed at meeting critical regional needs and by so doing provide West Indian society with an active intellectual discourse".[1]

Development and Growth

The Press opened its doors on the Mona campus of the UWI on 1 October 1992 and in its first five years published eighty-eight books. It began the process slowly: "In our first fiscal year 92–93," said Linda Cameron, director of the Press for the first five years, "we published two books, maybe three. In 93–94 seventeen books, 94–95 twenty-two books, 95–96 twenty-eight books, 96–97 eighteen books, and thus far in this 97–98 year we've published two."[2]

*Publisher's note: At the time this chapter was written, the Press was known as the Press University of the West Indies. In May 1999 the name was changed to the University of the West Indies Press.

In five years, the Press has positioned itself to overcome the difficulties identified by a UNESCO seminar (1972) on the problems of book production in CARICOM countries:

We very soon found that the problems of publishing and distributing scholarly work are but the top of a submerged reef lying in the path of Caribbean progress. The more we examined the problem, the more it appeared that development planning might well founder on that unsuspected but massive obstacle unless it became possible to provide the society with the kind of creative, educational and socially analytic literature which would help us to understand and to cope with our own situation, which would help us to acquire a sense of identity and purpose.[3]

It is worth recalling that at the same seminar, the late UWI pro vice chancellor, Professor Lloyd Braithwaite, recalled that when the UWI's journal *Social and Economic Studies* was first proposed in 1952–53, it was strongly opposed by the then principal of the university (an expatriate), on the grounds that the duty of academics in the West Indies was to get their work published in recognized international journals and that it was futile for the UWI to try to produce such a journal itself.[4]

Ironically, *Social and Economic Studies*, still published by the Institute of Social and Economic Research (ISER), is today a recognized international journal with metropolitan scholars vying for publication in its pages alongside their Caribbean peers. How times have changed. Similar competition exists for publication by the Press, although the majority of the authors it has published seem to be from the Caribbean. Says Cameron:

Although I haven't done an actual tally of what percentage, off the top of my head I would guess it's about fifty–fifty right now? It might be sixty–forty. Sixty Caribbean and forty outside. And those that are outside, many of those, and again I don't have a percentage, are Caribbean, but they are re-located some place else – teaching at some other institution or doing research some place else.[5]

Although it is not actually stated anywhere in their literature, the subject matter of the books submitted to the Press for publication must be related to the West Indies.

Structure and Governance of the UWI Press

The staffing and structure of the Press is as follows: the director reports to a board of directors chaired by the vice chancellor of the university. The board also has a representative from each of the campuses, a representative from the Caribbean Development Bank (CDB), as well as a representative from the private sector. From the inception of the Press up until 1997, the board met yearly, but starting in 1998 began to meet quarterly. The board does not decide on matters of publishing; its concern is with the structure and the financial picture of the Press.

The director also has three managers reporting to her, a managing editor, an accounting and financial operations manager, and a marketing manager. Each of these managers has at least one person working directly with her. So the managing editor has an assistant editorial and production person, the marketing manager has a marketing assistant, and the operations manager has an operations assistant. At the present time the operations manager also is responsible for the customer relations representative, the warehouse supervisor and the warehouse assistant/driver. The marketing manager and the managing editor also work with a field of freelance people. A pool of about twenty-five or thirty external persons work with the editorial department on a regular basis. The marketing manager, depending on the project – for instance the start-of-semester Great Book Sale – will have a crew of people to work with her on the particular event.

Matters relating to accounting and finances (payables, receivables, invoicing of books, customer relations, and keeping track of the budget) are the concern of the operations manager. The managers work together with the director to set the annual budget, then the operations manager keeps the group informed about how they are doing on that particular budget. Each of the managers is responsible for managing her particular area in relation to the budget. According to Cameron: "It is very much a participatory management set up, and everybody has a say in the decisions. It's not necessary that that particular opinion will be the one that carries the day, but everyone has a say."

Deciding What to Publish

The director also works with an editorial committee, and it is this committee that decides what will be published with the imprint of the UWI Press. This committee is made up of academics from the three campuses who come from many different fields. The way it works is that the director gets the materials together for a manuscript that the Press is considering. These materials include external peer reviews, plus a prospectus about the manuscript. Once the manuscript is reviewed, the Press invites the author to respond in writing to the reviews. It is a blind review in the sense that the reviewers know who the author is, but the author does not know who the reviewers are. When there is a prospectus, at least two reviews and the author's response, these are put before the editorial committee for a decision on whether to publish or reject the work.

Canoe Press

The Press actually uses two imprints for the books it publishes: the University of the West Indies Press, for the scholarly works that have survived the review process, and a subsidiary imprint, Canoe Press UWI. The Canoe Press imprint is used to publish material such as conference proceedings, textbooks and publishing for hire.

In other words [says Cameron], we sell professional publishing services through it. So with the exception of textbooks, anything that we use the Canoe Press imprint on has to be fully subsidized, and must cover the full cost of production; and then we agree to share the revenue between whoever sponsored the book and ourselves, because we assume the cost of marketing, promotion and sales but they must assume the cost of production.

Canoe Press receives as many as thirty submissions for subsidized publications a year, while the Press proper gets an average of a new manuscript submission every week. The Press has appointed sponsoring editors at the university campuses in Barbados and Trinidad, and submissions also come from those campuses, although many are submitted by the authors directly to Mona and not through the sponsoring editors.

Copublications

One dimension that the Press has fully embraced is the production of its books in conjunction with university presses in Canada and the United States. This activity is a direct offshoot of what Director Cameron considers her greatest strength in the job, her ability to negotiate contracts and "convince people they would like to publish with us". As a result the Press has thus far entered into joint publishing arrangements with Syracuse University Press, University Press of Florida, McGill-Queen's University Press, Wayne State University Press and University of Pennsylvania Press. These deals guarantee her Caribbean authors publication in North America as well as in the Caribbean and exposure to an international audience. Cameron explains further:

What we would like ideally is to establish a relationship, which we have done with University Press of Florida and McGill-Queen's University Press, one in the States and one in Canada, where we're going to co-pub three or four titles with each press each year. And that way we're not always starting from zero. Because there are no rules when you negotiate a contract, whether it's with an author or with another publisher. So if you can establish a relationship where you each respect what the other party is doing and have a level of confidence that they are going to deliver what they say they are going to deliver and it won't be an embarrassment to you once it's delivered, then it's much easier to do business. So we have worked hard at that. As with all businesses, part of [my success] comes from my contacts before I ever came here. You know, I was a member of one of the big publishers' associations in North America, so I knew the other directors. So when it was announced that I was coming here they were already thinking, 'OK. What have we got that can travel down there.' So McGill-Queen's came to us, but we went to Florida. And the other ones, sometimes it's them coming to us and sometimes it's us going to them.[6]

The Press has directories of publishers and when a manuscript is submitted which, it is felt, will appeal to a particular market the director looks very carefully at what each prospective university press has been publishing,

And we say, 'OK, well I think this title might fit with them.' So, then, on any given title I might write six or eight or twelve letters and find out who is interested. Maybe none. But maybe one or maybe two or three, and so then we send manuscripts and we send information, and it's a very long process and it takes a lot of doing.

Negotiating the rights and the markets is the ticklish part of the exercise:

The market areas are very clearly defined as part of the contract. So generally what we are trying to do is, we write a contract that says we have exclusive rights in the Caribbean, they have exclusive rights that, say it's a US publisher, they want all of North America usually. Sometimes I give them just the US, but they want all of North America. And then what we have tried to do is say 'let's share other world rights'. So that if we get an order from the UK or from someplace else, we can fill it. If they get it they can fill it.[7]

Ian Randle Publishers

Another Caribbean academic publisher who is heavily into copublications is the Jamaican-based Ian Randle Publishers (IRP). This publishing house opened its doors in 1991, a year before the UWI Press was started, and has had close links with the UWI community, publishing a number of highly respected historical works by UWI-based academics. It has, in the fiftieth anniversary year, just published *Modern Jamaican Art* on behalf of the University of the West Indies Development and Endowment Fund.

Ian Randle, president of IRP, is a graduate of UWI and for many years was the manager of Heinemann (Jamaica) Ltd prior to setting up his own publishing house. His books, like those of the UWI Press are attractive and well produced. Many of them are copublications. Like the Press, he explains that in copublishing:

There are situations in which we initiate, develop, create the books, and then sell on to overseas publishers. And it also works in exactly the opposite way, where we are taking books from publishers where they do all the work, and we are simply taking the editions and publishing locally. I went to Temple University Press in Philadelphia, and sold them a new book that we're doing. A book on reggae. And all they have seen is a manuscript. Now Temple trusts me enough to say, 'Please deliver to my warehouse two and a half thousand copies with my imprint details on it.' I don't have to show them anything. When I say we don't have to show them anything, obviously when we create the cover design we'll show it to them, they come back and comment on it; similarly when we change the imprint pages.

But what they do is, at manuscript stage they'll do exactly what we do. They'll send out the manuscript for evaluation, they come back with comments, they pass on the comments to us, we incorporate them. I'll send it to them at manuscript stage because, especially a university press, it has to go through the whole process of peer review. We have our own independent readers, so you merge the two sets of comments.[8]

Randle sees the copublishing deals as an essential part of IRP operations. He sees them in financial terms, as providing a safety net for his publishing ventures, because, he says, "very often the sale overseas virtually guarantees that the book is going to be profitable":

> I mean let's take *The Haunting Past*, for instance, which is a good example. When the book was at manuscript stage I sent it to three or four different publishers who I thought might have an interest in that book and in this market. And one came through and gave me a very substantial order. Were it not for his order I probably wouldn't have done the book. The order was for about 1,500 copies, of which 1,200 were paperback and 300 hardback. The American market always wants a hardback version, and that's great, because it means that they make more money off it, it's prestige for the author, and it gives us prestige too. So a lot of our books appear both in hardback and paperback. I get a print quotation for supplying these 1,500 books which would include imprint change; it would have their imprint on the book, so that in the United States, they are the publishers. I quote them a price, and we have a deal where on the signing of the contract they pay me one-third, when I deliver the books they pay me the other third, and the final payment comes sixty days later.
>
> However, what it means is that I have to undertake the total investment. I carry all the costs. They just simply send me the copyright changes that they want to put on to the book. When I give the print order, I say to my printer, I want you to print 1,500 copies with these changes. The books are printed and delivered straight to their warehouse. I don't even see the book sometimes, unless I ask for copies to be sent to me. It's very neat, and they pay in foreign exchange.
>
> The second point, though, is that you don't make a lot of money off those deals, because, when I get an order for 1,500 copies from an American publisher, I have to give it to him at a price that then allows him to make a profit. So I make considerably less profit doing that. My margins are low, but as far as I'm concerned, this is the only effective way of dealing with the American market, to

sell the rights. Number one, it gives me the safety net. Number two, I give my author the opportunity of being published overseas. And thirdly, if I were doing the book entirely on my own, I'd probably only do 750 copies, at say a unit cost of ten dollars – but because I now have an American partner, I'm doing 2,500 copies. My unit cost comes down to five or six dollars, so I can therefore sell my copies in my own market cheaper, and so in a way, these copublishing deals subsidize the production for the local market.

Differences Between the Press and IRP

The similarities between the work done by IRP and the Press are obvious. They are both producing scholarly works by Caribbean authors, and they are giving those authors wider exposure through copublishing deals with bigger publishers overseas. Yet, as Randle points out, there is a subtle difference between them:

My operation differs from the Press in that I don't have that restrictive mandate which says they must 'publish research aimed at meeting critical regional needs', in other words, academic books. I choose to publish at levels above A Level. And those books may or may not be textbooks.They can be textbooks but they're also academic books, and very often they are academic books which extend downward into classroom use: tertiary and undergraduate classrooms. So, for example, when I published *Caribbean Economic Development,* which is a reader in Caribbean economic development, it was conceived largely as an academic book. But now it is used in courses at UWI, it is used at CAST, and it is used in the schools for A Level programmes. So when I take on books, when I start to do the numbers, I'm saying, well if I produce this, then chances are, it might be used in the school system. I'll give you another example. One of the books we produced this year, Alvin Thompson's *The Haunting Past,* is prescribed as a textbook in survey courses in Caribbean Politics, or whatever, in quite a few US colleges. But it's not used that way here. It's seen essentially as an academic book here. So our publishing decisions very often attempt to bridge that gap between the straight academic and stuff which could be used in schools.[10]

But this observation overlooks the fact that the Press also operates the Canoe Press imprint for nonacademic books and for textbooks. Cameron describes Canoe Press publishing as:

Those materials that are relevant to the scholarly process but are not new works of scholarship themselves, and they are not textbooks. Things like conference proceedings, like a book we published last year for someone in Barbados called *The Administration and Conduct of Corporate Meetings*. Things like that are very detailed and exhaustive, but they are not new. It's just maybe the first time that all this information has been easily available between covers.[11]

This opens the door for consideration of the differences between academic or scholarly publishing and textbook publishing. Randle sees the difference this way: "Academic publishing is strictly those kinds of books where people are working, usually long-term, in an area of research and dissecting it and coming out with some conclusions about it. Whereas textbook publishing is specifically teaching people how to do certain things." The UWI Press will publish both kinds of books, although right now it is predominantly an academic publisher.

Teaching Texts and the Press

On the issue of teaching texts and the Press, Cameron had this to say:

We do have a textbook publishing component and we operate that under our Canoe Press imprint. It is a very intensive process to develop textbooks and one of the reasons that textbooks cost so much money is because the research and development that goes into them takes a long time. So, for instance, when we get a textbook manuscript, we have to have it reviewed very carefully and tested and we try to refine it as much as we can, because we know we are going to be in competition with firms that specialize in publishing textbooks, and academic publishing is totally different from textbook publishing. It's potentially very risky business at the university level because if you have the very same course taught within an institution by three different people, those three different people can each choose a different textbook. There is no rule that says they have to choose this one. So it's potentially very risky. However, if you do get in with a good textbook it's very lucrative. We presently have no plans to produce work for secondary schools. But some of our stuff goes in that direction naturally. We don't plan it that way. We look at that as a secondary, or even further, market. So it's wonderful if it happens, but we're not looking in that direction in the first instance.[12]

Developing Textbooks

Randle elaborates on what is needed to succeed as a textbook publisher:

It comes down to quality, marketing and making the right contacts. If it fits the curriculum and you market it properly, you have as good a chance as any others to get in. The problem is that there are very few local publishers in the Caribbean who can afford to make the kinds of investments in developing major textbook schemes, and spending all that money in the product development, and production of the books, and then the marketing, to have a reasonable chance of displacing any of the existing series.[13]

Meanwhile, the Press is currently preparing to publish four textbooks under the Canoe Press imprint. The first is in the area of government, authored by Trevor Munroe, which has done very well and been reprinted four times. The Press is now waiting for a revised version. They are also bringing out a textbook in sociology, one in social work, and another in chemistry. These are all being published to meet specific teaching needs because, as Cameron confesses: "We haven't got brave enough to do it on speculation yet."

It is a decision that Randle completely understands. At Heinemann he gained extensive experience in developing textbooks for the school market. At IRP he recognizes that he is in competition with the Press:

UWI Press's mandate is not to produce textbooks. In fact, if you speak to UWI Press, they are not textbook publishers at all. They are academic publishers. UWI Press's mandate is to publish the research work of faculty. That, if you ask me to define it, is what I think UWI Press's role is. And that's where it has to concentrate its resources if it has to justify its existence. In other words, UWI Press couldn't go out tomorrow morning and start to commission a range of textbooks for the new CAPE examination or for the BVI Community College while it had its own faculty members screaming at the door and saying, 'How come you're not producing my PhD piece, because I need that in order to keep my job at the university.' So in fact it has that strong pressure to respond to, and which is why it's difficult to be profitable.[14]

Cameron recognizes the competition from IRP:

Ian Randle is posing some interesting competition. I mean, for the most part we complement each other's programmes. But occasionally we are going after the same thing. So I think that that's good and healthy and I'm very pleased about that. We are going after the same authors and the same subject matter. Both. But I think that's healthy for both of us. So I'm not threatened by it and I don't think he is either.[15]

Caribbean Publishers and the Region's Textbook Needs

Both the UWI Press and IRP recognize that there is a textbook market in the Caribbean at all educational levels, but both recognize the risks involved in trying to service it, in trying to develop new texts specifically to meet curriculum needs. Currently, the Press is very strong in history and in cultural studies. And they are also, quite interestingly, getting a number of titles in theology, religious studies and economics. The Press, according to Cameron, is also branching out in new directions:

One of the things that we introduced this year that we're very proud of is something that we call the Press UWI Biography series. We've got two books in that series now. One is Douglas Hall's book about M.G. Smith and another is Bridget Brereton's book about John Gorrie, who was a Chief Justice in Trinidad in the late nineteenth century. We have two more books coming out in that series. One is about Lewis from Barbados who was a politician in the thirties and forties or whenever it was, it might have been in the forties and fifties, a very controversial fellow, and another manuscript coming out in that series is by Dr Giglioli who was in Guyana and who was very instrumental in solving the malaria problems in that area. Now, Dr Giglioli died. This is his autobiography. We're looking at a variety of other manuscripts. What we are trying to do with that series is not just focus on famous people. We're actually looking at manuscripts of people that nobody has ever heard of, but are representative of Caribbean peoples. So we're quite excited about that one. We also have manuscripts about the environment, housing in particular, the environmental impacts on housing, and the environment itself in relation to geography and geology. These of course are not produced primarily for teaching but they will get into the teaching area eventually.[16]

But neither Cameron nor Randle has any idea of the number or kinds of textbooks needed. When asked what percentage of needed texts were published by the UWI Press, Cameron laughed and said, "A tiny, tiny percent. Less than 1 percent, I would guess, at this point. I'd have to really think about that: how many different courses are taught, and what level of textbook is used."

Randle was asked: "Given the fact that there are so many subjects taught in a university or in a secondary school, is there any possibility in the near future, or even in the remote future, that we can supply all those areas?" His emphatic response was:

No, and I don't think we should try. What will happen is that, one, publishers will go first for those areas that have the largest numbers. That's the obvious thing that will happen. And the next influencing factor will be those people who are working in particular areas and have the confidence to write. They might write in an area that is not necessarily a big numbers area. For example, we are about to publish a *Reader in Caribbean Geography*. Now, geography isn't a big subject area, but it's a very nicely produced book and we think that small as the numbers are, we can make it work for that subject. So I think it will depend on those two things. The big numbers will get published first, then the good manuscripts will come afterwards, and if in fact a momentum builds up, then we will start to fill the void. But I don't think it is necessarily a goal to say that we have to publish everything locally. I don't believe that is necessary, because there are still some very good books being produced, and also you see, people talk glibly about globalization, and when they talk about globalization, they talk about it in terms of others gaining access to this global market – not realizing that they are part of the global market themselves, and therefore we can get access to the world. They are so used to people having access to us, that it's really revolutionary to think of us having access to them.[17]

Of course, Randle and Cameron are showing that globalization works, that publishers in the Caribbean can originate regional books and reach markets outside the region. But Randle also sees further:

I am coming around to the next stage, and it doesn't necessarily have to depend on the completion of stage one where we produce books about the Caribbean. We can start to produce books about other parts of the world. You can find attractive books, and I have one such book which I am publishing in a couple months' time.

I'm doing a deal with a small South African publisher who is producing a book called *Common Hunger to Sing* and it's the life stories of black women singers in South Africa, from the 1950s to the 1990s. They were all part of that whole anti-Apartheid protest. So I was interested in the book on several levels, one, obviously for the music market, the other one, from an almost feminist perspective, you know, you see the struggles of these women; and the third thing is that the text is complemented by some of the most beautiful photographs you could ever think of. Nice black and white photographs of beautiful black women, both young and old. And I think I can sell the book on those three levels. One of the good things about this particular deal is that I negotiated not just Caribbean rights, but the whole of North America. So you know, if I don't sell it here, I can sell it in the States. So you have to have the vision to think past the narrow confines of your own market and to not only say, I can sell the book in other markets, but also to have the confidence that other people from other parts of the world can come to you, because they think that you can produce a good book and can market it.[18]

Regional Publishing: No Statistics

Both Canoe Press and IRP produce books for the tertiary level market. But what about the provision of textbooks for the secondary and primary educational levels regionally? At all levels, the majority of textbooks used in the Caribbean come from the United States and the United Kingdom. Both Randle and Cameron estimate that 80 percent of the textbooks used in the region come from the United Kingdom. But both are quick to point out that they are guessing, and both deplore the absence of any statistics about the publishing industry in the region. When asked how many regional publishers there are and how they are doing, Cameron responded:

You know, I *wish* I could answer that question. And it's one of the things that I really think that the Book Industry Association of Jamaica (BIAJ) needs to be working with. One of the functions of an association like that should be to gather statistical information about the industry so that trends can be observed and plans can be made and people can, you know, plot their way and not just fumble from one place to the next. So I think the BIAJ is missing out on not carrying out that kind of activity.[19]

Randle joins Cameron in deploring the lack of reliable statistics, but by piecing together their views, the following impressionist picture of the textbook publishing scene in the Caribbean emerges.

Jamaica

The Press and IRP are the only publishers producing textbooks at the tertiary level, while at the secondary level there are:

1. Jamaica Publishing House, which has not produced a book in years. The publishing house grew out of an original association between Macmillan and the Jamaica Teachers' Association (JTA). Macmillan linked up with the JTA because it was felt that this was a direct link to the schools. At the time, the JTA was extremely well organized and very powerful, and there was every reason why that association should have worked. Similarly, William Collins linked with Sangster's Bookstores because it was felt that the publisher could get an advantage by linking with the most powerful bookseller in the island. But of course, the associations were never intended really to work. In both cases, the publishers were simply looking for local alliances which would allow their books from the United Kingdom to get into the market. So although local companies were established, the international publishers actually starved the local company. All the money and all the development went into producing books for the region out of England; and little has really changed.[20]

2. Kingston Publishers: Mike Henry had an interest in history. He was actually recruited in the United Kingdom by Collins, came to Jamaica, and started off as a representative for Collins. He is currently producing mass market trade books, doing a range of 'whatever Mike Henry is interested in' kind of books. The company used to publish secondary school publications and still have some books left over from the 1970s, when Kingston Publishers had an arrangement with a Far Eastern publisher, Far Eastern Press. All of those books were actually developed by McGraw Hill Far Eastern Publishers, but had a Kingston Publishers imprint on them.

3. West Indies Publishing is the rump of the old Heinemann. It really is not publishing any longer and is now called Carib Publishing. The company intends to continue specializing in textbooks for schools.

4. At the primary level, there is Carlong which is the local successor company to Longman.

Jamaican Government Ownership Policy in the Seventies

Many of the local publishing companies formed in the sixties and early seventies were linked with UK publishers. These linkages came under strain, due to government policies about Jamaican ownership of companies. Ian Randle explains:

When I was at Heinemann in the 1970s, we came under considerable political and social pressure at the time of the whole socialist thing and the Manley regime, and within two years of setting up, the company was forced to go local, and Heinemann actually had to sell majority shares in the Jamaican company. Because that was the policy at the time. And you know, it was absolutely disastrous. Because the company was undercapitalized and Heinemann simply stopped sending money. They didn't pull out, no, no. They stayed in, but they stopped sending any money at all. And their whole attitude changed. It was an absolutely wrong policy, it hasn't worked anywhere.[21]

Trinidad Textbooks Publishers

Neither Randle nor Cameron could identify any publishing house in Barbados, or indeed in any of the islands of the Eastern Caribbean or in Guyana. But Cameron found a different situation in Trinidad. She did a consultancy for the university a few years ago looking, not at publishing, but at printing throughout the region, to see who is doing what, where, and how much it cost. Her findings:

Actually there is quite a little bit of publishing done in Trinidad. I was astonished when I got there, because there were at least 350 printers in Trinidad. Many of them are small printers, but, still, that's quite a number of printers for a small country. And there are also publishers. I don't know the names of them off the top of my head. I knew a couple of them at that point because I would come up against them. One was called something like Imprint, with the *Express* newspaper people there. And then there was another one called, it started with P . . . I just can't remember.[22]

Paria Publishing

It is more than likely that the publisher Cameron had in mind is Paria Publishing Company which was started by a young Trinidadian advertising man, Gerard Besson, round about 1981. Since then the company has become such a success that Besson claims there are a number of benefits for his homeland in particular and the Caribbean in general from indigenous publishing. One, he says, is playing a role in recording the Caribbean's history, some of the subject matter of which, he reckons, would be too esoteric for overseas publishers. Among Paria's titles are *A History of Aviation in Trinidad and Tobago* by G.T.M. Kelshall (for the Airport Authority), *The U-Boat War in the Caribbean*, also by Kelshall, and *A Photograph Album of Trinidad at the Turn of the 19th Century* by Besson himself.

Paria also reprints long out-of-print books or monographs on various aspects of Trinidadian history. One of these is *Free Mulatto* by J.B. Philippe, first published in 1829. According to *Caribbean Week*:

Besson feels Caribbean publishing outfits like Paria also lend a hand in preserving the actual evidence of people's culture. In the case of Trinidad and Tobago, he described the archives and most other sources of historical information as 'chaotic and rapidly being devoured by cockroaches.' Besson disclosed that he personally has had to go around households collecting old photographs and interviews for some of his books. Now, among other achievements, Paria has the largest collection of photographs of the history of the Chinese ethnic population in Trinidad.[23]

Besson, who sits on the University Council of the St Augustine campus, publishes a wide variety of books, some academic, others not, with such titles as *150 Years of Business and Banking in Trinidad and Tobago*, *Legends of Trinidad and Tobago*, and *Treatments and Cures with Local Herbs* by Albertina Pavy, who is very much a grass roots person, and whose book is

Paria's best seller with more than 13,000 copies sold so far. "Paria," according to Besson, "has helped reverse a tradition in which almost every book in the region's bookstores and in educational institutions is brought in from big overseas publishers."[24]

Imprint

The other well known Trinidad publishing house, Imprint, seems to publish general trade books rather than textbooks, and they seem to produce a fair number of general titles. But our present focus is on textbook and academic publishing, and in Randle's view, there are no established publishers in these areas in Trinidad, except for Royurds. Is he contradicting Cameron's view about "quite a bit of publishing" in Trinidad? Not necessarily, because as he observes in the case of Guyana and Trinidad:

I can't think of anybody who is publishing consistently. But it comes down to what your definition of a publishing house is. And I think that to qualify to be considered a publisher, one really has to point to an organization that produces, I would think a minimum of one or two books a year, has some kind of a marketing structure for marketing the books, and displays some kind of consistency in output. If you produce one book every three years it's hard for me to describe you as a publisher, otherwise you would have to say that there are hundreds of publishers around the place, who publish only one book and disappear. The fact is that there are no established publishers in Trinidad. A lot of local entrepreneurs jump up and produce things because they think they can get books on school lists. But they have no publishing structures, no properly trained editorial people, no proper design of books. They simply put out materials to get them on to lists, and that really is the substance of Trinidad and Tobago textbook publishing with one exception. There is one company, Royurds, which has made an impact on the textbook publishing scene. Other than them, who else is there?[25]

Royurds Publishing Company, Randle explains, is a company formed by three Trinidadian educators who had, in fact, previously written for Thomas Nelson in the United Kingdom. The name of the company comes from Roy, Uriel and Clifford Narinesing. They had been long-standing authors for Nelson and then decided that they wanted to produce this course for themselves. Randle explains:

What they produce is an English series which started at the certificate level at CXC, and the first book was so successful, they then produced a complete course for the whole secondary school programme. And that to my mind is the first example of any kind of local breakthrough in a core subject area.[26]

It is not only now the lead course for CXC in Trinidad but, Randle thinks, for most places in the Caribbean: "It's being used, very much so, in Jamaica. Oh yes," he claims. "So that's one example of a Caribbean textbook producer who has broken through the UK domination of the field."

Primary School Science Texts

Randle also identifies another Caribbean textbook breakthrough of the UK dominance, this time at the primary level.

In Jamaica, Shirley Carby at Carlong has produced some books in science in particular, which have got into the Jamaican primary school system. Less so outside Jamaica because, again, if I interpret Shirley correctly, she limits her vision to producing for Jamaica. And to the extent that some of her stuff travels abroad, well, that's just additional. But she has set herself up and gone out, as far as I know, purely as a Jamaican publisher. Then, outside of that, there is as far as I am concerned, nothing.[27]

So who are the United Kingdom publishers that continue to lead in the region-wide sale of textbooks? Who predominates? According to Randle: "Longman, Macmillan and Nelson; the same ones that have been providing the books all along. Nothing has changed," and he finds this regrettable. He notes that in Trinidad and Tobago the government is trying to reverse the situation at the primary level:

The government there, I think, has gone to the other extreme. If you look at the list of books that they recommend for use in primary schools, for instance, 90 percent of them are done by, published by these, what I would call back-door Trinidad companies. I am actually one of the strongest advocates for getting a change from a situation where 80 to 90 percent of the textbooks are still produced by British publishers after thirty years of independence. I mean, I think that's a travesty. And that's true throughout the region, though it's more true in some areas than in others, and the interesting thing is that it's probably slightly less true in Trinidad. Because the system there allows what I consider inferior materials to get into the schools. So I am a strong advocate of removing the British domination of the textbook market, but I think it shouldn't be replaced by the first thing that comes along, or anything that comes along simply because it comes from within the region. And that really is the greatest challenge facing us now.[28]

Randle observes that a number of the United Kingdom educational publishers have set up satellite operations in African states not dissimilar to those in the Caribbean of recent memory: "One of the interesting things about the Caribbean at the moment, which is very significant," he argues, "is that no UK publishing house has an interest in any publisher in the Caribbean."

So will we see their return to the region in similar fashion as we have seen the return of Cable and Wireless? Unlikely, because the Caribbean is seen as a small book market which can be handily supplied from Britain without going to the trouble of setting up parallel companies in the region. In any case, there is more than one way to skin a cat, and more than one way to sell one's books, and the most favoured method at present is to enter into copublishing arrangements with Caribbean publishers.

Journal Publishing on Campus

But before there was a press at the UWI, there was still publishing. A great deal of publishing. The publishing was and continues to be done through journals and, eventually, it was the sheer number of journals published by various campus publishing houses that helped convince university authorities that a university press could be a viable proposition. Still, the journey from journal to press was long and convoluted.

Caribbean Quarterly

The university's first academic journal appeared on the Mona campus a year after the University College of the West Indies (UCWI) accepted its first students. The journal was *Caribbean Quarterly* (*CQ*), an interdisciplinary periodical started by Philip Sherlock and Andrew Pearse, which has been published continuously since 1949. It concerns itself with Caribbean culture in all its ramifications. Professor Rex Nettleford, the present editor of *Caribbean Quarterly*, explains the thinking that led to its creation:

In Jamaica the University's first Director of Extra Mural Studies who was also the Vice-Principal of the then University College and later the Vice-Chancellor of an independent UWI [that is, Philip Sherlock] was a poet and historian as well as a former advocate of cultural development throughout the region. He was to employ the Department of Extra Mural Studies as a base of operation for cultural research, the promotion of literature and the performing arts, as well as for the dissemination of material on Caribbean cultural life through the journal *Caribbean Quarterly*. The present incumbent [Professor Rex Nettleford] continues in this tradition. He not only creates dance works for what is regarded as a major dance-theatre company in the Commonwealth Caribbean, he also advises the Jamaican government on cultural policy.[29]

By 1951, *CQ* had a circulation of 3,000 copies, and the Extra Mural Department had enlarged its publishing programme to include other works:

The Extra Mural Department was proud of its record in publishing monographs specially produced for use by extra-mural classes and for building a well-informed public. Andrew Pearse produced and published *Caribbean Quarterly*, Cumper's *Social Structure of Jamaica*, and his *Social Structure of the British Caribbean* (Part I); *Caribbean Plays*, edited by Errol Hill; Gertrude Williams' *Everyday Economics for West Indians, A Sociological Manual for Extension Workers in the Caribbean* by M.G. Smith and G.J. Kruijer; *Focus,* an anthology of West Indian literature edited by Edna Manley; and an abridged version of Ligon's *Journal* of his stay in Barbados in the early days of the sugar-and-slave plantation, edited by Sherlock. As the names of Cumper and M.G. Smith suggest, the Department kept in close touch with Dudley Huggins, director of the newly-founded Institute for Social and Economic Research, and with his staff of research scholars.This collaboration underlines the importance of a close complementary relationship between departments responsible for extension programmes, research institutes and teaching departments. The story of the College's Extra Mural Department leads naturally to the story of ISER, the value of whose work is beyond calculation.[30]

Institute of Social and Economic Research Started

In 1948 ISER was set up at Mona with funds from the Social Science Research Council of Britain. This was before the Faculty of Social Sciences was established, and at a time when few studies had been made of Caribbean economy and society. In 1958 a branch was set up in Cave Hill and ten years later another at St Augustine.

The broad objective of ISER is to support research as the basis for scholarly excellence. There has been a concentration on development in general and Caribbean studies in particular. In this respect, ISER's aim is to act as a catalyst for understanding the Caribbean environment and to provide concepts, models and theories against which the performance of Caribbean societies and economies may be assessed. ISER also functions as the research arm of the Faculty of Social Sciences on all three UWI campuses. ISER's publications division processes about 150 articles and twenty monographs and working papers a year. The oldest of ISER's publications is the quarterly journal of *Social and Economic Studies*, which was founded in 1953 and has over 1,500 subscribers.[31]

Social and Economic Studies

The first issue of *Social and Economic Studies* (*SES*) carries the dateline February 1953 and came out under the editorial guidance of H.D. Huggins who was then the director of ISER. It was to be the first of a long line of publications issued by ISER:

When *SES* commenced publishing four decades ago there was very little serious systematic work to build up a knowledge base for scholarly research in the Social Sciences in the Caribbean region. The work of ISER and its scholarly journal *SES* has filled this gap with a high level of success, and *SES* now leads its field in communicating the results of research and reflection conducted at a sophisticated level on social, economic and political issues of relevance to the Caribbean . . . Every year *SES* receives over 150 manuscripts for possible publication from authors from all over the world, some of these from as far away as Australia and South Africa, indicating the wide acceptance it enjoys internationally as a leading journal in its field . . . there is no question of the leading position *SES* occupies as the indispensable and foremost journal for Caribbean socio-economic research.[32]

As Sir Philip Sherlock and Professor Rex Nettleford state in their history of the UWI:

The University College reached out into its supporting nations through its Department of Extra-Mural Studies and its Institute of Social and Economic Research (ISER). They complemented each other, the one lengthening the cords linking the College with the economic and social development of each supporting nation, the other strengthening the supporting stakes by deepening the people's understanding of themselves, their resources and their circumstances through research.[33]

Sherlock and Nettleford observe that: "By the end of its first ten years the University College of the West Indies had become indispensable because of the quality and relevance of its research." The principal, Arthur Lewis, emphasized this in his address to students at a matriculation ceremony in 1960. He asked: "Why not close the place down?" and replied:

The first answer is that we would not close the place down even if all the students disappeared, because the College doesn't exist merely to teach students. This is a great centre for research, and every country needs to spend money on research into its problems, whether it has students or not. For example, the Institute of Social and Economic Research was established here twelve years ago, without a single student of economics, and every one of the West Indian Governments is grateful for the fine work which it has done. Even if we sent all the medical students away, we should still have to keep the specialist doctors, who eat up such a large part of our budget. The College has an outstanding record in pharmacology, and in contributing to our understanding of malnutrition, which is one of the major problems of our people, and of its effects on pregnancy, on liver disease, or on heart disease. All this and other medical research must be continued, whether there are students or not. Equally important work is going on in Arts and Science. It would take all night to make a catalogue . . . every country in the world wants to have its own university, however much it may cost. It wants a body of specialists who are devoted to studying its problems on the spot. This is what we would lose if we were content merely to send our students to England. On the other hand, this presents to the College, to you and to me, a tremendous challenge. We have to justify ourselves not just by passing exams, which we could do anywhere, but rather by giving our minds to the problems of our country, and doing all we can to solve them – whether problems in science, or engineering, or politics, or aesthetics, or any other branch of knowledge.[34]

West Indian Medical Journal

Alongside of *Caribbean Quarterly* and *Social and Economic Studies*, with their reports on research in the humanities and the social sciences, there was also the *West Indian Medical Journal* (*WIMJ*), with its reports on medical research and medical procedures. A quick history of that journal was given by its editor Professor Vasil Persaud, on the occasion of the fortieth anniversary of the UWI:

With the establishment of the Faculty of Medicine of the then University College of the West Indies (UCWI), in 1948, there arose an urgent need for a medical journal which catered to the entire West Indian medical community. At that time there were two medical journals in the English-speaking Caribbean – the *Jamaica Medical Review* and the *Caribbean Medical Journal*. The latter was published in Trinidad. It still exists, but is concerned mainly with medical problems in that island. In 1951, the Publications Committee of the *Jamaica Medical Review* handed over its assets in formation of a *West Indian Medical Journal*, the first issue of which appeared in September, 1951 . . . Today, the quarterly issue of the *WIMJ* is released punctually during the final month of each quarter of the year.[35]

From the very start, those behind *WIMJ* stated in the first editorial that they intended that it would develop into "a reference journal of the diseases of the West Indies and as a medium for spreading knowledge of diseases in the West Indies among the local practitioners and/or the medical world as a whole".[36]

The journal has been successful in achieving that mission. It now has a circulation of about 1,200, and through the exchange programme of the UWI Library it reaches almost 100 libraries worldwide. The journal also attracts advertising support from international pharmaceutical corporations, and now receives around 100 manuscripts each year from which about 50 are published after careful peer review. As the editorial assistant of the *WIMJ*, Bridget Williams, stated some years ago: "It is a wonderful thing for a third world medical school to have a journal of the calibre of *WIMJ*."[37]

These three journals, *CQ, SES* and *WIMJ*, were the first scholarly publications of the university, but over the years they have been joined by others emanating from the various faculty departments, until by 1994–95 there were some twenty-four scholarly or cultural journals plus other periodicals originating from the three campuses of the university.[38]

From Journals to Books

Besides journals, the various publishing entities also from time to time produced monographs, working papers and books. Indeed, the expansion from journals to monographs and longer publications began with *CQ* and the Extra Mural Department. As the present editor, Professor Rex Nettleford, explains:

I was with the Extra Mural Department from 1953 as a student, and I was a reader for *Caribbean Quarterly*, for errors, etcetera. It was natural for *Caribbean Quarterly* to be seen as an outlet for scholarly work, particularly that emanating from the creative imagination, anthropology social and cultural. And the adjunct efforts of monographs, etcetera appeared fairly early. So it was a wonderful vehicle for academics on campus in the humanities, languages, history, literature, so that John Parry, Le Page, Sandiman, Coulthard in Spanish literature, M.G. Smith's *Dark Puritan*, and Andrew Pearse and Andrew Carr . . . were published in the 1950s under the imprimatur of the Extra Mural Department.[39]

The Institute of Social and Economic Research also began publishing occasional monographs and books, and in the 1970s under successive directors, Alister McIntyre, Vaughan Lewis and Edward Greene, ISER began a sustained publishing programme that made the institute the largest UWI publishing centre. The enterprise began with the publication of Norman Girvan's *Foreign Capital and Economic Development in Jamaica* in 1971, followed by Owen Jefferson's, *The Post-War Economic Development of Jamaica*, and Trevor Munroe's, *The Politics of Constitutional Decolonization Jamaica 1944–62*, both in 1972. That same year, George Beckford's *Persistent Poverty* was published by Oxford University Press, and that was put on sale by ISER along with its own books.

In the Department of History, Professors Douglas Hall, Elsa Goveia and Roy Augier brought out the *Journal of Caribbean History*, in collaboration with the UK publishers Ginn, and also worked out a comprehensive history of the West Indies, a multivolume history of the Caribbean, which was also to be published by Ginn. But both the journal and the history project went through a bewildering series of permutations. Ginn published some books under the imprint of Caribbean Universities Press, then the project collapsed when Ginn was bought out. The project moved to Heinemann, who published the journal for a some time, and then they declared that it was not worthwhile, so they abandoned it. Then funding was obtained from the Ford Foundation, and the proposal was to publish chapters of the history as they were produced, rather than have them lying around waiting for the slowest authors to turn in their chapters, and publishing all at once. But alas, there was a change of staff at Ford and policy changed, and they didn't continue to publish. With one thing and another, over time, the book project went into limbo, while the *Journal of Caribbean History* worked out a complex arrangement with the editor in Jamaica, but with the journal being produced in Barbados.[40]

More recently, the books of the Caribbean history project have been published by UNESCO, and for a short period the *Journal of Caribbean History* was marketed by Heinemann Caribbean, managed at the time by Ian Randle. At present, however, it is published by the UWI Press. So all is well that ends well. And in a sense, the ups and downs of the Caribbean history project and of the *Journal of Caribbean History* are a metaphor for the coming into being of a UWI press.

The idea of a press was mooted by many persons over many years, including Professors Augier, Nettleford, Beckford and Lloyd Braithwaite. Indeed, by the mid 1980s there were so many publishing units, and so many publications, that the ISER's then book review editor, sociology lecturer Herman McKenzie, likened the UWI publishing scene *vis-à-vis* a university press, to the situation of the Prussian states prior to the unification of Germany: "Now that all these journals are being published, you have a university press but it's not all in one place; like Germany before unification."[41]

But would the many UWI publishing principalities be willing to be pulled together under the federal umbrella of a university press? In this period, when there was active discussion about the need for a press, but before it became a reality, Professor Augier had a view that in some ways paralleled that of McKenzie's:

What we haven't examined, merely taking it for granted, is that there ought to be a UWI Press. But ought there to be? Isn't it true to say that we already have, not one, but several UWI presses? Would there really be any advantage to a combined press responsible for all the scholarly publishing on campus? What would be the advantage of such a federation as against the independent existence of the various journals?[42]

And Professor Nettleford, pointing to collaborative book production between the publishing arm of the Extra Mural Department and ISER to bring out a book about Garvey, the proceedings of a conference at Mona, opined that:

If we can develop a habit of copublishing, this may be the germ of the university press we've been talking about. But to be honest, I think both ISER and Extra Mural like to see their imprimatur on a book, rather than a university press. And in a sense, we do have a university press, that is, a mechanism to facilitate the output, high standard, and frequency of publications, either by way of journals, monographs or books, with the imprimatur of UWI. Some amount of funding is needed for this, to take care of editing, budgeting, forecasting, and planning the publication. And since many of these journals have hardly any budget, there is no reason why editors could not stay where they are but have things pulled together by a University press office.[43]

But the decisions that led directly to the formation of the UWI Press grew out of the activities of the journal editors at Mona, who in the 1980s formed themselves into the University of the West Indies Publishers' Association (UWIPA).

Precursor to UWIPA

Back in 1983, three years before UWIPA was formally launched in January 1986, the editors who were responsible for the production of *CQ, Caribbean Journal of Education* (*CJE*) and *SES* – Janet Liu Terry, Pam Mordecai and Wenty Bowen, respectively – began informal discussions about the common problems facing their journals. They agreed that their respective journals all needed to get more subscribers, and to be marketed in a more aggressive manner. They began circulating among themselves material of relevance to the editing and selling of scholarly journals, such as the *IASP Newsletter*, first brought to their attention by Nora Mailer of the university's Planning Unit, who had herself been once involved with ISER's publication unit.

Much of the thinking that went into the cooperation between *CQ*, *SES* and *CJE* was that while the expertise to edit and produce journals and books abounded on campus, what the individual journals did not have, and what it made no sense for each to develop individually, was a marketing arm. There needed to be developed an institution that would take on the marketing of all journals collectively, on behalf of all.

In pursuit of the quest for more subscribers and joint marketing, Pam Mordecai, publications officer of the *CJE*, in 1984 discussed the rental of a mailing list from the IBIS Information Service in London that provided 3,190 library addresses in the United Kingdom. *SES* and *CQ* agreed to join her in this promotional effort and to share the costs. The mailing was finally sent off in 1986. It should be understood that while the decisions and initiatives to cooperate came from the publications' editors, when the spending of money was involved, they needed and got the agreement of their respective heads of departments; and the director of ISER at that time, Professor Edward Greene showed his support of closer cooperation between the publishing units by inviting the editors of *CQ* and *CJE* to some of ISER's publications planning meetings.

Formation of the Association of Journal Editors

In January 1986, Margaret Mendes, lecturer in the Department of Management Studies, who had recently produced the first issue of the journal *Caribbean Finance and Management*, and who had encountered a number of problems in the process, invited the other editors of campus journals to a meeting in the lounge of the Senior Common Room, to see whether they shared similar problems which they could perhaps help each other to solve. This meeting was attended by several editors, including those of *CQ*, *CJE* and *SES*, and it was a surprise to discover that they did indeed have common problems. They decided to continue meeting on a monthly basis to air these problems, and perhaps find some solutions.

By the time of the March meeting, the editors learned that the three journals *CQ*, *CJE* and *SES* were planning a joint promotional mailing to UK libraries, and the meeting discussed the question of whether centralized distribution and promotion of all campus journals was needed, and what steps would be necessary for implementing such a distribution and promotion arm. The

March meeting agreed that the various campus journals would collaboratively promote subscriptions and sales of each other by running exchange advertisements in their respective journals, a practice that had already been implemented between *CQ*, *CJE* and *SES*.

By the time the May meeting came around, Margaret Mendes, who at that time was the main impetus behind the group, and who was instrumental in keeping the meetings going, announced that she had met a Peace Corps volunteer who was interested in publishing. Realizing that the Mona Campus Journal Editors group, as they then referred to themselves, could not go much further without some sort of secretarial help, the group backed Mendes' query as to whether she should approach the Peace Corps office in Kingston about getting a volunteer to work with the group.

The approach was made, and the Peace Corps agreed to provide a volunteer for one year. The volunteer, Sally Spencer, joined the group in July 1986. She came under the direct supervision of Margaret Mendes and worked out of her office in the Department of Management Studies. This was a rather bold and innovative step on the part of both the UWI journal editors and the Peace Corps, who had assigned their volunteer not to the UWI, but to a group representing UWI publication editors, a group that then had no formal recognition from the UWI's administration, and no official position in the university's establishment.

Needs Survey

In June 1986, the editors' group had agreed that a 'needs survey' of all campus journals would be a good place to begin to quantify the problems that they had. The job of conducting this survey was among the first tasks given to Sally Spencer. It was felt that such a needs survey would pinpoint the areas where the various journals needed most help, and for what purposes applications for funds might sometime in the future be solicited.

Besides collecting data for the needs survey, the Peace Corps volunteer worked on the production of *Caribbean Finance and Management* and other campus publications, copy editing, proofreading and liaising with printers. She had no decision making function as far as the content of these journals was concerned; her function was that of getting manuscript copy ready for the printers. She was also instrumental in organizing a number of exhibitions and displays of campus books and journals at the Tom Redcam Library and other libraries around the island, and at the College of Arts Science and Technology (CAST), now the University of Technology (UTECH).

In February 1987, UWIPA decided to apply for another Peace Corps volunteer. The group requested of the Peace Corps authorities that this new volunteer have a background in business and marketing. Acquisition of an additional volunteer would have two objectives. It would allow Sally Spencer to concentrate on production matters, while allowing the new volunteer to help the campus publications in the area that the needs survey had indicated that they needed most help – that of promotions and marketing.

This new volunteer, Michael Gill, joined the group in April 1987, and was assigned the task of preparing a joint catalogue of cross-campus publications.[44] While Gill went about the process of getting information from the various journal publishers for compiling the catalogue, UWIPA busied itself organizing for active participation in book fairs and exhibitions, both in Jamaica and elsewhere. In 1987 alone, the association took books and journals from the three campuses to the Black Book Fair in London, in March; the First International Caribbean People's Bookfair in San Fernando and Port of Spain, Trinidad, in June and July; and the Miami International Bookfair in Florida, in November.

Financial assistance to attend these fairs came from a variety of sources including the United States Peace Corps, the Jamaica National Export Corporation, and ISER. Participation in book fairs was part of UWIPA's marketing thrust to raise the profile of Caribbean produced books. It exhibited and sold books for twenty publishers in Trinidad, and in her report on that fair, Sally Spencer wrote:

Through participation in other bookfairs this year, the Association had publicity material available to take to Trinidad. The material included an all journals flyer (of three campuses), a bookmark with the UWI crest and the names of all the journals, individual flyers, and a red and white cloth banner. The UWI Publishers' Association received eighty six (86) requests for the catalogue and one hundred forty six (146) publications were sold. An annually updated UWI catalogue is a necessity. People were amazed at the number of UWI publications represented and each year the numbers increase. A lot of people asked if the UWI Publishers' Association would be able to publish individual books by West Indian authors.

The need to develop into not only a University Publisher but a West Indian publisher is apparent.[45]

UWIPA's Catalogue

If 1987 was UWIPA's 'Year of the Book Fair', 1988 was to be its 'Year of the Catalogue'. This was the year that the joint catalogue, put together largely by Gill, was published. The UWIPA Catalogue 1988, on its white cover, bore the crest of the UWI and above the crest the title *University of the West Indies Publishers' Association: 1988 Catalogue and Order Form*. Under the crest it said "The source for Caribbean scholarly materials". The catalogue was a note-sized publication with sixty pages. It listed three international agents, one in England, one in Italy and one in Singapore, and on the inside back cover said that UWIPA was "interested in setting up marketing and promotional agent relationships with other countries".

The first page of the catalogue stated in the introduction that:

The UWI Publishers' Association was founded as a non-profit organization in January 1986 and is composed of publishers from the three campuses and the contributing territories of the University of the West Indies and other associated West Indian publishers. Currently there are over 30 members in the Association representing a wide range of disciplines. The Association's main goal is to promote the published writings (including books, journals and teaching materials) of West Indian authors to the Caribbean and international markets.

The introduction continued:

This is the first catalogue of the University of the West Indies Publishers' Association. The Association has attempted to cast as wide a net as possible in order that publications from all institutions and individuals of the University of the West Indies are included, however, if publications are missing please complete a Catalogue Entry Form (contained in the end documents of this catalogue) and submit it for the next edition of the catalogue. The compilers of this catalogue decided that the cut off point should be 1980 but a few earlier publications have crept in as they are still available in print. The catalogue has been published in the assurance that it will be of special value to international scholarship with an interest in the Caribbean. Some 5,000 copies of the first issue of this catalogue will be distributed to potential users.

The catalogue contained seven pages listing a total of twenty-five Caribbean journals. UWIPA also assisted ISER in producing its catalogue. ISER's yearly report for 1987, under 'Publicity and Marketing' said that in that year:

The major publicity and marketing thrust for ISER publications is the catalogue of which 5,000 copies were printed. These have been mailed out to prospective customers worldwide. The catalogue is over 100 pages long and contains over 100 titles. It costs $15,000 to produce and comes out of central university funds as a benefit which ISER enjoys as member of the UWI Publishers' Association. Throughout the year customers have been kept informed of new publications by flyers. For each new publication the section sends out 4,000 to 5,000 flyers. In order to maintain a live list, the section has generated a mailing list of over 5,000 names and addresses. Mailing list maintenance is a major task and consumes a great deal of time and energy.

Peace Corps Volunteers

In all, UWIPA was to have three Peace Corps volunteers attached to the group, with overlapping periods of attachment; first Sally Spencer, then Mike Gill, then Aubrey Botsford. Sally Spencer was the UWIPA's production coordinator. She notified publishers about the catalogue and collected the catalogue entry forms. Mike Gill was the marketing coordinator at the time the first catalogue was prepared. He did the desktop computer work, entering the data and typesetting the catalogue. The third volunteer, Aubrey Botsford, having been a book editor in the United States, became actively involved in UWIPA's later foray into desktop publishing activities. With the assistance of these three volunteers, UWIPA underwent a process of development that began to give campus editors and university administrators an impression of the services that a university press might provide.

UWIPA and Help from UWI

Following the successful creation and distribution of the catalogue, UWIPA decided to use its computer capabilities to offer a desktop publishing service to members of UWIPA and the UWI campus generally. And with the phasing out of the Peace Corps volunteers, UWIPA inherited a desktop publishing system and took in typesetting jobs for campus persons and others. By this time Janet Liu Terry had moved from being publications officer with Extra Mural to being publications officer with ISER. She used her good relations with Professor Nettleford of Extra Mural, to get space to house the Peace Corps-provided desktop computer, and Professor Greene of ISER, and pro vice chancellor Roy Augier, who was chairman of the university's Publications Board, to get limited funds for UWIPA activities such as attendance at book fairs, and partial funding of part-time staff to man its desktop publishing operations. UWIPA would later thank the "University Publications Board for their encouragement, assistance and belief in the potential of UWIPA". The Publications Board had been started by vice chancellor A.Z. Preston as a pump-priming 'university' rather than 'campus' body, to fund publication requests from journal editors.[46]

Desktop Publishing

UWIPA developed its desktop capability to meet a need for typesetting by campus and off-campus publication units, and to raise money for its operations. It employed persons on a part-time basis to do these jobs.[47] At one stage, UWIPA was typesetting five books for different groups, including a major contract for IRP, a book for the Department of Spanish, a special issue of the *Jamaica Geological Society Journal* and a newsletter for the Save the Children Fund.[48] UWIPA was at that time also typesetting and arranging the publication and distribution of *Caribbean Geography*. The association also arranged a publishing seminar in 1989, with Botsford running the seminar, which was attended by many people interested but not yet involved formally in publishing. The seminar demonstrated that there was a potential market for such training.

UWIPA Newsletter

Besides doing typesetting for others, UWIPA, following the successful publication and distribution of its catalogue, turned to the production of a UWIPA newsletter, a bimonthly publication that went out to journal editors and those who had bought books from UWIPA, and to those on its mailing lists. The newsletter was an eight-page publication that contained book reviews, a list of upcoming book fairs and conferences, a list of new books, and advertisements for publishers, and just under the masthead it proclaimed "UWIPA – The complete source for Caribbean scholarly materials".

The newsletter also stated that UWIPA was creating a set of directories of Caribbean study associations, bookstores, libraries, schools, development and financial institutions, and publication promotional agencies, and it was offering these directories on adhesive labels for virtually the cost of the labels. Of course, mailing lists are a service readily available to publishers in the developed world. But as far as anyone could tell, this was the first time that such a service was being developed in the Caribbean, and being put at the disposal of Caribbean editors.

In *UWIPA Newsletter* volume 4, number 6, readers were given a view of how UWIPA saw itself:

The University of the West Indies Publishers' Association (UWIPA) was founded as a non-profit organization in January 1986. Its members include publishers from the three campuses and the contributing territories of the University of the West Indies (UWI), the largest of which is the ISER, and other associated West Indian publishers. Its main goal is to promote publishing within and about the Caribbean to the local and international markets. It also offers marketing, editorial and production services to its members. Membership is free and open to all publishers and to individuals associated with the UWI.[49]

Caribbean Review Of Books

In 1991 UWIPA discontinued the publication of the newsletter. In its place came the ambitious *Caribbean Review of Books* (*CRB*). It was one of the most important contributions made by UWIPA to expanding the data base about Caribbean books, and was due to the single-minded research of UWI's acquisition librarian, Samuel B. Bandara. Virtually single-handedly, he compiled and edited the *Caribbean Review of Books*. Issue number 1 was dated August 1991 and said below the masthead: "The complete source for Caribbean book news". In his editorial note, Samuel Bandara said:

For me this first issue of *Caribbean Review of Books* is the first step of a dream about to come true. I mean these words literally. It is the first step because I know that there will be more and still more to do in our second and third and later issues to achieve our aim which is to produce a single effective source for up-to-date book news of relevance to the Caribbean: a task that will take more than our enthusiastic and hard working *CRB* team, its parent UWIPA, and our friends around us now give: an achievement that will be beyond us unless most of our authors, editors, publishers, booksellers and librarians are willing to work together towards it.

In a sense a part of that editorial expressed the aims of UWIPA:

I believe, together with my colleagues in UWIPA, as we have believed from the first day when we began planning to team up, that the dream of a single sharing community of Caribbean book people working together for the common good can become a reality: that such a community who will share their experiences, efforts, and products, and will from that sharing reap mutual benefits is not a mere dream, but one that is already beginning to come true. It is a dream that we felt was within grasp in our more successful moments in UWIPA work, and it is a dream we refused not to believe in when we had our hard times and disappointments (for UWIPA in its short life has experienced both sides repeatedly . . .).[50]

The masthead of *CRB* declares that it is "published quarterly by the UWIPA, in August, November, February and May; editor Samuel B. Bandara and production editor and designer, Annie Paul". It had as editorial representatives, the Extra Mural representatives in the noncampus Caribbean territories, and the editorial advisers were Alan Moss (Barbados), Edward Baugh (Jamaica), and Selwyn Ryan (Trinidad and Tobago).

Sam Bandara had long nurtured the idea of launching the *CRB*. What finally got it off the ground in August 1991 was the news earlier in the year that the Caribbean Studies Association (CSA) was about to launch a newsletter. It was felt that unless UWIPA moved fast with *CRB* the older, better financed CSA newsletter would corner the market of Caribbean book buyers. The decision to take the plunge and publish *CRB* was taken and the first issue came out on schedule in August. By October the subscription list stood at ninety. Thanks and congratulations were expressed to Annie Paul for having done an excellent job of designing and producing *CRB*.

During the year, however, UWIPA and *CRB* suffered an almost irreparable loss. Bandara set it out on his editorial page:

We enter 1992 with the third issue after having experienced a great loss. Janet Liu Terry, a founder member of UWIPA has left the Caribbean for Australia. Janet was a key member of our team, a leading contributor to UWIPA's mission, not merely in carrying out the Association's work but in guiding and initiating activities; a member to whom UWIPA's business was indistinguishable from her own, so that she gave it time, concern, thought and care to an extent that no other participating member could match. We would like to use this page to record how much we miss Janet's knowledge and experience, and the advice, and guidance flowing from that base. We also miss the leadership, labour and friendship which we took for granted while she was with us. We want to publicly acknowledge Janet's contribution to UWIPA, indeed to publishing activity in the University of the West Indies, and to *CRB* which exists largely because of her.[51]

In *CRB* number 5, August 1992, UWIPA showed its commitment to joint marketing of Caribbean books by including a special advertising supplement – an eight-page catalogue – of books by IRP.

Jamaican Books in Print

Also included in *CRB* number 5, August 1992, was a compilation of books from Jamaican presses, some three pages of book titles, and the list of publishers took up a page and a quarter, both sections in fine print. The books came from nine different campus publishing locations as follows: Department of French and German; Department of History; Department of Management Studies; Department of Spanish; Faculty of Education; Faculty of Education, Department of Teacher Education; Faculty of Medical Sciences; and the Library.

This preliminary compilation continued in *CRB* number 6, and that was itself expanded into *Jamaican Books in Print, May 1993*, compiled by Samuel

B. Bandara and published not by UWIPA but by the Caribbean Books in Print Project, UWI, Mona (1993). This publication was assisted by a grant from the Research and Publications Fund Committee of UWI, Mona campus. The coordinator of UWIPA, Annie Paul, the publications editor of ISER, Mona, provided assistance by typesetting, designing and arranging for the production of the printed version.

In his introduction to *Jamaican Books in Print,* Bandara observes that:

UWIPA was now recognized in Jamaica and the Caribbean as an active body attempting to make a contribution to the Caribbean book industry. It is from this recognition that friends in the book industry, libraries and the academic circles provide assistance to *CRB* in accessing and publishing the data disseminated through its pages. It is perhaps too high a claim for *CRB* to make (even after 6 issues) that its reporting achieves anything more than 60% coverage of all Caribbean books published in English. For material in other languages *CRB*'s gleanings are very meager indeed. In spite of these shortcomings *CRB* is the only journal that devotes itself solely to the subject of Caribbean books . . .[52]

A measure of Bandara's industry was that he had recorded in the first six issues *CRB* citations for over 550 new Caribbean books during the period August 1991 to November 1992, and he expressed the hope that *Jamaican Books in Print* would be the prototype of a *Caribbean Books in Print* to follow later if funding could be found.

The UWI Press: UWIPA's Role

By the time of these developments, the UWI Press had been launched. The university had hired a consultant, David H. Gilbert, a former director of Cornell University Press (1986–89) and before that director of the University of Nebraska Press (1975–86). He was contracted as the consultant for a period of five weeks beginning 14 January 1991. On 8 February 1991 he submitted a twenty-seven-page "Report on the Proposed Establishment of a University of the West Indies Press".[53]

His detailed report recommended that the press be located on the Mona campus based on the fact that Mona had the heaviest publishing output and the strongest interest. He singled out UWIPA for praise, citing that in his opinion the university owed UWIPA a debt of gratitude for having established by sheer volunteer efforts the groundwork for a UWI press – a joint catalogue, joint book fulfilment, collection of mailing lists, desktop publishing services, amongst other things. Gilbert confirmed UWIPA's own belief that the activities of a university press would have to be subsidized. It was expected that the salaries and perquisites of the press personnel would be decided at a Publications Board meeting on 7 November 1991. It was felt by UWIPA members that its functions should be absorbed by the press once it was established.[54]

And this is indeed what happened. In April 1992 the vice chancellor of UWI, Sir Alister McIntyre, issued a news release which read in part:

By October of this year the University of the West Indies will have its own functional publishing house, The University of the West Indies Press. The University of the West Indies Press is expected to help rationalize the University's publication activities, and reduce costs of all types of publications. It is also expected to improve the efficiency, professionalism and effectiveness of all campus publishing activities through the provision of technical services such as editing, design and production, and training.[55]

UWIPA Absorbed by the Press

After enjoying the hospitality of the School of Continuing Studies and Professor Rex Nettleford for some years, UWIPA's part-time staff relocated to the offices of the UWI Press at 1A Aqueduct Flats on 25 November 1992.

This was done in order to facilitate the absorption of some of UWIPA's functions – book order fulfillment, catalogue production and marketing – by the new UWI Press (UWIP). It was felt that this was in keeping with the role UWIPA envisioned for itself after the establishment of the Press, the idea being to consolidate and build up publishing in the University and not to compete and duplicate such efforts.[56]

Linda Cameron herself commented on the move at a UWIPA management meeting on 19 January 1993. In a report she said:

On Wednesday 25th November 1992 I was pleased to welcome UWIPA part-time staff, Nasima Ahmad and Annika Lewinson, as co-inhabitors of the UWIP Offices located at 1A Aqueduct Flats . . . It has been a pleasure for me to share space with Nasima and Annika and I am glad of their company. Beginning on Monday 18 January Pam Stephenson, who has been working as a UWIPA part-time employee with campus courier and other duties, will be joining the UWIP payroll. She will continue her duties for UWIPA and will assume some additional duties for UWIP.

The Press and UWIPA – Catalogue 1993

The new arrivals began immediately to collaborate on the production of the Press' new catalogue which appeared in March 1993. It was UWIPA's last hurrah. Its life ended with a whimper, but it achieved its objective. Largely due to the work it had done, UWIPA had convinced the university's administration that a UWI press was no pipe dream, but a viable option. Meanwhile, some initiatives taken by UWIPA still remain to be resurrected: namely the *Caribbean Review of Books*, and its allied publications – *Jamaican Books in Print* and *Caribbean Books in Print*.

Notes

1. The full mission statement states: "Our mission, in harmony with the mission of the University of the West Indies, is to publish research aimed at meeting critical regional needs and by so doing provide West Indian society with an active intellectual discourse."
2. Interview with Linda Cameron, 28 September 1997. Ms Cameron, a Canadian, set up the UWI Press from scratch and was its director for its first five years.
3. "From Imitation to Innovation", report of a seminar on regional problems of book production and distribution, organized by the Trinidad and Tobago National Commission for UNESCO to mark International Book Year, UWI, St Augustine, Trinidad and Tobago, 13–15 April 1972, 2.
4. Ibid., 12
5. Interview with Linda Cameron, 28 September 1997.
   Publisher's note:

Authors published (1992 – Sept. 1997)	No	%
All categories	74	100
Caribbean	56	75[a]
Non-Caribbean	19	25[b]

   Notes
   [a] 7% (or 4) of this number are Caribbean authors located elsewhere
   [b] 26% (or 5) of this number are non Caribbean authors located in the region
6. Ibid.
7. Ibid.

8. Interview with Ian Randle, president of Ian Randle Publishers, 16 September 1997.
9. Ibid.
10. Ibid.
11. Interview with Linda Cameron.
12. Interview with Linda Cameron, 4 September 1997.
13. Interview with Ian Randle, 16 September 1997.
14. Ibid.
15. Interview with Linda Cameron, 4 September 1997.
16. Ibid.
17. Interview with Ian Randle, 16 September 1997.
18. Ibid.
19. Interview with Linda Cameron, 4 September 1997.
20. Ibid.
21. Interview with Ian Randle, 16 September 1997.
22. Interview with Linda Cameron, 4 September 1997.
23. Norman Faria, "Book-making Gamble", *Caribbean Week* (9–15 December 1989): 11.
24. Ibid.
25. Interview with Ian Randle, 16 September 1997.
26. Ibid.
27. Ibid.
28. Ibid
29. Rex Nettleford, *Caribbean Cultural Identity: The Case of Jamaica, An Essay in Cultural Dynamics* (Kingston: Institute of Jamaica, 1978), 158.
30. Phillip Sherlock and Rex Nettleford, *The University of the West Indies: A Caribbean Response to the Challenge of Change* (London: Macmillan Publishers, 1990), 62.
31. *UWIPA Newsletter* 4, no. 6 (November/December 1990): 1.
32. Evadne McLean, "Focus on Caribbean Journals: *Social and Economic Studies*", *Caribbean Review of Books*, no. 2 (November 1991): 1 and 23.
33. Sherlock and Nettleford, *The University of the West Indies*, 53.
34. As quoted in ibid., 63.
35. Vasil Persaud, "A Short History of *West Indian Medical Journal*", in *Medicine Then and Now: A Review of the First Forty Years*, edited by Brendan Bain (Kingston: Faculty of Medical Sciences, UWI, 1988).
36. Evadne McLean, "West Indian Medical Journal", *Caribbean Review of Books*, no. 5 (August 1992): 6.
37. Ibid.
38. For a listing of UWI and other Caribbean journals and periodicals see any of the catalogues of the Press UWI, but especially the catalogue for 1996/97, 15–18.
39. Interview with Professor Rex Nettleford, 11 May 1989.
40. Interview with Professor Roy Augier, 12 May 1989.
41. Interview with Herman McKenzie, 22 April 1989.

42. Interview with Professor Roy Augier, 12 May 1989.
43. Interview with Professor Rex Nettleford, 11 May 1989.
44. Wenty Bowen, "Background on the Association of Journal Editors, aka the UWI Publishers' Association (and the Involvement of Peace Corps Volunteers)", memorandum to Pro Vice Chancellor Roy Augier, 30 June 1987.
45. Sally Spencer, "Report of UWIPA's Participation in the First International Caribbean People's Bookfair, Trinidad, 26–30 June and 4–5 July 1987".
46. Interview with Professor Roy Augier, 12 May 1989.
47. Annie Paul, who became publications editor of ISER on the departure of Mrs Janet Liu Terry, began her association with UWI publishing as one of UWIPA's part-time staff involved in desktop publishing.
48. UWIPA Report 1991/92 to the Annual General Meeting, 15 December 1992.
49. *UWIPA Newsletter* 4, no. 6 (November/December 1990): 1.
50. Samuel B. Bandara, "Editorial", *Caribbean Review of Books*, no. 3 (February 1992): 2.
51. Samuel B. Bandara, "From the Editor", *Caribbean Review of Books*, no. 3 (February 1992): 2.
52. Samuel B. Bandara, "Introduction", *Jamaican Books in Print* (Mona, Jamaica: Caribbean Books in Print Project, 1993).
53. Linda D. Cameron, "Developing a Press in a Developing Region: Comparisons with Developing a Press in a Developed Country. Lessons We Have Learned and How They May Be Used to Help Other Presses to Make Their Books Available in the Region" (paper presented at the International Association of Scholarly Publishing, Vancouver, British Columbia, Canada 1–15 May 1997): 11.
54. From a report of the UWIPA Annual General Meeting, 24 October 1991
55. Cameron, "Developing a Press in a Developing Region", 13.
56. From a report of UWIPA 1991/92 to the Annual General Meeting, 15 December 1992.

13

From Ideas to Practice: The Development of the University of the West Indies Distance Education Policies and Programmes

Glenford D. Howe

Introduction

This paper analyses the policy[1] decision of the University of the West Indies (UWI) to incorporate distance education as an integral part of its educational service to the anglophone Caribbean.[2] The term distance education has varied interpretations,[3] but in this paper it is used in a broad sense and includes any organized arrangement by which teachers and students who are normally separated from each other in space, and often too, in time, are brought into regular relationships, through various means, including written correspondence and technology, for teaching and learning purposes.[4] My main argument in this paper is that both the typologies of policy analysis[5] (intended, rhetorical and implemented), as articulated by Joel Samoff,[6] and the concept of the Policy Cycle, as outlined by Dennis Palumbo,[7] among others, can be directly and meaningfully applied to provide a nuanced and substantive understanding of the iterative and interactive process of policy formulation, development and implementation as they relate to the UWI's distance education policy and programme. Although the paper looks at the three major phases in the development of UWI's distance education policy formulation and programmes, 1978–83, 1983–92 and 1992 to present, the main focus will be on the two latter periods when the real distance education thrust took place.

A Conceptual Framework

My focus on the UWI's distance education policy and programme for analysis is regarded as being important because, as Samoff argues, the analysis of education policy can "play a critical role in enabling the leadership and citizens to determine the direction of education and thereby of development more generally".[8] Furthermore, as he continues:

By comparing stated goals, realistic expectations, and actual outcomes, education policy analysis can identify successful and unsuccessful initiatives and examine the obstacles – both in general approach and in concrete implementation – to the achievement of national objectives . . . As it identifies constraints on implementation, education policy analysis can clarify the difficult choices that must be made and can suggest what will be required (financial resources, equipment, skills, political support) to translate proposed reforms into feasible programmes.[9]

This analysis of the UWI's distance education policies and programmes thus represents an attempt to explore the often complex and often skewed relationship between educational theory and practice. Analysing educational policy is a complicated and tricky task, however; not least because of the manifold difficulties of determining what exactly is the policy. It is therefore critical that the key concepts and terms which are operationalized in this essay be now defined.

- *Intended Policy*: This refers to what decision makers intend to accomplish through new or revised policy. In other words, intended policy is the stated or presumed intentions of the leadership that may or may not be translated into concrete actions.
- *Rhetorical Policy*: This alludes to official proclamations and publications that may be, but often are not, accompanied by concrete action. It represents what policy makers say they are going to do but do not do.
- *Implemented Policy*: This is the concrete actions that may or may not correspond with what is announced and which may be determined locally, informally and unofficially. The critical question to ask in relation to this type of policy is, *What, in fact, has been implemented?*

- *Policy Cycle*: The concept of the policy cycle as used by Palumbo is an abstract representation of the cyclical stages of policy making and is meant to convey the idea that the process involves the complex and at times contradictory characteristics of being, at various points and times, continuous, erratic, interactive, iterative and responsive. As Palumbo points out, "for the most part, policy making is a cyclical process even though it often skips various stages. In addition, policy is always being formed and reformed; it is never a single, clear, and non-contradictory set of objectives but most often a morass of conflicting goals, objectives and behaviours."[10] The complexity of policy making, as he rightly notes, is rooted in the fact that policy is not made only by the people at the top, or senior policy makers. Policy is also made on a daily basis by those Palumbo refers to as the "street-level bureaucrats", including school teachers, police officers, welfare workers, public health nurses, sanitarians, judges and prosecutors and the multitude of other people who work in governmental agencies.[11] The complex and iterative nature of policy making has also been noted by various other writers and analysts.[12]

Origins, Rationale and Early Initiatives 1978–1983

Although distance education is often spoken of as a recent development in terms of UWI policy, in reality the concept is one that has been utilized, albeit in a very limited way, by the university since 1970 when the University Council endorsed recommendations for the further development of its work in noncampus countries.[13] Early interest in distance education was generated by the belief that this mode of teaching had various benefits that would enable the university to enhance and increase its service beyond the campus countries. Distance education was seen as both a means of overcoming barriers of distance and as a way of significantly increasing educational opportunities of people who, because of their geographical location or socioeconomic position in society, would otherwise find it difficult to benefit from university level education.

Against the background of the perceived need for and benefits of distance education, the UWI through the Schools of Continuing Studies/University

Centres, launched in 1977–78 the Challenge Programme through the Faculty of Social Sciences at Mona, and subsequently at the other campuses, offering the BSc Part I to off-campus students situated in campus and noncampus countries. The objective was to allow these students the opportunity to register for and write or 'challenge' the UWI final examinations. Typically, students in noncampus countries registered at the campus nearest to their home country. Although it is possible to claim that in its early phase the programme did achieve some of its intended policy, its organization and implementation left much to be desired. As one report would later observe, the Challenge scheme was truly a challenge since the university only provided the syllabus, booklists and access to the library at each Extra Mural Centre but little else.[14] As a graduate of the Challenge Programme, this writer can attest to the truth of this assertion. In many instances, the reality of the programme was much removed from the intended policy and subscribed more closely to the rhetorical policy.

By the early 1980s, however, some of the problems of the Challenge initiative had been alleviated and there was an effort by the faculty to provide course material, visits from staff to noncampus territories prior to examinations to assist the students, recruiting of and liaison with local tutors and the offering of programmes to off-campus students in campus territories. This shift in the orientation and administration of the Challenge Programme meant that these students no longer existed in virtual isolation from the university. What developed instead was a moderately interactive relationship between the Challenge students and the university.[15] Many Challenge students, including this writer, eventually moved on to a campus country to complete or start a new degree. Many problems remained chronic in the Challenge enterprise, however.

What is more, by the early 1980s the UWI had also become interested in the further expansion of its distance education programmes to provide a better and broader range of services to its constituents, especially the noncampus countries. This interest was partly rooted in the university's development strategy which included, for example, a process of decentralization to, among other things, enable the individual campuses to respond to challenges and opportunities more effectively and rapidly. Decentralization, especially after the major restructuring initiative in 1984, however, had the unintended effect of compounding the problem of neglect of the noncampus countries as the various campuses became more inward looking and parochial in their outlook.[16] Change was, however, also a consequence of pressure from the noncampus countries for the university to play a more active role in the overall development in those territories.[17] These countries felt that they were missing out on such benefits as employment opportunities for nonacademic staff and benefits from research conducted mainly in and on the campus countries. At the same time, even campus countries such as Trinidad and Tobago were criticizing the university for, among other things, failing to adopt a leadership role in any national effort to promote science and technology.[18]

In addition, throughout the period of the Challenge Programme no real effort was made, as was a major objective of the programme, to foster the development of educational resources in the noncampus countries. What happened instead was the perpetuation of university/campus control over all aspects of the teaching and learning involved in Challenge.[19] An unwieldy management/organizational structure also created much delay and confusion in the implementation of the Challenge Programme. The successful administering of the programme depended on a great number of persons and administrative bodies dispersed over a wide geographical area, but there was no single unit which coordinated the programme. As a result, there was confusion among students and resident tutors as to whom complaints should be addressed, and other people described the Challenge Programme as often appearing "uncoordinated, haphazard and at best only incidental to the main on-campus operations".[20] Partly in an effort to counteract what they perceived to be neglect on the part of the UWI, but also as a result of their own national developmental plans, noncampus countries such as St Lucia, Antigua and Grenada began to develop or expand their own national tertiary institutions.[21]

Office of University Services and UWI Distance Teaching Experiment 1983–1992

In response to the various developments in and pressures from the non-campus countries, the university established the Office of University Services (OUS) to coordinate and manage its outreach programmes. The policy decision to create the OUS was based on the belief that this office could rationalize the delivery of the university's services, including those performed by the various extra mural centres that existed in all contributing

Caribbean countries.[22] This rationalization was, however, never realized. Instead, the OUS and the extra mural departments, which were grouped under the School for Continuing Studies (SCS), operated and developed as autonomous organizations with separate leadership. One consequence of this anomalous situation was that the expected benefits from the pooling of expertise and resources were not realized.[23]

Another major response of the UWI to these challenges and pressures was to launch in 1983 its Distance Teaching Experiment (UWIDITE). This enterprise followed on an earlier experiment in 1978 called 'Project Satellite' that linked, in the first instance, the Mona and Cave Hill campuses via two National Aeronautics and Space Administration (NASA) satellites. The success of the experiment led to the Caribbean Regional Communications Study (CARCOST), a feasibility analysis undertaken to determine whether and how interactive distance teaching and teleconferencing could contribute to education and the public service in the Caribbean.[24] UWIDITE represented an attempt to explore further the potential for utilizing telecommunications technology to expand the university's educational service to sites remote from the campuses of the UWI. The CARCOST report provided the blueprint for UWIDITE, and a three-year grant of US$600,000, the audio equipment for teleconferencing rooms, approximately US$220,000 for communication costs and funds for technical assistance and training were provided by the US Agency for International Development (USAID).[25] The project was implemented jointly under the auspices of the UWI and the Washington-based Academy of Educational Development (AED). Each UWIDITE site or centre was equipped with microphones, speakers and audiographic equipment for interactive teleconferencing, and various printed materials were used to support on-line and off-line interaction.[26] The initial teleconference was held in March 1983 between the five existing sites in Jamaica, Barbados, Trinidad, St Lucia and Dominica.[27]

With its limited resources and inadequate planning, however, the early UWIDITE operation was plagued with numerous problems that significantly affected the implementation process. One of the first difficulties to surface was the scepticism expressed by some faculty members who were concerned that the UWIDITE student would not be able to cover as much material as in a classroom setting, that the absence of face-to-face contact with lecturers would impact negatively on the amount and quality of learning and that the students would not be able to read sufficiently widely.[28] Even though some faculty and administrative staff, the 'street-level bureaucrats', eventually developed greater confidence in the UWIDITE initiative, there subsequently emerged a widespread attitude that distance education was an 'add-on', extra work and something of an 'outside child' of the university.[29] Some faculty members objected to writing material for the distance education students on the basis that this amounted to spoon-feeding, while others maintained that their subject could not be taught in this manner.[30]

It was also felt by campus staff that the work of distance education, in addition to their regular teaching or administrative work, was too strenuous and the renumeration in terms of assessment and promotion quite miserly. At the same time, the locally based staff at the tertiary institutions who assisted with the teaching of the university's courses felt isolated from their colleagues and departments in the campus countries.[31] One consequence of the negative attitude of UWI campus staff to UWIDITE was that the assignments done by the UWIDITE students were not always treated with the necessary urgency. Another problem that plagued UWIDITE was the breakdown and at times confusion with the teleconferencing facilities. Although the UWIDITE teleconferencing system was impressive, there were times when the equipment at a site could be down for an entire session in consecutive weeks, and there have also been times, as happened in Trinidad, when the system could be down for weeks.[32] In addition, many lecturers did not possess and did not develop the necessary familiarity and skills to be able to use the teleconferencing system effectively; there was no systematic or sustained training programme organized for these lecturers.

A number of complaints were made by the UWIDITE students about various problems, including the cost of transportation, as well as the difficulties encountered with transport in getting to and from the UWIDITE centres. For example, students in the rural areas of Dominica who could not get a bus to return home after 4 P.M. were therefore forced to remain overnight in the city until they could get a bus about 1 P.M. the following day. This meant that attending class at the UWIDITE centre often involved the loss of two full working days.[33] The easy and cost-effective education that the UWIDITE project was to facilitate for people in distance areas was thus often thwarted. Another difficulty which the students encountered was that the printed materials invariably arrived from the campus too late to allow students adequate time to prepare for the interactive sessions. Although this problem was in part a consequence of difficulties with the regular mail system, it was also rooted in the notion that distance education was viewed by campus staff as being of secondary importance. To compound the problem, the libraries and resource centres in the noncampus countries often lacked the necessary support and reference materials. Resident tutors and other teaching staff in the noncampus countries therefore often had to rely heavily on personal contacts in order to obtain timely responses from the faculties and administrative staff on behalf of the UWIDITE students.[34]

Difficulties also arose with the articulation of the Challenge and UWIDITE courses with the full degree programme on the campus. It was and still is possible, for instance, for students, such as those taking law or social sciences courses, to successfully 'challenge' the university exams in the home country, but subsequently find that there is no room for them on the campus to complete their degree.[35] In the Faculty of Law, this problem stems in part from the very rigid quotas for entry into the LLB programme. Country quotas, among other things, have meant that for years many students who want to pursue a career in law have found it difficult, if not impossible, to do so. Overwhelming pressure and fierce competition for places in the Faculty of Social Sciences has also meant that students completing Part I of any of the social sciences programmes by distance education are not guaranteed that they will be accepted by the faculty to complete their degree, even though the faculty has moved to significantly increase its intake of students. Clearly, in this case the university's promises of what distance education would mean, especially for noncampus students, have only been partially fulfilled, again highlighting the differences between intended, rhetorical and implemented policy. An unwieldy and bureaucratic system of organization of the distance education programme, and the university more generally, also contributed to many of the problems and frustrations experienced by UWIDITE students and staff in the noncampus countries.[36]

To stress the numerous problems and challenges UWIDITE has experienced since its conception is not meant to give the impression that the programme has been a failure, or that it was heavy on rhetorical policy and short on implemented policy. Any assessment of UWIDITE must necessarily seek to establish the extent to which it was or was not able to achieve what it was intended to do as outlined in its objectives, which included:

1. Demonstrating that a sufficient level of demand existed to support an operational system.
2. Creating within the UWI an interest in meeting identified demands by teleconferencing so that the institution would incorporate these as part of its armoury.
3. Establishing a core of experience and experienced workers, to allow the efficient design, staffing and implementation of a fully operational system for distance teaching and outreach.
4. Helping to develop mechanisms and expertise for the production of educational materials, for example, print, audio and audiovisual materials.
5. Developing a proposal for a permanent service.

This type of assessment was precisely what the 1986 Lalor and Marrett Report sought to do and it concluded that UWIDITE had gone far in terms of meeting these objectives.[37] The report noted that under UWIDITE multiple programmes had been organized for community aids, technicians, teachers, nurses, university undergraduates and government agencies. This, it argued, demonstrated that there was enough demand to support a distance education programme over the long term. Moreover, the report maintained,

the number and variety of programmes; the increasing number of programmes being developed in direct response to requests from governments or organizations in the countries on the network; the numbers of participants; and the extent of usage during term time; and the keenness of the other countries to join the system show clearly that a real demand exists to support an operational system.[38]

Significantly, between the inaugural teleconference in March 1983 and the present, UWIDITE sites have been increased from five to over twenty-five in fourteen countries around the region.[39] This expansion can be regarded as symptomatic of the demand for distance education services and has been critical in helping UWIDITE to overcome some of its problems and achieve its stated short-term objectives.

As regards the second stated objective, the report observed that UWIDITE had been accepted as part of the university's armoury. While there is much truth in this assertion, one has to be cautious in accepting this conclusion. As noted earlier, even though university official policies acknowledge the integral and important role of UWIDITE in its delivery of teaching, many faculty members, the 'street-level bureaucrats', still view the distance education enterprise as an 'add-on' and as peripheral to the university's mission. The third and fourth objectives, as the report rightly concluded, are still being pursued with some measure of success. Efforts are continuing to create a pool of expertise in the region to support the distance education programme, and to date various educational materials have been produced by the limited pool of experts so far developed.

There can be no doubt that the final objective has been met in large measure. This is, however, not the type of goal that can ever be completely achieved. Given that policy making and analysis is by nature an iterative and ongoing process, it can be expected that any plan or policy for UWIDITE, and more generally, for distance education, will be subject to a continuous process of evaluation, refining and reformulation. Indeed, it is this process that has led to what can be regarded as the third phase in the development of UWI distance education policy making and programmes. This third phase, it can be argued, started with the creation of the Board for Distance Education which held its first meeting in September 1993.

A New Dispensation, 1992–Present

The Board for Distance Education replaced the Advisory Committee which, when UWIDITE was established in 1983, was convened to advise on the structure and content of UWIDITE programmes and liaise with the wider university community. The main functions of the Board for Distance Education included the clarification of the goals and objectives for distance education; reviewing and restructuring of distance education at the UWI; and devising methods and techniques in distance education for the development and delivery of programmes, as well as rectifying the problems affecting the emerging system.

The many problems of the UWI distance education enterprise were in part revealed by the various mechanisms for feedback that the university had built into its planning and implementation process. These mechanisms included periodic visits and regular dialogue between campus-based distance education officials and the implementers in the noncampus countries, as well as the contracting of consultants to assess the implementation process. These reports were critical in not only highlighting deficiencies in the system, the recommendations incorporated in them were to lead to the rethinking and refining of the distance education policies of the UWI.

The most significant of the reports, the Renwick Report (1992), was to provide the blueprint for profound changes in the university's distance education policies and programmes. The Renwick Report recommended, among other things, that distance education be incorporated as an integral part of the UWI teaching and learning system, which meant that the university would become a dual mode institution. The report also recommended that a distance education centre be established to liaise with the faculties and manage and coordinate all distance education programmes.[40] A Caribbean Development Bank (CDB) appraisal report also provided the basis for the development of a new and more cohesive approach to distance education policy formulation. The appraisal report was, for instance, critical of the university's uncoordinated distance education programme, technical quality and delivery of teaching. It also called for closer relations between the UWI and the tertiary level institutions of the region, and emphasized the necessity for a needs assessment survey and for the quality and cost-effectiveness of the university's distance education programme to be improved.

In July 1992 the powerful decision making body, the University Academic Committee (UAC), decided that the UWI should become a dual mode institution as recommended by the Renwick Report. This decision was taken within the wider context of a major restructuring exercise gradually being undertaken in the university. The principal policy guide for this reform was the 1994 *Report of the Chancellor's Commission* which had been set up to review the governance of the university in light of its current and prospective developmental role in the region, and relevant developments in university administration and practice elsewhere.[41] In the execution of its task, the commission was to be fully cognizant of the resolve of regional governments, as expressed in the July 1989 Grand Anse Declaration, to maintain the university as a regional institution indefinitely. The commission's report was significant for the distance education process as it reiterated the numerous problems being experienced by the noncampus countries, endorsed the need for a major distance education thrust to help rectify these problems and called for a structural reform of the distance education system of governance.

Various reasons, some old and some new, were advanced by analysts and university officials to explain the urgency and necessity for a revived distance education programme. It was argued that because distance education was closely linked to modern telecommunications technology, it had the potential to extend its benefits to greater numbers of people than in the past.[42] Distance education was also seen as a response by the governments to the tremendous demands for educational services in the region. Moreover, it would enable the university to help the governments to extend the opportunities available for training and retraining, and in this way the institution could fulfil the wish of the governments that it maintain its regional character.[43] Distance education was also seen as a way for the university to shed its elitist image through greater enrolment, especially from the noncampus countries. This potential benefit of distance education was expressed in terms of helping the islands fulfil national goals by increasing access to higher education and thereby bringing about greater equality of educational opportunities. For others, distance education was a way to help stem the 'brain drain' or steady outward migration of the region's brightest and most skilled people. This view was linked to the belief that an effective UWI distance education programme was urgently required in order to survive the serious challenge and aggressive competition from off-shore universities in the United Kingdom and the United States.[44]

The threat from foreign universities took on additional importance given that the UWI desperately wanted to reverse a declining trend in student enrolment from the noncampus countries. In 1960–61, students from campus countries made up 66.5 percent of the total university enrolment, students from the Organization of Eastern Caribbean States (OECS) countries 11.8 percent and those from other territories constituted 21.7 percent. By 1988–89, however, students from the campus countries made up 93.5 percent of the total enrolment, while those from the OECS countries and the British Virgin Islands together only constituted 4 percent of the enrolment and those from Belize, Bahamas, Turks and Caicos and the Cayman Islands made up 1 percent.[45] This significant shift in enrolment from the OECS and other noncampus countries, it was recognized, was not simply a matter of the prohibitive cost of on-campus study. As part of its overall marketing strategy it was promised that under the new dispensation distance education would no longer be regarded as an 'add-on' or 'outside child', but as an integral part of the university. At the same time, there was a call for the university to become more customer oriented, and recognize, in this regard, that its key customers are the students.[46]

Consequent on the Renwick Report and the *Report of the Chancellor's Commission*, in early March 1995 a Distance Education Unit (Centre), headed by a director, was established at the Cave Hill campus in Barbados under the overall leadership of the pro vice chancellor for the now defunct Office of Academic Affairs. The centre's three main functional areas include curriculum development, programme delivery and the telecommunications network. It also engages in research and evaluation, training, and special projects and continuing education.[47] Another important structural change that resulted from the commission's report was the establishment of a Board for Non-campus Countries and Distance Education, to manage the distance education relationship and programmes in the noncampus countries. To complement these structural changes several other investigations were undertaken that focused on various distance education issues and areas. These included a needs assessment survey conducted by personnel of the Open University (United Kingdom) that aimed to establish the level and types of needs for distance education in the English-speaking Caribbean as voiced by potential students and their sponsors. This report, which clearly was performing an iterative function in the distance education policy process, reconfirmed the view of earlier reports that there was a tremendous need for UWI's distance education programmes in the noncampus countries.[48] Another report, this time by a local consultant, played a pivotal role in the creation of a Distance Education Unit, and the development of distance education awareness and work on the St Augustine campus in Trinidad.[49]

All of these developments were, in large measure, made possible through development loans provided under a US$82 million, Inter-American Development Bank (IDB) and CDB loan package to the university. US$9.1 million of the funds were utilized for a massive expansion and upgrading of the UWI distance education system and programmes aimed at, among other things, significantly broadening access (especially in the noncampus countries) to university level education. With the university attempting to increase its range of programme offerings and the number of enrolments to 20,000 (full-time equivalent) students by the year 2001, up from the current level of 16,000, it was anticipated that of this increase up to 1,000 students per year might be achieved through distance learning programmes.

From Ideas to Practice: Distance Education Policies and Programmes

This continuous process of evaluation and policy modification or reformulation resulted in and reflected an attempt by the university since the early 1990s to overhaul its distance education policies and programmes and to develop a new and comprehensive statement of policies, principles and procedures, the first draft of which was produced and adopted by the Board for Non-campus Countries and Distance Education in September 1996.[50] Recognizing that the establishment of a vibrant distance education programme is an ongoing process, the board, in the preamble to this statement, has acknowledged that the document will be modified in light of experience and consultation.[51] A strategic plan was also articulated for the university's distance education enterprise until the year 2001.[52] The plan focuses on identifying and meeting the higher education learning needs of a wider population of university students across the Caribbean and, where appropriate, beyond; identifying and developing or modifying programmes for areas in which there is high demand; developing programmes that will significantly increase UWI enrolments; developing programmes to meet the needs of all campus and noncampus countries; and developing programmes identified by the UWI and its stakeholders as important for economic, cultural and social development.

Conclusions and Future Prospects

Clearly, the university's distance education enterprise has over the years of its existence exhibited the three typologies of policy identified by Samoff. The successes and failures of the programme serve to highlight the distinctions between intended, rhetorical and implemented policies. Likewise, its three major phases of development and evolution, which have been built on past experiences, challenges and continuous evaluative research, demonstrate the vital importance of recognizing the cyclical, iterative, complex and even contradictory character of policy making and analysis. These overlapping and interactive processes and issues, as this review has shown, are integral to, and reflective of, how policy gets implemented in the real world. It therefore seems likely that the future development of the university's distance education policy and programme will out of necessity need to continue to be iterative and cognizant of how past experiences, failures, as well as successes, can be used to guide future policy decisions and programmes. Equally, it is evident that the success or failure of any future distance education initiatives will depend heavily on, among other things, the resources, resourcefulness and determination of both the university's officials and 'street-level bureaucrats'. It will, undoubtedly, also depend on how successfully such outstanding and problematic issues as students fees, compensation of faculty for distance education work and the future financing of distance education are resolved.

Notes

1. Policy refers to both statements of objectives and strategies and the process by which those objectives and strategies were specified. See Joel Samoff, "Education for What? Education for Whom? Guidelines for National Education Policy Reports" (paper prepared for UNESCO Project on Education Policy Analysis and Reviews in the LDCs, 31 March 1991), 3.
2. The anglophone Caribbean covers the area from Belize on the Central American mainland, across to Jamaica and the Bahamas Islands, then through the chain of islands between the Caribbean Sea and the Atlantic Ocean – from the British Virgin Islands in the north of the chain to Barbados in the south-east, to Trinidad and Tobago and further south to Guyana on the South American mainland.
3. See Winnifred M. Hall and Christine Marrett, "Quality Teacher Education via Distance Mode: A Caribbean Experience", *Journal of Education for Teaching*, 22, no. 1 (1996): 85–87.
4. See William Renwick, Doug Shale and Chandrasekhara Rao, *Appraisal of Distance Education at the University of the West Indies* (Vancouver: The Commonwealth of Learning, 1992), 11. Hereafter referred to as the Renwick Report.
5. Analysis refers to the review and evaluation, as well as the exploration of systematic connections and influences within and among the phenomena and relationships analysed. See Samoff, "Education for What?", 3.
6. Ibid., 6–7.
7. Dennis J. Palumbo, *Public Policy in America: Government in Action*, 2nd ed. (Toronto: Harcourt Brace College Publishers, 1994), 18–24.
8. Samoff, "Education for What?", 3.
9. Ibid.
10. Palumbo, *Public Policy in America*, 21.
11. Ibid.
12. See, for example, Brian W. Hogwood and Lewis A. Gunn, *Policy Analysis for the Real World* (New York: Oxford University Press, 1984), 10; Carl V. Patton and David S. Sawicki, *Basic Methods of Policy Analysis and Planning*, 2nd ed. (Englewood Cliffs, New Jersey: Prentice Hall, 1993), 21–73; E.S. Quade, *Analysis for Public Decisions*, 3rd ed., revised by Grace M. Carter (Englewood Cliffs, New

From Ideas to Practice: Distance Education Policies and Programmes

Jersey: Prentice Hall, 1989), 48–68; Duncan MacRae, Jr, and James A. Wilde, *Policy Analysis for Public Decisions* (Lanham: University Press of America, 1985), 3–12.

13. Marjorie Moyston, "Report on Challenge/UWIDITE Programmes", prepared for Distance Education Centre, Cave Hill Campus (1995–96), 2.
14. Gerald C. Lalor and Christine Marrett, *Report on the University of the West Indies Distance Teaching Experiment* (Mona, Jamaica: Senate House, University of the West Indies, 1986), 52.
15. Moyston, "Report on Challenge/UWIDITE Programme", 4
16. See Neville V. Nicholls and Ivan L. Head (co-chairmen), *A New Structure: The Regional University in the 1990s and Beyond. Report of the Chancellor's Commission on the Governance of UWI* (Mona, Jamaica: UWI, 1994), 32. Hereafter referred to as the *Report of the Chancellor's Commission.*
17. Zellyne D. Jennings, *Innovation in Tertiary Education in the Caribbean: Distance Teaching in the Faculty of Education at the University of the West Indies* (The Hague: Centre for the Study of Education in Developing Countries, 1990), 7
18. Ibid., 7.
19. E.P. Brandon, "Distance Education in the Restructured UWI: Policy and Problems" (unpublished paper, 1996).
20. Moyston, "Report on Challenge/UWIDITE Programme", 16.
21. See Patrick A.M. Emmanuel, "Academic Relations of Power: The case of UWI" (paper prepared for the Eighteenth Annual Conference of the Caribbean Studies Association, Jamaica, May 1993), 1–28.
22. Ibid., 25.
23. *Report of the Chancellor's Commission,* 34.
24. Jennings, *Innovation in Tertiary Education in the Caribbean,* 7.
25. Lalor and Marrett, *Report on the University of the West Indies Distance Teaching Experiment,* 12. Various organizations and regional governments also made contributions to the project. See ibid., 12.
26. Hall and Marrett, "Quality Education via Distance Mode", 87.
27. Gerald Lalor and Christine Marrett (with input from Robert Davis and Vilma McClenan), "UWIDITE: Report 1986–1993" (April 1994), 1–2.
28. Lalor and Marrett, *Report on the University of the West Indies Distance Teaching Experiment,* 74.
29. Verieux Mourillon, "A University's Desire to Be Rapidly Transformed to a Mixed Mode Institution: What Is the Role of Staff Development in this Transition?" (MEd thesis, University of Sheffield, 1995). See appendix 7 entitled "Excerpts of Statement to UWI Round Table on Distance Education, Pro-vice Chancellor Responsible for Distance Education (January 1995)"; see also *Report of the Chancellor's Commission,* 35.
30. Jennings, *Innovation in Tertiary Education in the Caribbean,* 15.
31. *Report on the Chancellor's Commission,* 35.
32. Lalor and Marrett, *Report on the University of the West Indies Distance Teaching Experiment,* 21; Jennings, *Innovation in Tertiary Education in the Caribbean,* 12.

33. Jennings, *Innovation in Tertiary Education in the Caribbean*, 13.
34. *Report on the Chancellor's Commission*, 35.
35. Brandon, "Distance Education", 2–3.
36. *Report on the Chancellor's Commission*, 34–36.
37. Lalor and Marrett, *Report on the University of the West Indies Distance Teaching Experiment*, 78.
38. Ibid., 78.
39. "The UWI Distance Education Centre", document produced by Distance Education Centre, 1996/97, 3.
40. Renwick Report, 5; *Report of the Chancellor's Commission*, 19.
41. *Report of the Chancellor's Commission*, 3
42. Renwick Report, 13.
43. *Report of the Chancellor's Commission*, 32.
44. Ibid., 35.
45. Ibid., 32.
46. *Report of the Chancellor's Commission*, 32.
47. "The UWI Distance Education Centre", 1; Edith Bellot et al., "The University of the West Indies Distance Education Unit: Mission and Policy, Course Development Procedures and Plans, Support Services for Distance Students", discussion draft prepared by Edith Bellot, David Geer, Don MacDonald, Vilma McClenan, John Moore and Bevis Peters, DEC (September 1995).
48. Alan Woodley, *Outcomes from the UWI Distance Education Needs Assessment Survey: Final Report* (London: Student Research Centre, Institute of Educational Technology, Open University, 1995).
49. Claudia Harvey, "Third and Final Report of the Consultancy on Distance Education 15th April–31st July, 1996 on the St Augustine Campus the University of the West Indies", report submitted to the Distance Education Centre, UWI, St Augustine, 2 August 1996.
50. Board for Non-Campus Countries and Distance Education, "Distance Education at the University of the West Indies: Statement of Policies, Principles, and Procedures, Board for Non-campus Countries and Distance Education", adopted September 1996.
51. Ibid.
52. Board for Non-Campus Countries and Distance Education, "Distance Education at the University of the West Indies, Strategic Plan August 1996–July 2001", adopted by Board for Non-campus Countries and Distance Education, September 1996.

14

Current Issues in Distance Education in the English-Speaking Caribbean: Challenges and Responses

Claudia Harvey

Introduction

At the Eighteenth World Conference of the International Council for Distance Education, the president of the Commonwealth of Learning (COL) posed seven issues for consideration of a panel on distance education in developing countries. As CARICOM governments cogitate on ways to entrench universal secondary education and to increase access and achievement at the tertiary level, these issues are of direct relevance to educators and decision makers of the region and it was opportune to examine the issues in the context of the English-speaking Caribbean.

The issues posed by the president of COL are listed below and the heading of the section in which each is presented in this paper is enclosed in brackets.

1. Governments are interested in distance education because it is a cheaper option, not because it is a (educationally) better option. [Government Interest]
2. Distance education does not attract the best and the brightest of academic scholars (because it is all about teaching and not about scholarships and research). [Academics and Distance Education]
3. Distance education continues to be seen as a second rate option for second class learners. (How true is this statement at present?) [The Target Group]
4. There is too much emphasis on credentialling and little on educational enrichment – one reason for the popularity of distance education in developing countries. [The Target Group: Different Kinds of Learners]

5. Good practice in distance education is little understood and much less practised in many of the developing countries' institutions. (Is there an appreciation amongst practitioners on what is good practice?) [The Practice of Distance Education]
6. The newly emerging multimedia technologies are an irrelevance to distance education practices in developing countries. [Technology in Distance Education]
7. Research on distance education is a prerequisite if distance education practices are to be improved in developing countries. [Research on Distance Education]

[Letter from president, Commonwealth of Learning, 30 April 1997]

Although occasional reference is made to other levels of the educational system, the paper addresses mainly distance education at the tertiary level in the English-speaking Caribbean. In so doing, it focuses on the case of the University of the West Indies (UWI).

The UWI and Its Contributing Countries

The UWI is a regional/international institution, serving fourteen countries in the Commonwealth Caribbean, including the three campus countries – Jamaica, Trinidad and Tobago, and Barbados, as well as the noncampus countries, St Lucia, Grenada, St Vincent and the Grenadines, Dominica, St Kitts/Nevis, Antigua/Barbuda, Montserrat, Belize, the Bahamas, the Cayman Islands and the British Virgin Islands. The university's support and main target group come from these fourteen islands.

Most of the contributing countries are in the mid economic range. The countries are challenged by globalization and some of the economies are severely threatened as they face open competition from larger, more viable providers in traditionally protected markets. Universal primary education has been achieved in most, but not all, the countries and universal secondary education is being aimed at by all. Relevant technology is available in all the countries and all have access to audiographic teleconferencing. Through the UWI and other providers, all the countries have access to distance education offerings at the tertiary level, and all are considering the use of distance education methodologies to expand educational offerings at the other levels of the formal system and in nonformal education.

Faced with the need to become internationally competitive, and recognizing that tertiary education provides a competitive edge in this knowledge and information driven age, the region has set itself a target of having 15 percent of its population enrolled in tertiary education by the year 2000, up from the present figure of between 2 percent and 4 percent. The increased use of innovative approaches, including distance and open education, is clearly indicated.

The UWI, in 1992, decided to expand its distance education offerings as part of the emerging new strategic direction for tertiary education in the region. This decision was also influenced by the fact that the competitive environment of the university has changed dramatically within recent times. Offshore educational institutions and internal private providers have been aggressively penetrating the region's higher education market, and have been meeting with increasing success. These competitors, frequently perceived within the region to be entrepreneurially aggressive but less academically sound than the UWI, exploit the tremendous potential of distance education as a revenue earner. The levels of success of the competing institutions in part have been due to their more flexible and accessible entry requirements and study arrangements. In part, too, sheer capacity issues have limited intake to the UWI in some important areas of need. Faced with these factors, the governments, especially those of the noncampus contributing countries, have been calling for wider access and more varied programming from the university. When such access proved to be difficult, some countries moved to seek alternatives to the UWI. The university responded to these and other challenges by instituting major changes in its governance and structure and embarking on new strategic directions in research, teaching and outreach. The expansion of distance education was a critical component of these changes.[1]

The Expansion of Distance Education at the UWI

The expansion of distance education at the UWI rested on three firm platforms. The first has already been outlined – the considerable support the expansion had from several of its major stakeholders. The governments and peoples of the region, especially from the noncampus countries, were fully supportive and indeed were pressure groups for distance education. Secondly, distance education also benefited from an injection of financial support from the regional development bank in the form of a grant and loan guaranteed by the contributing governments. This project is still in train and is funding the expansion of the physical facilities, upgrading of the technology and has provided seed money for staff training and the development of materials.

The third platform was the experience the institution has had in distance education. From as early as 1982, UWI had started distance delivery to campus and noncampus sites through the UWI Distance Teaching Experiment (later Enterprise), well known as UWIDITE, an audioconferencing system. There was also a core of staff, some of whom had worked with UWIDITE, who were firmly committed to the initiative. The UWI benefited, too, from international technical expertise, one which took the form of a COL consultancy, the findings and recommendations of which are captured in the report referred to as the Renwick Report.[2] This is the context, then, in which the current distance education operation exists at the UWI and the context in which I propose to discuss the questions posed for the consideration of the panel.

Government Interest

The first question posed related to whether governments are more interested in distance education because it is cheaper rather than because of its intrinsic educational worth. We have already seen that governments in the CARICOM region are particularly interested in distance education because of the value added that it would bring to their countries economically and socially. Thus at a 1997 meeting of ministers of education of the region, it was agreed that the countries needed to look at higher education in terms of the economic advantage it would bring to small countries in a period of expansion of knowledge industries, globalization and trade liberalization.[3]

To rapidly increase enrolment and achievement at tertiary level to improve levels of competence and competitiveness, it is imperative to ensure sufficient numbers of the qualified at the matriculation level. More flexible modes of delivery and more open entry are ways to increase enrolment rapidly. Both these requirements present persuasive arguments for the use of self-instructional distance methodologies. While cost savings would eventually result from these approaches, the governments' arguments seem in the first instance to be need rather than cost driven.

Over and above this, governments of the region do have an interest in quality education from at least two perspectives. On the one hand, almost all formal educational provisions in the region are provided by the state, and governments are, therefore, in one sense accountable for the quality of the product. On the other hand, it is the output from the educational system that would provide the quality input to other systems to service the country and ensure its competitiveness. While, therefore, governments may not get into the technical educational debate of the intrinsic value of one mode of delivery as against another, it is in their interest to be concerned with the quality of the output of distance education.

In the context of the English-speaking Caribbean, therefore, the articulations of governments would suggest that they are persuaded of the value of distance education not just because it is cheaper, but because they see it as a means of rapidly closing the gaps between their countries and others and between those segments of the population who are advantaged because of their access to education and those who are not because of their limited access.

Consequently, in the region attention is focused on the use of distance education at various levels. These include nonformal provisions to introduce basic skills (including literacy) for the most deprived of their population, attempts to attain universal primary and secondary education, and increasing participation at tertiary levels.

The region is also expressing increasing interest in the use of distance methodologies in nonformal and informal education to enhance civil society. There is an ongoing debate about the prevalence of social problems, cultural penetration and a general devaluation of the quality of life. It is felt that distance education methodologies can assist in addressing these problems. There is seen too the need to open avenues of adult and nonformal education to address these ends.

There is a broad consensus in educational policy circles today that educational reform can no longer be conceived as simply a linear expansion of the formal educational system but must now involve a complex articulation of formal with non-formal learning modes which open up learning opportunities as a permanent feature of modern society. HRD strategies must integrate all modalities of instruction and learning to maximize educational opportunity and the use of existing resources.[4]

On this point then, one can argue that while costs will always be a factor in government deliberations and decision making, the debate surrounding alternative ways to increase and maximize the educational provisions in the CARICOM region focus on wider issues of economic performance, international competitiveness, the reduction of inequalities and improvements in the quality of life. There continues to be faith that the right types of educational provisions, in the right quantities, would contribute to the resolution of these issues. To the extent that distance education is seen as increasing and enhancing these benefits, it is receiving increasing attention and support from governments and other interest groups in the region, including those at the UWI.

The Target Group – Different Kinds of Learners

The question as posed by the president of the COL seeks to determine the extent to which distance education is perceived as a second rate option for second class learners. The situation at the UWI suggests that the profile of the distance learner is a very varied one. At least three types stand out. It is true that in some faculties and on one campus in particular with high enrolment, the best students are selected for the face-to-face programme and others with lower matriculation requirements are allowed to do the distance programme. But even in this isolated case, most of the distance students may be poorer in terms of opportunity and economic circumstance than they are in educational potential.

More often than not, the distance student is someone with ability and is highly motivated but unable to afford the time to attend full-time classes. This is even more pertinent among noncampus countries where attendance at a campus will inevitably require relocation. Interestingly though, relatively high percentages of campus students pursue part-time study. The table[5] below shows the trend over a ten-year period.

The comparison shows a marked trend towards part-time study. Although official figures will not reflect it, campus authorities indicate that many of these students and their full-time counterparts follow courses *in absentia* and are, to all intents and purposes, distance students.

Table 14.1: UWI: Overall Registrations, 1985–86 and 1995–96

		Full-time	Part-time	percentage
Cave Hill				
undergraduates	(85)	1,246	499	28.6
undergraduates	(95)	1,768	1,053	37.3
higher degrees		38	30	44 1
		105	170	61 8
Mona				
undergraduates		3,033	661	17 9
		4,467	1,677	27 3
higher degrees		386	343	47.0
		520	1,007	65.9
St Augustine				
undergraduates		2,553	220	7 9
		3,454	396	10 3
higher degrees		210	300	58.8
		160	805	83.4

Included in the University Academic Committee (UAC) paper in which these figures are presented are the following recommendations:

In the case of undergraduate programmes the major long-term thrust should be to provide as full a range of Distance Education programmes as we can (bearing in mind what the market requires), so that students who cannot attend full-time will have more than adequate materials to pursue courses at all levels at something approaching their own pace. In the medium-term this may well mean that most of level 1, and a good deal else besides, need no longer be offered on-campus at all, especially since full-time on-campus students can take distance education courses too.[6]

Among this group pursuing undergraduate and graduate degrees, several part-time or distance students on transferring to full-time, face-to-face programmes do excel and in some instances surpass their counterparts who were always full-time registrants. Differences in performance may reflect other complexities in the region, including different educational opportunities or differences in the quality of pretertiary education.

A third group of distance students of particular interest are those pursuing continuing education courses. They may already have degrees but see the need for the continuous upgrading of skills to meet changing requirements in the world of work. Or they may need tertiary level courses without necessarily wanting or needing to complete a whole programme. Additionally, too, as economies change, not only do people have to upgrade their skills in a particular trade or profession, but more and more individuals are finding it necessary to change careers within their adult life; transitions that are necessary even as they continue to earn their livelihood in their current jobs. This argues therefore for the use of the more flexible methodologies made possible by distance approaches. Trends at the UWI support this argument. Needs analyses indicated that programmes in management for already practising professionals were the ones for which the greatest interest was expressed.[7] This has been supported by the response to the advertisement of new UWI distance programmes, where some two-thirds of the applicants opted for management type programmes or programmes that would allow entry to them. There is also a similar demand for programmes that are face to face but allow for a sandwich type approach with sessions interspersed with activity in the workplace.

In planning for the development of programmes for delivery by distance, the law, medical and engineering faculties all opted for continuing education type programmes rather than degree programmes. It would seem therefore that at the UWI, the consumers of distance education programmes are highly differentiated according to faculty and level of programme.

The comments in this section would also be relevant to the issue raised with respect to the debate over credentialling versus educational enrichment. The changing economic climate in the region suggests that governments, academics, university administrators and the student clientele have a genuine interest in educational upgrading beyond mere credentialling, although there is a demand for credentials because of the marketability.

To this extent considerable interest has been generated in the articulation of programmes across different types of tertiary level institutions, both to make better use of resources by avoiding duplication and to allow students to work towards a profile resulting from their cumulative tertiary experience, as against separate one-shot experiences in different institutions. Yet, this is not to pose an unrealistic picture of the performance of distance education students. Indeed, the paper to UAC notes:

Failure and drop-out rates remain high, especially for part-time (and distance) students. Internationally part-time and distance students do fail or drop-out at higher rates than full-time on-campus students, and indeed the reasons they have those statuses make it clear that they are likely to do so. But still too much of our teaching may be failing to address the learning difficulties of many of our students, while students continue to report attitudes that actively discourage their participation and effort.[8]

The case has not been established, therefore, that the learners are second rate, but that our provisions, not so much in terms of academic content, but in terms of student support may be second rate.

The UWI is attempting to address this problem. The aim is to provide student support in at least four different ways. One of these is through the tutor who will provide some face to face (or electronic contact) that allows students to interact directly with the tutor and with peers. This will provide both psychological and academic support. Additionally, tutor feedback on assignments will be a main mechanism for facilitating the learning of distance students. The second aspect of the support is by way of materials – both course manuals and guides, as well as non course specific materials such as a student handbook and other such materials to assist students in navigating their way through the university. A third form of support is the provision of student advisory services to assist students in addressing problems, including making course choices, mastering study skills and negotiating the difficult path of part-time study.

A fourth aspect of support has been adopted as a strategic activity for the entire university – for all students – becoming more student friendly. This strategy will attempt to introduce administrative mechanisms that are more responsive to the needs of students and is of particular importance to those who cannot visit campus offices to have issues addressed. Such strategies of support widen the concept of the practice of distance education beyond different ways of delivering instruction to include the creation of an institutional environment, actual or virtual, that cushions the effects of contact from a distance. The creation of a supportive environment may be a particularly critical element in situations where students may be first generation educated, facing deprived conditions and requiring support even more intensely than students in other situations.

The Practice of Distance Education and the Role of Academics

Requirements for the professional practice of education has for quite some time been under debate. Indeed, in many systems, it is still thought that mastery of the cognate discipline is sufficient to make one a proficient teacher. That belief and practice is even more widespread in tertiary education, where more often than not the style of induction to teaching is by unconscious apprenticeship. The graduate student, by virtue of performance in a subject area, becomes first tutor or teaching assistant and then by further mastery of the discipline moves up the rank to lecturer, senior lecturer or their equivalent, with seldom any reference to competence as a teacher. Indeed, as one professor put it in a recent discussion:

Teaching is taken for granted. You are expected to be a good teacher. Exceptionally bad performance may be noted and penalised but there is no specific reward for good teaching.

In several other systems, the validity of education as an academic discipline or as a area of genuine professional practice is still questioned. The status of education as an area of professional practice is still unclear enough for its presence on the schedule of universities to be questioned. In recent times, with the need to become more client focused, many universities have tabled the issue of instructional development and the practice of teaching at the tertiary level is firmly on the agenda in terms of stated policy.

In terms of rewards, however, teaching is still the less favoured of the activities at the university. A good researcher may easily be forgiven the sins of poor teaching and move easily up the academic ladder. Many a good university teacher, however, has been denied promotion or even renewal of contract on the basis of unsatisfactory research. It is in this wider context of the status of teaching at universities that one needs to look at the practice of distance education. If teaching is considered the poor cousin in the hierarchy of functions for the university academic, then distance teaching, seemingly one step more removed, will face the same fate.

In many ways, teaching at a distance puts the focus on assisted self-instruction. The preparation of materials – be they print, audio, video or on-line – assumes an understanding of the basic principles of curriculum and instruction; teaching and learning; assessment and evaluation. This may pose problems in an academic setting where different scenarios may obtain as follows:

1. Academics may value pedagogy and have the skills to practise it effectively.
2. They may value and be willing to learn the skills or collaborate with those who have them.
3. They may assume that once the academic content is right, pedagogy will follow.
4. They may be contemptuous of such matters.

With these different views obtaining in the academic setting, the distance educator may be hard pressed to persuade his or her academic colleagues to engage in materials preparation. The UWI has instituted, as a matter of policy, that it is a dual mode institution and, consequently, that distance education is everybody's business. It has attempted to address this issue of differing levels of skill and interest in pedagogy by adopting a team approach to the preparation of distance materials. Every team will include a content expert, a curriculum specialist/instructional designer, an editor and a relevant media specialist depending on the medium in use. Since, however, in many instances it is the same staff who teach face to face who are involved in the production of materials, the process is frequently a slow one.

In the interest of quality control, it is intended that all materials will be subject both to academic review by peers and professional review by other curriculum/instructional experts. An attempt is also being made to do pilot runs of courses before more permanent packaging is undertaken. These considerations deal largely with the materials preparation aspect of the practice of distance education. There are, however, very real considerations in other respects of distance education. These are notably areas affecting delivery, student support and sensitive but valid student assessment.

When traditional universities go distance, then several of their normal practices get called into question. For example, registrarial practices that require registration to proceed by face-to-face contact to confirm acceptance or change of course now need to be more amenable to treatment from a distance. Fortunately, technology allowing easy transfer of information facilitates these arrangements.

For, in fact, the task of instruction becomes more diffuse and is delegated to several different actors. Unlike the face-to-face situation, where the lecturer may be presenter, marker and mentor all rolled into one. Indeed, it explains the response of one academic to the distance education enterprise.

If you can have curriculum writers who can write materials, then maybe you would need fewer academics, because the teaching function is being divested to tutors, curriculum specialists and other such persons.

Am I disempowering myself by 'giving in to' this new collectivist, mechanistic culture?

Distance education removes the very essence of academia: that is the contestation of ideas and engagement with different world views. Will distance education devalue a tradition that is an essential part of my tradition?[9]

The dilemmas and the inherent role change for academics continue to pose a challenge to the UWI. But it also further changes the role of the academic. In the UWI model, the campus academic is being called upon to assume the role of course coordinator: facilitating the role of the tutor in delivery, setting the standards for marking and moderating the marking of tutors. This in turn requires the preparation of the coordinators to play this role. A certain dilemma is presented, therefore. On the one hand, there is the argument that the face-to-face faculty should remain involved in distance education to ensure the academic integrity of the programmes and to ensure the unity of the product offered by the university – that is, a BSc degree offered by the UWI is of the same worth, whichever campus or whatever the mode of delivery.

To maintain this, however, requires a high degree of diversification in the role of the university lecturer. There is some argument, therefore, that special staff should be employed with different job specifications to engage in the distance programmes. The policy makers have resisted this tendency for the reasons given earlier, to the extent that new academic recruits are having responsibility for distance teaching explicitly written into their contracts.

No doubt as distance becomes more entrenched into the practice of the university, different modalities will be worked through by different faculties and in different programmes. Nevertheless, questions of the reward structure will again help to shape how these modalities are worked through. There is strong argument for academic institutions to place greater weight on teaching if the distance teaching practice is to receive the attention that it requires.

Distance Education Technologies and Their Relevance to Developing Countries

It has become popular in some circles to talk of 'high tech' versus 'low tech' approaches to technologies in use in distance education, with print and radio considered to be at the low end, and the creation of virtual classrooms of learners and teachers distant in time and space, but being connected by computer interactivity, at the high end. It has been pointed out, however, that the choice of technology should not be dominated by considerations of levels of technology but by appropriateness to the learning situation, in terms of pedagogical appropriateness, availability, user friendliness and cost.

The initial investment in distance education at the UWI was marked by the concept of bringing the university lecturer to the student, and using then state of the art technology to do so. The system which has been hailed for its sustainability has existed from 1982 and is dominated by an audioconferencing facility. Each audioconference site is equipped with microphones, a loudspeaker system and a telewriter. All sites are connected by two pairs of dedicated phone lines. At each site, both pairs function simultaneously, receiving and transmitting information, respectively. A message from any given site is transmitted to a bridge in St Lucia which then redistributes it to all other sites.

The telewriter is a graphics tablet with a stylus that is linked through appropriate software to the computer at the site. In turn, this computer is connected by a pair of modems to the two pairs of telephone lines serving the site. These telephone lines also perform the task of transmitting and receiving information from the computer. The system at first linked the three campus sites to two noncampus sites and then was expanded so that all noncampus countries of the UWI now have at least one audioconference site.

So persuasive has been the technology and so strong its impact on access and on the popular imagination, that in the region the acronym UWIDITE is almost synonymous, not just with audioconferencing, but with distance education on the whole. Many are the decision makers whose access to tertiary education began with UWIDITE. Indeed, the system is still being expanded. A marked trend is seen in the campus country of Jamaica, the largest island member of the contributing countries, where communities are opting with the support of business enterprises in the locality to establish their own sites, frequently based on the compound of and closely linked to a tertiary or secondary institution.

A major platform of the current expansion of distance education at the UWI has been the upgrading of the technology and increase in the number of rooms on each site. On completion, each site will have a ten-station computer laboratory which will be available to distance students not only for stand-alone use, for example word processing and working with CAI packages, but also for networking. The computer network facility will link all non- and off-campus sites to each other, to the campuses and to the Internet. In time, the network will make possible computer based interaction between tutors and students, students and students and on-line group activity as well as provide access to the World Wide Web.[10]

As much impact as the enterprise has had, it has not been without its challenges. One immediate challenge is achieving full new functionality of existing sites that are not part of the funded technology upgrade. The audiographic system as existed was intended to be conducive of interactive tutorials between lecturer and student. However, the difficulties of providing library support in the noncampus countries and of providing support print materials to the audioconference sessions led to the emergence of the concept of the facility being the forum for the academic to deliver weekly lectures and for the resident tutors (the site coordinators of the system) to institute a local tutorial support system. Thus the technology was used to mirror the dominant on-campus teaching style of weekly or bimonthly expository lecture and interactive tutorial, with the first being by distance and the second face to face.

With the UWI decision to offer many of its campus courses by distance, the limitations of a synchronous system immediately can be seen. The number of students able to access the lectures will be limited to the number of students who can fit in the audioconference rooms at any one time. The logistics of scheduling will also place limitations on the number of courses that can be mounted at any one time. The provision of computers for student use on the off-campus sites is a necessary, and in some cases overdue, addition. If complete degree programmes are available by distance, however, then instead of having one year group using the machines, there would be three year groups for any one programme *and* an increased number of programmes. The logistics are currently being worked out and threaten to pose quite a challenge.

The response of the Distance Education Centre (DEC) has been to promote a print-based system with audioconferencing, audio and video tapes, computer aided instruction and interactivity as supports. The centre is now exploring collaboration with a regional media house to add broadcast radio and television to the mix. It is believed that a multimedia approach such as described will allow for greater flexibility and greater choice of media to match pedagogical intent, while at the same time taking advantage of the latest technology.

Given the tendency for practitioners to use modes with which they are most comfortable and which lend themselves to least difficulty in implementation, at this time several courses will continue to be delivered largely by audioconference with face-to-face tutorials and some print support. Indeed, even as the curriculum planners indicate that full print support will make it possible to decrease the number of tutorials, the local site coordinators are presenting a case that argues that if students are to gain maximum benefits from the course offerings, full print support must be added and the same number of tutorials maintained. Additionally, difficulties associated with the preparation of print materials may leave audioconferencing, which is consonant with the dominant mode of delivery on the campuses, as the dominant mode in distance delivery.

Even as that debate proceeds in the field among those who will be delivering the programmes, however, there is another debate at the policy making level concerning whether a major investment should be made in videoconferencing because of the interactivity and visual impact that it allows. Given the difficulties of synchronous modes as outlined earlier – the relatively high costs, the efforts involved in winning acceptance and widespread use of such new technology as already available, and the marginal pedagogical value added to be gained – the DEC has argued for a delay in the acquisition of yet another new technology. But there are strong proponents for accepting this new and persuasive mode.

Kuboni points out, "In reality, maintaining a clear perspective on technology acquisition is never an easy task."[11] It is made the more difficult as the debate continues among those favouring the conferencing environment of synchronous modes and those advocating the flexibility of asynchronous modes; those arguing the virtues of relatively low cost with higher chances of sustainability and those pursuing the need to buy into the fast paced technological environment in order to benefit from the several advantages it allows.

Nor is the task of choice made easier by

the strong likelihood that corporate interests will always be seeking to convince the university authorities to buy into their product line. (Under these circumstances) it is absolutely necessary that the university ensures that its decision-making regarding the selection and acquisition of new media technologies is always grounded in relevant and appropriate information.[12]

This argument holds not just for universities, but for all sectors of the education system and particularly in developing countries when the best use must be made of limited resources. Indeed, decision making about choice of technology for institutions in developing countries is frequently painful. It almost always requires an agonizing decision of keeping up with the latest so as not to get left behind, while at the same time trying to ensure sustainability and greater access. Frequently, the technology that is most up to date and attractive may reach only a small cross-section of the target group and may be most susceptible to obsolescence.

The UWI Distance Education Centre (UWIDEC) supports the use of technology that allows flexibility and interactivity; that is supportive of an appropriate, and as far as possible, learner centred pedagogy; that allows access to international data sources and that is affordable and sustainable – not easy criteria to apply in an era when the technology changes on an almost daily basis.

Research on Distance Education

There is no doubt that research on distance education, especially in developing countries, is imperative if the practice in terms of pedagogy is to improve, but of equal importance if the impact and costs are to be determined. This is especially so since every investment decision implies that to choose one path, is to forego another. Given the budgetary constraints and the perpetual struggle of the developing world to catch up and to keep up, relevant research is needed to inform the best investment decisions. Once the decisions are made, relevant research assists in ensuring that best use is made of the investment. In this way, maximum use can be made of scarce resources in a hostile global environment where the decision to have some stay up to date is to deny some the means to a basic livelihood.

Although conducting research and using research findings are critical areas for truly informed and progressive work in distance education, it is very likely that institutions or units engaged largely in distance education activities may be hard pressed to also engage in research. This is all the more so in light of the earlier discussion on the choices that academics must frequently make between research and teaching if they are to progress up the academic ladder. Indeed, if safeguards are not instituted, distance education may suffer the fate of units or individuals within tertiary level institutions who find themselves relegated to what is considered to be less worthy positions, doing the drone work of the organization without reaping the prestige or other rewards.

Equally dangerous would be to run the risk of being so caught on a treadmill of development and delivery as to neglect the need to keep up to date with findings that would inform and improve practice. This is a particular risk in developing countries that may not naturally fall into the loop of regular academic exchanges or the international publication networks. This risk has been greatly reduced because of the ready access to research information via the Internet, but even here access may not be as easy for individuals and institutions in developing countries.

Recognizing the critical role of research, the UWIDEC attempted to capture the essential elements and purposes of research in its Strategic Plan.[13] In brief the DEC seeks to enhance practice by reference to research; improve the insightfulness of research by combining the perspectives of the educator with that of academics in the cognate disciplines; and embark on research that deals with various areas of policy and practice in distance education. It is planned that research within the DEC will therefore rest on the following pillars:

- As an area of scholarship for all academic staff of the centre
- As a source of data for decision making for all staff
- As an avenue for staff development
- As a mechanism for marketing the work of the DEC
- As a mechanism to promote quality in the development and delivery of programmes

To achieve the latter, research will be promoted in the following areas:

- Needs assessment, demand and feasibility studies
- Student and staff responses to the organization of distance education, student support systems, curriculum content and delivery

- Comparative analyses of the impact of different methods and technologies
- Assessment and accreditation of programmes with a view to articulating programmes across the region and modifying programmes to suit Caribbean needs
- Instructional and staff development

Given that the DEC faces the usual constraints of limited resources, it sought to identify strategies to assist in the achievement of its goals. One such strategy is the attempt to involve graduate students in various disciplines in research activity related to distance education. One can envisage engineering students doing work on computer technology related to distance education; management students investigating the comparative costs and benefits of different teaching modes and research on the marketing of distance education; and communication students investigating the use of different media for distance delivery. To date, one cannot yet report on any specific action in this area, but there is potential. Thus, if postgraduate students are indeed apprentices to the academic trade, such a measure will ensure that they are apprenticed not only to their cognate discipline or to face-to-face teaching but also to distance education.

Conclusion

Good practice in distance education, like all good practices, argues for contextual relevance. It must strive to benefit as far as possible from the latest and best (acknowledging that 'best' is contextually defined). At the same time, it must be specifically crafted to suit the economic and social imperatives of the context in which it is being applied, while maximizing the intrinsic learning experience and extrinsic benefits for the target group.

Notes

1. See Claudia Harvey and Gwendoline Williams, "Using a Stakeholder's Analysis to Plan for Quality Assurance: A Case Study of the Expansion of Distance Education at the University of the West Indies" (paper presented at the Quality Assurance and Distance Learning Conference, Sheffield University, September 1996), Neville V. Nicholls and Ivan L. Head (co-chairmen), *A New Structure: The*

Regional University in the 1990s and Beyond. Report of the Chancellor's Commission on the Governance of UWI (Mona, Jamaica: UWI, 1994).

2. William Renwick, Doug Shale and Chandrasekhara Rao, *Appraisal of Distance Education at the University of the West Indies* (Vancouver: The Commonwealth of Learning, 1992).
3. CARICOM, *Report of the Special Meeting of CARICOM Ministers Responsible for Education* (Bridgetown, Barbados: CARICOM, 1997).
4. Didacus Jules, *Information, Non-Formal Education and Training: The Situation of Small Island States,* UNESCO/CARNEID Caribbean Education Annual, vol. 3, 93–94.
5. This table is taken from UAC paper 14C, prepared by the Office of Academic Affairs for the University Academic Committee, 1996.
6. Ibid.
7. See Alan Woodley, "Outcomes from the UWI Distance Education Needs Assessment Survey", Final report, 1992.
8. See UAC Paper 14C.
9. As quoted in Harvey and Williams, "Using a Stakeholder's Analysis".
10. See Olabisi Kuboni, "An Appraisal of Educational Technology Needs within the Education System of CARICOM Countries" (background paper to the Special Meeting of the Standing Committee of Ministers Responsible for Education [SCME], May 1997).
11. Ibid.
12. Ibid.
13. The UWI Board for Non-Campus Countries and Distance Education, Strategic Plan for Distance Education at the University of the West Indies, August 1996–July 2001, adopted September 1996.

15

Management Information Systems in Universities: Is the University of the West Indies on Target?

Gloria Barrett-Sobers

Introduction

Shrinking financial and other resources combine with increasingly complex operations and structures to dictate the need for more and better information in many organizations, including the University of the West Indies (UWI). The development and explosive expansion of the Internet with its vast information resources, now so easily accessible from any part of the globe, and the persuasive promotional efforts of vendors of the various packaged software solutions may, however, seduce the unsuspecting and uninitiated into believing that introducing computerized administrative systems is a 'cinch'. The experiences of those who have implemented such systems suggest otherwise and indicate, *inter alia*, a frequent failure to fully grasp the costly problems that can arise when organizations fail to plan carefully for the introduction of automated management information systems (MIS). Those who have successfully done so boast, on the other hand, of the benefits that flow from conducting a detailed planning exercise and using the blueprint as the framework for implementing the systems.

There is a new institutional chaos, according to Tom Peters, which relates to the constant innovations in computers and telecommunications technologies, and the shattering and accelerating change which these bring to organizations and in which environment successful institutions must thrive.[1] Massey, in his keynote address to the Twenty-Second International Conference on Improving University Teaching, in reflecting on how the university has changed because of technology, reminds us that, in addition to becoming more expensive, it has become a very chaotic place for students, faculty, staff and administrators alike.[2] He goes on to link the use of technology to the very essence of the university, declaring that *technology has the potential to either make or break the university.*[3] There can be no doubt that technology has had a significant impact on the teaching and learning process, the delivery modes for teaching and the access to data and information, considering that in addition to the traditional card catalogues and periodical indices, the researcher can now tap into various search engines, digitized and housed in bits, bytes and web pages in cyberspace.

For administrators, no less than faculty and students, issues related to technology are compelling. The cost and difficulty of keeping track of new information are major concerns but are not the only ones. The questions challenging administrators are relentless. How can the technology help us track our students? Is there a system that will effectively handle the variety of contract types and reflect the peculiar weightings of research and publications alongside teaching for our faculty? To what extent should the systems be integrated, and how is this best done? What computer platform is best? What database management system? Which software? Who needs what technology, and how do we decipher what is essential and what is superfluous? How will we identify and pay for the increasingly expensive and elusive information technology professionals, to design, implement and maintain the systems?

This paper focuses on the issues involved in introducing technology in the administrative systems of the university and examines the experience of the UWI in its efforts to establish automated MIS, a process still in train. The approaches used by the university in its quest for viable, effective, computerized administrative systems are reviewed against key issues and challenges gleaned from experience, and the lessons others have learned that could serve as a guide to this university and perhaps other institutions that are trying to get it right in time to meet the challenges of the twenty-first century.

Issues in Implementing MIS

Tony Simon and John Fielden, in the first of a series of Practical Management Guides produced by the Commonwealth Higher Education Management Service (CHEMS), define MIS as the organization of the basic operating systems of the university that provide the information that managers at all levels need. For example, the system used by a Finance Office clerk to process payments provides overall financial totals for the Bursar and contributes to trend or unit cost data for the Vice-Chancellor. The main rationale for an MIS is to assist the internal management of the institution; it is possible, also, to incorporate data and statistics from external sources.[4]

In developing and implementing MIS in any organization, a number of issues usually arise and several important questions need to be answered. Does the institutional strategy endorse the use of MIS? Is there a coherent management structure into which the technological and the management aspects of the MIS properly fit? Is there a technology strategy and/or a management information strategy in place? Is there a plan for the introduction of the MIS? Who prepared it or will prepare it? Does that person have the time, and the technical and relevant experience to apply to the task? To what extent must consulting assistance be sought? Must the system be integrated? What is a realistic budget estimate to allocate to MIS? Should the systems be developed in house or should packaged software be procured? How will the development and implementation phases be managed? Has the organization made adequate provision for the allocation of resources, staffing, hardware environment, software support, physical location? Is maintenance adequately provided for?

Strategic Planning for the MIS

According to Simon and Fielding, an effective MIS is being recognized as one of the two pillars of university management, the other being a strategic plan.[5] The juxtapositioning of MIS and strategic planning is not accidental. Although some institutions continue to respond haphazardly to perceived needs, experience suggests that without a strategy for developing the MIS, within an agreed long-term framework and based on agreed understandings of the university's information requirements, efforts are doomed to fail or, at best, become extremely costly. Preparing a plan for the introduction of MIS, the experts admonish, is not and should not be thought of as a trivial task. It should be prepared by persons with the time, and technical and relevant experience to apply to the task. This is one area where the use of external consultants, experienced in the field, is strongly recommended. In addition to the very critical factor of having the support and commitment of the vice chancellor, the plan should contain the following elements:

- The results of the review of existing systems and procedures, including their problems, strengths and weaknesses,
- a broad statement of the functional requirements of each of the systems of the proposed MIS,
- analysis of the various hardware, application software, networking and support options available to the university, including the process to be used to acquire each component,
- descriptions and justification of the selected option,
- an implementation plan incorporating timings, priorities and resources,
- analysis of the organizational implications of implementing the MIS, including possible levels of involvement of staff in the implementation and indication of practices and procedures that may need re-design,
- a statement of the training needs of all management and staff,
- an estimate of capital and recurrent costs associated with implementation and operation of the MIS,
- a statement of the performance indicators to be applied to measure the progress of the implementation and operation of the MIS,
- recommendation of the appropriate management structure for the project, including composition and terms of reference of the steering committee and project management.[6]

Project Management

The planning and development of the systems should be guided and directed by a steering committee comprising senior staff drawn from the administration as well as from the information technology unit of the university. This assumes that the university has established an information technology unit with a senior person having overall responsibility for MIS development. Simon and Fielden have proposed the management structure outlined in Figure 15.1 below. They suggest that success is better guaranteed where the vice chancellor, perhaps via the pro vice chancellor responsible for information systems strategy, is directly involved at the institutional level. A steering committee comprising the pro vice chancellor responsible for information systems, the registrar, academic registrar, director of finance, head of the information technology unit, the MIS project manager and some independent representatives, should concentrate on monitoring progress against a defined plan and expenditure against a defined budget. It does not matter if this committee is not strongly technical, as this will probably result in obvious questions being asked without embarrassment. One pitfall to avoid, however, is changing the membership of this committee to any significant degree. It is important to maintain continuity and a core of members should remain constant throughout the life of the project. It is also critical that the committee is chaired by a person with 'clout'.

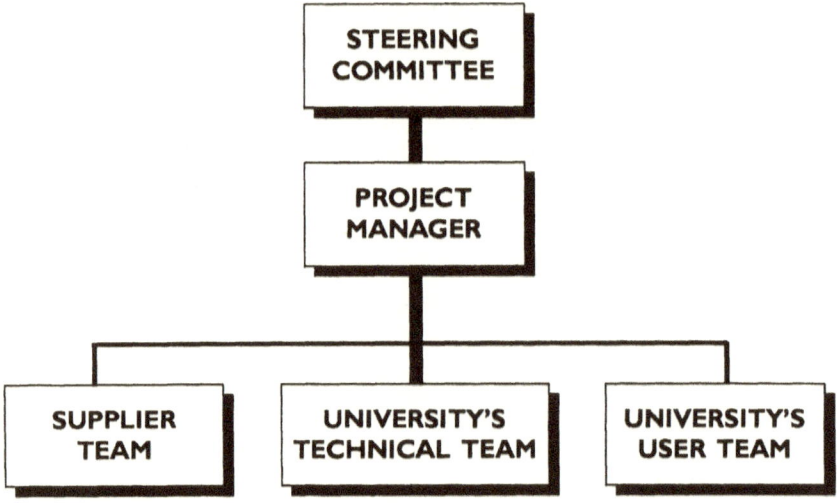

Figure 15.1: Management of the MIS Implementation Cycle.
Source: ABCD, no. 132 (1998).

The project manager is accountable to the steering committee for the success of the MIS project. He or she should be competent in project management as well as experienced in MIS implementation. This position is, no doubt, the most important one in the project and should be a full-time position. It appears that it is not uncommon to find an inappropriate person appointed to this post, or else that the post is filled by a staff member who continues to perform his or her normal duties supposedly on a part-time basis. Although it is often convenient for the project manager to be located within the computer centre, ideally he or she should be part of the planning or institutional research function and should not have to report formally to the head of the computer centre.

In the development and implementation stages there should be a supplier team comprising staff from the supplier or allied consultants, a technical team of university staff and a user team or teams for each particular application. Key to the success of the MIS project is appointing the right persons to these teams. Often departments or functional heads either make inappropriate appointments, or when operational demands become heavy, rescind the appointments or override the project demands.[7]

Implementing the MIS

An information system is not implemented until it is able to produce the desired output – print cheques, enrol students, print staff data, timetable examinations, and so on. The milestones of the implementation plan are defined as these functions are brought into service. The plan should define tasks, associated resources, scheduling, priorities and the milestones, as well as performance indicators to measure and monitor progress. It should be prepared in consultation with all relevant parties such as suppliers, end users, and information systems staff. The literature asserts that a common pitfall in developing MIS is that such detailed plans are not produced, or if produced, they are incomplete, with details such as the allocation of responsibilities and tasks, resources required and priorities omitted.[8]

An important and early decision to be made by management is the choice between purchasing packaged software or developing software in house. The trend seems to be towards procuring packaged software. In the United Kingdom, for example, in certain critical areas such as financial systems, payroll, library, timetabling and executive information systems, more that half the applications currently in place are packaged software.[9] Packaged software is now the norm in universities in North America. At a users' conference in 1996, one supplier (PeopleSoft) registered some fifty-seven universities using its products across that continent.

The problems associated with developing systems in house have been documented.[10] They include high expenditure for the engagement of analysts and programmers; long lead time (a minimum of several years) between start-up and final implementation of the project; staff leaving the organization, each one taking valuable and relevant knowledge with him or her; involvement of staff at all operational levels, even while they continue to perform their normal tasks; and the absence of the benefits of sharing ideas and innovations with other universities through user groups during the development period and after the system becomes operational.

These days, software packages are usually developed using a 'model' specification of requirements of users within a particular industry. There are a significant number of packages that have been specifically designed and developed to cater to the needs of universities. Although the information and data processing requirements will vary between universities, it should not be difficult to find a package to substantially satisfy particular needs or to resolve any such variations by changing internal procedures to suit the way the package is developed and/or modifying the software to suit the internal procedures. Careful selection of the package and proper management of its implementation are essential if the option of packaged software is followed. If the wrong product or supplier is selected the financial, operational and management implications can be serious. Researchers have found that with careful selection and proper management, the chances of implementation success are higher with the packaged software option.

It is important in preparing the requirements specification that it must be complete, accurate, comprehensive and structured. A strategy for evaluating the supplier responses should be developed to include a weighting and scoring scheme for the various features, such as software functionality, support capability, training programmes and documentation. Since the selection of the right package is so critical, if the project team has no experience in the procurement of software and associated services, it is advisable to seek the assistance of a consultant in assuring the choice of a 'best fit' in the software package.

The next critical success factor in implementing the MIS is the effective training of all staff involved with the systems – the technical team as well as the administrative and clerical staff who will use the system, and managers who will lose control of their operations if they do not understand and influence the new procedures.

A training plan, properly costed, should be an integral part of the project implementation plan. If packaged software is used, the suppliers will play a key role in the training exercise – from installation through any customization, implementation and maintenance. A special training facility dedicated to the project and for use by the teams and user groups should be set up and should include a place for discussions, training sessions, demonstrations, testing and teaching.

The conduct of implementation workshops to examine and review the project plans from time to time has proven to be useful. The objectives of such workshops would be to review and revise the project plan with the users involved in the installation and application of the system; and to obtain the commitment of users to the viability and execution of the plan. An important outcome should be a user-driven project management team controlling the implementation at each major operational phase. The occasions of the workshop should, in addition to the publication of regular newsletters, provide for reporting on the project and keeping the university community informed of the progress and results of the system.

Appropriate Technology

Notwithstanding the findings in favour of packaged software, there is much evidence of the ineffective and often costly acquisition and utilization of technology that occurs because local technological capacities have not been developed and sustained. Kiggundu defines appropriate technology as any innovation that enhances the technological capacity of the organization and enables it to perform its critical operating and strategic management functions with greater efficiency, economy and effectiveness on a sustained basis.[11]

Appropriate technology, Kiggundu reminds us, is a function of the hardware – machinery, equipment and tools; the software – programmes and manuals for operating and maintaining the hardware; and the 'organware' – the organizational arrangements, management processes, environmental factors and human resources and cultural factors which all combine to make the technology work. It would be unwise to focus on only one of the above at the expense of the others if the acquisition and utilization of the technology are to be effective and sustainable.[12] Universities, particularly those in developing countries such as those of the Caribbean region, must provide leadership in seeking ways to improve the technological capacities of their nations and regions. One way is to exploit fully every opportunity for the introduction and diffusion of new and appropriate technology that can be linked to national development in general.[13]

Resourcing the MIS

One of the most critical success factors for the MIS implementation is the allocation of adequate staff resources with appropriate expertise and availability. John McDonagh suggests that it is unwise to plan to have more than two functions being installed concurrently, as this places an excessive burden on both the technical and the functional staff.[14] Ideally, key staff on the project should have their normal responsibilities delegated, and it may become necessary to recruit new personnel on short-term contract during the life of the implementation project. The need for appropriately skilled and experienced technical staff cannot be overemphasized. Consideration should be given, if necessary, to seeking secondment of personnel from other institutions who have already undertaken an MIS implementation, preferably using the same application software.

It is assumed that detailed planning will have ensured that the appropriate hardware environment is in place for the selected software and that the requisite software support has been procured. If, in the course of the ongoing project reviews, it is confirmed that the implementation cannot be accommodated within the overall project framework due to the lack of resources, something will have to give, be it the cost, the time scale, the scope of the project, or perhaps a combination of the above. The project team, best placed to propose any compromises, should bring these issues promptly to the attention of the steering committee and university management to obtain additional resources or redefine the project.

Often, if the planning team does not have the appropriate expertise, cost estimates are inadequate. It is not only the project budget that can be off target, but the budget allocation for technology and technology support in the university may be well below the industry average. Table 15.1 gives the percentage of operating expenses spent on functional areas for the universities listed. On average, Ontario universities spent 4.4 percent of operating expenses on central computing and communication.

In the United Kingdom, much of the MIS costs are shared nationally and as a result individual university MIS expenses are reduced. The Joint Information Systems Committee (JISC) of the Higher Education Funding Council (HEFC) facilitates the cost-effective exploitation of information systems within higher education. JISC provides a pervasive network of

Table 15.1: Percentage of Operating Expenses by Functional Area by Institution for the Fiscal Year Ended 30 April 1996

Functional Area Institution	Instruction and Research	Library	Central Computing and Comm.	Student Services	Administration	Physical Plant	Other	Total
Brock	61 8	6 6	5 1	2.5	7 1	14.4	2 5	100
Carleton	64 9	7 3	3 4	5 7	6 5	10 8	1.4	100
Guelph	65 4	5.7	3.8	3 6	5 1	13 2	3.2	100
Lakehead	65 1	6.2	2 5	4.3	7.4	13 2	1.3	100
Laurentian	67.2	6 4	2 5	2 8	8.0	10.7	2 4	100
Algoma	47 0	11 8	2 7	5 7	17 1	11 9	3.8	100
Hearst	56 4	7.4	0.8	0 6	21 7	13 1	0	100
McMaster	64 0	7 1	4 4	2 9	6 2	11 6	3.8	100
Nipissing	58 9	5 9	2 4	8 1	15.7	9 0	0	100
Ocad	60 9	4 0	0 7	1 5	14.8	13.5	4 6	100
Oise	63 7	7.3	4 1	3 0	8 4	12.9	0 6	100
Ottawa	65 8	6.8	4 6	4 1	5 7	11 3	1.7	100
Queen's	71 2	6 8	3 3	3 7	3.6	9 4	2.0	100
Ryerson	63.0	3 9	6.0	3 5	7 5	11.8	4.3	100
Toronto	62 3	9 2	4 0	6.3	3 7	11 8	2 7	100
Trent	62 5	7.5	4 1	5 2	7 9	9.1	3 7	100
Waterloo	62 5	6 4	5.5	4 9	7 1	12 4	1.2	100
Western	65 7	7.5	4 7	6.4	4 3	8 9	2 5	100
Wilfrid Laurier	63.9	6 4	3.3	5 2	8 6	9.9	2 7	100
Windsor	61 0	7 4	4 8	6 2	5 7	12 5	2 4	100
York	62 4	6 9	5 9	4.2	8 5	10 2	1 9	100
Average All Institutions	**64.1**	**7.2**	**4.4**	**4.8**	**5.9**	**11.2**	**2.4**	**100**

Source: Financial Report of Ontario Universities, Council of Ontario Universities, 1996.

infrastructure and central information review and, in this way, the cost of MIS to individual institutions is reduced. For example, the Universities Central Council on Admissions (UCCA) provides a centralized national system for student admission that must reduce considerably the cost of student information systems in individual universities.

MIS projects have suffered from certain frequent mistakes that should be avoided:

1. Taking key members of the user team off the project because other operational tasks require their attention;
2. Failure to provide users with adequate training in the new software because the head of department decides they cannot afford the time;
3. Failure to report on and publicize the progress and results of the project to the university community at large. Organizations are beginning to acknowledge the importance of the human factor in any organizational change. People need to know in order to buy into the changes. The use of regular newsletters and departmental user group meetings can address this particular challenge, to a large extent;
4. Selecting inappropriate technology that fails to address the 'organware' along with the hardware and the software;
5. Inadequate allocation of resources, staff, both technical and administrative, hardware and software support and physical facilities.

How Do Universities Organize and Manage Their Information Systems?

The following overviews of the environment, organization and management of information systems at McMaster University in Ontario, Canada, and Bath University in the United Kingdom are presented mainly to indicate two different models currently in use in universities. There was no scientific selection of these universities. Of the several universities invited to provide data on their MIS environment, McMaster and Bath were most comprehensive and representative of different approaches in dealing with MIS. Information on their systems was supplied directly by information systems administrators in these universities.

McMaster University, founded in 1887, has an enrolment of over 12,000 full-time and 6,000 part-time students and more than 1,000 full-time plus several hundred part-time faculty members, with an additional 2,000 staff members. McMaster is one of the top research institutions in Canada.

The University of Bath, founded in 1966, is one of the smaller modern universities in the United Kingdom, with student enrolment of just under 6,000. Having grown up in the age of technology, it appears to have responded well to the changing demands placed on higher education. In the national Research Assessment Exercise of 1996, it was ranked highest outside of Oxford, Cambridge and London universities.

Overview of the Services offered by the Computer Information Systems at McMaster University

At McMaster, the data services section of Computer Information Systems (CIS) offers computing and information services to customers who are the sponsors of administrative systems throughout the university. Customers include all faculty, staff and students, as well as administrative staff in all departments.

The CIS provides

- core university data processing services,
- administrative application system support,
- customer support, and
- management of a stable and reliable network with both on- and off-campus access.

These services are applied to develop and support the mission-critical systems of the university administration. They also apply to the administrative systems that are local to work groups or individuals.

Strategies and plans with respect to data and technology employed are formulated and developed in parallel with the customer demand and priorities for development. These are planned with reference to an analysis of the fundamental business processes of the university, the goal of improving data systems quality and access, and the marketplace for information technology. Implementation occurs through the ongoing systems solutions arising out of development demand and priorities.

Priorities for the data service's high impact agenda are set and approved by a steering committee which includes the vice president, administration and the assistant vice president, information services and technology, with representation from the central administrative areas, as well as from the academic and the health sciences areas.

Importance to the University Mission

CIS supports the basic activity of the university by ensuring that faculty, staff and students are provided with reliable administrative services such as marks processing, degree audit and payroll. Continuous response to change, while in pursuit of university goals and objectives, requires a computing infrastructure foundation that has been specifically designed to easily support change.

Cost

Information technology hardware and software cost approximately Cdn$900,000 annually. McMaster's approach to MIS appears to be common to many of the Ontario universities.

University of Bath

Information technology services, under the leadership of the university director of information technology, provides services for students, and academic, research and administrative staff. The University of Bath spends 1.2 percent of its total operating budget of £70,373,000 on MIS. We must bear in mind, however, that student admissions is centralized nationally through the UCCA system and does not appear in the university's operational budget, and at Bath also the payroll (a major cost item in the information systems) is contracted out and is not included in the 1.2 percent allocation to MIS. Their records management system is also handled independently and not through the information technology services unit.

The information strategy of the university is designed to support the university's mission and complement its strategic plan. The strategy shows how information is to be used to meet organizational objectives and suggests what actions must be undertaken to achieve those ends. Its aim is to provide a framework within which information can be produced and used in the most effective and efficient manner.

The vision that underpins the information strategy is of a university where information about teaching, learning, research, scholarship and administration is easily available and systematically disseminated to all of its members. The university administration, which supports the core activities of the institution, makes a commitment to the transparency of the information that it produces. The university commits itself to sharing information about itself and its activities, within the limits imposed by the law and financial viability, with relevant external communities.

Bath University Computer Services (BUCS) has responsibility for the quality and capability of the common information technology infrastructure, especially the functionality and maintenance of the campus network and communication system. Specifically, BUCS provides advice and consultancy in all aspects of computer services, including software applications support, network support, World Wide Web and e-mail services.

As regards its information systems, the strategy is to coordinate the ways in which information systems are used in the university and, hence, to promote the effective and efficient use of these systems for research, teaching and learning, and in the management and administration of these activities.

Information systems are subject to continual development and innovation and the strategy is expected to be reviewed regularly and modified to take account of such factors and changes within the university.

For students, the university will provide access to information systems with networked computer workstations provided by the computing service and by some schools. A target of one workstation to seven students on campus by 1998 has been set.

The university's plan specifies the continued development of its client-server systems environment; computers will normally be PCs using Microsoft Windows software or UNIX systems and servers based on UNIX systems. The decision has been taken that administrative applications are to be based on the ORACLE database system and made accessible across the network to authorized staff and students within the university.

The continued development of the campus network and its connections to JANET and the rest of the Internet is a key part of the strategy as it provides the means to connect the personal workstations to all types of information servers both on campus and off.

The university has recognized and articulated the view that information generation and dissemination is one of the most vital features of its operations. The responsibility for the information strategy inside the university lies with the Information Services Committee which is a committee of Senate. Its recommendations have ultimately to be approved by Senate and Council. The chair of this committee is taken by a pro vice chancellor. The responsibility for external information strategy rests formally with the director of public relations who reports directly to the vice chancellor. It is the responsibility of the Information Services Committee to update the information strategy annually and to incorporate it in the university's Strategic Plan.

Is UWI on Target with MIS?

Early in the 1980s, the UWI took cognizance of the global trend towards greater use of computer technology and began to computerize certain systems, and later the campuses at large.

Earlier efforts at automating systems had been isolated, related specifically to payroll or general ledger, or both, and could only be characterized as partially automated systems since many of the processes continued to be manual.

The financial systems developed on all three campuses in the early 1980s each used different software platforms: at Mona, an IBM mainframe was installed; at Cave Hill, it was the ICL 1901A; and at St Augustine, the NCR 9010 and later the ICL DR820. Table 15.2 summarizes the various administrative systems developed or installed since 1980 on all three campuses. It does not include the library systems that appear to be more consistent across the campuses as the systems moved from a 'low tech' access through the local external communications network to the Library of Congress and later to other cooperative library groups. Library systems appear to be more standardized and homogeneous globally and may explain why the systems on the three campuses seem to be developing in tandem and with greater commonality in evidence.

Table 15.2 lists the administrative systems along with the software platforms, salient features of the systems and comments on the issues, outcomes and challenges encountered in each system. The table shows that the early diversity and lack of cohesiveness and integration have only very recently

Table 15.2: The University of the West Indies Computerized Management Information Systems (MIS): A Historical Synopsis

INFORMATION SYSTEM	SOFTWARE PLATFORM	PROJECT DURATION	SALIENT FEATURES	COMMENTS
Financial System	IBM Mainframe	1980s–92 (Mona)	General Ledger Accounts Payable Accounts Receivable	Bespoke system developed for IBM platform by Bursary IS staff. Batch processing with centralized data processing operations at the Computer Centre *Problems:* • Slow performance • Access problems, lacked on-line processing with decentralized operations • Need to utilize emerging technologies and move to UNIX platform with Oracle as relational database
Financial System	ICL 1901A	1983–86 (Cave Hill)	General Ledger Accounts Payable Accounts Receivable	Bespoke batch processing system, consultant developed and implemented by Bursary staff. As at Mona, too centralized. Lacked networking capabilities
Financial System	NCR 9010	1980–85 (St Augustine)	General Ledger	System developed by Complete Computer Systems Programme developed in house. System handled batch processing
CIS Cobal Financial System	ICL DRS20	1986–91 (St Augustine)	General Ledger Accounts Payable Accounts Receivable	*Problems:* • Slow performance • Hardware not upgradeable, outgrew hardware
Powerhouse Financial	Powerhouse Powerhouse HP9000	1987–96 (Cave Hill) 1991–97 (St Augustine)	General Ledger Accounts Payable Accounts Receivable	Programme customized in house. Data entered at source *Problems:* • Knowledge of system highly localized • Inadequate documentation • When staff left the knowledge of the system left with them. • Need to utilize emerging technologies and move to Oracle as relational database

Table 15.2 continued

INFORMATION SYSTEM	SOFTWARE PLATFORM	PROJECT DURATION	SALIENT FEATURES	COMMENTS
Banner Financials	Client-server (windows terminals linked to NT server) Oracle, relational database management system on UNIX platform	1993–present (Mona) 1997–present (Cave Hill) 1997–present (St Augustine)	General Ledger Accounts Payable Accounts Receivable	1 The first system v1.10 went into production August 1994 at Mona 2 At Cave Hill v2.1.8 implemented in 1 January 1997 3 At St Augustine v2.1.8 implemented in August 1997 Upgraded to v2.1.11 in March 1998 4 Implemented an upgrade from v1.10 to v2.1.5 at Mona in March 1998 Currently using the General Ledger and Accounts Payable module However, limited use of the Accounts Receivable module because Banner will require customization to meet UWI requirement (eg staff receivables) 5 The vendor SCT provides technical support and training at all campuses Otherwise the system is maintained by Bursary IS staff with inputs from MISU/Computer Centre staff ***Challenges:*** • Inadequate campus-wide network hampers the maximizing of the system at Cave Hill and St Augustine • Lack of adequate training for both end-users and technical staff • The package was not designed for easy customization (The Accounts Receivable, Inventory and Fixed Asset modules are not working as per requirements at Mona) V 2.1.11 has a better fit in terms of Fixed Assets • Limited period of support from the vendor for each version

Table 15.2 continued

INFORMATION SYSTEM	SOFTWARE PLATFORM	PROJECT DURATION	SALIENT FEATURES	COMMENTS
Payroll (IBM)	IBM Mainframe (Mona)	1980s–95		Payroll system was on the IBM mainframe in the 1980s; however, they were experiencing problems such as • Space problems • Insufficient number of digits for some fields UWI had outgrown the system *Challenges:* • Some difficulty interfacing with Banner Financials and potential problems to interface with PeopleSoft HRMS
Powerhouse Payroll	Powerhouse HP9000	1989–present (Cave Hill) 1991–present (St Augustine)		Satisfies all current requirements. *Challenges:* • Hardware and software not Year 2000 compliant

Table 15.2 continued

INFORMATION SYSTEM	SOFTWARE PLATFORM	PROJECT DURATION	SALIENT FEATURES	COMMENTS
Student Information System (SIS)	IBM Mainframe (Mona)	1976–90 (Mona)		The Computer Centre maintained the system that was a batch system. Most financial processes were semi-manual. *Problems* • Introduction of semester programmes created new demands on the MIS • General dissatisfaction with a centralized, batch processing system. On-line access to more users was essential.
	Powerhouse	1989–present (Cave Hill)	Admissions Registration Examination	• Customized in house • Satisfactory and stable for a while • Needs maintenance and upgrading • Lacks adequate documentation • Hardware and software not Year 2000 compliant

Table 15.2 continued

INFORMATION SYSTEM	SOFTWARE PLATFORM	PROJECT DURATION	SALIENT FEATURES	COMMENTS
Student Information System (FoxPro)	FoxPro on workstations -- DOS/windows 3.1, 95. Moving to Web clients Novell 3.11 File Server for Registry staff Access to other departments is through NT Server (acts as gateway to Novell Server)	September 1990--present (Mona and St Augustine)	Registration Examination Admissions Graduation grades Transcripts	In 1989, the Registry hired programming staff and led by a committee, they developed a prototype using FoxBASE. The original prototype was sent to St Augustine for their use. The intention at the time was that the prototype would provide framework for development of a student information system using a more sophisticated relational database management (Informix). *Current Status:* The system provides extensive features with on-line access to registration information. It accepts 9,000 applications and maintains 11,000 registered students. It is fairly stable though constantly evolving based on new requirements and technologies. Two programmer/analyst staff in the Registry, who have comprehensive knowledge of the system, maintain it *Challenges:* • Need to move to more sophisticated relational database with inherent security features • Deployment to more users delayed because of lack of proper network infrastructure • System needs streamlining

Table 15.2 continued

INFORMATION SYSTEM	SOFTWARE PLATFORM	PROJECT DURATION	SALIENT FEATURES	COMMENTS
Powerhouse Student	Powerhouse HP9000	1991–present (St Augustine)	Student Accounts	All current requirements satisfied *Challenge* • Hardware and software not Year 2000 compliant
SIMS	INFORMIX relational database system	1995–present (St Augustine)	Administration Registration Examination Student Accounts	1. Designed in house by RTSG of Engineering Faculty 2. Intended for university-wide use but this has failed to materialize 3. Admissions and Registration modules in Production 4. Examination module being tested Semester 2 – 1997/98 5. Student Accounts module to be tested Semester 2 – 1997/98 *Challenges:* • Inadequate documentation • Staff movements resulting in reduction in members of staff with knowledge of the system • Inadequate arrangements for dissemination and maintenance of the system

Table 15.2 continued

INFORMATION SYSTEM	SOFTWARE PLATFORM	PROJECT DURATION	SALIENT FEATURES	COMMENTS
Human Resource System	FoxPro on DOS/Windows 3.1 or Windows 95	Implemented May 1992 (Mona)	• Personnel data of UWI academic and senior administrative staff • Benefit processing including leave • Prior work experience	Bespoke system developed by Office of Administration with the cordial services of Mona campus centre staff to computerize some of their manual processes. It was used to maintain basic personnel information for academic staff. Most processes continued to be manual. For nonacademic staff all processes were manual.
PeopleSoft Human Resource MIS	Client-server (Windows 95 workstations linked to NT Server) Oracle, relational database management system on a Unix platform	Acquired in December 1994 but installation was delayed for almost 2 years. Implementation planned for mid-1998	• Personnel Administration • Recruitment • Position Management • Career/Succession Planning • Benefit Processing	*Background:* UWI purchased PeopleSoft v 4 in 1994 based on analysis of requirements. However, adequate implementation budget was not in place. Implementation was delayed. The system is being implemented on all UWI campuses in its current version, v 7 *Current Status:* Implementation budget was approved for 1997/98. In the first phase, personnel administration, recruitment and position management modules will be implemented by mid-1998. There is now a team of full-time persons comprising technical and functional persons at Mona and to a lesser extent at Cave Hill and St Augustine. PeopleSoft provides technical support and technical training *Challenges:* • Suitable location for project team • Need for additional systems analyst and functional staff input • Considerable maintenance and training costs

363

begun to give way to a new attempt at homogeneity and integration of the systems throughout the regional university, although full integration is not yet a reality. It was about that time we noted the beginnings of common systems, viz., Powerhouse Financials and Payroll at Cave Hill and St Augustine, and the FoxPro-based student information systems at Mona and St Augustine.

Notwithstanding these initiatives, the lack of integration in systems persisted. In 1995 at the St Augustine campus, for example, the financial and payroll systems were still on a Powerhouse platform, but preparing to move to the Oracle-based Banner system; the FoxPro-based student information system was giving way to the Informix-based in house bespoke systems; and Student Information Systems (SIMS) and the Oracle-based PeopleSoft HRMS were about to be installed. Since 1993, arising from recommendations made by MIS consultants under the UWI Centre Project funded by the Inter-American Development Bank (IDB), Banner Financials and PeopleSoft Human Resource Management Systems and Payroll have been installed and are now being implemented across all the campuses. Due to lack of adequate documentation and training support, SIMS developed in house by the Real Time Systems Group (RTSG) of the Faculty of Engineering at St Augustine, which should have been implemented across all campuses, has reached no further than the St Augustine campus, where it was developed. Changes in staff involved with the development of the system resulted in the employees moving on with the knowledge of the system, with not enough persons left behind to provide the requisite installation, maintenance and training support.

The literature and the cases considered earlier emphasize the importance of planning to the successful achievement of effective MIS. How successfully has the UWI planned the development of its systems, and to what extent have these plans been achieved?

In 1990–91, with the assistance of external consultants the UWI prepared a detailed project with a primary objective "to strengthen its management and operational capabilities in areas critical to the decision-making process..."[15] This objective gave rise to a major subproject, the institutional strengthening of the university, the other subproject being in training. Under the institutional strengthening subproject, the development of MIS dominated the eight activities planned. The plan spoke to "the design of an integrated network of computers (mainframe and PC-based) for the purpose of communication, authority and control of information pertinent to the management of UWI".[16]

It included the overview of existing systems and user needs, the development of detailed plans and programmes for pooling and conversion that would include relevant support technology. The activities specified that a comprehensive needs analysis would be conducted to identify areas that required upgrading in order to implement a formal human resource planning function, and that an appropriate human resources information systems package would be put in place to support this function. The necessary training would be provided according to the plan.

The project plan detailed activities to ensure manpower information capacity, financial planning and budgeting, resources allocation, management of information related to government contributions and student fees, management and operational audits, generation of management reports and a system of archives and records management. The project gained the support of international funding agencies and consultant services were engaged to assist in achieving the plan. This was a giant step in the right direction for the UWI. The institution recognized MIS as a key pillar of university management and took the first steps to set these systems in place.

At about the same time that this project was taking off, in 1991, the Mona campus administration seized an apparent opportunity to purchase a convex supercomputer, listing among the benefits of this move that the administrative software offered could greatly improve the administrative systems. The purchase was a controversial one, not only because it involved a significant loan-financed capital outlay, but also because it failed to take into account the university-wide initiatives pursued in the Institutional Strengthening Project (ISP). Arising from the purchase of the convex supercomputer, however, were some intensive planning initiatives led by the principal of the Mona campus that gave rise to an enlightened information systems plan to be managed and implemented through the Mona Information Systems Unit (MISU). Detailed management and organization structures were developed along with detailed terms of reference for each key position and the four subunits, viz., the Operations Management Unit, the Technical Services Unit, the User Support Services Unit and the Systems Development Unit. User subcommittees were set up with explicit terms of reference to facilitate the scheduled implementation of the various systems.

The plan to put in place the requisite fibre optic network, to assure the infrastructure necessary to facilitate an integrated communication network for the university linking all campuses and centres across the region, is currently being implemented under an IDB/Caribbean Development Bank (CDB)/UWI loan agreement. This is expected to promote and expedite not only the expansion of distance education programmes but also to facilitate the development of UWI Intranet links using the Internet and optimistically, the integration of the information systems across all the campuses.

It is evident that the university has engaged in considerable planning for the MIS. What then explains the circumstances where seven years later the progress towards the integrated information network and the generation of information pertinent to the management of UWI has been so slow? Save for the library information system and the automated archives and records management systems, none of the other systems can claim to have achieved its target.

Several reasons suggest themselves for the failure of UWI to achieve its targets on time. One is the poor selection of consultants for the ISP, referred to as the Centre Project. Most of the activities related to administrative systems were primarily about the development of computerized information systems, whether financial, human resources, student information, project management, manpower planning or fund raising. Seasoned MIS practitioners have pointed out the importance of selecting consultants who have both the expertise and the relevant experience. The suggestion was earlier made that consideration should even be given to engaging, on a visiting basis, personnel from other universities who have already undertaken similar MIS exercises. It is noteworthy that the more successful activities of the project referred to earlier were led by experts from other universities, who had some experience in the relevant information systems.

The critical factor of having a single person technically competent and experienced in MIS, at pro vice chancellor–director level, to drive the university's information strategy and MIS implementation, has not been addressed at the UWI. Different persons on the three campuses have at various times taken up the challenge and championed the cause. The appointment of an information strategist and technologist at the university Centre, whatever title he or she goes by, is still to be implemented. The absence of such a position may be contributing to the impression of a yet unclear and unfocused information strategy and may have had a negative impact on the pace of implementation of the MIS.

Another contributing factor to the delays would be the failure to release key members of the user teams for full-time dedication to the project. This is indirectly related to the cost factor. There is relentless pressure to attempt to establish and implement new systems without any additional personnel costs, despite the fact that all the evidence points to the weakness of this approach. This leads only to prolonged and problem-prone implementation that costs more in the long run.

The cost factor is a serious contributor to the delayed and inconsistent outcomes. Compared to the average percentage expenditure of 4.4 percent on central computerized systems in Ontario universities (this includes salaries and wages, employee benefits, purchases, rental and maintenance of equipment, operational supplies and expenses, utilities, and other miscellaneous costs), UWI budgeted 2.6 percent of its operating expenses for its computerized systems for 1997–98. (See Table 15.3 below.)

Other factors affecting implementation were recognizing the immense amount of training and retraining associated with the development and implementation of MIS and budgeting adequately for this. The Mona plan for MIS recognized the training factor but failed to allocate a budget for it, hence requests for training in the application of the various systems software have had to be put on prolonged hold.

Table 15.3: Operating Expenses in Computerized Systems Compared to Total Operating Expenses for the University of the West Indies, 1997–98 (in millions of dollars)

Campus	Currency	Computerized systems	Total	Percentages
Centre	JA	3 12	9 32	0.3
Cave Hill	Bds	1 65	35 17	4 7
Mona	JA	88 14*	3,052 26	2 9
St Augustine	Bds	4 75	193.6	2 5
TOTAL	Bds	8 38	324.26	2 6

(*Does not include current project costs associated with the IDB-funded Local Area Networks and some aspects of the Banner Project, and the WIGUT negotiated Technological Grant for each staff.)

Conclusion

It is important to recognize that the experience of the UWI in seeking to implement and maintain MIS is not unique. The difficulties, delays and deficiencies encountered along the way are not uncommon. The university is, without a doubt, on the right track in taking the decision to establish integrated information systems throughout the regional university. Without this, UWI will not be able to face the challenges of the approaching new century.

It is instructive, however, that the UWI's Strategic Plan 1997–2002 does not include an information strategy and does not address in a cohesive manner a strategic plan for information technology and MIS within the university. References to information systems are scattered and unfocused. This is a reflection of the absence of a director of information services – a position strongly recommended by the Commission on Governance in 1994.[17] Unless the university appoints someone of the calibre and with the expertise and experience recommended by Simon and Fielden to take hold of this vital pillar of university management, the development of MIS will continue to be unco-ordinated and sloppy. It is essential that the UWI appoint an experienced, competent, technically relevant director of information services and technology who can inspire confidence and articulate the vision and strategy for the university's information services, and its MIS in particular. Such a person would necessarily drive and monitor the development and implementation of the systems throughout the university, ensuring that they are coordinated and integrated as far as is possible.

With the appropriate leadership in place, it can be expected that an adequate strategy and structure will be established to deliver effective MIS services and that the right staff with relevant expertise will be mobilized for the systems.

A centralized information technology unit, properly equipped and resourced at each campus is essential for the delivery of effective MIS services. Both McMaster and Bath universities have employed this mechanism to deliver information services with fair success. The UWI has begun to move in this direction but must now accelerate the process, moving quickly away from the scattered independent attempts at computerization. A structured, integrated approach, managed and controlled through a central unit, will, it is hoped, assure greater efficiency in resource utilization and more effective services.

The training factor cannot be overstated. With the rapid growth in the number of computers on all the campuses, the installation and implementation of the new MIS and the regular upgrades to each system, there will be constant need for user training. To date, the budgets for the computerized systems have been lamentably inadequate, and user training in particular has not been accurately forecasted and budgeted for, although the Strategic Plan affirms high priority for training and staff development. The new rolling biennial budgeting system adopted by the university in 1996 happily provides an early opportunity to address this deficiency.

The university has been able to develop a Five-Year Strategic Plan, which, whatever its deficiencies may be, has propelled the institution into the discipline of examining its own management and carefully planning and budgeting towards specific targets. The university's efforts at developing and implementing MIS have not been without problems and delays, some related to lack of resources but many arising from poor planning and lack of the appropriate expertise, particularly to articulate the vision and lead the development of the systems.

There are signs, however, that the systems are beginning to merge and move towards the strategic target of integrated, responsive, relevant information services. Is the UWI on target with its MIS? Not yet, but the goals are clear and some encouraging steps have been taken. As soon as the right leadership for information services and technology is put in place the chances of success in attaining the targets will be enhanced.

Notes

1. Tom Peters, *Thriving on Chaos* (New York: Alfred A. Knopf, 1988), 10
2. T. Benjamin Massey, "Technology and the University", in *Proceedings of the 22nd International Conference on Improving University Teaching,* edited by T B. Massey (Rio de Janeiro. Faculdade da Cidade, 1997), 5.
3. Ibid., 11.
4. Tony Simon and John Fielden, "The Ideal MIS and How Not to Achieve It", in *Introducing Management Information Systems in Universities* (CHEMS Practical Management Guides), no. 1 (1997): 1.
5. Tony Simon and John Fielden, "Pitfalls in Implementing Management Information Systems", *ABCD,* no. 132 (February 1998): 20.
6. Simon and Fielden, "The Ideal MIS and How Not to Achieve It", 8.
7. Simon and Fielden, "Pitfalls in Implementing Management Information Systems", 21–22
8. Ibid., 24.
9. Ibid , 25
10. Simon and Fielden, "The Ideal MIS and How Not to Achieve It", 10

11. Moses N. Kiggundu, *Managing Organizations in Developing Countries* (Connecticut: Kumarian Press, 1989), 190.
12. Ibid., 191.
13. UNESCO, *Science and Technology in Developing Countries* (Paris, UNESCO, 1992).
14. John McDonagh, "Implementation – Installation and Commissioning", in *Introducing Management Information Systems in Universities* (CHEMS Practical Management Guides), no. 1, (1997): 20.
15. "UWI/CDB Project for the Implementation of the University Centre Concept", Grant agreement between CDB and UWI, Schedule 3, 1991.
16. Ibid.
17. Neville V. Nicholls and Ivan L. Head (co-chairmen), *A New Structure. The Regional University in the 1990s and Beyond Report of the Chancellor's Commission on the Governance of UWI* (Mona, Jamaica: UWI, 1994), 42–43.

Contributors

Gloria Barrett-Sobers is the UWI's Director of Administration and the University Registrar. She has broad experience in management and management information systems.

Wenty Bowen is formerly Director of the Creative Production and Training Centre (CPTC) Limited. He has extensive experience in the publishing industry in the Caribbean and was part of the original group of Caribbean editors whose activity laid the basis for the establishment of the UWI Press.

Alan Cobley is currently Dean of the Faculty of Humanities at the UWI Cave Hill campus.

Jeff Cumberbatch is Deputy Dean and Head of teaching in the Faculty of Law at the UWI Cave Hill campus.

Claudia Harvey is the UNESCO Area Representative for the Caribbean. She is a former Director of the Distance Education Centre of the UWI.

Glenford Howe is Research Officer for the Board for Non-Campus Countries and Distance Education, UWI.

Keith D. Hunte is Principal of the Cave Hill campus of the UWI.

Orville Kean is President of the University of the Virgin Islands, St Thomas. He has worked as a Family Assistance Worker for the Virgin Islands Department of Social Welfare, and Director of Research and Statistics for the Virgin Islands Department of Social Welfare and the Department of Commerce

Don Marshall is Research Fellow at the Institute of Social and Economic Research, Cave Hill campus. He has published a number of journal articles on globalization, social change and development theory.

Errol Miller is Professor of Education and Director of the Institute of Education at the Mona campus of the UWI. He has written extensively on issues pertaining to Caribbean education and society.

Rex Nettleford currently serves as Vice Chancellor of the UWI. He has written extensively on Caribbean culture, politics and society.

Earle Newton is Director of the School of Education in the Faculty of Humanities, Cave Hill campus. He specializes in Educational Administration and Leadership.

Carlisle A. Pemberton is Senior Lecturer and Head, Department of Agricultural Economics and Extension Department, UWI, St Augustine campus.

Rita Pemberton is lecturer in the Department of History at UWI's St Augustine campus.

Bevis Peters is Director of the Tertiary Level Institutions Unit (TLIU) based at Cave Hill. He has acted as Director of the UWI's Distance Education Centre.

Roger Prichard has served as Pro Vice Chancellor (Research) at the UWI. He has previously held positions as President of the Canadian Association of University Research Administrators and Expert on University Research Administration, Commonwealth Fund for Technical Cooperation.

Sarojini Ragbir is Communications Coordinator in the Department of Agricultural Economics and Extension, UWI, St Augustine.

Don Robotham has served as Pro Vice Chancellor with responsibility for Graduate Studies at the UWI.

www.ingramcontent.com/pod-product-compliance
Lightning Source LLC
Chambersburg PA
CBHW021815300426
44114CB00009BA/187